Do Markets Corrupt Our Morals?

"Storr and Choi ask: Do markets corrupt our morals? Their answer supports two propositions: (1) If there is no morality there can be no markets; (2) Markets enable liberalism and people to flourish."

—Vernon L. Smith, *Professor of Economics and Law, Chapman University; 2002 Nobel Laureate in Economics*

"Even self-proclaimed socialists grudgingly concede that economic markets are productive. However, they set participants against each other, rely entirely on self-interest rather than community, reward greed, and generally elevate money over virtue. About the best that can be said for them is that they can serve as the cash cow allowing massive redistribution.

If this is the common wisdom, then Storr and Choi offer an uncommon corrective. They argue along several pathways that markets buttress virtue, promote sociability, bring out the brighter lights of our nature. That is, economic society isn't just instrumentally worth holding on to but makes us better people. With carefully curated evidence and lucid explanation, *Do Markets Corrupt Our Morals?* demonstrates that neither economic society nor economics deserves its reputation as dismal."

—Loren E. Lomasky, *Cory Professor of Political Philosophy, Policy & Law, University of Virginia; author of* Persons, Rights and the Moral Community

"The collapse of Lehman Brothers in 2008 was a catastrophe in itself, and a symptom of something bigger. We came to see our financial markets as an orgy of greed. But why 2008? It is not as if that was the year when greed was invented. So, what transformed an omnipresent germ of greed into 2008's flesh-eating superbug? What new policy goals and new financial instruments taught people to think that the aim of investing is to "get rich quick" rather than to build a long-term portfolio of cautiously balanced risk? Storr and Choi understand that 2008 was not humanity's first crisis; neither will it be the last. But why do some economies recover, while chaos and poverty seem endemic in other economies? What establishes and sustains the moral foundations of thriving market societies?"

—David Schmidtz, *Kendrick Professor of Philosophy, University of Arizona; author of* The Elements on Justice

"Virgil Storr and Ginny Choi jump with both feet into a centuries old debate on whether the market economy while delivering us material progress does so at the cost of corrupting our moral sense. *Do Markets Corrupt Our Morals?* sets out to weigh the various sides of the arguments and in this carefully reasoned book they bring conceptual clarity and empirical analysis to a topic too often marred by conceptual confusion and empirical vacuousness. It is an engaging read from start to finish, and a work vitally needed for our times. Storr and Choi have produced a must-read book for scholars across the social sciences and the humanities and provide us with the necessary starting point for a productive conversation on markets and morality."

—Peter J. Boettke, *University Professor of Economics and Philosophy,*
George Mason University; author of Living Economics:
Yesterday, Today, and Tomorrow

"This is a lively, original and timely book. Turning the standard arguments against markets on their head, Storr and Choi stress the educational function of markets. Where democracy relies upon the idea of "ruling and being ruled in turn," markets encourage the ideal of "serving others and being served in turn." Markets thus are mutually beneficial not only in a material sense. Markets are also morally mutually beneficial, encouraging virtue on the part of individuals and strengthening cooperative bonds across communities as a whole. This is a deeply humane study of markets. May it be widely read!"

—John Tomasi, *Romeo Elton Professor of Natural Philosophy, Brown University;*
author of Free Market Fairness

"The common sentiment regarding markets is that they bring out the worst in people by rewarding and reinforcing selfish if not corrupt behavior. As Storr and Choi argue in this insightful, important, and timely book, not only does the market coexist with morality, it actively promotes it, supporting and enhancing our participation in our communities and creating a more prosperous society in terms of virtue as well as wealth."

—Mark D. White, *Chair of the Department of Philosophy, College of Staten Island/*
CUNY; editor The Oxford Handbook of Ethics and Economics

"Storr and Choi have brought economics and politics back to ethics, which should never have been left. Of course values matter. Of course markets smooth off the rough sides of humans. Of course 'sweet commerce' reigns, and should. Of course. But it took a brilliant book like this one to show it."

—Deirdre N. McCloskey, *author of* The Bourgeois Virtues: Ethics for an Age of
Commerce

Virgil Henry Storr • Ginny Seung Choi

Do Markets Corrupt Our Morals?

palgrave
macmillan

Virgil Henry Storr
Department of Economics
George Mason University
Fairfax, VA, USA

Ginny Seung Choi
The Mercatus Center at George Mason
University
Arlington, VA, USA

ISBN 978-3-030-18415-5   ISBN 978-3-030-18416-2   (eBook)
https://doi.org/10.1007/978-3-030-18416-2

This Palgrave Macmillan imprint is published by the registered company Springer Nature Switzerland AG
The registered company address is: Gewerbestrasse 11, 6330 Cham, Switzerland

Preface and Acknowledgments

On September 15, 2008, Lehman Brothers filed for bankruptcy protection. Although people who paid attention to these kinds of things were aware that something was wrong with global financial markets long before Lehman collapsed, it became clear on that day to even the casual observer (and became even more apparent in the weeks and months that followed) that markets simply were not working as they had worked in the past. There was a global financial crisis underway. This was followed by the Great Recession. In countries around the world, wealth seemed to evaporate overnight, incomes fell dramatically, and unemployment rose precipitously. While there is still some debate over what caused the crisis and the recession that followed, many people have singled out acquisitiveness as one of the chief culprits. That the market system seemed to have encouraged consumers (especially home buyers) to want more than they could afford and seemed to have encouraged businesses (especially financial firms) to put profits over principles appeared to be key reasons behind the global downturn. For many, the economic downtown, and the greed that seemed to be behind it, proved that there was just something wrong with the market system.

On the night of September 17, 2011, a few hundred activists set up camp in Zuccotti Park in the financial district in Lower Manhattan, New York. Originally, the Occupy Wall Street protestors slept in sleeping bags and under blankets. Within a few weeks, however, they had set up tents, a kitchen, a library, and even wireless internet and had inspired Occupy protests in cities around the globe. Some of the protestors were unhappy with the inequality, exploitation, and corruption that seemed to be endemic in market economies. Some were annoyed with how little the wealthiest in their communities seemed to have been affected by the financial crisis of 2008 and how much ordinary citizens were still suffering from the economic downtown. Some were self-described "anti-capitalists." Others had specific goals like raising taxes on the wealthy or forgiving consumer debt. Although no single issue united the hundreds who encamped in Zuccotti Park or the hundreds of thousands who participated in the various Occupy protests in cities around the globe, an overwhelming majority of the protesters would have agreed that there was just something wrong with the market economy.

On May 26, 2015, Vermont Senator Bernie Sanders launched his campaign for the Democratic Party's presidential nomination. A few weeks later, on June 16, 2015, then-businessman Donald Trump launched his campaign for the Republican Party's presidential nomination. Although there were considerable policy differences between the two presidential candidates, aspects of their campaigns were quite similar. For instance, both candidates argued that the economic and political systems in the United States no longer worked for the average American and were rigged in favor of the rich and the politically connected. American corporations, they argued, had simply betrayed the American worker. This message resonated with voters. Both political figures attracted considerably large and energized crowds throughout their campaigns. Sanders, Trump, and their respective supporters disagreed on everything from immigration to various social policies, but they seemed to agree that there was just something wrong with the market economy.

What, if anything, is wrong with the market economy? One common answer to that question is that markets corrupt our morals. *Do Markets Corrupt Our Morals?* is an attempt to assess this claim. Specifically, we rely on what we believe to be the most convincing theories about how markets can work and the best available evidence regarding how markets have worked to explore the relationship between markets and morality. Admittedly, the arguments and evidence we present are suggestive rather than conclusive. That said, we find that markets are not morally corrupting. In fact, we argue that there are compelling reasons to believe that the reverse is true, that is, that markets are moral training grounds that support moral improvement.

Of course, *Do Markets Corrupt Our Morals?* could not have been written without a lot of help. In fact, we owe thanks to a number of people who aided in the development of this project. We owe a tremendous debt to our mentor and grand-mentor, the late Donald C. Lavoie. Our shared research project, which focuses on the sociality and morality of markets, is directly inspired by, and draws considerably on, Don's work. We also owe a huge debt to our colleague and friend Peter J. Boettke. Among the many hats that he wears, Pete is the director of the F.A. Hayek Program for Advanced Study in Philosophy, Politics, and Economics at the Mercatus Center, George Mason University. Pete's guidance has been critical as we pursued this project. Additionally, with the Hayek Program, he has created an amazingly supportive research environment.

We would also like to thank Paul Aligica, Neera Badhwar, Jennifer Baker, Don Boudreaux, Chris Coyne, Rosemarie Fike, Laura Grube, Stefanie Haeffele, Dan Houser, Arielle John, Cate Johnson, Jayme Lemke, Paul Lewis, Loren Lomasky, Deirdre McCloskey, John Pascarella, Dan Russell, Dave Schmidtz, Chad Van Schoelandt, Solomon Stein, Megan Teague, and Mark White for very helpful discussions and comments on earlier drafts of the arguments presented here. The usual caveat applies. We would also like to thank Alice Calder, Jessica Carges, Logan Hansen, Marcus Shera and Linden Chamlee Wright for helpful research support. Special thanks are owed to Elizabeth Graber (Commissioning Editor), Sophia Siegler (Editorial Assistant), and everyone else at Palgrave Macmillan who helped to guide this book from development through to production. We would also like to thank all of the scholars, colleagues, and students at George Mason University, Saint Vincent College, and elsewhere not listed above who have offered helpful comments on this subject since we started talking about it several years ago. A special thanks is owed to the faculty, staff, and students at the Universidad Francisco Marroquín for helpful feedback during the early stages of this project.

We would like to thank Beloit College Press for allowing us to reuse portions of our article "Markets as Moral Training Grounds." We would also like to thank the *Journal of Markets and Morality* for allowing us to reuse portions of our articles "Why the Market? Markets as Social and Moral Spaces" and "The Moral Meanings of Markets" (that Virgil co-authored with Ryan Langrill).

This book could not have been written without the financial support of the Mercatus Center at George Mason University. Nor could it have been written had Daniel Rothschild not built and maintained a vibrant intellectual environment at Mercatus.

Finally, we would like to thank our family and friends for their love, patience, and support while we developed this book. Virgil would especially like to thank his wife Nona for her understanding and her feedback on multiple drafts of this book. And, he would like to thank his daughter Winnie for being the perfect research assistant. Ginny would like to thank her cats, Ody and Jasper, for being the cutest distractions.

Fairfax, VA, USA	Virgil Henry Storr
Arlington, VA, USA	Ginny Seung Choi
March 2019	

Contents

List of Figures

List of Tables

1

Can Markets Be Moral?

Even people who are typically sanguine about markets worry that we risk losing our souls when we engage in market activities. Specifically, the concern is that the more we engage in market activity, the more likely we are to become, at best, selfish and corrupt, and, at worst, rapacious and debased.

The same Adam Smith who famously celebrated the potential of markets to deliver material wealth believed that there were moral costs associated with life in market societies. Smith thought that markets could be alienating and corrupting of our morals. In *The Wealth of Nations* ([1776] 1981: 782), for instance, Smith argued that the typical laborer in market societies, because of the division of labor, spends his life performing a "few very simple operations" and, as a result, has "no occasion to exert his understanding, or to exercise his invention in finding out expedients for removing difficulties which never occur." Because most of our jobs are a monotonous drudgery, Smith (Ibid.) believed that the typical worker in a market society,

> generally becomes as stupid and ignorant as it is possible for a human creature to become. The torpor of his mind renders him, not only incapable of relishing or bearing a part in any rational conversation, but of conceiving any generous, noble, or tender sentiment, and consequently of forming any just judgment concerning many even of the ordinary duties of private life.

While the act of repeating the same task over and over leads a worker to develop dexterity in his appointed task, it "renders him incapable of exerting his strength with vigor and perseverance, in any other employment than that to which he has been bred. His dexterity at his own particular trade seems, in this manner, to be acquired at the expense of his intellectual, social, and martial

© The Author(s) 2019
V. H. Storr, G. S. Choi, *Do Markets Corrupt Our Morals?*,
https://doi.org/10.1007/978-3-030-18416-2_1

virtues" (Ibid.). Life in market economies, according to Smith, can corrupt our morals.

Similarly, in *The Theory of Moral Sentiments*, Smith ([1759] 1982: 181) offered an account of the moral poverty that occasioned the poor man's son's pursuit of material prosperity and described how commercial society actually benefits from the poor man's son's moral degradation. The poor man's son, Smith explained, is ambitious and envies the comforts enjoyed by the rich. He fools himself into believing that if he had more money he would be more content. So, he devotes "himself forever to the pursuit of wealth and greatness" (Ibid.). The irony, Smith described, is that in order to attain the tranquility and comfort that only money can buy, the poor man's son disturbs the tranquility and comfort that he might have enjoyed all his life had he lacked ambition and not pursued wealth so doggedly. It is not until the end of his life that the poor man's son realizes that his ambition misled him. "It is then, in the last dregs of life, his body wasted with toil and disease," Smith (Ibid.) wrote, "that he begins at last to find that wealth and greatness are mere trinkets of frivolous utility, … more troublesome to the person who carries them with him than all the advantages they can afford him are commodious." The poor man's son's envy and the efforts it inspired proved to be in vain.

While a personal tragedy of sorts, Smith explained that society benefits from the poor man's son's act of self-deception. The poor man's son is not an enviable person. But, his turpitude inspires his labors which ultimately benefit society as a whole. In fact, Smith explained, many of us engage in this kind of useful self-deception, perhaps for different reasons than the poor man's son. "The pleasures of wealth and greatness," Smith (Ibid.: 183) explained, can "strike the imagination as something grand and beautiful and noble, of which the attainment is well worth all the toil and anxiety which we are so apt to bestow upon it." According to Smith (Ibid.: 183),

> It is this deception which rouses and keeps in continuous motion the industry of mankind. It is this which first prompted them to cultivate the ground, to build houses, to found cities and commonwealths, and to invent and improve all the sciences and arts, which ennoble and embellish human life.

The industry, ingenuity, and innovation that drive economic progress would seem to depend on ambition, envy, and ultimately self-deception.

While concluding that the benefits associated with markets outweigh the moral costs of engaging in market activity, even Adam Smith believed that there were potentially real moral costs associated with engaging in market activity. This concern is at the center of all serious criticisms of markets on moral grounds.

Is There Something Wrong with Markets?

Concerns about the potentially negative moral effects of engaging in market activity have a long history. Aristotle, for instance, argued that there were two types of wealth acquisition: one moral and the other immoral. According to Aristotle (*Pol.* I.10, 1258a38–1258b2), "There are two sorts of wealth-getting … one is a part of household management, the other is retail trade: the former necessary and honorable, while that which consists in exchange is justly censured; for it is unnatural, and a mode by which men gain from one another." Household management is the practice of using household resources efficiently. It might involve increasing your wealth by working harder on the farm, or adopting new strategies for husbanding resources, or simply doing more than you have in the past while using less than you used in the past. It might also involve barter and potentially selling surplus produce. But, household management, which Aristotle thought was necessary, honorable, and natural, did not involve selling that surplus produce for a profit. Pursuing profit, for Aristotle, was unnatural and illegitimate because he believed it necessarily involved taking advantage of others. Aristotle (*Pol.* I.8, 1256b27–31) was particularly concerned with wealth-getting that went beyond providing "such things necessary to life, and useful for the community of the family or state." And, he was especially critical of usury because it involved using money to make money rather than to facilitate exchange which is its natural function. For Aristotle, then, retail trade and usury, which arguably drive market economies, were justly censored.

St. Thomas Aquinas essentially shared Aristotle's concerns about unchecked wealth acquisition through retail exchange. Although Aquinas (ST II-II, q. 77, a. 4) was not opposed to market exchange, he viewed it as neither virtuous nor opposed to virtue, and nonetheless worried that there was something illegitimate about gains from trade beyond a certain level. Aquinas (ST II-II, q. 77, a. 1) believed that there was a "just price" that sellers should charge buyers. According to Aquinas (Ibid.), "if someone would be greatly helped by something belonging to someone else, and the seller not similarly harmed by losing it, the seller must not sell for a higher price: because the usefulness that goes to the buyer comes not from the seller, but from the buyer's needy condition." Aquinas believed that this "just price" should not be determined by the buyer's willingness to pay, as it typically is in market economies, but by the costs the seller incurred in producing the good (Ibid.).

Karl Marx was particularly concerned with the dehumanizing effects of markets. Most notably, he argued that money exchange and the division of labor necessarily led to exploitation and alienation. Workers in market economies are necessarily parties to inequitable wage-for-labor relationships where they typically receive less than their fair share of what they produce (i.e. their labor time is stolen by others). Workers in market economies also become estranged from themselves, their labor, the product of their labor, and one another. Workers in market societies are, thus, spiritually and physically transformed in negative ways by their market experiences. According to Marx ([1821] 1994: 49), the greater the scope of market exchange relations, "the more *egoistic* and asocial man becomes."

Several contemporary scholars from several disciplines and from a variety of perspectives have echoed this concern that the greater our exposure to markets the more likely we are to lose our souls (e.g. Anderson 1995; Bowles 2016; Falk and Szech 2013; MacIntyre 1981, 1999; Roth 2007; Shleifer 2004). Michael Sandel in *What Money Can't Buy: The Moral Limits of Markets* (2012), for instance, argued that markets undermine morality. Sandel (Ibid.: 7) was particularly worried about the expansion of markets and market values that has occurred over the last 30 or so years. Although he believed that an increase in greed has undoubtedly accompanied this "market triumphalism," the most worrisome consequences of this growth of markets have been "the expansion of markets, and of market values, into spheres of life where they don't belong" (Ibid.). There are perverse moral consequences, he said (Ibid.: 15), associated with becoming a world "where everything is up for sale." Specifically, Sandel (Ibid.: 64) explained, "markets leave their mark on social norms. Often, market incentives erode or crowd out nonmarket incentives."

Additionally, Sandel (Ibid.: 111) argued that markets in certain goods and services under certain scenarios are likely to be unfair; "the fairness objection points to the injustice that can arise when people buy and sell things under conditions of inequality or dire economic necessity." This suggests that market exchanges are not always voluntary and that desperation can force people to buy or sell goods and services that they would not buy or sell if they were in less dire economic circumstances.[1] In addition to his fairness concerns, Sandel also stressed that market relationships can be corrupting in some circumstances. "[T]he corruption objection … points to the degrading effect of market valuation and exchange on certain goods and practices. According to this objection, certain moral and civic goods are diminished or corrupted if bought and sold" (Ibid.). This implies that giving away certain goods and services can be morally neutral or even virtuous while exchanging the same goods and services for

---

[1] Notice that this echoes Aquinas' concern about a "just price."

money can be morally problematic. This also suggests that introducing money matters into certain relationships can pervert or poison those relationships.

These claims that markets corrupt our morals should be taken seriously. Since markets clearly make us materially better off, one reason to not embrace markets enthusiastically would be if in doing so we invite an alarming level of moral risk.

Does It Matter if Markets Are Morally Corrupting?

Markets do make us wealthier. The United States, Western Europe, and parts of Asia, Africa, Latin America, and Eurasia where markets thrive (i.e. where property rights are secure and contracts are enforced) are richer than the parts of the world where markets are constrained. The wealth-creating capacity of markets can be confirmed with conventional measures of wealth like gross domestic product (GDP) per capita. In 2015, for instance, GDP per capita was over $35,000 in the richest commercial countries like Hong Kong, Singapore, New Zealand, and Switzerland while it was well below $3500 in noncommercial societies like Zimbabwe and Chad (The World Bank 2016). The wealth-creating capacity of markets can also be shown using other measures. People in commercial societies tend to live longer than people in noncommercial societies. In 2015, for instance, life expectancy at birth was 84 years in Hong Kong, 82 years in Singapore, 81 years in New Zealand, and 83 years in Switzerland. Compare that to life expectancies of less than 60 years in Zimbabwe and 52 years in Chad (Ibid.). People living in market societies also tend to be better educated, healthier, and enjoy a higher standard of living than people living in nonmarket societies. Perhaps most conclusively, immigration tends to flow from less commercial societies to more commercial societies.

Exposure to markets has also dramatically improved the material well-being of societies over time. In his 1755 paper, Adam Smith (quoted in Stewart [1795] 1829: 64) made the claim that "little else is requisite to carry a state to the highest degree of opulence from the lowest barbarism, but peace, easy taxes, and a tolerable administration of justice; all the rest being brought about by the natural course of things." Smith's recipe of simply allowing markets to work has proven to be effective at raising incomes around the globe over the last few centuries. Deirdre McCloskey (2010) referred to the amazing increase in wealth since the Industrial Revolution as the "great fact." As

McCloskey (Ibid.) detailed, for most of human history the average person survived on $3 a day. In the last 250 years, average income has grown to $30 a day; average income is over $100 a day in the richest countries. McCloskey (Ibid.) argued that this dramatic upturn in average incomes occurred when pursuing success through market activity came to be viewed as dignified and honorable. Ascribing dignity to market activity led to an expansion of markets and an explosion of innovation.

While market economies have undoubtedly made people better off, other economic systems have proven to be unworkable and even disastrous. For instance, socialism—a system of economic organization where the means of production are collectivized and economic activity is centrally planned—has repeatedly failed to deliver prosperity. When they were actively pursuing socialist policies, average income levels in the former Soviet Union, China, and Cuba were dramatically lower than those in the market societies of the West. Most starkly, in 2015, average income in the market economy of South Korea was 21 times higher than income per capita in the command economy of North Korea (Central Intelligence Agency 2018).

Additionally, planned economic systems in socialist countries are often accompanied by repressive political systems. For example, the Cuban government restricts freedom of expression and the Cuban Criminal Code permits the government to imprison individuals who act in ways that contradict socialist norms and values. Recently, the Cuban Commission for Human Rights and National Reconciliation received reports of thousands of "arbitrary detentions" during 2016 (Human Rights Watch 2017). Although the Vietnamese and Chinese governments have introduced market reforms in the last few decades, they still maintain restrictions on freedom of association, speech, movement, and the press. Similarly, a 2014 U.N. Human Rights Council Commission of Inquiry found that "systematic, widespread and gross human rights violations have been and are being committed by the Democratic People's Republic of Korea" (Human Rights Watch 2015).

Market economies are, of course, not without their issues. Inequality, for instance, is arguably a problem in many market societies. The literature on the relationship between economic freedom and inequality, however, is somewhat mixed. A cross-country study on the relationship between economic freedom and income equality by Berggren (1999) reported that while positive *changes* in economic freedom between 1975 and 1985 resulted in lower income inequality, a country's *level* of economic freedom in 1985 correlated positively with income inequality. Contrarily, Scully (2002) found that higher *levels* of economic freedom correlated negatively with income inequality. Still, the gap between the rich and the poor in some market economies is particularly wide.

Gini coefficients, which measure the degree of income inequality, can be as high in both market and nonmarket economies.[2] For example, the United States (45.0) has a higher degree of income inequality than Venezuela (39.0) and Cambodia (37.9) and ranks as the 39th (out of 157 countries) most unequal society according to the CIA World Factbook (Central Intelligence Agency 2018).

Although markets contribute a great deal to our material well-being, it still matters to many critics, defenders, and students of commercial life whether or not there are moral costs associated with engaging in market activity. Unfortunately, most defenses of the morality of markets do not address the core concerns of the critics. Again, regardless of the specifics of any particular critique, a central component of the strongest moral criticisms of markets is that we risk losing our souls when we engage in market activities. In response to the belief that engaging in the market necessarily comes at a tremendous moral cost, the defenses are oftentimes what Lavoie and Chamlee-Wright (2000) have convincingly described as *minimalist defenses* of the morality of the market. These minimalist defenses either try to sidestep the issue or affirm but seek to downplay the potential moral harms associated with engagement in market activity.

One type of minimalist defense stresses that markets are merely tools. The markets-as-mere-tools defense claims that individuals can utilize markets to purchase Bibles as well as pornography, to purchase lifesaving medication as well as illicit and dangerous drugs, to purchase an airline ticket that takes them home to visit their families as well as to purchase airline tickets that they can use to abandon their families. Markets are, thus, like knives, or automobiles, or any other tool that can be used for good or bad purposes but are neither good nor bad in and of themselves. They cannot be fairly described as being moral or immoral.

The other type of minimalist defense of the morality of markets that is typically offered either implicitly or explicitly enlists the arguments advanced by Mandeville in his *Fable of the Bees* ([1714, 1729] 1988). In that fable, Mandeville asserted two key points: first, markets transform private vice into public virtue and, second, attempts to eliminate private vice like greed could undermine markets. An albeit weaker version of this defense invokes Smith's famous claim that interests, not benevolence, drive market activity and lead to

---

[2] It might be argued that the more important worry relates to the quality of life of the poorest in these countries, that the gap between the rich and the poor in a particular country is an irrelevant consideration, and that mobility rather than inequality should be the principal consideration. Additionally, as we discuss in Chap. 4, economic inequality is more of an issue in nonmarket societies. Still, it would be wrong to dismiss economic inequality as a legitimate concern or to say that economic inequality is not a phenomenon that we observe in market societies.

the positive social outcomes that we observe in markets. Recall, Smith ([1776] 1981: 26–27) argued that "it is not from the benevolence of the butcher, the brewer, or the baker, that we expect our dinner but from their regard to their own interest. We address ourselves, not to their humanity but to their self-love, and never talk to them of our own necessities but of their advantages." Although Smith intended to highlight the limits of benevolence in this and the surrounding passages, the arguments that he advanced in this section of *The Wealth of Nations* are sometimes recounted as if they are a celebration of selfishness.

Rather than constituting a defense of the market, these responses arguably constitute an indictment of the market. If the charge is that the market is morally corrupting, neither protesting that this kind of allegation is irrelevant and/or invalid nor expressing agreement with the charge while highlighting the resultant material benefits constitutes a convincing defense against that charge.

Resolving the debate between the critics and defenders of markets on moral grounds is to answer the following questions both theoretically and empirically: Are markets moral? Are there moral costs associated with engaging in market activity? Do markets corrupt our morals? The belief that markets often deliver the material goods but rarely deliver the social or the moral goods appears to be mistaken. The evidence suggests that, rather than necessarily destroying social bonds, markets can and often do encourage their development (Storr 2008). Furthermore, the evidence also suggests that, rather than making us selfish and corrupt, markets both work better when peopled by virtuous people and encourage virtuous behavior.

This is admittedly not a unique observation. Others have argued that we do not tend to lose our souls in markets (see especially McCloskey 2006, 2010, 2016). This book builds on these efforts and argues that markets are not morally corrupting.

What Are These Things Called Markets?

At this stage, please permit us a short note on terms. A market is a space where the buying and selling of goods and services takes place. In markets, sellers compete with one another to attract buyers and buyers compete with one another to secure the goods and services that they desire. In markets, people also cooperate with one another to produce and purchase goods and services. The term "market" could refer to an actual space like a local flea or farmers' market. It could also describe a conceptual market like the labor market or the housing market. Markets work well when market participants can effectively exchange with one another. Well-functioning markets, thus, depend on clear and respected property rights, reliable contract enforcement, and mechanisms for resolving disputes. Markets depend on clear and respected distinctions between *mine and thine* and a clear sense of what can be done with one's own property (including one's own person). Similarly, contract enforcement is necessary if trading partners are to engage in any trades where the payment for goods and services and the delivery of goods and services do not occur simultaneously or there is a need to establish long-term trading relationships. Should disputes materialize, trading partners need a forum for resolving disputes and a belief that they will be dealt with fairly in that forum. Markets, then, are social arenas that are characterized by buying and selling, and that are made possible by certain institutions which facilitate buying and selling. Markets are also spaces where entrepreneurship and innovation thrive. Of course, markets can and do still operate when these institutions are weak or weakly enforced. But people are less able to use markets to coordinate their activities with others, to satisfy their desires, and to earn a living when property rights are not widely respected, when contracts are not routinely enforced, and where the rule of law does not exist.

Market societies, market economies, market-based societies, and commercial societies will be used interchangeably to describe areas, countries, or regions where markets are permitted to thrive, that is, spaces where property rights are respected, contracts are enforced, and the rule of law exists. Stated another way, market societies are spaces where the market system not only operates but operates without significant interference.

Capitalism is often used to describe this type of economic system. We will, however, generally avoid using capitalism to describe a market system because it is somewhat misleading. Market economies, of course, do facilitate the acquisition of capital goods (meaning here the accumulation of useful stuff) as well as the growth and development of a community's capital stock. But market societies do not depend solely or even primarily on capital acquisition. Market economies also require innovation. Globalization has been used to describe the spread of markets around the world. We will, however, not use this term because globalization not only refers to the spread of markets but also describes the spread of ideas and institutions. Neoliberalism has also been used to describe an ideology that supports market economies. That term will not be enlisted here because it is unclear to our minds exactly how supportive many so-called neoliberals truly are of market economies. Many people who are described as neoliberals are quite comfortable with weakening market institutions.

It should also be noted that market economies both have much in common and vary tremendously. The size of the welfare state, for instance, can differ significantly in different market societies. Take the Nordic countries—Sweden, Norway, Finland, Iceland, and Denmark—all of which are known for their generous welfare systems that include elaborate social safety nets, publicly provided healthcare and education, public pensions, and high tax burdens. Despite having larger governments than other market societies, these countries have strong property rights, reliable contract enforcement, and low barriers to trade and so are still characterized as market societies. The type of political systems that accompany market economies can also differ significantly. Market economies flourish within democratic political systems, like the United Kingdom, as well as more autocratic political systems, like Singapore. As long as the political systems in these countries secure property rights, enforce contracts, and safeguard a rule of law, we will describe them as market societies.

We will refer to all other societies as nonmarket societies.[3] Admittedly, our label for nonmarket societies might appear misleading to some readers. We acknowledge that one interpretation of the label paints nonmarket societies as primitive societies where there is no buying and selling and where there is no respect for property rights, contracts, or the rule of law. That is not what we mean here. By nonmarket societies, we simply mean societies whose institutional environments significantly impinge on the operation of markets. For instance, we describe Indonesia as a nonmarket society. It had a dictatorship under Suharto until 1998 and continues to suffer from cronyism and nepotism. While to a lesser degree since the fall of Suharto, the state continues to exercise its power to restrict genuine competition in the market and distributes special privileges to the socioeconomic and political elite. In other words, although markets definitely exist in Indonesia, they are not allowed to operate freely in Indonesia. Another example of a nonmarket society is Spain. Spain underwent a peaceful transition from a dictatorship to a democracy after the death of its dictator, Francisco Franco, in 1975. Since Spain's induction into the European Union in 1986, it has experienced rapid economic modernization and achieved vast improvements in freedom and human rights. However, it lags behind many other European countries in its economic competitiveness (Schwab et al. 2017: 272). In particular, an inefficient government bureaucracy and restrictive labor regulations are some of the top issues that prevent Spain from being more competitive economically (Ibid.). While markets exist and even flourish in Spain, its institutional shortcomings, highlighted above, are why we describe it as a nonmarket society.

---

[3] See Appendix for the list of market and nonmarket societies.

If engagement in market life comes at a moral cost, then we should expect those moral costs to be higher in market societies since market life is more prevalent in market societies. Thus, we should also expect qualitative evidence of these negative moral consequences to be more readily available in market societies. Similarly, we should expect quantitative measures of morality to be lower in market societies than in nonmarket societies. This book will examine both the qualitative and quantitative evidence. The evidence suggests that market societies outperform nonmarket societies on material as well as moral grounds.[4]

How Is This Book Structured?

Most scholars accept that people are materially better off in market societies, and that people are materially worse off in nonmarket societies. There is, however, a debate among the critics, defenders, and students of commercial life concerning whether the wealth that societies gain by embracing markets comes at too high a moral cost.

This book, thus, attempts to answer the questions: Are markets moral? Do markets depend on and encourage vices like greed and envy? Or do they rely on and encourage virtues like trust? Is engaging in market activity morally problematic? Do markets corrupt our morals? We find that rather than corrupting our morals that the opposite is true. The evidence suggests that the market actually improves our morals. There are two main arguments that we advance in support of this claim. First, we argue that people can improve their lives through markets. People in market societies are wealthier, healthier, happier, and better connected than people in nonmarket societies. This material fact, we contend, is morally significant. Second, we argue that the market is a moral space that both depends on its participants being virtuous and also rewards them for being virtuous. Without principled participants both the market and society can deteriorate into general despair and disorder. Moreover, rather than harming individuals ethically, the market is an arena where

---

[4] This, of course, will not be fully satisfying to anyone who worries that markets are morally corrupting. A critic of markets concerned about the potential of moral corruption as a result of market activity could always complain (a) that they are not committed to the view that nonmarket societies are less morally corrupting than market societies, or (b) that our approach does not account for all of the complexity involved in linking market activity to moral outcomes. However, the arguments and evidence that we offer are reasons to be skeptical of the claim that markets are morally corrupting. At the very least, we advance a response to the question, "Do markets corrupt our morals?," that directly engages that question. If we inspire others to look for more compelling ways to assess whether or not market activity is morally corrupting, we would have surpassed our ambition.

individuals are encouraged to be their best selves. More provocatively, successful markets not only require but also produce principled participants.

The next two chapters explore one of the central moral criticisms of markets (i.e. that markets are morally corrupting) and the way that scholars who disagree with this proposition have defended the market against that charge. Chapter 2 reviews and critically engages a variety of moral criticisms of the market including those by St. Thomas Aquinas, by Rousseau, and by Marx. This chapter will also review and critically engage some of the more recent criticisms of the moral aspects of markets. We argue that a common thread running through all of these arguments is the notion that markets are morally corrupting. Although this claim is often discussed in the language of moral philosophy, and the most damning critiques along these lines are deontological claims that do not allow for the possibility that market exchange can be moral, what we are calling the common central concern of the moral critics of markets (i.e. that markets are morally corrupting) is at root an empirical, rather than a philosophical, claim. As such, we can evaluate whether or not it is true that markets are likely to be morally corrupting using our theoretical understanding of how markets can and should work, and on the basis of evidence regarding how markets do in fact work.

Unfortunately, traditional moral defenses of the market do not really address the central moral criticism leveled against markets by their critics. Rather than (theoretically or empirically) evaluating the claim that markets are morally corrupting, the traditional defenses either avoid or (implicitly or explicitly) endorse the view that markets are potentially corrupting. In Chap. 3, we review and discuss the way that the market is traditionally defended on moral grounds. Specifically, we argue that both claims that the market neither promotes nor suppresses morality and claims that the market transforms private vice into public virtue are inadequate responses to the central moral criticism of markets. If the moral critics of markets are worried that markets promote vice, a response that says that markets are amoral or that highlights the material benefits that result from engaging in market activities does not constitute a strong defense nor does it speak to whether or not markets corrupt our morals.

If the central moral concern of market critics is to be evaluated, the question of whether or not engaging in market activities is morally corrupting has to be answered directly. The remaining chapters ask and answer the question: Do markets corrupt our morals? Are markets moral spaces that depend on and cultivate our morality or are markets immoral spaces where vice thrives and is encouraged? Is virtue endogenous to markets?[5] Chapter 4 demonstrates

---

[5] Munger and Russell (2018) asked a similar question about profit seekers.

that the market is an arena where individuals can work to improve their lives. People who live in market societies are wealthier, healthier, happier, and better connected than people who live in nonmarket societies. Additionally, these benefits are not only enjoyed by the privileged few in these communities. The least advantaged in market societies are better off than the least advantaged in nonmarket societies and may be better off than the most well-off in some nonmarket societies. This material fact, we argue, is of moral significance.

We then argue in Chap. 5 that markets function better when participants are virtuous, although markets *could* function without especially virtuous beings. Additionally, we show that market participants tend to be virtuous. McCloskey (2006, 2010, 2016) has forcefully and convincingly made the same point that markets are compatible with and depend on virtuous behavior. The bourgeois virtues are both bourgeois (i.e. born of markets) and virtuous (i.e. exhibiting the very virtues we have long admired). Beyond exhibiting the seven virtues that McCloskey highlighted (love, faith, hope, courage, temperance, prudence, and justice), we show that people in market societies tend to be more altruistic, are less likely to be materialistic and corrupt, and are more likely to be cosmopolitan as well as trusting and trustworthy.

In Chap. 6, we argue that markets actually have the ability to make us more virtuous. We show how market participants respond to trustworthy and untrustworthy trading partners and highlight the mechanisms through which moral development occurs in markets. Rather than being morally corrupting, markets are spaces of moral development because they offer us opportunities to discover others who have the moral qualities that we admire as well as because virtuous behavior is rewarded, and immoral behavior is punished in markets.

Finally, Chap. 7 teases out the implications of our conclusion that markets are moral spaces that depend on and encourage morality. It is important to note that saying that markets are not morally corrupting is not to say that markets should exist in everything. It is possible to accept that we are correct that markets are moral and still maintain that certain markets in certain goods and services are noxious and should be limited. Our arguments do imply, however, that, rather than there being moral costs associated with engaging in market activity, there are moral costs that will result from curtailing market activity. The moral critics of markets seem to have it exactly wrong. As such, implementing policies that attempt to respond to their moral concerns about markets might very well lead to the immoral outcomes that they themselves want to avoid.

Bibliography

Anderson, E. 1995. Feminist Epistemology: An Interpretation and a Defense. *Hypatia* 10 (3): 50–84.

Aquinas, T. [1485] 1918. *Summa Theologica*. Trans. English Dominican Province. London: Burns, Oates & Washbourne.

Aristotle. [350 BC] 1984, 2013. *Politics*. Trans. Carnes Lord. Chicago/London: University of Chicago Press.

Berggren, N. 1999. Economic Freedom and Equality: Friends or Foes? *Public Choice* 100 (3–4): 203–223.

Bowles, S. 2016. *The Moral Economy: Why Good Incentives Are No Substitute for Good Citizen*. New Haven: Yale University Press.

Central Intelligence Agency. 2018. The World Factbook 2018. https://www.cia.gov/library/publications/the-world-factbook/index.html

Falk, A., and N. Szech. 2013. Morals and Markets. *Science* 340 (6133): 707–711.

Human Rights Watch. 2015. *World Report 2015: North Korea: Events of 2014*. New York: Human Rights Watch. https://www.hrw.org/world-report/2015/country-chapters/north-korea

Human Rights Watch. 2017. *World Report 2017: Events of 2016*. New York: Human Rights Watch. https://www.hrw.org/sites/default/files/world_report_download/wr2017-web.pdf

Lavoie, D., and E. Chamlee-Wright. 2000. *Culture and Enterprise: The Development, Representation and Morality of Business*. London/New York: Routledge.

MacIntyre, A. 1981. *After Virtue: A Study in Moral Theory*. Notre Dame: University of Notre Dame Press.

———. 1999. *Dependent Rational Animals: Why Human Beings Need the Virtues*. Chicago: Open Court Publishing.

Mandeville, B. [1714, 1732] 1988. *The Fable of the Bees or Private Vices, Publick Benefits*. With Commentary by F.B. Kaye. Indianapolis: Liberty Fund.

Marx, K. [1821] 1994. *Karl Marx: Selected Writings*, ed. L.H. Simon. Indianapolis: Hackett Publishing.

McCloskey, D.N. 2006. *The Bourgeois Virtues: Ethics for an Age of Commerce*. Chicago: University of Chicago Press.

———. 2010. *Bourgeois Dignity: Why Economics Can't Explain The Modern World*. Chicago: University of Chicago Press.

———. 2016. *Bourgeois Equality: How Ideas, Not Capital or Institutions, Enriched the World*. Chicago: University of Chicago Press.

Munger, M.C., and D.C. Russell. 2018. Can Profit Seekers Be Virtuous? In *The Routledge Companion to Business Ethics*, ed. E. Heath, B. Kaldis, and A. Marcoux, 113–130. London/New York: Routledge.

Roth, A.E. 2007. Repugnance as a Constraint on Markets. *Journal of Economic Perspectives* 21 (3): 37–58.

Sandel, M.J. 2012. *What Money Can't Buy: The Moral Limits of Markets*. London: Macmillan.

Schwab, K., X. Sala-Martin, and R. Samans. 2017. *The Global Competitiveness Report 2017–2018*. Geneva: World Economic Forum.

Scully, G.W. 2002. Economic Freedom, Government Policy and the Trade-Off Between Equity and Economic Growth. *Public Choice* 113 (1–2): 77–96.

Shleifer, A. 2004. Does Competition Destroy Ethical Behavior? *American Economic Review* 94 (2): 414–418.

Smith, A. [1776] 1981. *An Inquiry into the Nature and Causes of the Wealth of Nations*. Indianapolis: Liberty Fund.

———. [1759] 1982. *The Theory of Moral Sentiments*. Indianapolis: Liberty Fund.

Stewart, D. [1795] 1829. *The Works of Dugald Stewart. Vol. 7. Account of the Life and Writings of Adam Smith*. Cambridge: Hilliard and Brown.

Storr, V.H. 2008. The Market as a Social Space: On the Meaningful Extraeconomic Conversations That Can Occur in Markets. *Review of Austrian Economics* 2 (2–3): 135–150.

The World Bank. 2016. *World Bank Open Data*. https://data.worldbank.org/. Accessed 15 Mar 2016

2

Markets as Monsters

In Kenyan author Ngugi wa Thiong'o's (1982) mythical novel *Devil on the Cross,* the devil ("Satan, the King of Hell") hosts a competition between Kenyan businessmen to see which one of them is the biggest thief and robber. Businessman after businessman takes the stage to brag about their wealth and their women, to tell of their conquests, and to share their philosophies on business. "He will tell us how he first came to steal and rob and where he has stolen and robbed," the master of ceremonies announced, "and then he will tell us briefly his thoughts on how to perfect our skills in theft and robbery" (Ibid.: 87).

Before the proceedings got underway, however, the master of ceremonies invited the head of the foreign delegation of entrepreneurs that was there to witness the competition to offer opening remarks. The remarks by the head of the delegation were a celebration of the corruption that undergirds economic life in the more developed world. The leader (Ibid.: 89) remarked,

> I think there is no one who does not know that theft and robbery are the cornerstones of American and Western civilization. Money is the heart that beats to keep the Western world on the move. If people want to build a great civilization like ours, then kneel down before the god of money. … It's far better to drink the blood of your people and to eat their flesh than to retreat a step.

Embracing the pursuit of money over everything else, the leader told the assembly, was the reason that the developed world had grown wealthy and was the surest path to wealth in the developing world.

Each contestant in this peculiar competition offered similar explanations for why they were able to succeed. In every case, greed and dishonesty were at

© The Author(s) 2019
V. H. Storr, G. S. Choi, *Do Markets Corrupt Our Morals?*,
https://doi.org/10.1007/978-3-030-18416-2_2

the root of their economic successes, and at the heart of the capitalist system. For instance, one of the competitors, Gĩtutu, explained that he believed in "the catechism of the lord … Reap where you never planted, eat that for which you never shed a drop of sweat and drink that which has been fetched by others" (Ibid.: 101). Also, as Gĩtutu asked, "How do think you think Grogan and Delamere became rich? I would sleep with my mother before I believed that it was their own sweat that made them so wealthy. … Who has ever become rich by his own sweat? Who has ever become rich through his salary alone?" (Ibid.: 102). Similarly, Mwireri, another "entrepreneur" in the competition, explains that he has "studied thoroughly the system based on the theft of the sweat and blood of workers and peasants – what in English we call *capitalism*. The system is this: the masses cultivate; a select few (those with talents) harvest" (Ibid.: 166). In Ngugi's tale, entrepreneurs are parasites, not producers. The system that empowers them is a devil who would make a hell for us on earth and so should be crucified.

Ngugi's fanciful tale resonates because it captures a common concern about capitalism, that is, that it is a corrupt system that corrupts us. While Ngugi's portrayal of capitalism as a devil that must be destroyed seems rather extreme, capitalism and capitalists are nonetheless often portrayed as monsters within popular literature and in the scholarly debate over the morality of capitalism. Vampire capitalism sucks the blood of workers, further enrichening the wealthy and impoverishing the disadvantaged. Demon capitalism possesses us all, turning us into slavish, soulless creatures who produce only what we are told to produce, and consume only what we are told to consume. Zombie capitalism is lumbering around the landscape, hungry for human flesh, eating human brains, transforming us into mindless, withered things who are empty inside and act on our urges rather than because of any higher motives.

These monster metaphors seem to get to the heart of what so many feel as they experience commercial society and what so many moral critics of markets seem to find when they examine market societies. Medley and Carroll (2004), for instance, argued that global capital is not a godsend, traveling around the globe, improving lives whenever and wherever it lands. Rather, it is a hostile force; in their words, "a hungry ghost." "Capitalist institutions," they claimed, "interpolate individual workers into factory regimes that will consume not only their labor, but also their whole being, body and spirit" (Ibid.: 146). Likewise, Harman (2010: 12) argued that "21st century capitalism as a whole is a zombie system, seemingly dead when it comes to achieving human goals and responding to human feelings, but capable of sudden spurts of activity that cause chaos all around." Similarly, Kennedy (2016) suggested that modern commercial societies are populated by firms engaged in forms of "vampire capitalism," that is, not reinvesting revenues into production but instead reorienting their wealth toward risky financial investments.

Additionally, McNally (2011) argued that monsters ought to be the central figures in any narrative about commercial society. In fact, stories of monsters are so popular in these communities because, McNally (Ibid.: 3) contended, "tales of body-snatching, vampirism, organ-theft, and zombie-economics all comprise multiple imaginings of the risks to bodily integrity that inhere in a society in which individual survival requires selling our life-energies to people on the market." These narrative forms become the "refuge" for discussions of the monstrosity of the market because contemporary politics in the developed world drives those kinds of concerns underground. According to McNally (Ibid.: 4), however, in the tales about the "monsters of the market," monsters are,

> both perpetrators and victims. In the former camp, we have those monstrous beings – vampires, evil doctors, pharmaceutical companies, body-snatchers – that capture and dissect bodies, and bring their bits to market. In the camp of the victims, we find those disfigured creatures, frequently depicted as zombies, who have been turned into *mere bodies*, unthinking and exploitable collections of flesh, blood, muscle and tissue.

McNally viewed not only the workings of the capitalist system but the rise of capitalism itself as a kind of horror story. Capitalism disrupted the communal forms of economic organization that preceded it and dissected the social bonds that previously connected individuals, replacing them with money relations (Ibid.: 37). Once cut adrift, it became impossible for us to avoid becoming victims of vampires and turning into soulless zombies.

Again, the concern is not just that markets are themselves monsters and that markets are largely populated by demons, vampires, and zombies. The risk of engaging in market activity is not just that we risk becoming victims of markets and other market actors, or that we are vulnerable to all manner of monsters within market settings. The concern is that markets can actually transform us. The view is that "the division of labor [makes] man as far as possible an abstract being, an automaton, and [transforms] him into a spiritual and physical monster" (Marx [1821] 1994: 49). If the market is morally corrupting, then the moral costs associated with engaging in market activity are potentially tremendous.

Key Critics of the Morality of Markets Agree That They Are Morally Corrupting

Moral philosophy gave birth to political economy a few centuries ago and political economy gave birth to economics just over a century ago. The science of how societies allocate scarce resources efficiently, the science of consumption and production, the science of exchange is, thus, rooted in the study of right and wrong, the study of justice, the study of how we might live better together. Since before Adam Smith to present-day virtue ethicists, moral philosophers have been concerned with whether our commercial dealings were compatible with the exercise of virtue and if our commercial dealings depended on or promoted vice. That concern has sometimes led them to conceive of the community and the market as distinct spheres of life, with distinct moral possibilities. The potential for moral growth that exists in the *polis* is, on these views, contrasted with the probability of moral decline in the *agora*. This section offers a brief review of the key claims by some of the strongest critics of commercial society about the moral costs associated with the growth of market society.

St. Thomas Aquinas did not believe that market activity was necessarily morally problematic. If an item was bought and sold for what it was worth, there was nothing inherently sinful in the transaction. But, Aquinas did think that selling an item for more or buying it for less than the "just price" was immoral. Additionally, while Aquinas did not condemn market activity, he believed that there was the potential to take advantage of others in every transaction and that market life was not particularly edifying.[1]

For Aquinas, our relationships with others ought to exhibit an equality of justice; people should give to others what they owe them and should expect

---

[1] Aquinas also believed that usury ought to be condemned. He (ST II-II, q. 78, a.1.) specified that "[t]o take usury for money lent is unjust in itself, because this is to sell what does not exist, and this evidently leads to inequality which is contrary to justice." Money, he (Ibid.) elaborated,

> was invented chiefly for the purpose of exchange: and consequently the proper and principal use of money is its consumption or alienation whereby it is sunk in exchange. Hence it is by its very nature unlawful to take payment for the use of money lent, which payment is known as usury: and just as a man is bound to restore other ill-gotten goods, so is he bound to restore the money which he has taken in usury.

However, Aquinas (ST II-II, q. 78, a. 2.) clarified that,

> there would be no sin in receiving something of the kind [e.g. benevolence, and love for the lender, and so forth], not as exacting it, nor yet as though it were due on account of some agreement tacit or expressed, but as a gratuity: since, even before lending the money, one could accept a gratuity, nor is one in a worse condition through lending.

from others what they deserve. As such, we should attempt to establish an equality of justice in all of our interactions with one another. This means doing good and refraining from evil (ST II-II, q. 79, a. 1.), expecting our judicial decisions to restore an equality of justice wherever an inequality is discovered (ST II-II, q. 62, a. 3.), and buying and selling at the just price (ST II-II, q. 77, a. 1.).

Trading at anything other than the just price, Aquinas expounded, injures one of the parties to the trade and so is sinful and rightly condemned. This is the case even when neither party engages in fraud in order to obtain more than their due. According to Aquinas (ST II-II, q. 77, a. 1.),

> buying and selling seem to be established for the common advantage of both parties, one of whom requires that which belongs to the other, and vice versa … Now whatever is established for the common advantage, should not be more of a burden to one party than to another, and consequently all contracts between them should observe equality of thing and thing. Again, the quality of a thing that comes into human use is measured by the price given for it, for which purpose money was invented … Therefore if either the price exceed the quantity of the thing's worth, or, conversely, the thing exceed the price, there is no longer the equality of justice: and consequently, to sell a thing for more than its worth, or to buy it for less than its worth, is in itself unjust and unlawful.

Trade exists to benefit both parties to the exchange. Again, a trade is unjust if one trading partner received more than they deserved and the other less than they deserved.

According to Aquinas, trades at prices other than the just price are sinful, even if one party is willing to live with the injustice because they have a particular need for the good or service being traded. As Aquinas (ST II-II, q.77, a. 1) explained,

> if the one man derives a great advantage by becoming possessed of the other man's property, and the seller be not at a loss through being without that thing, the latter ought not to raise the price, because the advantage accruing to the buyer, is not due to the seller, but to a circumstance affecting the buyer.

So, in this perspective, charging a desperate man who needs a particular good more than the just price for that good is sinful. Similarly, paying a desperate man who needs the money from a sale less than the just price for his goods is also sinful. Although this kind of unbalanced trade is understandably permitted by human law,[2] it is inconsistent with divine law according to Aquinas because it means taking advantage of another's needy condition.

The question of the morality or immorality of market life in any particular time or place would, then, appear to be an empirical question for Aquinas. If most things in a particular market are bought and sold for what they are worth, then most market dealings in that market establish an equality of justice and are consistent with divine law. If, however, most trades in a market are above or below the just price, then most trade in that market involves some kind of exploitation (i.e. either the buyer is taking advantage of the seller or vice versa), and market transactions (at least as they tend to exist in that market) are morally suspect.

That the prevalence of trades at or away from the just price determines the moral character of a market in an Aquinian system means that understanding what Aquinas meant by the just price is critical to understanding what he believed about the morality of market activity. It is evident, for instance, that the just price of a good is not something that is inherent in that good. According to Aquinas (ST II-II, q. 77, a. 1.), in a situation where the seller will suffer without the good, "the just price will depend not only on the thing sold, but on the loss which the sale brings on the seller." Under this scenario, it would be acceptable to sell the good for more than it is worth in and of itself; what matters is what the thing is "worth to the owner." What the good in question is worth to the parties in the exchange, that is, the subjective evaluations of the buyer and the seller, determines the just price.

But, while the subjective evaluations of the buyer and seller jointly determine the just price, the just price is not simply the price that was agreed to by the buyer and seller. It is possible on Aquinas' account to buy and sell a good for other than the just price. Furthermore, he did not seem to be referring to the price that would have emerged in a competitive market, or even the price that others agreed to in the market.[3] While Aquinas certainly condemned fraud, price gouging, and taking advantage of fire sales, he acknowledged that there are justifiable reasons for the just price to differ from the price elsewhere in the market (e.g. when both the buyer desperately needs it and the seller would suffer from being without it).

---

[2] It is possible to read this as simply a condemnation of price gouging (e.g. raising the price of a needed good or service after something like a hurricane or flood). However, he also seems to be condemning what economists refer to as price discrimination, where a producer or a firm charges different prices to different consumers for the same product. As such, Aquinas seems to be denouncing price discrimination of the kind that is commonplace in markets.

[3] However, there are articles, including Friedman (1980), that argue that the just price is simply the market rate. See also Guzmán and Munger (2014) for an interesting discussion of these issues.

Aquinas might have viewed the just price as the price that ensures that both the buyer and the seller are made equally better off by the exchange. To deploy the technical jargon of economics, the just price might be the price where the consumer surplus is equal to the producer surplus. There is conceivably no reason, however, to expect that this would be achieved in any actual market transactions, except by coincidence. Deciding to only trade at the just price would require sellers to refuse to accept exchanges where the buyer is not made equally better off (i.e. not engage in profit maximization). Similarly, deciding to only trade at the just price would require buyers to reject trades that do not equally benefit the sellers (i.e. not engage in cost minimization). Yet profit maximization and cost minimization are regular, if not essential, features of the market. Moreover, it is impossible to know a buyer's willing-ness to pay or a seller's willingness to accept an offer without their admitting it before consummating an exchange. Simply stating the defects of the par-ticular item being sold or offered in an exchange would not guarantee that both parties benefit equally from the exchange. Trading at the just price would seem to require buyers and sellers to confess their willingness to pay or accept and then to split the difference when agreeing to an exchange. Haggling, bar-gaining, wrangling, quibbling, and all the other activities that tend to be asso-ciated with market activity would, thus, appear to be sinful in Aquinas' view. Most exchanges in real-world markets, even in the markets of Aquinas' day, would have to be considered unjust and so immoral if we were to employ this standard.

Still, Aquinas did believe that it was possible for market activity to be moral or at least not immoral so long as trades were conducted at the just price, even if trade at the just price is likely to be quite rare. Moreover, he even believed that some trade is "commendable because it satisfies a natural need" so long as other trade that "satisfies the greed for gain, which knows no limit and tends to infinity" is justly censured (Ibid.: q. 77, a. 4.).[4] His was not a blanket condemnation of gain but of gain that was misdirected away from serving

---

[4] According to Aquinas (ST II-II, q. 77, a. 4.),

> trading, considered in itself, has a certain debasement attaching thereto, in so far as, by its very nature, it does not imply a virtuous or necessary end. Nevertheless gain which is the end of trading, though not implying, by its nature, anything virtuous or necessary, does not, in itself, connote anything sinful or contrary to virtue: wherefore nothing prevents gain from being directed to some necessary or even virtuous end, and thus trading becomes lawful. Thus, for instance, a man may intend the moderate gain which he seeks to acquire by trading for the upkeep of his household, or for the assistance of the needy: or again, a man may take to trade for some public advantage, for instance, lest his country lack the necessaries of life, and seek gain, not as an end, but as payment for his labor.

some social or public good and instead steered toward some purely personal advantage. Again, a great deal of exchanges that occur in markets would likely run afoul of this standard.

Aquinas also believed that market activity was not particularly edifying, regardless of how one used the proceeds from market exchange. Describing why clerics should avoid trade where possible, Aquinas (Ibid.: q. 77, a. 4.) argued that,

> Clerics should abstain not only from things that are evil in themselves, but even from those that have an appearance of evil. This happens in trading, both because it is directed to worldly gain, which clerics should despise, and because trading is open to so many vices, since "a merchant is hardly free from sins of the lips" ['A merchant is hardly free from negligence, and a huckster shall not be justified from the sins of the lips'] (Ecclus. 26:28). There is also another reason, because trading engages the mind too much with worldly cares, and consequently withdraws it from spiritual cares; wherefore the Apostle says (2 Tim. 2:4): "No man being a soldier to God entangleth himself with secular businesses."

Of course, clerics were permitted to engage in trade "directed to supply the necessaries of life" (Ibid.: q. 77, a. 4.). Aquinas, however, emphasized that there is something potentially debasing about engaging in retail trade. Market activity is necessarily directed toward worldly gain and the market actor is prone to moral error. A more modern translation of the passage that Aquinas quotes from the Ecclesiasticus, which is a part of the Apocrypha, stated more clearly that "it is difficult for a merchant to avoid doing wrong and for a trader not to incur sin." There was a certain kind of moral danger involved in market activity.

Rather than focusing on the morality or immorality of engaging in market activity, Jean-Jacques Rousseau focused on the negative moral effects that market society had on some of its participants. Specifically, Rousseau reasoned that we should expect to observe high levels of deceit and greed in commercial societies. Because people in commercial society were necessarily dependent on the opinions of others, they constantly had to pretend to be someone that they were not in order to stay in others' good graces. Rousseau also believed that commercial society gave rise to endless desires.

Rousseau's concerns about the moral effects of markets are sprinkled throughout his writings but are perhaps clearest in his second discourse. Rousseau began *A Discourse on Inequality* by suggesting that there are two kinds of inequality among human beings. According to Rousseau ([1754] 1984: 77),

I discern two sorts of inequality in the human species: the first I call natural or physical because it is established by nature, and consists of differences in age, health, strength of the body and qualities of the mind or soul; the second we might call moral or political inequality because it derives from a sort of convention, and is established, or at least authorized, by the consent of men. This latter inequality consists of the different privileges which some enjoy to the prejudice of others – such as their being richer, more honoured, more powerful than others, and even getting themselves obeyed by others.

While we should expect to observe differences between the old and the young, the healthy and the sick, and the strong and the weak in every place and time, Rousseau stated that many of the inequalities that we observe between human beings in commercial society are artificial. Moreover, the moral failings of humans (e.g. greed, vanity, and pride) that would seem to be the source of artificial inequalities (i.e. differences in power or privileges) are really the result of these inequalities.

Interestingly, Rousseau's view of humans in the state of nature is decidedly non-Hobbesian. As he (Ibid.: 98) wrote, "let us not conclude with Hobbes that man is naturally evil just because he has no idea of goodness, that he is vicious for want of any knowledge of virtue." "We conclude," Rousseau (Ibid.: 104) explained,

> that savage man, wandering in the forests, without work, without speech, without a home, without war, and without relationships, was equally without any need of his fellow men and without any desire to hurt them, perhaps not even recognizing any one of them individually. Being subject to so few passions, and sufficient unto himself, he had only such feelings and such knowledge as suited his condition; he felt only his true needs, saw only what he believed it was necessary to see, and his intelligence made no more progress than his vanity.

Savage man, Rousseau concluded, was neither deceitful nor greedy. While it is true that he was incapable of virtue, it is also true that he was not prone to vice.

But, with the advent of commercial society everything changed. According to Rousseau, commercial society saw the introduction and expansion of artificial inequalities. As a result, Rousseau argued, humans became softer, smarter, more industrious, dependent on one another, and developed the capacity for virtue and a tendency toward vice. More pointedly, the introduction of the division of labor and the expansion of markets that accompanied and made society possible meant that humans became deceitful and greedy.

To be sure, the introduction of the division of labor and the specialization it encourages results in an increase in our productive capacities and an improvement in our material conditions. But, according to Rousseau (Ibid.: 119), a person is no longer "free and independent" under the division of labor and is instead "diminished … into subjection … to his fellow men, men of whom he has become the slave, in a sense, even in becoming their master; for if he is rich he needs their services; if he is poor he needs their aid; and even a mid-dling condition does not enable him to do without them." In commercial society, humans must rely on others in order to survive. Under the division of labor, you succeed by convincing others to work for or to employ you, con-vincing others to buy the stuff that you might have for sale, or to sell you the stuff that you desire. As such, in commercial society, we must constantly con-vince others that making us better off will make them better off as well. "[A]ll of which," Rousseau (Ibid.) rationalized, "makes him devious and artful with some, imperious and hard towards others, and compels him to treat badly the people he needs if he cannot make them fear him and does not judge it in his interest to be of service to them."

Rousseau did not seem to accept that the coincidence of wants that allows for robust trade to occur (i.e. that buyers truly want what sellers have to offer and vice versa) is a common enough phenomenon to facilitate robust trade. Instead, sellers must sometimes trick buyers or compel them in some way to get them to buy their goods and services. The division of labor unleashes not only our productive capacities, but also our worst traits because we need one another so much.

In addition to leading us to deceive one another about the goods and ser-vices that we have for sale, Rousseau noted that the market also drives us to deceive one another about our possessions, strengths, and capabilities. A man's status in a commercial society depends on "the quantity of his possessions," "his power to serve or to injure," and his "intelligence, beauty, strength, skill, merit or talents" (Ibid.). "[S]ince these qualities were the only ones that could attract consideration," Rousseau (Ibid.) explained, "it soon became necessary either to have them or to feign them." However, Rousseau did not expect that many people would have those qualities. As such, people are forced to pretend to be what they are not in a commercial society. In a commercial society, Rousseau (Ibid.) stated, it is,

> in one's own interest to seem to be other than one [is] in reality. Being and appearance became two entirely different things, and from this distinction arose insolent ostentation, deceitful cunning and all the vices that follow in their train.

The moral concerns that we have about our engaging in market activity, Rousseau confirmed, are warranted. It is not just that markets give free reign to certain vices; markets seem to promote and even depend on certain vices.

Rousseau considered greed to be another vice that colors our market interactions. Moreover, for him, greed is attended by a series of other vices including jealousy and a disregard for others. According to Rousseau (Ibid.),

> a devouring ambition, the burning passion to enlarge one's relative fortune, not so much from real need as to put oneself ahead of others, inspires in all men a dark propensity to injure one another, a secret jealousy which is all the more dangerous in that it often assumes the mask of benevolence in order to do its deeds in greater safety; … there is competition and rivalry on the one hand, conflicts of interest on the other, and always the hidden desire to gain an advantage at the expense of other people.

Rather than seeing market interactions as positive sum games, Rousseau regarded them as zero-sum games. Despite what they pretend to be doing, market actors are not really in the business of serving others. They are actually in the businesses of taking advantage of others. Because commercial society places us in a condition of dependence where our survival and success are entirely determined by how others view and treat us, we are transformed by the market into creatures with "a dark propensity" to "gain an advantage at the expense of other people" (Ibid.). This "evil," Rousseau explained, is a consequence of property and the division of labor, and is at the root of many, most, maybe all market interactions.[5]

It is fair to say, as Rasmussen (2008: 15) declared, that "Rousseau repudiated nearly every aspect of commercial society and that his critique of it is one of the most comprehensive offered." Still, we believe that Karl Marx is rightly viewed as *the* critic of capitalism.[6] Marx offered an economic, a social, and a moral critique of markets.[7] Marx's economic critique of capitalism turns on the inevitability of crisis within the capitalist economic system (see Marx

---

[5] Rousseau was deeply critical of the introduction of private property. While he thought the creation of private property was likely inevitable, and while he credited it with the creation of society, he nonetheless believed that property was the source of countless ills. According to Rousseau (Ibid.: 109),

> The first man who, having enclosed a piece of land, thought of saying 'This is mine' and found people simple enough to believe him, was the true founder of civil society. How many crimes, wars, murders; how much misery and horror the human race would have been spared if someone had pulled up the stakes and filled in the ditch and cried out to his fellow men: 'Beware of listening to this impostor. You are lost if you forget that the fruits of the earth belong to everyone and that the earth itself belongs to no one!'

[6] A version of this discussion of Marx has appeared on *Liberty Matters* (Storr 2018).

[7] Marx also argued, with Friedrich Engels, that the capitalist system had to be overturned and replaced with a socialist system in which the workers owned all the enterprises (see Marx and Engels [1848] 1967).

[1821] 1994). Marx's social critique of capitalism stresses the necessary antagonism between classes in commercial society.[8] Marx's moral critique of capitalism, although he would not have recognized it as a moral critique, concerned the inevitability of exploitation and alienation under capitalism.[9]

At its core, Marx argued, the market system was deeply unjust because workers in a market system did not get their due.[10] The owners of the means of production received more than their fair share of what was produced, and the laborers received considerably less than they deserved.

The exploitation of the worker in a market economy, Marx asserted, was an economic fact. Marx offered a technical definition of exploitation. According to Marx ([1867] 1990), exploitation occurs when the owners of capital in a market system capture the "surplus value" created by their workers (i.e. the value of the products that workers produce above what the workers need to subsist). Workers did not enjoy the fruits of their labor in capitalism. The very objects into which workers poured their labor are sold to others. And, the employers, rather than employees, capture the profits associated with these sales. Stated another way, labor hours were stolen from the laborers. Marx believed that we should expect exploitation to be pervasive in a market system, because the owners of capital will tend to bid down wages to the lowest levels possible. "The ordinary wage," Marx ([1844] 2009: 20) explained,

---

[8] See Marx and Engels ([1848] 1967) where they claimed that capitalism has evolved into a war between the bourgeoisie (i.e. the capitalist class that owns the means of production) and the proletariat (i.e. the working class).

[9] Admittedly, it is not always clear that Marx meant his discussions of exploitation and alienation to be "moral" critiques of markets. At various places in his writings (see, for instance, his "Critique of the Gotha Program"; Marx [1891] 1938), he seemed to explicitly reject that he is engaging in a moral argument. It is certainly the case that Marx did not believe that moral appeals from within the market system would ever lead to a correction of those moral ills (without, of course, a complete replacement of that system). Still, even if we were to accept that Marx was not ultimately engaged in a moral critique of the market system, his discussions of exploitation and alienation certainly have moral implications. As will be discussed, Marx believed that markets transformed us into a kind of monster. Human beings in a market system would not and could not flourish. Laborers in a market system had their labor stolen from them. There is a sense in which these are unavoidably moralized claims.

[10] Although our focus here is on the unjust extraction of surplus labor (i.e. the stealing of the laborer's labor time), Cohen (1995) explained that there are at least two senses in which exploitation is unjust. According to Cohen (Ibid.: 195–208),

> we can indeed say ... both that the extraction is unjust because it reflects an unjust distribution and that the asset distribution is unjust because it generates that unjust extraction. ... First, forced extraction of a surplus is wrong because of what it is, and not because it inherits the wrong of something else. Second, on our reasonable assumption that the sole purpose of means of production is to make product, a distribution of means of production is unjust only if and because it enables an unjust transfer of product.

is the lowest compatible with common humanity (that is a cattle-like existence). … The worker has become a commodity, and it is a bit of luck for him if he can find a buyer. And the demand on which the life of the worker depends, depends on the whim of the rich and the capitalists.

In order to survive, workers must simply accept lower wages than they deserve.[11]

Exploitation, for Marx, was an unavoidable feature of the market system.[12] Marx and Engels ([1848] 1906: 34), for instance, asserted that "modern bourgeois private property is the final and most complete expression of the system of producing and appropriating products, that is based on class antagonisms, on the exploitation of the many by the few." Similarly, Marx ([1867] 1915: 708) argued that,

within the capitalist system all methods for raising the social productiveness of labour are brought about at the cost of the individual labourer; all means for the development of production transform themselves into means of domination over, and exploitation of, the producers; they mutilate the labourer into a

---

[11] Admittedly, Marx ([1867] 1990) believed that there were circumstances where this wage might end up above subsistence levels.

[12] It might not be obvious from this account, but there is an issue with Marx's exploitation thesis. Marx's "proof" of exploitation under capitalism rested (in part) on the now-refuted labor theory of value. As Marx took pains to demonstrate, the only way that the capitalist can earn a profit is if he pays the worker less than the value that the worker creates. But, we should admit, Marx's criticism of capitalism might still stand even if we jettison the labor theory of value. To modernize the claim, all we would have to do is define exploitation as occurring whenever an employee's wage is lower than her marginal revenue product. In fact, one way to read Marx's discussions in the 1844 manuscripts is as an expression of Marx's hyper-concern with the differential power of employers and employees. Moreover, if neoclassical economic theory is correct, most workers in any profit-maximizing firm will be paid less than their marginal revenue product; in other words, most workers will be exploited according to a modernized version of Marx's critique.

There have been several studies that have explored whether workers in particular industries or firms are paid their marginal products. Not surprisingly, the answer is that some workers are paid their marginal product, some are paid more, and some are paid less. Where we see workers being paid less it is because of wage compression in fields where wage disparities would disrupt collaboration or because workers lack bargaining power. Consider the study by Macdonald and Reynolds (1994) of salaries of Major League Baseball players. Their study did not challenge previous findings that baseball players were not paid commensurate with what they contributed to the team's revenues before free agency. However, after free agency, veteran players appeared to be paid their marginal revenue product, while young players were still being "exploited," that is, paid less on average than their marginal revenue products. The findings in this study suggest that Marx's concern about some people getting less than they deserve could be a very real worry under some market structures. Moreover, as Wertheimer (1999: x) argued,

the important moral core of the Marxist view is not unique to Marxism. When Marxism claims that capitalist class exploits the proletariat, it employs the ordinary notion that one party exploits another when it gets unfair and underserved benefits from its transactions or relationships with others.

Note that rather than updating or modifying Marx, Wertheimer articulated a view of exploitation that does not rely on Marx.

fragment of a man, degrade him to the level of an appendage of a machine, destroy every remnant of charm in his work and turn it into a hated toil; … they distort the conditions under which he works, subject him during the labour process to a despotism the more hateful for its meanness.

At the center of the market process, Marx believed, was the exploitation of the many by the few. Moreover, the market system was not only profoundly unjust but was also demeaning and destructive. The market system and the capitalists who drive it were necessarily vicious.

For Marx, the moral invidiousness of the market system was not limited to how the market exploited workers. Additionally, he explained, workers in a market system necessarily become estranged or alienated from the product of their labor, the act of labor, their true natures, and their fellow men. This estrangement was both demeaning and dehumanizing. Rather than workers being able to improve their lives through their labor, they were made worse off through their labor. In fact, "the worker becomes an ever cheaper commodity the more commodities he creates" (Marx [1844] 2009: 71). Although the connection between an individual and the goods she produces should be an intimate one, Marx (Ibid.) contended that "the worker is related to the product of labor as an alien object" in a market system. More worrying, this alien object assumed power over the worker. According to Marx (Ibid.: 71–72),

> the more the worker spends himself, the more powerful the alien objective world becomes which he creates over-against himself, the poorer he himself – his inner world – becomes, the less belongs to him as his own. … The worker puts his life into the object; but now his life no longer belongs to him but to the object. … The *alienation* of the worker in his product means not only that his labor becomes an object, an *external* existence, but that it exists *outside him* independently, as something alien to him, and that it becomes a power on its own confronting him.

Because in a market system, the worker does not own the product of his labor, it gives birth to a dark irony: *mere tools become masters and those who should be masters become mere tools*. The worker produces an object that should be his to command but instead becomes a slave to the object that he produced.

According to Marx, because the product of a worker's labor is an alien thing in a market economy, the act of producing ceases to be a process where workers feel like themselves. "In his work," Marx (Ibid.: 74) wrote, he does not affirm himself but denies himself, does not feel content but unhappy, does not develop freely his physical and mental energy but mortifies his body and ruins his mind. The worker therefore only feels himself outside his work, and in his work feels outside himself. He is at home when he is not working, and when he is working he is not at home.

40 hrs/week

Work should be a source of dignity. But, in a market system, work is not ennobling. Instead, "it is activity as suffering, strength as weakness, begetting as emasculating, the worker's *own* physical and mental energy, his personal life or what is life other than activity – as an activity which is turned against him, neither depends on nor belongs to him" (Ibid.: 75). Because the product that the worker produces is an alien thing, the process of production is an alienating process.

There is a third sense in which labor in a market economy was alienating. Work in a market economy "estranges man's own body from him, as it does external nature and his spiritual essence, his *human* being" (Ibid.: 78). Human beings in a market system were transformed into something not altogether human. Unlike animals, who only produce what they need for themselves and their offspring, humans also produce when their physical needs have been satisfied as a way to express their sense of beauty and their sense of self. Because workers in a market context were robbed of their labor product, they were also robbed of their humanity, and they were robbed of their "advantage over animals." Alienated labor, for Marx, was necessarily debased labor.

Finally, labor in a market system also alienated workers from their fellow men. According to Marx (Ibid.: 78),

> An immediate consequence of the fact that man is estranged from the product of his labor, from his life-activity, from his species being [i.e. nature] is the *estrangement of man* from *man*. If man is confronted by himself, he is confronted by the *other* man. What applies to a man's relation to his work, to the product of his labor and to himself, also holds of a man's relation to the other man, and to the other man's labor and object of labor.

Rather than being connected to his fellow man, man was distanced from his fellow man during the process of production. The man divorced from his labor product, himself, and his humanity, cannot be connected to others. The estrangement of the worker that occurs in the market was a total estrangement.

To summarize, for Marx, individuals in market systems become alienated from their labor product, the production process, their human nature, and one another. The market system, thus, transforms humans into a kind of creature. Marx ([1844] 1994: 49) asserted that the division of labor in a market system transformed an individual into a spiritual and physical monster.[13]

If morality is in any way an expression of our humanity, then, this spiritual and physical monster does not have the capacity to be a truly moral actor.[14] A man who is estranged from himself and his fellow men cannot possibly be virtuous. The money system, which is responsible in Marx's theory for the worker's alienation, exhibits a "distorting power both against the individual and against the bonds of society, etc., which claim to be entities in themselves. It transforms fidelity into infidelity, love into hate, hate into love, virtue into vice, vice into virtue, servant into master, master into servant, idiocy into intelligence, and intelligence into idiocy" ([1844] 2009: 128). Again, the confusion, the loss of self that Marx described was profound and total. Estranged from his true nature, man is bewildered and "the world is upside down" (Ibid.: 129). There is simply no scope for true virtues in Marx's concept of the market order. We should expect workers to be debased because labor in a market system debases. We should expect him to be undignified because labor in a market system robs him of his dignity. We should expect him to be egoistic and asocial because labor in a market system alienates him from his human nature and his fellow men.

If true, the Aquinian, Rousseauvian, and Marxian accounts of the market paint a horrifying picture. There are obviously differences between their positions. But, they share a common and potentially devastating moral criticism of markets: our participation in the market corrupts our morals by engendering antisocial and overly self-interested sentiments, attitudes, and behaviors. It may be true that some of us may gain riches by engaging in market activity but any riches that we might gain come at the expense of others and at the price of our souls. The market system, they describe, would seem to be at best a moral quagmire.

---

[13] More fully,

> Just as the mutual exchange of products of *human activity* appears as *trading* and *bargaining*, so does the mutual reintegration and exchange of the activity itself appear as the *division of labor* making man as far as possible an abstract being, an automaton, and transforming him into a spiritual and physical monster. (Marx [1844] 1994: 49)

[14] Another way to make this point is to claim that markets do not allow for the emergence of a truly human morality. According to Engels ([1878] 1959: 132), "a really human morality which stands above class antagonisms and above any recollection of them becomes possible only at a stage of society which has not only overcome class antagonisms but has even forgotten them in practical life."

Contemporary Critics of the Morality of Markets Agree with These Earlier Market Critics[15]

Echoing the concerns about markets articulated by Aquinas, Rousseau, and Marx, a diverse group of scholars have argued that markets grow at the expense of communities and that markets promote selfishness, greed, and other vices. The communitarian critics, for instance, focus on the negative social consequences and the problematic moral outcomes that result from our reliance on and the expansion of the market (e.g. Bell 1976; MacIntyre 1981; Etzioni 1988; Putnam 2001; Sandel 2012). They explained that market-based societies fundamentally rely on autonomous actors pursuing their own ends and competing against each other. As the space occupied by the market expands, the space that community can occupy necessarily shrinks. *Gemeinschaft* necessarily surrenders to *Gesellschaft*. The growth of the market system has unwound the social bonds that knit our communities together. The communitarians lamented that we were once embedded in community, but that we are now all alone because of the expansion of markets. In a society based on market exchange, social bonds give way to rivalry, community fragments into a body of competitors, and loyalty is replaced by self-interest. Therefore, said the communitarians, the modern economic order inevitably transforms human beings into isolated atoms. And, arguably, isolated human beings cannot be truly moral.

Others have shared this belief that market values, by which they mean acquisitiveness and selfishness, are at odds with and eventually come to replace our virtues as the market expands.[16] According to this view, the market brings out the worst in us because it necessarily pits seller against seller, seller against buyer, and buyer against buyer. Once we were virtuous and cared about each other, but now we are only concerned with private gain and care only about ourselves. Although the market has improved our lives materially, they argued, it has also made us bad people.

---

[15] This section relies substantially on Storr (2009).

[16] Cohen (2009) pointed to greed and fear as being the two "values" that motivate market activity. According to Cohen (2009: 39),

> The immediate motive to productive activity in a market society is (not always but) typically some mixture of greed and fear, in proportions that vary with the details of a person's market position and personal character. It is true that people can engage in market activity under other inspirations, but the motives of greed and fear are what the market brings to prominence, and that includes greed on behalf of, and fear for the safety of, one's family. Even when one's concerns are thus wider than those of one's mere self, the market posture is greedy and fearful in that one's opposite-number marketeers are predominantly seen as possible sources of enrichment, and as threats to one's success. These are horrible ways of seeing other people, however much we have become habituated and inured to them, as a result of centuries of capitalist civilization.

Below we briefly review some of the most trenchant critiques of the market on moral grounds. This in no way is meant to be comprehensive. As such, we do not review some of the critics of markets that you might think that we ought to review; there are important critics of the market whose arguments we do not engage here.[17] However, our contention is that the critics whose arguments we do recreate below and attempt to respond to in subsequent chapters (and those critics whose work we do not engage here) agree that markets are potentially morally corrupting, despite admittedly important differences in the specifics of their arguments. Indeed, a central claim of many of the critiques of the market on moral grounds is that engaging in the market is materially beneficial but morally detrimental. The sample of these critiques presented below is meant to highlight this similarity rather than emphasize any differences between them.

Moreover, we do not review some of the criticisms of markets that you might think we should engage. There is no real discussion of the phenomenon of inequality except as it is articulated as evidence of the moral failure of markets.[18] Likewise, there is no discussion here and no real effort in subsequent chapters to argue against the position that some things should not be for sale (e.g. Satz 2010).[19] Similarly, while we do engage several critics of markets who worry about the effects of markets on community, our focus here is not on the communitarian critiques of markets (e.g. Putnam 2001; Bell 1976, 1993). Our silence should not suggest that we think that there is no merit to these lines of market criticism nor that we think there is no way to defend against them. Rather, we have chosen to limit our discussions here to recounting and responding to the empirical claim that markets are corrupting and that the expansion of the market has resulted in moral decline.

---

[17] For instance, we do not engage Karl Polanyi's critique of market fundamentalism (see Block and Somers 2014). Similarly, we do not engage conservative objections to laissez-faire like the one advanced by Röpke ([1958] 2014), who worried that free markets could undermine the very moral foundations that they require to function well if we were not careful. We do, however, engage Schumpeter's ([1942] 1950) similar claim that markets may contain the seeds to their own destruction in Chap. 6. Additionally, we do not engage a number of important virtue ethicists that have argued that the values of the market are at odds with traditional virtues (e.g. MacIntyre 1981). Like the critiques of the market that we do engage, however, many of these critiques are at root a charge that markets deliver the material goods but cannot deliver the moral or social goods. To the extent that the critics that we ignore offer additional or alternative criticisms of markets, nothing in our effort should be viewed as challenging or endorsing those critiques.

[18] As such, we do discuss Piketty (2014) in Chap. 4. Our concern there, however, is whether or not inequality is particularly a problem for market societies. While we present some of the most trenchant criticisms of Piketty's findings, we agree with Piketty's view that if inequality were peculiar to market societies that it would constitute a moral failing of market societies.

[19] As we clarify in Chap. 7, nothing we argue here challenges the possibility that some markets are noxious.

The Marxist philosopher Henri Lefebvre worried about the encroachment of the space of the market into other social spaces. According to Lefebvre, in order to grow, capitalism must create a particular kind of space. This space— what might be called market space and what Lefebvre called at different times the space of work, exchange, and consumption—is a space of alienation, domination, and exploitation. According to Lefebvre (1991: 325), capitalism's survival depends on the extension of capitalist space to "space in its entirety." The expansion of the economic sphere gobbles up households, towns, nature, and even outer space. As the extent of the market expands, we are increasingly able to take advantage of the division of labor and so, as a community, we become increasingly prosperous. Lefebvre would assert, however, that we have paid dearly for this progress. This process of market spaces devouring communal spaces is quite harmful. Capitalism also creates new global and fractured spaces through processes like urbanization and globalization.[20] According to Lefebvre (Ibid.: 336), "the mobilization of space for the purposes of its production makes harsh demands." Indeed, the production of new space and the occupation of all pre-existing space which accompanies the growth of the market are not benign processes. Most significantly, it requires "the entirety of space [to] be endowed with *exchange value*," which is ultimately alienating (Ibid.: 336). Following Marx, Lefebvre noted that within capitalist spaces man's labor products become alien objects, foreign things, which have a power over him. His labor product belongs to another and so he, ultimately, belongs to another.

Market space is what Lefebvre called "abstract space." Abstract space is not only a space of work, exchange, and consumption but also a space of political power and social control. It is "the space of accumulation (the accumulation of all wealth and resources: knowledge, technology, money, precious objects, works of art and symbols)" through a variety of means, some straightforward and some quite devious, some dexterous, and some quite vicious (Ibid.: 49). According to Lefebvre (Ibid.), because capitalism requires a space where the accumulation of money and power reigns supreme, abstract space becomes "the dominant form of space" in capitalist contexts; and, because capitalism requires a subjugated proletariat, abstract space is also necessarily a "space of

---

[20] Capitalist space is global in that "it abolishes distinctions and differences" (Lefebvre 1991: 355) and "its circulatory systems and networks may occupy space worldwide" (Ibid.: 341). It is fragmented and fractured because it "locates specificities, places or localities, both in order to control them and in order to make them negotiable" (Ibid.: 282). Interestingly, as Lefebvre (Ibid.: 355) explained, "it is not … as though one had global (or conceived) space to one side and fragmented (or directly experienced) space to the other – rather as one might have an intact glass here and a broken glass or mirror over there. For [capitalist] space 'is' whole and broken, global and fractured, at one and the same time."

dominance." It is a space "manipulated by authorities" who are prepared to use force when necessary to "shape," "socialize," and "crush" the users of space, to reinforce the distance between members of different classes, to bring about conformance with the edicts of the owners of space (Ibid.: 285). The alienating and hegemonic nature of capitalist space and the potential of market space to transform and corrupt its inhabitants are central to Lefebvre's critique of capitalism.[21]

Marxian geographer David Harvey (2001) proposed that the fragmentation and loss of identity that Marx and Lefebvre described has only intensified in recent years. According to Harvey (Ibid.: 123), since the 1970s, capital accumulation has resulted in what he called "time-space compression." Technological innovations accelerate production processes and speed up transactions, compressing time. Improvements in transportation and communications, such as jet transport and the Internet, reduce spatial barriers, compressing space. "We have recently been going through a strong phase of ... 'time-space compression,'" Harvey (Ibid.) wrote, "the world suddenly feels much smaller, and the time-horizons over which we can think about social action become much shorter." This compression of time and space, Harvey explained, is not a positive development, but is a source of deep anxiety. Because "our sense of who we are, where we belong and what our obligations encompass—in short, our *identity*—is profoundly affected by our sense of location in space and time," Harvey (Ibid.: 124) argued, the technological innovations as well as transportation and communication revolutions have created "crises of identity." These crises of identity are also at the same time *crises of virtue*. Not knowing who we are or where we belong, we are unlikely to know how we should behave or which qualities we should exhibit. Still, in this milieu, Harvey (Ibid.: 125) predicted, despite our efforts to respond to our profound alienation, "capital accumulation, market materialism and entrepreneurial greed rule the roost." The spaces of capital are, thus, immoral spaces and immoralizing spaces.

Economic anthropologist Stephen Gudeman was, similarly, concerned about the expansion of the space of the market into nonmarket spaces.[22] In

---

[21] In fact, alienation is a central concept of all of Lefebvre's work from his writing on dialectical materialism where he casts Marx as primarily a theorist of alienation to his critique of everyday life and his discussion of the production of space (Elden 2004: 41).

[22] Gudeman "is one of the leading economic anthropologists of our time" (Löfving 2005: 8). His contribution to our understanding of local and universal models and the embeddedness of daily life and anthropological practice cannot be exaggerated.

The Anthropology of Economy (2001), Gudeman argued that the economy is made up of two transactional realms: the market and community.[23] The market is characterized by anonymous exchange and rational calculation and is peopled by individuals, families, and corporations pursuing profits and attempting to accumulate wealth. In the market realm, Gudeman (Ibid.: 10) explained, "self-interest of the unit – whether an individual, a family, or a corporation – is a primary motive and value." The communal realm, on the other hand, is characterized by sociality, reciprocity, and mutuality. The communal realm places us "within a matrix of social relationships" (Ibid.: 9).

Though distinct, these two spaces (i.e. the market and the community) are interwoven. We simultaneously live and work in both spheres. "The two realms of market and community," Gudeman (Ibid.: 11) wrote,

> complement one another, conjoin, and are separated in acts, institutions, and sectors. No trade or market system exists without the support of communal agreements, such as shared languages, mutual ways of interacting, and implicit understandings. Communities also are inside markets, as households, corporations, unions, guilds, and oligopolies, and contain them as nation-states that provide a legal structure for contracts and material infrastructure.

Gudeman believed that the relationship between the market and community is dialectical (Ibid.: 12). We simultaneously "make and live" both spaces; market life is socially constituted; social life can be conditioned by market phenomena (Ibid.: 15). Furthermore, activities and entities can appear under both guises. The corporation is both a market entity "embedded in exchange" (Gudeman and Rivera 1990: 184) and "a community that is nestled in larger communities" (Gudeman 2001: 22). Although the house is "not built around the need to exchange," it does engage in trade; house members do produce goods for sale and consume goods purchased in the market (Gudeman and Rivera 1990: 185).

While Gudeman insisted that the market has a critical role to play in maintaining the communal sphere, he nonetheless had a very limited view of that role. According to Gudeman (2001), individuals sometimes engage in market activities to create, maintain, and extend the base. The base is whatever the individuals in a community possess that links them to each other. The base, he (Ibid.: 27) explained, "is the patrimony or legacy of a community and refers to anything that contributes to the material and social sustenance of a

---

[23] See Gudeman (2016) where he argued that economies are divided into five abstract spheres: the house, community, commerce, finance, and meta-finance.

people with a shared identity: land, buildings, seed stock, knowledge of practices, a transportation network, an educational system, or rituals." The community, he noted, often depends on trade to attain its prized possessions, its religious and cultural symbols, and the materials it needs to build its community centers, churches, and schools. Additionally, for the members of some communities, engaging in a certain market activity is a way of expressing their community identity (e.g. ethnic Chinese traders and middlemen in Indonesia). But, in his view, the space of the market is not the realm of "real" sociality. It is not the realm where meaningful social relationships develop. In Gudeman's view, the market sphere taints, rather than supports, social relationships; "real community may enter the market today as a successful producer of goods, but find itself transformed by the experience" (Ibid.: 160).

As the market sphere expands, Gudeman claimed, community members will be forced to engage in market activities. In doing so, however, they put themselves at moral risk. The more time we spend in the corporation instead of the house, the more time we spend being driven by interest rather than interacting with others based on mutuality. As the space of the market expands, people spend less time fostering meaningful social relationships and more time pursuing material desires. "As the market develops and the drive for profit expands," Gudeman (1992: 144) wrote, "the corporation takes over the space of the house, pushing it to the periphery physically, in everyday functions, and in competitive production." According to Gudeman (2001: 144),

> spreading rapidly and on a global scale, markets are subsuming greater portions of everyday life. Increasingly, we commoditize things, leisure, body parts, reproductive capacities, DNA, and social relationships. As people flock to cities, sell their hardwood trees, change clothing styles, and watch television, community ... shrinks.

For Gudeman (Ibid.: 140, 144), as was true of Lefebvre, this ever-increasing expansion of the sphere of the market into the communal sphere is both alienating and destructive. "When capital expands, we often find the *debasement of community* as its values evaporate in support of the market" (Ibid.: 22; emphasis added).[24]

Likewise, in *What Money Can't Buy: The Moral Limits of Markets* (2012), Sandel argued that markets undermine morality and worried about the recent

---

[24] Admittedly, Gudeman was not wholly pessimistic about the potential of the communal sphere to survive capitalist expansion. As Gudeman (2001: 22) continued, "the creation, maintenance, and expansion of [the communal sphere] also may transform market life."

expansion of markets and market values (Ibid.: 7).[25] According to Sandel (Ibid.: 10), in recent times, "we drifted from *having* a market economy to *being* a market society" (Ibid.: 10). A market economy, Sandel (Ibid.: 10–11) explained, is "a tool – a valuable and effective tool – for organizing production" while a market society represents "a way of life in which market values seep into every aspect of human endeavor" and "a place where social relations are made over in the image of the market." Although Sandel believed that an increase in greed has undoubtedly accompanied this "market triumphalism" (Ibid.: 10), the most worrisome consequences of this growth of markets has been "the expansion of markets, and of market values, into spheres of life where they don't belong" (Ibid.: 7). There are perverse moral consequences, he claimed, associated with our moving to a world "where everything is up for sale" (Ibid.: 15). Specifically, as Sandel (Ibid.: 64) explained, "markets leave their mark on social norms. Often, market incentives erode or crowd out nonmarket incentives." Moreover, for Sandel, markets in certain goods and services under certain scenarios are likely to be unfair and corrupting.

According to Sandel (Ibid.: 111), "the fairness objection points to the injustice that can arise when people buy and sell things under conditions of inequality or dire economic necessity." This suggests that market exchanges are not always voluntary and that desperation can force people to buy or sell goods and services that they would not buy or sell if they were in less dire economic circumstances. "Market choices," Sandel (Ibid.: 112) described, "are not free choices if some people are desperately poor or lack the ability to bargain on fair terms. So, in order to know whether a market choice is a free choice, we have to ask what inequalities in the background conditions of society undermine meaningful consent." Think here of the child forced to work in a sweatshop, the man forced into prostitution, and the woman forced to sell an organ because they are extremely poor. Also think of the indigenous producer of some export commodity in the developing world who is not able to bargain for fairer terms for her product when transacting with her certainly richer and potentially more sophisticated trading partners in the developed world. As Sandel (Ibid.: 111) explained, "a peasant may agree to sell his kidney or cornea to feed his starving family, but his agreement may not really be voluntary. He may be unfairly coerced, in effect, by the necessities of his situation."

In addition to his fairness concerns, Sandel also worried that market relationships can be corrupting in some circumstances. As he (Ibid.) clarified,

---

[25] Sandel's view is not all that different from the arguments advanced by MacIntyre in *After Virtue* (1981). According to MacIntyre (Ibid.: 254), "the tradition of virtues is at variance with central features of the modern economic order and more especially its individualism, its acquisitiveness, and its elevation of the market to a central social place." McIntyre worried that the profit motive and competition, both essential elements of the market, undermine virtue.

"the corruption objection … points to the degrading effect of market valuation and exchange on certain goods and practices. According to this objection, certain moral and civic goods are diminished or corrupted if bought and sold." This suggests that giving away certain goods and services can be morally neutral or even virtuous while exchanging the same goods and services for money can be morally problematic. This also suggests that introducing money matters into certain relationships can pervert or poison those relationships. Think here of the monetization of certain activities like sex as occurs during prostitution, which many view as being inherently degrading to both the buyer and the seller. Think also of the sister who charges her brother for doing a favor and the attempt to buy a friendship rather than earning it. Both types of relationships would be damaged by the introduction of market dealings. Sandel also mentioned the selling of blood which he claimed ends up reducing, rather than increasing, the availability of blood relative to the current system that relies on donations (Ibid.: 122–125).

With markets increasingly expanding into spaces where they do not belong, the prevalence of these often unfair and potentially corrupting exchanges only increases. "Economists," Sandel (Ibid.: 9) complained, "often assume that markets are inert, that they do not affect the goods they exchange. But this is untrue. Markets leave their mark. Sometimes, market values crowd out non-market values worth caring about." Nor is it judgment-free; the market endorses utility-maximizing attitudes and commends some practices and goods while stigmatizing others. Consequently, while Sandel acknowledged that the market is productive, effective in allocating goods, and functions as a social space, he argued that it may warp meaningful relationships and is morally problematic.

Political philosopher John Gray (1998: 36) has also worried about "the unintended consequences of … freeing up markets." According to Gray (Ibid.), the expansion of markets has resulted in "a fracturing of communities, and a depletion of ethos and trust within institutions, which muted or thwarted the economic renewal which free markets were supposed to generate." While he recognized that the moral costs associated with engaging in market activity did not automatically imply that other economic systems are ethically better, Gray (2008: 5) strongly felt that "a modern market economy cannot do without a measure of moral corrosion." Markets often reward our worst traits. "The traits of character most rewarded by free markets," Gray (Ibid.: 4) claimed,

> are entrepreneurial boldness, the willingness to speculate and gamble, and the ability to seize or create new opportunities. It is worth noting that these are not the traits most praised by conservative moralists. Prudence, thrift, and the ability to press on patiently in a familiar pattern of life may be admirable qualities, but they do not usually lead to success in the free market.

Gray (Ibid.: 5) supposed that a society of people from whom high degrees of mobility and willingness to exit partnerships that are no longer profitable are required for economic success is "unlikely to be a society of stable families or to be notably law-biding." Freer markets, he believed, have not improved us socially or morally, but have made us worse on both dimensions.

While admitting that markets do a good job of delivering the material goods, Orthodox rabbi and philosopher Jonathan Sacks also believed that markets do a poor job of delivering the spiritual and community goods and can cause social ills (e.g. because of large income inequalities). According to Sacks (2002: 89), the growth of markets,

> has done more than open up extremes of poverty and wealth. It has subverted other institutions—families, communities, the bonds that link members of a society to a common fate, the moral discourse by which, until now, we were able to maintain a critical distance between 'I want' and 'I ought.'

"The perennial temptations of the market," Sacks (Ibid.: 89) wrote, are "to pursue gain at someone else's expense, to take advantage of ignorance, [and] to treat employees with indifference."[26] All too often, he lamented, we yield to these temptations.

Along similar lines, Ray Fisman and Tim Sullivan praised the market's ability to allocate resources and amass wealth but argued that it cultivates the wrong values. Because they are avid supporters of the market as an allocation mechanism, they worried about the negative image of markets. As Fisman and Sullivan (2016: 156) elucidated, those who find markets distasteful view them as instruments of exploitation. This image of the market blocks us from implementing a market mechanism when it is appropriate to do so and tends to compel us to settle for a suboptimal, often nonmarket allocation mechanism (Ibid.: 153):

> Why does [the image problem] concern us? Because that image problem gets in the way of using markets to do some good for society. Markets are a means of resource allocation, and often a really effective one at that. But they're not good for everything – or at least not without a lot of engineering and tweaking. That's something both free-market advocates, as well as those who find markets wholly repugnant, need to hear.

---

[26] These temptations, he insisted, need to be guarded against, even if that means interfering with markets. "[C]anons of fair trading and conditions of employment have to be established and policed" (Sacks 2002: 89).

When judged on its ability to achieve economic efficiency and thus materially improve lives, they concluded, the market is undeniably our best available instrument. But, they stated, it tends to disproportionately compensate an elite few. Consequently, market values introduce a new set of preferences and priorities that clash with the social order.

They illustrated their point with a 1965 movie on the lives of prisoners of war during World War II near Singapore, *King Rat* (Ibid.: 175–177).[27] Among other things, *King Rat* focused on the black market that thrived in the prisoner of war camp during the war.[28] Fisman and Sullivan (Ibid.: 177) concluded,

> Although markets often help keep people alive and better off than they might be otherwise ... they also provide the King with outsized rewards, leading to inequitable and seemingly unfair results. He is better fed, better dressed, and wields far more power than nearly anyone else at Changi. Markets also disrupt traditional social order, despite Lieutenant Grey's best efforts to maintain it. The market can be a source of turmoil that, whatever its virtues, can be tough to live through.
>
> Markets can also transform who we are. They can make us behave in ways that – in contrast to the beauty of the metaphor of the invisible hand – make us all worse off ... And competition itself, part of the lifeblood of how markets work, not only drives away profits but can drive out concerns of morality and compassion that may come to be seen as an unaffordable indulgence.

Fisman and Sullivan were critical of the way markets mold our morality. The market injects certain priorities and preferences into our interactions. For instance, they suggested that market competition will prompt people to maximize their immediate profits and drive out moral concerns.

According to Fisman and Sullivan, people will sometimes behave unsavorily in the marketplace, as we tend to go great lengths to achieve our goals. By revealing themselves to be unpleasant individuals, repeated business may become less likely. Subsequently, people operating on market values end up poorer in the long run without realizing it. This is not always and the only outcome of markets. According to Fisman and Sullivan (Ibid.: 180),

> The owners of a company with fat profit margins and an unassailable position in the marketplace ... can afford to be honest and charitable. But business owners in the cutthroat business of textile production in Bangladesh, say, might not have this luxury. As competition for contracts drive prices ever lower, there's inevitably the temptation to cut corners on worker or product safety just to make a living.

---

[27] The movie was adapted from a novel with the same name by James Clavell.

[28] See Radford (1945) for a discussion of economic activity in prisoner of war camps.

Therefore,

> We may not even realize it, but "the market" makes us selfish in such a way that undermines the common good. ... This irony shows how the market, by undermining our concern for others and beliefs in the intentions of others, can end up shrinking rather than growing the economic pie (Ibid.: 179).

They concluded that competitive markets "have the potential to make us not just selfish but downright unethical" and "bad people" (Ibid.: 180).

There are obviously considerable differences in the critiques of the market on moral grounds discussed above. We hope, however, that their affinity to the earlier critiques of the market is quite evident. Moreover, we hope that the key similarity between these critiques stands out in sharp relief, that is, markets are morally corrupting.

The Most Damning Moral Criticism of Markets

The most damning critique of markets on moral grounds is that engaging in market activity places us in a kind of moral jeopardy. The market, on this view, is a kind of monster that is not content with simply consuming us but is insistent on transforming us into monsters in its own image. There is, goes this argument, an unavoidable moral risk associated with buying and selling in the marketplace. Since markets so clearly reward our worst traits, according to this view, they have the potential to crowd out virtue and to corrupt the virtuous. As the market expands, we might grow wealthier but might also grow vicious. We can surely gain the whole world by adopting and participating in markets, but we will just as surely lose our souls.

If this critique is true, the material benefits of markets might still be tempting enough to push us toward an embrace of markets. But, if we truly lose our souls in markets, we should probably not be thrilled that we have been placed in this moral predicament.

Notice that the claim that markets are morally corrupting is not a deontological claim about the moral character of markets but a theoretical and empirical claim about what happens to people when they engage in market activity or live in market societies. As such, the central moral criticism of markets (i.e. that markets are morally corrupting) cannot be evaluated philosophically, at least not entirely. It must be evaluated using our theoretical understanding of how markets can and should work, and on the basis of evidence regarding how markets do in fact work.

Both theory and history suggest that markets are not the *immoralizing* spaces that some have imagined them to be. If markets are really morally corrupting, then we should expect the social scientific models and concepts which explain how markets function, to the extent that they do so effectively, to highlight, or imply, or at least leave space for the moral corruption that so many critics assert. More importantly, if markets really do in fact crowd out virtue and corrupt the virtuous, this should be borne out in the evidence. If the moral critics of markets are correct, at least one of the following propositions should hold:

Proposition 1: *Vice is more prevalent in market societies than in nonmarket societies and virtue is less prevalent in market societies than in nonmarket societies.*
Proposition 2: *As a society becomes more market-oriented and as the scope of the market in a society expands, more vice and less virtue will exist in that society.*
Proposition 3: *The more a person engages in market activity, the less virtuous they are likely to be.*

Figure 2.1 represents what we should expect to find when we examine the data on the relationship between markets and morality if these propositions are correct. If the moral critics of markets are correct, then we should expect to observe measures of morality being higher in nonmarket societies than in market societies and measures of immorality being higher in market societies than in nonmarket societies.[29]

Rather than finding support for these propositions, we find (overwhelming) evidence to the contrary.[30] We simply do not find evidence that markets are monsters, transforming us into evil creatures; more greedy, more selfish,

---

[29] This is a purposefully blunt empirical strategy. To be clear, societies are complex and other differences between them besides their *marketness* might explain any observed differences in measures of virtue and vice. But, if markets are really morally corrupting, we believe that we should see some hint of it in these comparisons. See Appendix for a discussion of our empirical strategy.

[30] Much of the evidence we present in subsequent chapters speaks directly to Proposition 1 and only indirectly to Propositions 2 and 3. We adopted this strategy for two reasons. First, the evidence for Proposition 1 is much easier to attain and interpret across a number of different measures of morality and immorality. Second, we believe that if Proposition 1 is proven to be incorrect then Propositions 2 and 3 are also likely to be incorrect. Admittedly, this is an untested belief. It is possible that market societies might outperform nonmarket societies on measures of morality but still be suffering from moral decline as they become more market-oriented (i.e. Proposition 1 might be false but Proposition 2 might be correct beyond some threshold). Additionally, it is possible that average morality is greater in market societies but that the individuals in market societies who are most enmeshed in the market are less virtuous (i.e. Proposition 1 might be false but Proposition 3 might be correct). (See the Appendix for further discussion.) If our belief about the relationship between the three propositions is not correct, then our effort here should be viewed as speaking only to Proposition 1. That said, where possible we reference social scientific studies and evidence that speak to all three propositions.

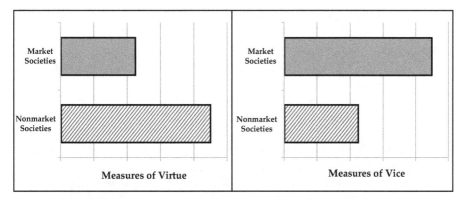

Fig. 2.1 If markets corrupt our morals… If markets are truly morally corrupt, we should observe market societies displaying lower levels of virtue and higher levels of vice compared to nonmarket societies

more materialistic, less trustworthy, less tolerant, and less connected than we would have been had we been able to avoid these monstrous markets. The evidence, in fact, suggests that markets are moral spaces that not only depend on virtue but also reward virtue and punish vice. If we are transformed by our experiences in markets, the evidence suggests that we are transformed for the better. There is reason to believe that virtue is more prevalent in market societies than nonmarket societies and that we become more moral the more that we engage in market activity.

Ironically, many of the strongest defenders of markets proceed as if they believe, perhaps deep down, that the moral critics of markets are correct. Instead of meeting the critiques head on, there is a tendency to try to sidestep or minimize the moral criticisms of markets. If the charge is that the market is a monster, the defense cannot simply be that it is not the only monster in town, nor is it a satisfactory defense to concede that the market is a monster that devours our souls but to remind us that it always leaves us food for our stomachs. In the next chapter, we review some of these defenses of markets on moral grounds and argue that they are not adequate responses to the moral criticisms of markets that we surveyed in this chapter.

Bibliography

Aquinas, T. [1485] 1918. *Summa Theologica*. Trans. English Dominican Province. London: Burns, Oates & Washbourne.

Bell, D. 1976. The Cultural Contradictions of Capitalism. In *Modernity: Critical Concepts*, ed. M. Waters. London/New York: Routledge.

————. 1993. *Communitarianism and Its Critics*. Oxford: Clarendon Press.

Block, F., and M.R. Somers. 2014. *The Power of Market Fundamentalism: Karl Polanyi's Critique*. Cambridge/London: Harvard University Press.

Cohen, G.A. 1995. *Self-Ownership, Freedom, and Equality*. Cambridge: Cambridge University Press.

————. 2009. *Why Not Socialism?* Princeton: Princeton University Press.

Elden, S. 2004. *Understanding Henri Lefebvre: Theory and the Possible*. London/New York: Stuart Elden.

Engels, F. [1878] 1959. *Anti-Dühring: Herr Dühring's Revolution in Science*. Moscow: Foreign Languages Publishing House.

Etzioni, A. 1988. *The Moral Dimension: Toward A New Economics*. London/New York: Free Press Collier Macmillan.

Fisman, R., and T. Sullivan. 2016. *The Inner Lives of Markets: How People Shape Them and They Shape Us*. New York: Public Affairs.

Friedman, D.D. 1980. In Defense of Thomas Aquinas and the Just Price. *History of Political Economy* 12 (2): 234–242.

Gray, J. 1998. *False Dawn: The Delusions of Global Capitalism*. New York: New Press.

————. 2008. It Depends. In *Does the Free Market Corrode Moral Character?* Conshohocken: John Templeton Foundation. https://www.templeton.org/market

Gudeman, S. 1992. Remodeling the House of Economics: Culture and Innovation. *American Ethnologist* 19 (1): 141–154.

————. 2001. *The Anthropology of Economy: Community, Market, and Culture*. Hoboken: Blackwell Publishing.

————. 2016. *Anthropology and Economy*. Cambridge: Cambridge University Press.

Gudeman, S., and A. Rivera. 1990. *Conversations in Colombia: The Domestic Economy in Life and Text*. Cambridge: Cambridge University Press.

Guzmán, R.A., and M.C. Munger. 2014. Euvoluntariness and Just Market Exchange: Moral Dilemmas from Locke's *Venditio*. *Public Choice* 158 (1–2): 39–49.

Harman, C. 2010. *Zombie Capitalism: Global Crisis and the Relevance of Marx*. Chicago: Haymarket Books.

Harvey, D. 2001. *Spaces of Capital: Towards a Critical Geography*. London/New York: Routledge.

Kennedy, P. 2016. *Vampire Capitalism: Fractured Societies and Alternative Futures*. London: Palgrave Macmillan.

Lefebvre, H. 1991. *Critique of Everyday Life, Vol. 2: Foundations for a Sociology of the Everyday*. Virginia: Verso.

Löfving, S. 2005. Introduction. In *Peopled Economies: Conversations with Stephen Gudeman*, ed. S. Löfvin. Uppsala: Uppsala University.

MacDonald, D.N., and M.O. Reynolds. 1994. Are Baseball Players Paid Their Marginal Products? *Managerial and Decision Economics* 15 (5): 443–457.

MacIntyre, A. 1981. *After Virtue: A Study in Moral Theory*. Notre Dame: University of Notre Dame Press.

Marx, K. [1867] 1915. *Capital: A Critique of Political Economy*, ed. F. Engels. Chicago: Charles H. Kerr & Company.

———. [1891] 1938. *Critique of the Gotha Program*. New York: International Publishers.

———. [1867] 1990. *Capital*. London: Penguin Books.

———. [1821] 1994. *Karl Marx: Selected Writings*, ed. L.H. Simon. Indianapolis: Hackett Publishing.

———. [1844] 1994. Excerpts – Notes of 1844. In *Karl Marx: Selected Writings*, ed. L.H. Simon, 40–53. Indianapolis: Hackett Publishing.

———. [1844] 2009. The Economic and Philosophic Manuscripts of 1844. In *Philosophers on Shakespeare*, ed. P.A. Kottman. Stanford: Stanford University Press.

Marx, K., and F. Engels. [1848] 1906. *Manifesto of the Communist Party*. Chicago: Charles H. Kerr & Company.

———. [1848] 1967. *The Communist Manifesto*. London: Penguin.

———. [1844, 1848] 2009. *The Economic and Philosophic Manuscripts of 1844 and the Communist Manifesto*. Amherst: Prometheus Books.

McNally, D. 2011. *Monsters of the Market: Zombies, Vampires and Global Capitalism*. Leiden: Brill Online Books and Journals.

Medley, J., and L. Carroll. 2004. The Hungry Ghost: IMP Policy, Global Capitalist Transformation, and Laboring Bodies in Southeast Asia. In *Postcolonialism Meets Economics*, ed. E. Zein-Elabdin and S. Charusheela, 145–164. London/New York: Routledge.

Piketty, T. 2014. *Capital in the Twenty-First Century*. Trans. A. Goldhammer. Cambridge: Harvard University Press.

Putnam, R.D. 2001. *Bowling Alone: The Collapse and Revival of American Community*. New York/Philadelphia: Simon and Schuster.

Radford, R.A. 1945. The Economic Organization of a P.O.W. Camp. *Economica* 12 (48): 189–201.

Rasmussen, D.C. 2008. *The Problems and Promise of Commercial Society: Adam Smith's Response to Rousseau*. University Park: Pennsylvania State University Press.

Röpke, W. [1958] 2014. *A Humane Economy: The Social Framework of the Free Market*. New York City: Open Road Media.

Rousseau, J.J. [1754] 1984. *A Discourse on Inequality*. Trans. M. Cranston. New York: Penguin Random House.

Sacks, J. 2002. *The Dignity of Difference: How to Avoid the Clash of Civilizations*. London: Bloomsbury Publishing.

Sandel, M.J. 2012. *What Money Can't Buy: The Moral Limits of Markets*. London: Macmillan.

Satz, D. 2010. *Why Some Things Should Not Be for Sale: The Moral Limits of Markets*. Oxford: Oxford University Press.

Schumpeter, J.A. [1942] 1950. *Capitalism, Socialism, and Democracy*. New York: Harper and Brothers.

Storr, V.H. 2009. Why the Market? Markets as Social and Moral Spaces. *Journal of Markets and Morality* 12 (2): 277–296.

———. 2018. Marx and the Morality of Capitalism. *Liberty Matters: An Online Discussion Forum.*

wa Thiong'o, N. 1982. *Devil on the Cross.* Portsmouth: Heinemann.

Wertheimer, A. 1999. *Exploitation.* Princeton: Princeton University Press.

3

Markets as Unintentionally Moral Wealth Creators

Bernard Mandeville's poem *The Grumbling Hive* is a fable that speaks to the relationship between markets and morality. The hive was a wealthy and well-governed society and the bees who inhabited it were industrious but immoral. Production and consumption in this society was motived by vice. According to Mandeville ([1732] 1988: 66),

> Vast Numbers throng'd the fruitful Hive,
> Yet those vast Numbers made 'em thrive;
> Millions endeavoring to supply
> Each other's Lust and Vanity.

Moreover, the industrious in that society, Mandeville ([1732] 1988: 67) wrote, were thieves and charlatans, no different from "Sharpers, Parasites, Pimps, Players, / Pick-pockets, Coiners, Quacks, [and] South-sayers."[1]

Indeed, cheating and deceit seemed to pervade every industry in the Hive. The lawyers, for instance, colluded with each other to stoke conflicts between their respective clients and exaggerated the work they had to do so that they could overcharge their clients. Similarly, the doctors were more concerned with their own fame and wealth than with improving their own skills or even their patient's health. While some priests were truly ascetics, many more were lazy, lustful, greedy, and prideful. Additionally, while some soldiers were

---

This chapter relies on Langrill and Storr (2012).

---

[1] By south-sayer or soothsayer Mandeville likely meant a fortune teller or diviner.

© The Author(s) 2019
V. H. Storr, G. S. Choi, *Do Markets Corrupt Our Morals?*,
https://doi.org/10.1007/978-3-030-18416-2_3

honorable, most were cowards. Finally, the kings' ministers were often unethical, and justice was not blind but favored the wealthy. According to Mandeville (Ibid.), "All Trades and Places knew some Cheat, / No Calling was without Deceit." The environment that Mandeville portrayed is one where greed, selfishness, hedonism, and materialism drive the activities of every member of the community and govern their dealings with each other.

Despite vice pervading every sector of the economy, the Hive was a "Paradise" (Ibid.: 69). This society where vice thrived was nonetheless the envy of all the neighboring hives. According to Mandeville (Ibid.), the bees in the Hive were,

> Flatter'd in Peace, and fear'd in Wars,
> They were th' Esteem of Foreigners,
> And lavish of their Wealth and Lives,
> The Balance of all other Hives.

Rather than being a barrier to their success, Mandeville explained, their vice was the source of their success. Vices, such as vanity and greed, generated societal prosperity. Their vices led to industry, innovation, and a happy existence filled with comfort and material conveniences. "Such were the Blessings of that State," Mandeville (Ibid.) wrote,

> Their Crimes conspir'd to make them Great:
> And Virtue, who from Politicks
> Had learn'd a Thousand Cunning Tricks,
> Was, by their happy Influence,
> Made Friends with Vice: And ever since,
> The worst of all the Multitude
> Did something for the Common Good.

Moreover, Mandeville (Ibid.) claimed, their virtues served them well only when they were paired with and learned from their vices;

> The Root of Evil, Avarice,
> That damn'd ill-natur'd baneful Vice,
> Was Slave to Prodigality,
> That noble Sin; whilst Luxury
> Employ'd a Million of the Poor,
> And odious Pride a Million more:
> Envy it self, and Vanity,
> Were Ministers of Industry.

Their greed and profligacy worked together to make them work harder. Their sumptuousness and pretentiousness worked together to encourage them to put others to work. Their industry was driven by their envy and vanity. For Mandeville, it was their vices and not their virtues that lifted the poor out of poverty and lead to a prosperous society.

In Mandeville's poem, the Hive was troubled by the vice that was rampant in their society, despite the riches that they enjoyed. So, they prayed to Jove to rid their society of vice, not understanding the role that it served. And, unfortunately for the Hive, Jove granted their wish. Almost immediately production halted, and their economic successes were reversed. The Hive quickly learned that their private vices were the source of their public benefits.

This claim that markets transform private vice into public benefits is perhaps the most popular defense of the morality of the market. Sometimes people advance stronger versions of the claim that sound reminiscent of Mandeville's account. Sometimes they advance weaker versions of the claim that describe markets as not depending on vice but nonetheless being able to channel vice in socially beneficial directions. Both the strong and weak versions of this defense ground the moral goodness of the market in its ability to generate good results for society despite the bad motives of individuals.

Neither strong nor weak versions of the *private vice into public benefits* defense of the morality of markets, however, are likely to satisfy the critics of markets who worry that engaging in market activity leads to moral decline. In fact, this "moral defense" of markets fails to challenge (in the weak version) and actually endorses (in the strong version) the belief that markets corrupt our morals.

Another claim that people defending the market often advance is the assertion that markets are amoral spaces that promote neither virtue nor vice. Instead, goes this defense, markets are simply tools that like almost all other tools can be used for good or for ill. Many tools can be used for moral or immoral ends. A knife can be used to cut fruit and to commit murder. A hammer can be used by a carpenter to build a house and can also be used by an aggressor to assault someone. A radio can be used to transmit vital information about evacuation routes during a major storm and can be used to direct armed militia intent on genocide. In each of these cases, it would be a mistake to condone or condemn the tool for the praiseworthy or blameworthy purposes that it was used to advance. Neither its positive nor its negative uses redound to the moral status of the tool. Any positive or negative moral outcomes that result from their use should be attributed to the user and the user's moral or immoral purposes.

The market is sometimes described as a morally indifferent tool that links prospective buyers with prospective sellers. Specifically, the market has been viewed as a coordinative mechanism that allocates resources efficiently to those who most value them in the economy. It provides the space within which consumers compete with one another for products and producers compete with one another for suppliers and customers. If a consumer and a producer agree on the terms of the trade, the former gives the latter a payment in cash or a cash equivalent in exchange for the product that the latter is offering. Buyers are said to be succeeding in the market when they purchase desired products at prices less than or equal to the maximum prices that they were willing to pay. Similarly, sellers are said to be succeeding in the market when the price at which their sales occur is greater than their cost. Since people bring and live their values out in the market, it can easily and happily accommodate both sinners and saints. It is, thus, exempt from moral praise or reproach.

This *markets-as-mere-tools defense* does not, however, speak to the concern that there are moral costs associated with engaging in market activity. Moreover, even if the market is just a tool, every tool is better suited for some purposes than others. Markets might be properly viewed as tools and might still be open to the charge that they are tools that are likely to be used by immoral people to do immoral acts in pursuit of immoral ends. Also, the more that you use a particular tool, the more adept you become at wielding it. Markets might be properly viewed as tools and might still be open to the charge that they cultivate certain immoral skills and that certain other moral traits might atrophy because they are unlikely to be exercised.

A third defense of the morality of markets that is frequently advanced is to admit (at least implicitly) that many negative things are associated with markets but to argue that nonmarket settings are associated with even worse moral problems. Markets left unchecked may result in the moral degradation and material deprivation of the proletariat, goes this defense, but the casualties associated with the various experiments with market alternatives like socialism number in the millions. Moreover, the moral decline that occurs when individuals engage in market activity also occurs and possibly occurs to a greater extent in nonmarket settings (see Otteson 2014). To paraphrase Churchill, these defenders of markets agree that markets are the worse economic systems in terms of their impact on morality, except for all the others that have been tried.

Ironically, many of the most popular moral defenses of the market do not defend the morality of market. Moreover, they do not (theoretically or empirically) evaluate a central claim of the market critics, that is, that markets are morally corrupting.

Many Traditional Defenses Do Not Defend Against the Charge That Markets Are Corrupting

Traditionally, defenders of the market on moral grounds advanced weak or strong versions of Mandeville's contention that markets transform private vice into public benefit; or, argued that markets are tools and, thus, immune from moral criticism; or, argued that markets were more moral than other economic systems; or, advanced all three arguments more or less simultaneously. This was arguably true of a number of classical and post-classical writers who sought to defend the market on moral grounds. This was certainly true of the moral defenses of the market advanced by Montesquieu, Adam Smith, and Philip Wicksteed. This section offers a brief review of the key claims by three of the strongest defenders of commercial society.

The *doux commerce* thesis stands in contrast to Mandeville's thesis and stands out as one of the most powerful arguments in favor of the moralizing effect of markets (Hirschman 1977, 1982).[2] Forcefully articulated by Montesquieu, but also endorsed by Voltaire, Adam Smith, Thomas Paine, and, more recently, Deirdre McCloskey, the *doux commerce* thesis points to the moralizing and civilizing effect of commerce.[3] "Commerce," Montesquieu ([1748] 1989: 338) argued in *The Spirit of the Laws*, "cures destructive prejudices, and it is an almost general rule that everywhere there are gentle mores, there is commerce and that everywhere there is commerce, there are gentle mores." Additionally, Montesquieu argued, commerce "polishes and softens barbarous mores" (Ibid.). Specifically, in commercial society, better judgment is rewarded, hard

---

[2] It is admittedly possible to cast the argument that we advance in subsequent chapters as a version in *doux commerce* thesis. Indeed, in Chap. 5, we agree with Montesquieu that wherever there is trade we are likely to find gentle mores. And, in Chap. 6, we fully agree with Montesquieu that markets reward virtue and punish vice. As we discuss below, however, Montesquieu maintained a worry that markets might be corrupting that we do not believe is supported by the evidence.

[3] For instance, Voltaire described commerce as a force that encourages people to become more tolerant toward others despite religious (and other) differences. In the Royal Exchange in London, "a place more venerable than many courts of justice, where the representatives of all nations meet for the benefit of mankind," "the Jew, the Mahometan, and the Christian transact business together, as though they were all of the same religion" ([1733] 1901: 281). Likewise, Thomas Paine, in *The Rights of Man* ([1792] 1995: 265), depicted commerce as "a pacific system, operating to cordialize mankind, by rendering nations, as well as individuals, useful to each other." "If commerce were permitted to act to the universal extent it is capable," he (Ibid.: 266) continued, "it would extirpate the system of war ... The invention of commerce ... is the greatest approach towards universal civilization." Adam Smith, in his *Lectures on Jurisprudence* ([1763] 1982: 538), spoke about the influence of commerce on manners; "[w]henever commerce is introduced into any country, probity and punctuality always accompany it. ... Of all the nations in Europe, the Dutch, the most commercial, are the most faithfull to their word." Finally, McCloskey (1998: 310) asserted that "who we are depends on what we do, our ethics depend on our business. Commerce is a teacher of ethics. The growth of markets promotes virtue, sometimes."

work is rewarded, being thrifty is rewarded, and being honest and trustworthy is rewarded. Moreover, unlike in pre-commercial or noncommercial societies, individuals are penalized for indulging their worst traits (e.g. abrasiveness, bigotry) in market societies. Markets also check our passions, making us less prone to religious and political enthusiasm as well as other passions that might create social tensions or conflicts. As such, commerce encourages a set of virtues including but not limited to tolerance, prudence, industriousness, frugality, and probity. Commerce, Montesquieu (Ibid.) contended, also encourages peace.[4] Commerce offers nations an alternative to conquest. "Two nations that trade with each other," he (Ibid.) wrote, "become reciprocally dependent; if one has an interest in buying, the other has an interest in selling, and all unions are founded on mutual needs." Commerce makes it possible to obtain the goods that are possessed by a different group of people living in a different place without having to use force to gain them. It also raises the cost of belligerence. Any conflict between trading partners will necessarily hurt both sides, at least temporarily.

Montesquieu (Ibid.: 341) offered the example of Marseilles as a community whose mores were transformed by commerce. According to Montesquieu (Ibid.), Marseilles became a major commercial port because its geography was not fit for agriculture. This forced focus on commerce, he suggested, transformed Marseilles' citizens, turning them into a different kind of people. Montesquieu (Ibid.; emphasis added) asserted that,

> They had to be *hardworking* in order to replace that which nature refused them; *just*, in order to live among the barbarian nations that were to make their prosperity; *moderate*, in order for their government always to be tranquil; finally, of *frugal mores*, in order to live always by a commerce that they would the more surely preserve the less it was advantageous to them.

As we would expect in any commercial society, commerce has made the people of Marseilles hardworking, just, moderate, and frugal.

Montesquieu (Ibid.: 339) explained that commerce had a moderating effect on those who engaged in it. "The spirit of commerce," he (Ibid.; emphasis added) wrote, "produces in men a certain feeling for *exact justice*, opposed on the one hand to banditry and on the other to those moral virtues that make it so that one does not always discuss one's own interests alone and

---

[4] There appears to be evidence for this. For example, Friedman (1996) mentioned how no two countries in which a McDonald's, the fast food chain, exists has ever fought a war against each other. This seems to have also been borne out by the scholarly literature that has examined it. See, for instance, Jervis (2002), Gleditsch (2008), Martin et al. (2008), Koerber (2009), and Strong (2009).

that one can neglect them for those of others." Commerce creates a circumstance where a person's interests are made to stand against her passions (Hirschman 1982). Stated another way, commerce checks our strongest passions and redirects them into socially beneficial directions. On the one hand, commerce makes us less likely to think of others as enemies. It encourages us to think of ways that we can gain what we might need or want from others by appealing to their self-love rather than by thinking of ways to acquire it from them through fraud or force. It encourages positive sum, rather than negative sum, thinking. On the other hand, commerce discourages us from thinking of each other as brothers and sisters. It encourages us to view one another as means rather than ends. It encourages us to think of the interests of others only as a way of convincing them to help to further our own goals. While the absence of commerce leads to banditry, Montesquieu acknowledged that the presence of commerce does not result in a perfectly benevolent citizenry.

Interestingly, Montesquieu ([1748] 1989: 338–339) also believed that, while gentling certain mores, commerce could also be corrupting. "We see that in countries where one is affected only by the spirit of commerce," Montesquieu (Ibid.) wrote, "there is traffic in all human activities and all moral virtues; the smallest things, those required by humanity, are done or given for money."[5] In commercial society, things tend to become commodified and relationships tend to become commercialized. Another way to read this is as an endorsement of the claim that market values can and do crowd out (certain) moral values.[6]

Montesquieu's articulation of the *doux commerce* thesis is, thus, arguably both powerful and unsatisfying. It raises the possibility that markets can improve mores. But, it notes that there are very real limits to the moral transformation that markets can bring about. In fact, markets do not always change mores for the better. For instance, altruism seems to give way to egoism, sisterhood seems to give way to isolation, generosity seems to give way to a

---

[5] Here, Montesquieu anticipated concerns advanced by Satz (2010) and Sandel (2012) about the expansion of markets into what should be nonmarket spaces. Satz (2010: 3) discussed how "as markets expanded their reach, new controversies have arisen concerning the morality of markets." Markets, she described, can shape our politics, culture, and even our identities. Most troublingly, "[s]ome markets thwart desirable human capacities; some shape our preferences in problematic ways; and some support objectionably hierarchical relationships between people" (Ibid.: 4). These markets, such as the ones in human organ, blood diamonds, and sex, "strike many people as noxious, toxic to important human values" and "evoke widespread discomfort and, in the extreme, revulsion." Similarly, Sandel (2012) anguished over the "the expansion of markets, and of market values, into spheres of life where they don't belong" (Ibid.: 7) and over how "certain moral and civic goods are diminished or corrupted if bought or sold" (Ibid.: 111). Interestingly, Falk and Szech's (2013) experiment revealed how market negotiation lowered subjects' willingness to pay to save the lives of mice.

[6] According to Montesquieu ([1748] 1989: 339), "total absence of commerce produces the banditry that Aristotle puts among the ways of acquiring. Its spirit is not contrary to certain moral virtues; for example, hospitality, so rare among commercial countries, is notable among bandit peoples." Others have written about the incompatibility of commerce with certain traditional values (MacIntyre 1981).

cold exact justice where everyone gets no less but also no more than they deserve. At a societal level markets encourage peace. At an individual level, however, markets are potentially corrupting. As such, Montesquieu ended up (partially) repeating, rather than refuting, the central moral critique of markets—that markets are morally corrupting.

Although Adam Smith endorsed the *doux commerce* thesis, he was primarily a student of commercial society, and did not offer a defense of the morality of markets, per se. Moreover, as we have already discussed, Smith focused on some of the moral failings of markets. Smith's tale of the poor man's son, his discussion of the role of self-interest, and his discussions of the invisible hand, for instance, all treat markets as mechanisms for transforming private interests and even private vices into public benefits. Stated another way, Smith articulated both the weak and strong versions of Mandeville's defense of markets on moral grounds.

Admittedly, Smith attempted to distance himself from Mandeville ([1714] 1989).[7] It is, however, difficult not to see Mandeville's influence in Smith's tale of the poor man's son. Remember, the poor man's son envies the comforts enjoyed by the rich and tricks himself into believing that if he were wealthy that he would be more content. However, on Smith's account, the envy of the poor man's son and the efforts it inspired proved to be in vain. The riches he chased all his life did not bring him the contentment that he had hoped to find. But, Smith noted, society benefits from self-deception of the kind engaged in by the poor man's son; economic progress depends on ambition, envy, and self-deceit.[8]

---

[7] Arguably, Smith did not object to that portion of Mandeville's argument that assumed public virtue is rooted in private vice. As Smith ([1759] 1982: 309) acknowledged, "[w]hether the most generous and public-spirited actions may not, in some sense, be regarded as proceeding from self-love, I shall not at present examine." Instead, Smith objected to Mandeville's suggestion that all apparent virtues are in fact motivated by vice. "Dr. Mandeville," Smith (Ibid.: 308) observed, "considers whatever is done from a sense of propriety, from a regard to what is commendable and praise-worthy, as being done from a love of praise and commendation, or as he calls it from vanity." This blurring of the line between virtue and vice, and this insistence that even the motives which purport to be the purest are in fact fraudulent, Smith (Ibid.) explained, is incorrect and destructive. Although Smith continued to discuss Mandeville's "favorite conclusion" in derisive tones, Smith's objection to Mandeville's view that public virtue depends on private vice is that Mandeville makes too much of the claim. Smith may have agreed with Mandeville that markets can channel private vice in such a way that it leads to public virtue, but Smith disagreed with Mandeville's conclusion that this means that vice has become virtue.

[8] According to Smith ([1759] 1982: 183), in times of ease, we are apt to view the pleasures of wealth as being "something grand and beautiful and noble," something necessarily connected to the even grander "order, the regular harmonious movement of the system, the machine or the oeconomy" which the quest for wealth makes possible. But, viewed apart from the part that it plays in this grand system, the pleasures of wealth "will always appear in the highest degree contemptible and trifling" (Ibid.). In times of ease, then, we are likely to engage in a kind of self-deception, to imagine the trinkets we are striving for as more than *mere* trinkets. It is an open question whether or not this is the same self-deceit that the poor man's son engaged in or an altogether different brand of self-deception. But it appears to be the case that the quest for wealth, at least in these passages in Smith ([1759] 1982), is motivated by some kind of self-deception.

According to Smith ([1759] 1982: 183), "[i]t is this deception which rouses and keeps in continuous motion the industry of mankind." Interestingly, Smith positioned this self-deception as the engine of industry. "It is this," Smith (Ibid.) wrote, "which first prompted them to cultivate the ground, to build houses, to found cities and commonwealths, and to invent and improve all the sciences and arts, which ennoble and embellish human life." Admittedly, Smith was silent on how many people in a society must deceive themselves in this way in order for economic development to occur. He did not say how many people in a society will be or must be blinded by their own ambitions, envy, and deceit for that society to become prosperous. It is possible that he viewed ambition, envy, and self-deception as being neither necessary nor sufficient for progress. It could be that this is a kind of robustness claim here; in other words, even the ambitious, the envious, and the self-deceived can contribute to society through markets. Additionally, when he credited deception with inspiring labor which changed the "whole face of the globe," he could have been describing an historical accident and not expressing a theoretical claim about the link between private vice and public virtue. It could be that he believed that self-deception was the fount of the economic progress that actually occurred, but that progress is still possible (even potentially more likely) if market actors were not so self-deceived.

Others have suggested that this more generous interpretation of Smith's parable of the poor man's son is exactly the interpretation that we should adopt. Hanley (2009: 105), for instance, argued that there are "good reasons to regard the story of the poor man's son less as a window into Smith's vision of the truth of the conditions of life in commercial society, and more as a cautionary tale that illustrates the possible or potential degradation of life in such a society, one that provides incentives for citizens of such a society to embrace the remedies proposed in his account of prudence."[9] Yet, even read as a cautionary tale, Smith's parable would suggest that there is a particular kind of moral risk associated with life in commercial society. And, there is nothing in the reading of the poor man's son as a cautionary tale that breaks the link between private moral deprivation and social material development that Smith seemed to draw in the tale.

---

[9] Smith, Hanley (2009: 106) argued, believed that vanity could be checked and channeled toward "the pursuit of other goods more conducive to both virtue and happiness." And, Smith ([1759] 1982: 149), worried that "[t]he person under the influence of any of those extravagant passions [i.e. avarice, ambition and vain glory], is not only miserable in his actual situation, but is often disposed to disturb the peace of society, in order to arrive at that which he so foolishly admires." Smith believed that we not only could but should escape the moral pitfalls that ensnared the poor man's son. Additionally, it is not only personally problematic but also socially problematic if we do not escape these extravagant passions.

Although it is possible that Smith believed that self-deception mattered for progress in the past but need not in the future, there is no real evidence for such a generous reading of his parable of the poor man's son. In fact, it is a less strained interpretation of what is going on with the poor man's son parable to read Smith as lamenting the moral consequences associated with admiring and seeking to emulate the rich but viewing these vices as the price that we pay for material prosperity. Smith surely believed that it would be better for any individual to pursue wisdom and virtue over vice. However, like Mandeville, Smith seemed to be suggesting with this parable that our material progress would be stunted if too many in our society attempted to constrain their own ambitions. Smith seemed to be saying that, as Hill (2017: 21) wrote, "it would be economically and socially disastrous if everyone pursued 'real happiness' at the expense of the happiness of individual wealth accumulation and conspicuous consumption that, in the long view, makes a society progressive and prosperous."[10]

It is also easy to hear echoes of Mandeville in Smith's discussions of the invisible hand. Shortly after the parable of the poor man's son in the *Theory of Moral Sentiments,* Smith ([1759] 1982: 184–185) explained that the rich in commercial society provide for the poor, even though they may have little regard for them. According to Smith (Ibid.; emphasis added),

> The produce of the soil maintains at all times nearly that number of inhabitants which it is capable of maintaining. The rich only select from the heap what is most precious and agreeable. They consume little more than the poor, and in spite of *their natural selfishness and rapacity*, though they mean only their own conveniency, though the sole end which they propose from the labours of all the thousands whom they employ, be the *gratification of their own vain and insatiable desires*, they divide with the poor the produce of all their improvements. They are *led by an invisible hand* to make nearly the same distribution of the necessaries of life, which would have been made, had the earth been divided into equal portions among all its inhabitants, and thus without intending it, without knowing it, *advance the interest of the society*, and afford means to the multiplication of the species.

Of course, Smith was not suggesting here something as crass as private vice is necessary for public virtue. But, he definitely was not challenging that conclusion. In fact, he lent support for that view. The rich, he suggested, are selfish

---

[10] Interestingly, Weber ([1905] 2002) seemed to offer a different basis for people's work ethic than the one that Smith and Mandeville are advancing. Weber rooted his work ethic in worldly asceticism and not greed or self-deceit.

and rapacious. They are driven to employ laborers in productive enterprises by their vanity and their "insatiable desires." The rich do not intend the social good that results from their actions.

Smith's reference to the invisible hand in *An Inquiry into the Nature and Causes of the Wealth of Nations*, similarly, supports, rather than challenges, the notion that public virtue is rooted in private vice. Although intending "only his own gain," Smith ([1776] 1981: 456; emphasis added) described how every individual in commercial society,

> is in this, as in many other cases, *led by an invisible hand to promote an end which was no part of his intention.* Nor is it always the worse for the society that it was no part of it. *By pursuing his own interest he frequently promotes that of the society more effectually than when he really intends to promote it.* I have never known much good done by those who affected to trade for the publick good. It is an affectation, indeed, not very common among merchants, and very few words need be employed in dissuading them from it.

Again, while not the same thing as suggesting that vice is necessary for public good, like Mandeville, Smith was here separating intentions from outcomes. In fact, Smith was suggesting that if merchants were to consciously attempt to do what they believed was in the public interest, they would not accomplish "much good." The social good that the commercial actor creates is unintentional. As such, it is hard to factor this unintended result into any moral accounting concerning the actor. The actor has acted to help herself. By coincidence, and perhaps against her will, she has helped others. In such a scenario, it might make sense to celebrate the system as being moral, but we are left with no basis on which to conclude that the people within that system are particularly moral.

Indeed, if Smith's other statements about market participants are to be taken at face value, we have reason to believe that Smith was suspicious of the morality of market participants. For instance, Smith (Ibid.: 82–104) discussed how employers work together to suppress the wages of their laborers.[11] Smith

---

[11] "Masters," Smith ([1776] 1981: 84) stated,

> are always and every where in a sort of tacit, but constant and uniform combination, not to raise the wages of labour above their actual rate. To violate this combination is every where a most unpopular action, and a sort of reproach to a master among his neighbours and equals. We seldom, indeed, hear of this combination, because it is the usual, and one may say, the natural state of things which nobody ever hears of. Masters too sometimes enter into particular combinations to sink the wages of labour even below this rate. These are always conducted with the utmost silence and secrecy, till the moment of execution, and when the workmen yield, as they sometimes do, without resistance, though severely felt by them, they are never heard of by other people.

(Ibid.: 145; emphasis added) also noted that "[p]eople of the same trade seldom meet together, even for merriment and diversion, but the conversation ends in a *conspiracy against the publick*, or in some contrivance to raise prices." Although he doubted that much can be done to prevent these conspiracies, and he worried that some regulations actually make these conspiracies more likely (if they force people from the same trade to interact with one another more frequently), Smith clearly did not expect merchants to be motivated by the public good.

Smith's "defense" of the morality of the market, thus, is not a very strong one. While the market system can perhaps be viewed as a kind of morality converter which can translate vice at the individual level into virtue at the societal level, market participants qua their roles as market participants are at best amoral and at worst immoral. Moreover, the material success of the system is driven by their self-interest and maybe their selfishness.

Whereas Smith argued that market activity was propelled (in part) by vice but was nonetheless likely to be socially beneficial, Phillip Wicksteed stressed that market activity could be driven by moral as well as immoral motives and could result in socially beneficial as well as socially wasteful outcomes. Markets, for Wicksteed, were like empty moral vessels that market participants fill with whatever moral or immoral material they bring with them as they engage in market activity. As such, in Wicksteed's view, markets were both morally neutral and thoroughly awash with moral content.

In *The Common Sense of Political Economy* ([1910] 2003), Wicksteed argued that it was a mistake to think of the "desire to possess wealth" as that ultimate end which drives market participants. To be sure, market participants almost always seek the lowest price for the goods they want to buy and the highest price they can attain for the goods that they wish to sell, all else equal. But, the profits or savings that result from their ministrations in the market are not ends in themselves. They are merely means that the market participants will deploy in order to obtain some ultimate end. As Wicksteed (Ibid.: 163) explained, "to regard the 'economic' man (as he is often called) as actuated solely by the desire to possess wealth is to think of him as only desiring to collect tools and never desiring to do or to make anything with them." We might chase after trinkets our whole lives. We do not, however, want to acquire trinkets for the sake of acquiring and possessing them. Rather, our hope is often that by gaining and owning these trinkets our lives will become more comfortable and content. That said, there are other, less self-centered and less selfish reasons that we might desire wealth. We might want wealth so as to help those who lack the skills or opportunities to acquire wealth without our help. We might want to acquire trinkets in order to place them in the service of others.

Wicksteed argued that it is arbitrary to characterize only self-interested motives as economic motives when other regarding motives also induce market activity. According to Wicksteed (Ibid.: 165), if we are concerned with why market actors behave as they do, we "must be prepared to recognize all motives that are actually at work." And,

> We may either ignore motives altogether, or may recognise all motives that are at work, according to the aspect of the matter with which we are concerned at the moment; but in no case may we pick and choose between the motives we will and the motives we will not recognise as affecting economic conditions. There seems little sense, then, in using the term "economic motive" at all; for the whole conception appears to be a false category (Ibid.).

Market space, for Wicksteed, must either be viewed as a space of both egoism and altruism, of both vice and virtue, or it must be viewed as a neutral, amoral space, where the motives and morals of the actors are treated as separable and separate phenomena.[12]

For Wicksteed (Ibid.: 180), the key feature of our economic connections is not that we enter into them because it is in our interest to do so and certainly not the altruism that can characterize many of our relationships. Instead, "the specific characteristic of an economic relation is," Wicksteed (Ibid.) argued, "its 'non-tuism.'" By this, he meant that market participants are not especially interested in those with whom they are transacting. They are only interested in how to get the person on the other side of the exchange to make the exchange. He explained that this is not simply a form of egoism because, although market actors are not really thinking about others when exchanging, they are also not thinking about themselves. For Wicksteed (Ibid.), a market participant is only,

> thinking of the matter in hand, the bargain or the transaction, much as a man thinks of the next move in game of chess or of how to unravel the construction of a sentence in the Greek text he is reading. He wants to make a good bargain or do a good piece of business, and he is directly thinking of nothing else.

---

[12] According to Wicksteed ([1910] 2002: 165), "[e]very man has certain purposes, impulses, and desires. They may be of a merely instinctive and elementary nature, or they may be deliberate and far-reaching; they may be self-regarding or social; they may be spiritual or material." Also, "the economic relation, then, or business nexus, is necessary alike for carrying on the life of the peasant and the prince, of the saint and the sinner, of the apostle and the shepherd, of the most altruistic and the most egoistic of men" (Ibid.: 171).

Wicksteed acknowledged that moral considerations may exist in the back of the market participant's mind at all times and may even be brought to the forefront of his thinking when he reflects on them.[13] But, according to Wicksteed (Ibid.: 181), for the most part, "he is exactly in the position of a man who is playing a game of chess or cricket. He is considering nothing except his game." As Wicksteed (Ibid.) asserted, you would not call a chess player selfish for protecting his king or a cricket player selfish for protecting the wicket. Similarly, you would not call a teacher altruistic for helping a student learn her lessons nor would you call a surgeon selfless for saving a patient. Those moments do not speak to whether the chess player, or cricket player, or teacher, or surgeon, is egoistic or altruistic. To determine if a person is selfish or selfless you would have to look at the rest of their lives. "At the moment [of the exchange]," Wicksteed (Ibid.) explained, "the categories of egoism and altruism are irrelevant."

Markets, for Wicksteed (Ibid.: 184), are "ethically indifferent instruments." By this, he meant that markets are essentially tools that individuals use to further their ends, regardless of their ends. Markets work to deliver the goods and services that people desire through the most cost-effective channels that are available. However, they do not pass judgment on the motives that inspire people to enter the marketplace. Wicksteed (Ibid.) explained that markets "take no count" of these admittedly very important morally significant considerations. Instead, market participants are either left to decide themselves which motives to follow or must rely on some third-party mechanism to enforce any societally adopted moral limits on market transactions. On this view, the players and the umpires can, thus, be moral, immoral, or both; the game itself is neither moral nor immoral.

Although our market interactions are categorized by their non-tuism, and markets are morally neutral mechanisms, Wicksteed thought that it would be incorrect to describe them as amoral or unmoral. According to Wicksteed (Ibid.: 182),

---

[13] Wicksteed ([1910] 2003: 180) continued that,

> All manner of considerations of loyalty, of humanity, of reputation, and so forth, are no doubt present to his mind ... but in making his bargain the business man is not usually thinking of these things ... Neither is he thinking of the ultimate purposes to which he will apply the resources he gains. He is not thinking either of missions to the heathen or of famine funds, or of his pew rent, or of his political association. But neither is he thinking of his wife and family, nor yet of himself and the champagne suppers he may enjoy with his bachelor friends, nor of a season ticket for concerts, nor of opportunities for increasing his knowledge of Chinese or mathematics, nor of free expenditure during his next holiday on the Continent, nor of a week at Monte Carlo, nor of anything else whatever except his bargain.

Any relation into which I enter for the fulfilment of my purposes may, in a sense, be called unmoral, inasmuch as it is a means and not an end. But if by unmoral we mean unaffected by moral considerations, or not subject to moral restraints, then the economic relation is no more unmoral than the relations of friendship, the relations of sex, the relations of paternity, or the family relations generally.

The market sphere is in a sense a thoroughly moralized sphere.

The market is a space, Wicksteed argued, where actors are constantly choosing to either follow or disregard their moral restraints, where they are constantly choosing whether to work and trade with others that have particular moral or immoral goals, where they are constantly choosing whether or not to pursue strategies that are likely to lead to morally acceptable or morally unacceptable results. Wicksteed (Ibid.) wrote that "to say that the economic relations, or even the economic forces, are unmoral, is in one sense perfectly true, and in another sense entirely false, and in the sense which it is true it is in no special way characteristic." Our interactions in the market, Wicksteed (Ibid.: 182) suggested, are no less shaped by moral considerations and no less governed by moral restraints than our interactions in other spheres. But, although markets are thoroughly moralized, our interactions in them are also no more or less moral than our interactions in other settings. While "the taint of inherent sordidness which attaches itself in many minds to the economic relation" is certainly mistaken, Wicksteed (Ibid.: 183) claimed, "the easy optimism that expects the economic forces, if only we give them free play, spontaneously to secure the best possible conditions of life, is equally fallacious, and even more pernicious." Wicksteed appeared to be disagreeing with both Rousseau and Smith on this point.

By insisting that markets are morally indifferent instruments, he hoped to defend markets against those who would claim that they are morally corrupting as well as criticize those who would claim that markets necessarily promote public virtue.[14] "It is idle," Wicksteed (Ibid.: 184) asserted, "to assume that

---

[14] Wicksteed discussed how the moral accounting regarding markets is more complicated than many pretend. According to Wicksteed ([1910] 2003: 183–184),

> That London is fed day by day, although no one sees to it, is itself a fact so stupendous as to excuse, if it does not justify, the most exultant paeans that were ever sung in honour of the *laissez-faire laissez-passer* theory of social organization. What a testimony to the efficiency of the economic nexus is borne by the very fact that we regard it as abnormal that any man should perish for want of any one of a thousand things, no one of which he can either make or do for himself.

But, Wicksteed (Ibid.) continued,

ethically desirable results will necessarily be produced by an ethically indifferent instrument, and it is as foolish to make the economic relation an idol as it is to make it a bogey."

Arguably, Wicksteed's defense of the morality of the market is unlikely to satisfy those who worry that the market is morally corrupting. Wicksteed acknowledged that at least some, and perhaps all, market actors will be driven by ethically problematic motives. Additionally, in markets, even market actors with a well-developed and functioning moral compass will end up assisting others whose aims are potentially morally dubious. Moreover, Wicksteed noted that there are several moral disadvantages that must be placed alongside any moral advantages that might result from the existence and expansion of markets in commercial society. He was also silent on whether those with moral aims are more or less likely to succeed in the market, whether acting in markets is more or less likely to produce ethically desirable results than acting in other spheres.

Montesquieu, Smith, and Wicksteed each offered a somewhat ambiguous account of the morality of the market. They each illustrated the market as a system that could generate (public) virtue. But, each also admitted that markets did not eliminate vice, even if it sometimes reoriented it toward virtuous ends. Moreover, at times, each seemed to suggest that markets actually depended on and even promoted vice. There is a peculiar agreement between the critics of the market on moral grounds and the defenders of the morality of the market: all seem to believe that markets are morally problematic in some respects and can even be morally corrupting.

---

we must look at the picture more closely. The very process of intelligently seeking my own ends makes me further those of others? Quite so. But what are my purposes, immediate and ultimate? And what are the purposes of others which I serve, as a means of accomplishing my own? And what views have I and they as to the suitable means of accomplishing those ends? These are the questions on which the health and vigour of a community depend, and the economic forces, as such, take no count of them.

Also, Wicksteed (Ibid.) wrote,

When we draw the seductive picture of 'economic harmony' … we insensibly allow the idea of 'help' to smuggle in with it ethical or sentimental associations that are strictly contraband. We forget that the 'help' may be impartially extended to destructive and pernicious or to constructive and beneficent ends, and moreover that it may employ all sorts of means. We have only to think of the huge industries of war, of the floating of bubble companies, of the efforts of one business or firm to choke others in the birth, of the poppy culture in China and India, of the gin-palaces and distilleries at home, in order to realize how often the immediate purpose of one man or of one community is to thwart or hold in check the purpose of another, or to delude men, or to corrupt their tastes and to minister to them when corrupted.

More Contemporary Defenses Do Not Do a Better Job of Responding to the Critics

Not surprisingly, the more recent defenses of the morality of the market have echoed the defenses offered by the earlier students of commercial society. In these contemporary moral defenses, the market is often described as a morally neutral space (like Wicksteed) or as a space that converts private vice into public virtue (like Mandeville and Smith). These contemporary defenses also often point to the moral and other horrors that occur in nonmarket settings and nonmarket systems.

This section offers a brief review of some of the strongest moral defenses of the market that emerged in the past few decades. We do not attempt to engage every important defense, nor do we try to present an exhaustive review of the defenses we do engage.[15] As with our examination of the contemporary critiques of the morality of the market in the previous chapter, our contention is that the various defenses are alike in at least one important respect. Specifically, none of these defenses, in our view, adequately respond to the central critique of the market on moral grounds; that is, none respond to the argument that engaging in market activity can corrupt our morals.

Milton Friedman's ([1962] 2002) defense of the morality of markets, for instance, is in many ways an indirect one. Friedman argued that the market system is the only system that gives economic actors the freedom to choose their own projects and paths, and so by extension is the only truly moral economic system. For Friedman, the basic economic problem of a society was one of coordination between large numbers of people. A society can only achieve

---

[15] One interesting account of the relationship between markets and morality that we do not engage is Hodgson (2013). Although principally concerned with how moral considerations should affect economic analysis, Hodgson does arrive at several conclusions about the morality of markets. According to Hodgson (Ibid.: 130),

> I do not claim that capitalism is a noble example of ethical achievement. On the contrary, we have abundant evidence of corruption and injustice under capitalism. Capitalism has exploited the weak and driven many into a life of mind-numbing labor. ... It is predominantly a system of getting and spending, driven by greed. ... But whatever their failings, humans are not *entirely* motivated by self-interest, even under a social order that encourages and depends on private acquisition and consumption. ... Business strategies are touched by ethical impulses of some kind, ... Competition does not extinguish moral sentiment. Capitalism depends on significant residues of morality for its very existence.

On Hodgson's account, markets are very bad morally but are not wholly immoral spaces. Some "residue" of morality remains in markets. See also Smith and Wilson (2019) that advances an integrated approach to understanding human life that combines Adam Smith's both economic and moral insights.

mass coordination through either a system based on ~~voluntary exchange~~ and mutual gains from trade (i.e. a free enterprise economy) or a system where the state dictates and executes exchanges (i.e. a socialist economy). Only the market, however, can generate social coordination and cooperation while preserving freedom. By relying strictly on a person's right to choose, Friedman explained, the market limits the extent to which certain groups of people can control others. According to Friedman (Ibid.: 14–15),

> So long as effective freedom of exchange is maintained, the central feature of the market organization of economic activity is that it prevents one person from interfering with another in respect of most of his activities. The consumer is protected from the coercion of the seller because of the presence of other sellers with whom he can deal. The seller is protected from coercion by the consumer because of other consumers to whom he can sell. The employee is protected from coercion by the employer because of other employers for whom he can work, and so on. And the market does this impersonally and without centralized authority.

Friedman regarded the market as the first step to guaranteeing both economic and political freedom. As such, it is not surprising that he viewed the denouncement of the market to be equivalent to lacking faith in freedom. Friedman (Ibid.: 15) argued that,

> this characteristic [of the market] also has implications that go far beyond the narrowly economic. Political freedom means the absence of coercion of a man by his fellow men. The fundamental threat to freedom is power to coerce, be it in the hands of a monarch, a dictator, an oligarchy, or a momentary majority. The preservation of freedom requires the elimination of such concentration of power to the fullest possible extent and the dispersal and distribution of whatever power cannot be eliminated ... by removing the organization of economic activity from the control of political authority, the market eliminates this source of coercive power. It enables economic strength to be a check to political power rather than a reinforcement.[16]

Where markets are limited, economic strength depends on political strength. As such, in countries that are not economically free, the political elite are necessarily also the economic elite, and vice versa. The greatest bulwark against political coercion, Friedman suggested, is economic freedom, which pits economic power against political power.

---

[16] There is a considerable literature on the relationship between markets and democracy, including Bowles et al. (1993), Lindblom (1995), Prychitko (2002), Dallmayr (2015), and Boycko and Shiller (2016).

Besides describing the free enterprise system as an economic order that protects freedom, which is morally desirable, morality as such does not play an explicit role in Friedman's case for the market. For Friedman, repurposing the market towards the achievement of moral ends (or to insist that it accounts for morality) is beyond its capabilities, and would be unreasonable and irresponsible. The social responsibility and so the moral obligation of every businessperson, Friedman (Ibid.: 133) argued, is to maximize profits; in a market system, "there is one and only one social responsibility of business – to use its resources and engage in activities designed to increase its profits so long as it stays within the rules of the games, which is to say, engages in open and free competition, without deception or fraud." To earn a profit, a firm must offer a good or service that consumers value more than the value that they place on the various inputs that were combined to produce that good or service. Profits, then, are evidence that firms are behaving in socially beneficial ways. Since earning profits in free and competitive markets means that a business is using resources in socially beneficial ways, if a corporate manager were to prioritize an objective above profit maximization, she would be violating her societal obligations (Friedman [1970] 2007).

It is important to remember, however, that Friedman's insistence that businesses prioritize profit-making is not unconstrained. He also insisted that businesses follow the rules, and accepted that these rules can and should be established by society. According to Friedman ([1962] 2002: 133), it is "the responsibility of the rest of us to establish a framework of law such that an individual in pursuing his own interest is, to quote Adam Smith again, 'led by an invisible hand to promote an end which was no part of his intention.'" Friedman, thus, would seem to accept that some business practices and some markets could be deemed socially unacceptable.[17]

Friedman also insisted that the market is ultimately an amoral economic system. To be sure, people can carry out their moral projects within markets. But, the market itself is morally neutral. According to Friedman (Ibid.: 12),

> in a society freedom has nothing to say about what an individual does with his freedom; it is not an all-embracing ethic. Indeed, a major aim of the liberal is to leave the ethical problem for the individual to wrestle with. The "really" important ethical problems are those that face an individual in a free society – what he should do with his freedom. There are thus two sets of values that a liberal will

[17] As we will discuss in Chap. 7, our conclusion that markets do not corrupt our morals, like the case Friedman articulated here, opens the door for the possibility of noxious markets or of banning certain practices like insider trading or price gouging.

emphasize – the values that are relevant to relations among people, which is the context in which he assigns first priority of freedom; and the values that are relevant to the individual in the exercise of his freedom, which is the realm of individual ethics and philosophy.

The market is a space where actors decide whether or not to behave ethically.

Admittedly, even if we were to add to his arguments the likelihood that ethical behavior is sometimes or even frequently rewarded in real-world markets, Friedman stopped short of a full defense of the morality of markets. Instead, Friedman's arguments suggest that the moral concerns about the market are, in a sense, beside the point. Market actors decide to act ethically or unethically, market actors may choose to reward or punish ethical or unethical behavior, the rules governing market interactions may permit or prohibit certain practices, but the market itself is not in any way morally responsible.

Henry Hazlitt ([1964] 1994) offered a similar defense of market morality, stressing the moral neutrality of market spaces and justifying the pursuit of self-interest. Hazlitt argued that markets act as vehicles that we use to achieve social cooperation in an economy and through which we balance egoism (or self-love) and altruism (or love for others). "Even if we assume that everyone lives and wishes to live primarily for himself," Hazlitt (Ibid.: 313) wrote, "we can see that this does not disturb social life but promotes it, because the higher fulfillment of the individual's life is possible only in and through society." Acting in the market is not purely altruistic since market participants cooperate with others primarily because it furthers their own interests. But, it is also not purely egoistic since market participants necessarily concern themselves with the interests of others. Had the market economy truly only promoted selfishness (in a narrow sense), Hazlitt contended, it would not be as successful as it is. Successful market participants tend to be rule followers and markets that are successful are peopled by rule-following participants. "People who try to improve their own fortunes by chicanery, swindling, robbery, blackmail, or murder," Hazlitt (Ibid.: 311) clarified, "do not increase the national income. Producers increase the national welfare by competing to satisfy the needs of consumers at the cheapest price. A free economy can function properly only within an appropriate legal and moral framework." For Hazlitt, then, markets are not morally neutral.

Hazlitt argued that there is another sense in which markets are moral: markets compensate individuals for their economic contributions to society and, thus, produce morally desirable results. Market rewards, Hazlitt explained, tend to flow to those who create value in proportion to the value that they create. As such, the distributions of incomes that we observe in the markets, however unequal, are not appropriately described as unjust. They are a result of a process where everyone tends to get what they deserve.

Anticipating an argument that was later developed by Hayek, Hazlitt criticized the desire for social justice, meaning here income equality. Efforts to even out inequality, he argued, attempt to remedy an injustice that has not occurred and hamper economic growth and development. The market system, Hazlitt (Ibid.: 316) wrote,

> tends constantly to reward individuals in accordance with their specific contribution to production. By the constant play in the market of prices, wages, rents, interest rates, and other costs, relative profit margins or losses, the market tends constantly to achieve not only maximum production but optimum production. That is to say, through the incentives and deterrents provided by these ever-changing relationships of prices and costs, the production of thousands of different commodities and services is synchronized, and a dynamic balance is maintained in the volume of production of each of these thousands of different goods in relation to each other.

As such, "[a]ny serious effort to enforce the ideal of equality of income, regardless of what anyone does or fails to do to earn or create income – regardless of whether he works or not, produces or not – would lead to universal impoverishment" (Ibid.: 317).

Redistributing income would dampen the incentives that market participants face to work hard and to gain new skills. Hazlitt (Ibid.: 322) argued that "a system that provides us better than any other with our material needs and wants can never be dismissed as ethically negligible or ethically irrelevant. Morality depends upon the prior satisfaction of material needs" (Ibid.). Although the market system will result in different individuals earning different incomes, it nonetheless promotes general prosperity and so raises the incomes of everyone.[18] Hazlitt conceived of morality as a kind of luxury good. As such, a baseline level of wealth is necessary for morality to exist.

---

[18] "The wealth of the rich," Hazlitt ([1964] 1994: 317) explained,

> makes the poor less poor, not more. The rich are those who have something to offer in return for the services of the poor. And only the rich can provide the poor with the capital, with the tools of production, to increase the output and hence the marginal value of the labor of the poor. When the rich grow richer, the poor grow, not poorer, but richer. This, in fact, is the history of economic progress.

Yet, Hazlitt recognized that some market actors are unethical. Moreover, he asserted that markets can sometimes reward unethical people. "Of course," Hazlitt (Ibid.: 306) admitted,

> there are isolated instances in which competition seems to work unjustly. It sometimes penalizes amiable or cultivated people and rewards churlish or vulgar ones. No matter how good our system of rules and laws, isolated cases of injustice can never be entirely eliminated. But the beneficence or harmfulness, the justice or injustice, of institutions must be judged by their effect in the great majority of cases—by their over-all result.

On net, Hazlitt believed that the market is a moral system. As such, he disagreed with Wicksteed's contention that markets were morally neutral.[19]

Despite the legitimacy of any moral criticisms that might be leveled at the market system, Hazlitt stressed that other economic systems are more morally problematic. The alternatives to the market system like the alternatives to democracy are necessarily coercive. Without a doubt, Hazlitt (Ibid.: 324) wrote, on moral grounds, the market system is "infinitely superior to its coercive alternatives" because,

> Only when men are free can they be moral. Only when they are free to choose can they be said to choose right from wrong. When they are free to choose, when they are free to get and to keep the fruits of their labor, they feel that they are being treated justly. As they recognize that their reward depends on their own efforts and output (and in effect *is* their output) each has the maximum incentive to maximize his output, and all have the maximum incentive to cooperate in helping each other to do so. The justice of the system grows out of the freedom it insures, and the productivity of the system grows out of the justice of the rewards that it provides.

---

[19] "It is true," Hazlitt ([1964] 1994: 321–322) wrote,

> that capitalism, as it functioned in [Wicksteed's] time and today, is not yet a heaven filled with cooperating saints. But this does not prove that the system is responsible for our individual short-comings and sins, or even that it is ethically 'indifferent' or neutral. Wicksteed *took for granted* not only the economic but the ethical merits of the capitalism of his day because that was the system he saw all around him, and therefore he did not visualize the alternative. What he forgot ... is that modern capitalism is not an inevitable or inescapable system but one that has been chosen by men and women who live under it. ... True, this system of freedom, ... presupposes an appropriate legal system and an appropriate morality. It could not exist and function without them. But once this system exists and functions it raises the morality of the community still further.

Unfortunately for our purposes here, Hazlitt asserted but did not show how markets raise the morality of the community or of community members.

The market system is moral, on this view, because it gives participants the freedom to pursue their moral projects.

Ultimately, Hazlitt's moral defense of markets is not a forceful defense of markets against the charge that they are morally corrupting. Hazlitt maintained that markets are moral spaces because they allow people to pursue their moral projects and because they promote social cooperation and economic progress. He suggested that markets are the only economic system that allows us to be moral. Although market participants are sometimes unethical, Hazlitt stressed that markets tend to promote ethical behavior. Arguably, this is an appropriate and accurate moral accounting. In fact, we make a similar argument in later chapters. Hazlitt, however, offered arguments but no real evidence. Simply stating that, on net, the market will encourage more ethical than unethical behavior raises an empirical question, it does not settle it. Moreover, declaring that the market system is morally better than its alternatives does not in and of itself answer the critics' concern that markets are corrupting.

Like Friedman and Hazlitt, F.A. Hayek's defense of the morality of markets rested on his understanding of the market order as the result of a process that no single person or group can or does control. Hayek described the price system as a vast telecommunications system that allows market participants to overcome the knowledge problem. This problem centers on how a large group of individuals in a society should coordinate their economic activities when relevant information is private, often tacit, inconsistent, and dispersed among them (Hayek 1945: 519). As such, economic actors are themselves best positioned to comprehend their immediate circumstances and the consequences of their actions. Since the "economic problem of society is mainly one of rapid adaptation to changes in the particular circumstances of time and place," we require a system that can rapidly transmit relevant information throughout the economy (Ibid.). Hayek proposed the price system as this system; it ensures that "only the most essential information is passed on and passed on only to those concerned" (Ibid.: 527). By transmitting this essential but dispersed information, markets "serve the general interest to a greater extent than any direct altruistic behavior ever could" (Lavoie and Chamlee-Wright 2000: 107).

Importantly, Hayek argued, no other system can replicate or outperform the market economy on economic grounds, not even one with a well-intentioned and benevolent central planner. If Hayek was correct that only the market system offers its participants liberty and secures better economic outcomes overall (even when the economy is in constant disequilibrium), there is a case, albeit an indirect one, for characterizing it as a moral order. Furthermore, the market might also be characterized as a moral order because it can accommodate diverse goals, including moral goals.

However, the market itself is morally neutral in Hayek's view. It would be a conceptual error to credit the market for the ethical behavior of market participants or to blame it for the unethical acts of market actors. "Surely," Hayek (1962) wrote,

> it is unjust to blame a system as more materialistic because it leaves it to the individual to decide whether he prefers material gain to other kinds of excellence, instead of having this decided for him. …If [a market system] gives individuals much more scope to serve their fellows by the pursuit of purely materialistic aims, it also gives them the opportunity to pursue any other aim they regard as more important.

The market is not morally responsible for the allocation of benefits and burdens that emerge within it.

Interestingly, Hayek did not believe that defenses of the justness of profits or even ordinary returns on investments were warranted. Essentially, Hayek viewed justice as a personal and interpersonal virtue that made sense only at the level of interpersonal interactions. For example, Hayek believed that discussions of whether workers deserved more or less than their marginal product or whether entrepreneurs deserved more or less than the profits they were able to capture missed the point.[20] He argued against concluding that markets treat individuals justly or unjustly by giving some what they deserved and others more or less than their due. Although it is appropriate to discuss justice at the level of individuals, it is inappropriate to demand that the results of the market process or any other game be just. This, he argued, anthropomorphized the market. "Justice," Hayek (1976: 70) contended,

> clearly has no application to the manner in which the impersonal process of the market allocates command over goods and services to particular people: this can be neither just nor unjust, because the results are not intended or foreseen, and depend on a multitude of circumstances not known in their totality to anybody.

---

[20] Contrary to Hayek, Israel Kirzner, who also viewed the market as a discovery process like Hayek, argued that that the returns that profit seekers receive are deserved. As such, profits are just. Although the profits that entrepreneurs obtain in the market are not like the returns from production (which no one would begrudge the producer), Kirzner ([1989] 2016) explained that they are very different from the fruits of luck (which many might begrudge the recipient). Instead, acts of discovering pure profit opportunities are in a different category, a category between production and luck. "An act of discovery, even though it is not an act of deliberate production," Kirzner (2004: 165) explained, "is the expression of human motivation and human alertness. That which has been discovered might never have been discovered but for this motivation and alertness; it is quite wrong to see the discovery as merely the product of blind chance." In other words, it is possible to hold that the discoverer "deserves" the fruits of his discovery when the market process is viewed as a discovery process and discovery is viewed as a creative act (i.e. the thing that was discovered did not exist in an economically meaningful sense prior to its being discovered).

Anthropomorphizing complex processes allows people to make moral judgments about them but, in Hayek's view, doing so is inappropriate.

Although Hayek resisted applying moral judgments to the outcomes of emergent orders like markets or games, it is possible to challenge him on this point (see Haeffele and Storr Forthcoming). If, in order to win a game, you had to engage in what would normally be considered bad behavior (e.g. the kind of behavior that it would take to win games like Liar's Poker or Star Trek's Kobayashi Maru training exercise or the Game of Thrones), it would not be absurd or even an error to describe that game as a bad game. Similarly, if a game tended to reward virtuous behavior and to punish unethical behavior (e.g. reward hard work and punish cheating), then it would make sense to characterize it as a moral game. And, if it is possible that some games can be condemned as immoral and others described as moral, then the market can certainly be condemned or praised on moral grounds. That said, even if it is correct that markets are not appropriately characterized as moral or immoral, this says nothing about whether or not the market is morally corrupting. Hayek's efforts to inoculate the market from moral considerations are not as effective as he hoped.

While Peter Boettke agreed with Wicksteed and Hayek that "[m]arkets themselves are neither moral nor immoral" (2004: 49), he also agreed with Kirzner and others who believe that profits are deserved because "in a truly contractual society one cannot do well unless by doing good" (Ibid.: 47). He, thus, proposed social cooperation as a standard for judging the morality of markets. Where markets promote social cooperation, Boettke continued, we should judge them as morally good. Where markets fail to promote social cooperation, we should judge them as morally bad since the alternatives to social cooperation are exploitation, violence, and oppression. Because, for Boettke (Ibid.: 48), the morality of an economic system depends on the degree to which it promotes social cooperation, "the rules which enhance social cooperation and as such allow the simultaneous achievement of liberty, prosperity, and peace are *moral* rules."[21] Conversely, "[m]oral rules which promise justice, but deliver reduced liberty, lower levels of prosperity, and the breakdown of peaceful harmony do not deserve to be described by terms such as 'just' and 'moral'" (Ibid.: 48–49).

The market system performs quite well when social cooperation is used as the central moral standard. The moral critics of markets, however, might be

---

[21] "When markets are embedded in a private property order governed by the rule of law," Boettke (2004: 49) wrote, "then they can be reasonably relied on to allocate resources effectively and to channel behavior in a manner consistent with the values of individual liberty, personal responsibility, honesty in dealing, respect for the property of others, etc."

described as being principally concerned with how markets fare when judged against other moral standards. Additionally, it remains an open question, on Boettke's account, as to whether or not and to what extent social cooperation is compatible with immorality, where, say, morality is conceived of as justice. Boettke was, simply, silent on a number of issues that concern the critics of markets on moral grounds.

Similar to Adam Smith's contention that the market does not depend on beneficence, J.R. Clark and Dwight Lee asserted that the market should primarily be recognized for its "ability to generate desirable outcomes without relying on what is widely seen as moral behavior" (Clark and Lee 2011: 2). They argued that human beings operate with two alternative moral systems: magnanimous morality and mundane morality. Magnanimous morality describes the type of duty-based rectitude where friends and family incur some personal sacrifice to help each other. This is the type of behavior people who lived in small communities needed to survive. "Survival," they (Ibid.: 5) stated, "was critically influenced by how people reacted to the behavior of each other, and those reactions with the greatest survival value evolved into emotional responses that helped enforce what became to be considered desirable, or moral, behavior." On the other hand, mundane morality can be generally defined as "obeying the generally accepted rules or norms of conduct such as telling the truth, honoring your promises and contractual obligations, respecting the property rights of others, and refraining from intentionally harming others" (Ibid.: 6).

The market, Clark and Lee argued, depends on mundane morality. The market does not need magnanimous morality to function properly. Moreover, they conceded, the market encourages behavior that could be considered immoral. Echoing Mandeville, Clark and Lee (Ibid.: 8) explained that,

> the importance of the invisible hand characterization of the market is that the truly impressive performance of the market at motivating mutual help and assistance does not involve intention, personal sacrifice, or identifiable beneficiaries. According to the invisible hand case for markets, more help is provided because people do not intend to provide it; the help is motivated and generally accomplished by personal gain; and the benefits go to the society, in other words to no one in particular. So not only does the market not require the behavior that most see as moral, it is seen as motivating a level of indifference to that morality that is widely seen as immoral – in particular, regarding greed and willingness to profit from the problems of others.

It is clear from their account that the mundane morality that the market depends on is so thin a notion of morality that it is compatible with a great deal of immorality.

Moreover, Clark and Lee asserted, trying to replace mundane morality with magnanimous morality would be a mistake. First, our altruistic sentiments are strongest toward those who are socially close. But, they explained, the number of people for whom we feasibly and realistically can care is proportionately minuscule compared to the number of people for whom we must care in order to achieve global economic cooperation. Second, even if it were possible to care for such a large number of people, an economy requires information on their wants and desires. To Clark and Lee, the price system does an impressive job at transmitting information, but it relies on impersonal exchange and self-interested motivations to determine market prices, both of which are contradictory qualities to magnanimous morality.

Additionally, Clark and Lee argued that we should not be so quick to dismiss mundane morality. Social harmony and human liberty are virtues that emanate from and depend on mundane morality. According to Clark and Lee (Ibid.: 23),

> No matter how great one believes the marginal social value of caring for others is, the optimal amount of it is very limited, which suggests we should use our limited capacity to care where it does the most good and rely on market exchange as a substitute for caring – that is we should view the market's mundane morality as a good substitute for magnanimous morality. Private ownership, voluntary exchange, and the mundane morality of the marketplace do a far better job, at a far lower cost, of promoting productive cooperation and social harmony over multitudes of diverse and dispersed people than relying solely on magnanimous morality.

Mundane morality is simply a more workable and more profitable form of morality than magnanimous morality.

If they are correct, Clark and Lee would have articulated an important rationale for not replacing the market system with an alternative economic system that depended more on magnanimous morality but did not perform as well on economic grounds. They would have done so, however, by conceding that the critics are correct that markets depend on immorality and are likely to be morally corrupting.

As with the various critiques of markets on moral grounds, there are obviously considerable differences in the defenses discussed above. There are, however, key similarities between these defenses, and many of the others that you might have encountered. While the morality critiques of markets stress the potential for moral corruption when individuals engage in market activities, many of the defenses either agree with the critique or attempt to minimize the importance of that claim rather than directly responding to it.

Answering the Question, Are Markets Morally Corrupting?

Many of the critics of markets on moral grounds have described it as a kind of monster. This monster, however, is not simply content with attacking and consuming us. This monster wants to transform us into creatures in its own image. Arguably, the most damning criticism of markets is that it places market participants in a kind of moral jeopardy where they must risk their souls to satisfy their material needs and wants. Markets, goes this view, reward our worst traits and, in so doing, crowd out morality.

Indeed, multiple prosecutors have accused the market of being an *immoralizing* space and, on that basis, have attempted to convict it, often recommending imprisonment or even death as its sentence. Rather than defending their client against this charge by claiming its innocence, however, many of the attorneys for the market have simply conceded the prosecution's interpretation of the underlying facts of the case, offering only mitigating evidence. The market does crowd out morality, say its defense attorneys, but it has contributed to society (in the form of wealth and social cooperation), despite its obvious failings. Ironically, those few attorneys for the market who do claim that their client is innocent often acknowledge that there was a crime and even that the market was somehow involved. The market, goes this defense, is simply a morally neutral tool, an amoral space, an unwitting accomplice, perhaps itself a victim.

Many of the moral defenses of markets are, thus, not adequate responses to the moral criticisms of markets that have been advanced. Lavoie and Chamlee-Wright (2000) accurately characterized these as *minimalist moral defenses of the market*. These minimalist moral defenses, they explained, are merely attempts to redirect our moral judgment away from the market and toward the behavior of market actors, or the nature of the social rules governing markets, or the positive social outcomes associated with markets.[22] These minimalist moral defenses

---

[22] Minimalist moral defenses of the market "[rest] not on the individual's ability to intentionally improve the lives of others and the community in general, but rather on the idea of unintended consequences" (Lavoie and Chamlee-Wright 2000: 105). It makes no explicit assumption regarding the morality of economic agents; they need only obey the rules. As long as they obey the law, the greedy businessmen acting in their self-interests unintentionally satisfy the needs and desires of others and are even pushed to

do not really respond to the central moral criticism of the market, that is, they do not challenge the claim that the market is potentially morally corrupting.

Of course, there have been some moral defenses that have attempted to directly respond to the complaint that markets are corrupting. Lavoie and Chamlee-Wright (Ibid.), for instance, attempted to move beyond the minimalist moral defenses of markets that they criticized. Likewise, Meadowcroft (2005) articulated an ethical defense of the market that rested on the market's ability to improve the lives of market participants, the space that markets give individuals to pursue their own moral projects, the justness of economic distributions, and the ability of markets to regulate conduct. Similarly, McCloskey (2006) wrote quite persuasively that markets are peopled with individuals who exhibit the bourgeois virtues of prudence, temperance, courage, justice, faith, hope, and love. Additionally, Brennan and Jaworski (2016) directly engaged what they called the "corruption objection" to markets and argued quite forcefully that this particular criticism of markets fails. In order to be successful, Brennan and Jaworski argued, a corruption objection would have to provide evidence, not conjecture, and be devoid of logical leaps or errors. None of the major corruption objections, Brennan and Jaworski (Ibid.) pointed out, pass this test.

In our view, in order to assess the guilt or innocence of the market on the main charge in the indictment, the question of whether or not engaging in market activities is morally corrupting must be answered directly. We believe that the claim that markets are morally corrupting is simply wrong. Markets do not work in theory or in practice the way the moral critics and some of the moral defenders of markets contend. Additionally, rather than the evidence confirming that markets depend on or promote vice, the evidence points in the opposite direction. It is, we believe, possible to offer and support the following responses to the propositions discussed in Chap. 2 that are advanced or implied by those critics and defenders of commercial society who believe that markets are morally corrupting:

Response 1: *In fact, virtue is more prevalent in market societies than in nonmarket societies and vice is less prevalent in market societies than in nonmarket societies.*
Response 2: *In fact, as a society becomes more market-oriented and as the scope of the market in a society expands, more virtue and less vice will exist in that society.*
Response 3: *In fact, the more a person engages in market activity, the more virtuous they are likely to be.*

---

better serve others. Here, the market is a moral order not because market participants deliberately pursue moral purposes (although they are capable of doing so) but because the market inadvertently achieves social cooperation or distributive justice.

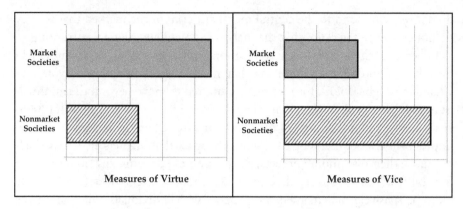

Fig. 3.1 If markets do not corrupt our morals… If markets are truly morally enriching, we should observe market societies displaying higher levels of virtue and lower levels of vice compared to nonmarket societies

Figure 3.1 represents what we should expect to find when we examine the data on the relationship between markets and morality if our responses to the moral criticisms of markets are correct.[23] If we are right, we should expect to observe higher levels of measures of virtue and lower levels of measures of vices displayed in market societies compared to nonmarket societies.

Markets are not, in fact, the monsters, transforming us into evil creatures, that so many accuse them of being. Instead, there is compelling evidence that markets are moral spaces that not only depend on virtue but also rewards virtue while punishing vice. The moral critics of markets are correct that we cannot engage in market activities and emerge unaffected by the experience. We are changed and, arguably quite profoundly, by our dealings in the market. But, contrary to what some may believe, we are changed for the better. We become better people as a result of our interactions in the market. The evidence suggests that we not only become wealthier but become less greedy, less selfish, less materialistic, more trustworthy, more tolerant, and better connected, as a result of our exposure to markets.

The remaining chapters attempt to answer the question: Do markets corrupt our morals? There are two main arguments that we advance in response to this question. In the next chapter, we argue that people can improve their lives through markets and that this fact is morally relevant. In subsequent chapters, we argue that the market is a moral space that both depends on its participants being virtuous and also rewards them for being virtuous. Rather than harming individuals ethically, the market is an arena where morality is encouraged.

---

[23] Note that Fig. 3.1 offers the opposite image of Fig. 2.1.

Bibliography

Boettke, P.J. 2004. Morality as Cooperation. In *Morality of Markets*, ed. P.J. Shah and P. Shah, 69–82. Delhi: Academic Foundation.

Bowles, S., H. Gintis, and B. Gustafsson. 1993. *Markets and Democracy: Participation, Accountability and Efficiency*. Cambridge: Cambridge University Press.

Boycko, M., and R.J. Shiller. 2016. Popular Attitudes toward Markets and Democracy: Russia and United States Compared 25 Years Later. *American Economic Review* 106 (5): 224–229.

Brennan, J., and P.M. Jaworski. 2016. *Markets Without Limits: Moral Virtues and Commercial Interests*. London/New York: Routledge.

Bruni, L., and R. Sugden. 2013. Reclaiming Virtue Ethics for Economics. *Journal of Economic Perspectives* 27 (4): 141–164.

Clark, J.R., and D.R. Lee. 2011. Markets and Morality. *Cato Journal* 31: 1–26.

Dallmayr, F. 2015. *Freedom and Solidarity: Toward New Beginnings*. Kentucky: University Press of Kentucky.

Falk, A., and N. Szech. 2013. Morals and Markets. *Science* 340 (6133): 707–711.

Friedman, T.L. 1996. Foreign Affairs Big Mac I. *The New York Times*, December 8. https://www.nytimes.com/1996/12/08/opinion/foreign-affairs-big-mac-i.html

Friedman, M. [1962] 2002. *Capitalism and Freedom: Fortieth Anniversary Edition*. Chicago: University of Chicago Press.

———. [1970] 2007. The Social Responsibility of Business Is to Increase Its Profits. In *Corporate Ethics and Corporate Governance*, ed. W.C. Zimmerli, M. Holzinger, and K. Richter, 173–178. Berlin: Springer.

Gleditsch, N.P. 2008. The Liberal Moment Fifteen Years On. *International Studies Quarterly* 52 (4): 691–712.

Haeffele, S., and V.H. Storr. Forthcoming. Is Social Justice a Mirage? *The Independent Review*.

Hanley, R.P. 2009. *Adam Smith and the Character of Virtue*. Cambridge: Cambridge University Press.

Hayek, F.A. 1945. The Use of Knowledge in Society. *American Economic Review* 35 (4): 519–530.

———. 1962. The Moral Element in Free Enterprise. Reprinted in *Foundation for Economic Education* from a Symposium on The Spiritual and Moral Element in Free Enterprise. https://fee.org/articles/the-moral-element-in-free-enterprise/

———. 1976. *Law, Legislation and Liberty, Vol. 2: The Mirage of Social Justice*. Chicago: University of Chicago Press.

———. [1988] 1991. *The Fatal Conceit: The Errors of Socialism*, ed. W.W. Bartley III. Chicago: University of Chicago Press.

Hazlitt, H. [1964] 1994. *The Foundations of Morality*. Irvington-on-Hudson: Foundation for Economic Education.

Hill, L. 2017. "The Poor Man's Son" and the Corruption of Our Moral Sentiments: Commerce, Virtue and Happiness in Adam Smith. *Journal of Scottish Philosophy* 15 (1): 9–25.

Hirschman, A.O. 1977. *The Passions and the Interests: Political Arguments for Capitalism before Its Triumph*. Princeton: Princeton University Press.

———. 1982. Rival Interpretations of Market Society: Civilizing, Destructive, or Feeble? *Journal of Economic Literature* 20 (4): 1463–1484.

Hodgson, G.M. 2013. *From Pleasure Machines to Moral Communities: An Evolutionary Economics Without Homo Economicus*. Chicago: University of Chicago Press.

Jervis, R. 2002. Theories of War in an Era of Leading-Power Peace 'Presidential Address, American Political Science Association, 2001'. *The American Political Science Review* 96 (1): 1–14.

Kirzner, I.M. 2004. The Ugly Market: Why Capitalism is Hated, Feared and Despised. In *Morality of Markets*, ed. P.J. Shah and P. Shah, 69–82. Delhi: Academic Foundation.

———. [1989] 2016. *The Collected Works of Israel M. Kirzner: Discovery, Capitalism and Distributive Justice*, ed. P.J. Boettke and F. Sautet. Indianapolis: Liberty Fund.

Koerber, C.P. 2009. Corporate Responsibility Standards: Current Implications and Future Possibilities for Peace Through Commerce. *Journal of Business Ethics* 89 (4): 461–480.

Langrill, R., and V.H. Storr. 2012. The Moral Meaning of Markets. *Journal of Markets and Morality* 15 (2): 347–362.

Lavoie, D., and E. Chamlee-Wright. 2000. *Culture and Enterprise: The Development, Representation and Morality of Business*. London/New York: Routledge.

Lindblom, C.E. 1995. Market and Democracy – Obliquely. *PS: Political Science & Politics* 28 (4): 684–688.

MacIntyre, A. 1981. *After Virtue: A Study in Moral Theory*. Notre Dame: University of Notre Dame Press.

Mandeville, B. [1714, 1732] 1988. *The Fable of the Bees or Private Vices, Publick Benefits*. With Commentary by F.B. Kaye. Indianapolis: Liberty Fund.

Martin, P., T. Mayer, and M. Thoenig. 2008. Make Trade Not War. *The Review of Economic Studies* 75 (3): 865–900.

McCloskey, D.N. 1998. Bourgeois Virtues and the History of P and S. *The Journal of Economic History* 58 (2): 297–317.

———. 2006. *The Bourgeois Virtues: Ethics for an Age of Commerce*. Chicago: University of Chicago Press.

Meadowcroft, J. 2005. *The Ethics of the Market*. London: Palgrave Macmillan.

Montesquieu. [1748] 1989. *Montesquieu: The Spirit of the Laws*, ed. A.M. Cohler, B.C. Miller and H.S. Stone. Cambridge: Cambridge University Press.

Otteson, J. 2014. *The End of Socialism*. Cambridge: Cambridge University Press.

Prychitko, D.L., ed. 2002. *Markets, Planning, and Democracy: Essays after the Collapse of Communism*. Cheltenham: Edward Elgar Publishing.

Sandel, M.J. 2012. *What Money Can't Buy: The Moral Limits of Markets*. London: Macmillan.

Satz, D. 2010. *Why Some Things Should Not Be for Sale: The Moral Limits of Markets*. Oxford: Oxford University Press.

Smith, A. [1776] 1981. *An Inquiry into the Nature and Causes of the Wealth of Nations*. Indianapolis: Liberty Fund.

———. [1759] 1982. *The Theory of Moral Sentiments*. Indianapolis: Liberty Fund.

———. [1763] 1982. *Lectures in Jurisprudence*. Indianapolis: Liberty Fund.

Smith, V.L., and B.J. Wilson. 2019. *Humanomics: Moral Sentiments and the Wealth of Nations for the Twenty-First Century*. Cambridge: Cambridge University Press.

Strong, M. 2009. Peace Through Access to Entrepreneurial Capitalism for All. *Journal of Business Ethics* 89 (4): 529–538.

Voltaire, J. Morley, and T. Smollett, eds. [1733] 1901. *The Works of Voltaire. A Contemporary Version. A Critique and Biography*. Trans. W.F. Fleming. New York: E.R. DuMont.

Weber, M. [1905] 2002. *The Protestant Ethic and the "Spirit" of Capitalism and Other Writings*. Trans. P. Baehr and G. Wells. London: Penguin Books.

Wicksteed, P.H. [1910] 2003. *The Common Sense of Political Economy, Including a Study of the Human Basis of Economic Law*. London/New York: Routledge.

4

People Can Improve Their Lives Through Markets

There are surely victims of markets. Think of the business owners and their employees who lose their livelihoods because they no longer make a product that consumers want to buy, because there are cheaper or better alternatives, or because consumer tastes have changed. Think of the worker who is paid too little or is forced to work too much or labors in unsafe environments. Think of the consumers who mistakenly buy defective and potentially dangerous products. Think of the poor who are necessarily disadvantaged in an economic system where wealth leads to all sorts of advantages. Think of the community member who is forced to breathe air or drink water polluted by a nearby factory.[1]

Think of enslaved Africans in the New World. In their study of life on a Bahamian plantation, archeologists Laurie Wilkie and Paul Farnsworth (2005) tell the story of Boatswain. Boatswain was "a tall and slender African

---

[1] Consider, for instance, that Blockbuster, once a Goliath of the video rental industry, could not keep pace with changes in technology and customers' preferences and filed for bankruptcy in 2010. Toys R Us, a toy store, ceased its operations in 2018 in the United States, citing, "shoppers flocking to online platforms like Amazon.com Inc (AMZN.O) and children choosing electronic gadgets over toys" as two of the main reasons for its closure (Ruckinski 2018). For similar reasons, Borders, a bookstore, and Tower Records, a music store, went out of business in 2011 and 2006, respectively. Additionally, California's Division of Occupational Safety and Health opened an investigation against Tesla, the electric car company, based on current and former employees' concerns about the Fremont factory prioritizing production over worker safety (Ehrenkranz 2018). In 1997, Ernst & Young revealed in a report that workers at a Nike shoe factory in Vietnam "were exposed to carcinogens that exceeded local legal standards by 177 times in parts of the plant and that 77% of the employees suffered from respiratory problems" and "were forced to work 65 hours a week, far more than Vietnamese law allows, for $10 a week" (Greenhouse 1997). Apple has worked hard to address similar criticisms and improve its reputation on this margin in the recent years, but another supplier to Apple has been accused of subjecting its employees to work in "an unsafe environment for long hours earning low wages" in early 2018 (Chong 2018).

© The Author(s) 2019
V. H. Storr, G. S. Choi, *Do Markets Corrupt Our Morals?*,
https://doi.org/10.1007/978-3-030-18416-2_4

... of an upright carriage" (Wylly 1821 quoted in Wilkie and Farnsworth 2005: 89). He was brought to the Bahamas as a young adult and enslaved on the Clifton plantations owned by William Wylly on New Providence, Bahamas. Boatswain was married to Chloe who had "a tawney complexion" and "a remarkably good countenance" (Ibid.). When she was 15 years old and prior to her marriage to Boatswain, Chloe had given birth to Mary Anne, who was likely the child of Wylly or one of his relatives.

A mason by trade, Boatswain was an important figure on the plantation. Like the other tradesman on the Wylly plantation, Boatswain was allowed to spend at least two days a week working for himself. This meant that in exchange for giving up his claim to half of his ration of corn, he was allowed to go into Nassau, the central town on New Providence, to sell his services to whoever he wished. "A skilled craftsman like a mason," Wilkie and Farnsworth (Ibid.: 88) explained, "would be in great demand throughout the city of Nassau, where stone buildings abounded." In fact, the plantation documents suggested that Boatswain was rarely involved in activities on the plantation, and, so, likely had "more lucrative wage options beyond the confines of the plantations" (Ibid.: 89). Boatswain was pretty successful and, as a result, became well known throughout Nassau, with an established reputation and a large base of customers (Ibid.: 89).

Although Wylly was a gentler plantation owner than his peers and Boatswain was able to earn an even better life than his peers through his market efforts, there is really no way to soften slavery.[2] The enslaved may be given more or less autonomy on a particular plantation, plantation owners may be more or less brutal in some particular instance, but the loss of real freedom is always absolute and the terror associated with slavery is always extreme. Despite being enslaved by a planter who "fancied himself a reformer, and perhaps even a savior, of the enslaved population on the island" (Ibid.: 69), and having achieved an even better standard of living than others on the plantation through his market activities, Boatswain, Chloe, and their four children ran away from the plantation on January 17, 1821. Unfortunately, Boatswain and his family were ultimately reacquired by Wylly and were sold to Henry Moss

---

[2] According to Wilkie and Farnsworth (2005: 306),

> Wylly saw himself as enlightened and benevolent, and perhaps – compared to planter peers who included a couple that tortured a teenaged slave girl to death – he was. In the rules of Clifton Plantation, he set out a series of behavioral and work conditions that had to be met by the enslaved community. The benefits [Wylly] offered in return [to the slaves] included the right to worship according to [their own] religious doctrine, the right to live in a house of [their own] construction, the limited right to learn to read and write, the right to support oneself on a small parcel of land, and the right to participate with his blessing in the Nassau market.

a few years later (Ibid.: 90). Sent to Crooked Island, one of the more rural islands in the Bahamas, "Boatswain lost the prestige of being a craftsman, and in 1834, he is listed as working in the salt pans of Long Cay, away from his family" (Ibid.). Working in the salt pans was then, as it is now, backbreaking work.[3] There is no reprieve from the sun, made more unbearable by the glare from the salt crystals. Any open wound would refuse to heal because of the ever-present and all-preserving salt. Additionally, Boatswain was separated from his family. As a market participant, Boatswain was able to benefit from his market activities. As a possession, his involvement with markets wrecked an already disadvantaged life.

The market for enslaved Africans and the markets that depended on their labor were truly noxious markets (Satz 2010).[4] Chattel slavery was an indisputably deplorable system, the horrors of which cannot be overstated. Under chattel slavery, human beings were bought and sold as if they were the personal property of other human beings. And, being perceived as no more than mere property, slaves were often treated no better than (and sometimes were treated worse than) physical property. More than 12 million Africans were captured and shipped to the New World as a part of the trans-Atlantic slave trade from 1525 when it began to when it was ended in 1866 (Eltis 2017). Those Africans who survived the Middle Passage as well as their descendants were forced to work as servants in households, in various trades, and on plantations (see Handler 2009). When they resisted their servitude in any way, they were brutally punished. When they complied, they were horribly abused. There was little that enslaved Africans could do to protect themselves from the unspeakable and near constant threats of violence that characterized this socioeconomic system.

If ever there were victims of markets, enslaved Africans in the Americas during the sixteenth, seventeenth, eighteenth, and nineteenth centuries would be chief among them. But, when given access to markets, not as property but as producers and consumers, enslaved Africans were able to make important personal gains. In the Bahamas, for instance, enslaved Africans (like Boatswain) were able to improve their standards of living because of their access to markets.

Admittedly, slavery in the Bahamas was an especially peculiar institution (Johnson 1991). The advertisements published in the *Bahama Gazette* and the *Royal Gazette*, two of the main local newspapers at the time, spoke to the

---

[3] See Thiagarajan (2017) that describes life and work of a modern-day salt harvester.
[4] Satz (2010) defined noxious markets as those markets that are "toxic to important human values" (Ibid.: 3) and that "undermine the conditions that people need if they are to relate as equals" (Ibid.: 94). In Chap. 7, we discuss Satz's notion of noxious markets with more detail.

strangeness of slavery in this British colony. One advertisement, for instance, offers "To Hire by the Month … Several Negro Women, who are good Cooks, Washers and Ironers, and capable of doing all kinds of House Work" (*Royal Gazette*, 4 September 1804). Another advertised a job for "Four Negro Women as Nurses and Washers at the Hospital at Fort Charlotte. For whom liberal Wages will be paid by applying at the Office" (*Bahama Gazette*, November 29, 1799). Interestingly, the people of African descent who were sought in these advertisements were not just liberated Africans but also Africans who were still enslaved.

In the Bahamas, there was a firmly established practice of self-hire where the enslaved in urban contexts and in maritime centers were allowed to seek their own employment and to retain whatever wages they earned above a pre-determined weekly fee they agreed to and paid to their owners (Johnson 1996: 1). As Governor of the colony Sir James Carmichael-Smyth explained, "it has long been a custom in this Colony to permit the more intelligent of the Slaves, and more particularly Artificers, to find employment for themselves & to pay to their owners either the whole or such a proportion of what they may gain as may be agreed upon between the Parties" (quoted in Johnson 1996: 5). Under this system of self-hire, "male slaves … found employment as steve-dores and porters and as labourers in stone-quarrying, wood-cutting and road-building" (Ibid.: 6). And, "female slaves on the self-hire system were employed primarily as domestics and itinerant vendors" (Ibid.). These enslaved workers on self-hire were often paid the same wages as liberated Africans and even whites doing the same jobs. Occasionally, enslaved workers on self-hire dominated the trades in which they worked (Ibid.: 36).

The self-hire system benefited both slaves and their owners. As Johnson (1996: 34) detailed,

> For the slave owners, the self-hire system provided a steady cash income from slaves who assumed responsibility for their own maintenance. For the slaves, the system presented an opportunity to remove themselves from their owners' surveillance and enjoy a status that fell somewhere between chattel slavery and freedom.

At the time, the Bahamas had no stable export crop because the soil in the colony could not sustain large-scale agriculture. Consequently, slave owners could not keep their slaves employed productively and had trouble meeting the maintenance needs of their slaves. Under self-hire, enslaved Africans took responsibility for their own upkeep and so relieved slaveholders of that burden. The enslaved, on the other hand, gained some autonomy, a kind of quasi-freedom where they could work where they pleased for wages that they agreed to (or sometimes dictated) so long as they paid their owners the agreed to sum (Ibid.: 43).

People, even enslaved people, can improve their lives through markets. On occasion, slaves on self-hire could earn enough to significantly improve their lives. According to Johnson (Ibid.: 42),

> After discharging their contractual obligations to their owners, some slaves (particularly those who lacked special skills) probably had little disposable income. A significant number, however, earned enough money to indulge in leisure-time activities like drinking and gambling on a regular basis and to purchase inexpensive consumer items. Many slaves accumulated enough savings to buy their own freedom.

Again, this does not mean that the sting of slavery was eliminated. Of course, quasi-freedom is not freedom, a relatively wealthy slave is still a slave, and being able to buy your own freedom means that you were once chattel. But, because self-hire was so widespread in the Bahamas, Bahamian slaves were considerably better off than slaves elsewhere at the time (Craton and Saunders 1992: 288; also Wilkie and Farnsworth 2005; Johnson 1991, 1996).[5]

People can improve their lives through markets. If, on one side of the ledger, the concern is that markets are corrupting, on the other side of the ledger must be the very real possibility that we are better off in market societies. Societies that embrace markets have higher standards of living and a better quality of life. People residing in countries with markets are wealthier, healthier, happier, and better connected.

There are clearly material benefits that accrue to the societies that embrace markets. Through markets, as Adam Smith ([1776] 1981) asserted, we are able to pursue and acquire more of our material wants than we could without markets. Indeed, most people would likely agree that at least some people could improve their material lives through markets. The benefits associated with markets, however, are not limited to the rich; a "general plenty diffuses itself through all the different ranks of society" and "universal opulence... extends itself to the lowest rank of people" (Ibid.: 22). People can improve their lives through markets, even the least advantaged.

This chapter will argue that people in market societies are wealthier, healthier, happier, and better connected than people in nonmarket societies. We will

---

[5] The practice of provision plots and weekend markets also contributed to the advantages that Bahamian slaves had over slaves elsewhere (Storr 2004). The practice involved giving the enslaved use rights to a plot of land on the plantation, allowing them to grow crops for their own use in their "free time," and allowing them to sell surplus crops in weekend markets.

also explore whether or not these (material) benefits of markets are only enjoyed by the few or are also enjoyed by the least advantaged in market societies. The potential for material betterment by engaging in market activity, we argue, is of moral significance.

A Tale of Two Estonias

There are considerable differences between the Estonian Soviet Socialist Republic and the Republic of Estonia. The Soviet Union annexed Estonia in 1940, lost it to Nazi Germany in 1941, and recaptured it in 1944. Estonia then remained a Soviet satellite until it asserted its sovereignty in 1988 and gained its independence in 1991. During both periods of Soviet occupation, Estonia's economy suffered considerably. In the first period, banks and major industries were nationalized and smaller firms were forced to close (Smith 2001: 33). Moderate savings accounts were confiscated. Regulations to restrict the free movement of labor and to extend the working day were introduced. Privately held land in excess of 75 acres along with land owned by the Church and local authority were placed into a reserve and distributed to the poor in rural areas (Ibid.: 34). This was, however, only a first step toward introducing collective agriculture. As Smith (Ibid.) described, "around a hundred collective farms were created in Estonia during 1940–41, while medium-sized farmers and so-called 'kulaks' were subjected to punitive taxation and compulsory deliveries to the state at artificially low prices."

Once the Soviets regained Estonia, these efforts to create a Soviet-style economy in Estonia resumed or intensified. After the war, Taagepera (1993: 81) explained,

> Forced collectivization of agriculture … eliminated the last segment of private enterprise. It was preceded by four years during which land redistribution was aimed at eliminating the large farms, with the goal of forming invariably small new ones and creating social tensions between those who lost and those who gained land. Increasing taxes and obligatory deliveries at ridiculously low prices made individual farming well-nigh impossible by 1948.

Additionally, Soviet state-led industrialization efforts attempted to expand industry and increase mechanization within industries. But, despite achieving increased output in some sectors, the Soviet system proved less efficient than the more market-oriented economic system it replaced. For instance, according to Taagepera (Ibid.: 83), "in oil-shale mining, which was Estonia's main industrial base, the amount produced per worker was slightly lower in 1950 than in 1939."

Life improved some in subsequent years. But, Estonians remained (materially) worse off during the Soviet era than their neighbors who had remained market societies.[6] Prior to Soviet occupation, national income in Estonia was on par with its neighbor Finland. Although income per capita in Estonia remained higher than other parts of the Soviet Union throughout its occupation, it had fallen well behind Finland by the time it gained its independence. In 1990, GDP per capita (at current U.S. prices) in Estonia was $3589 compared to $28,326 in Finland. Health indicators in Estonia at the end of Soviet rule were also quite poor relative to its neighbors; for instance, life expectancy at birth in Estonia was 70 years compared to 75 years in Finland in 1990 (United Nations 2017).

In addition to the considerable differences in the standards of living in Soviet Estonia and in its neighbor Finland by the end of the Soviet Era (Raun [1987] 2002: 208), the differences between Soviet Estonia and contemporary Estonia are also quite striking. After its independence in 1991, Estonia transitioned its economy from a Soviet-style command economy to a market economy. Its integration into the European Union in 2004 accelerated that transition. Since 2002, Estonia has consistently ranked as one of the top 20 economically free countries in the world in the Fraser Institute's Economic Freedom Rankings. As a result, GDP per capita (at current prices) had grown to $17,782 by 2016 and life expectancy had grown to 77 years by 2012. Admittedly, Estonia has not yet caught up with its neighbors, but Estonians are clearly (materially) better off in the post-Independence market society they have developed than they were in the nonmarket society that they endured under Soviet rule.

A Tale of Two Koreas

The differences between North and South Korea also highlight the key role that markets can play in the prosperity and well-being of a country and its people. In 1945, the Korean peninsula was liberated from the oppressive rule of the Japanese Empire with the victory of the Allied forces in World War II. The United States and the Soviet Union agreed to jointly supervise the surrender of the Japanese forces and divided the peninsula into two zones at the 38th parallel line (i.e. latitude 38° N). They instituted provisional governments in their respective zones with the intent that they would be dissolved

---

[6] Of course, Estonians were worse off than their neighbors in more significant ways. During the Soviet era, there were forced deportations of Estonians to other parts of the Soviet Union and colonialization by Russians. Moreover, the political system remained an oppressive one throughout.

when the Korean peninsula achieved independence or was placed into an international trusteeship. However, the Soviets and the Americans were unable to arrive at an agreement regarding the implementation of the Joint Trusteeship over Korea and, later, the Soviets refused to partake in the first Korean democratic election, which was organized and supervised by the United Nations (UN). As a result, the UN recognized the government in the American zone as the sole legitimate government on the peninsula in 1948. Along with the rising tensions between the Soviet Union and the United States, the Armistice Agreement at the end of the Korean War left the peninsula separated by the 38th parallel in 1953.

Seventy years after separation, the two Koreas cannot be more different in all aspects of life. South Korea has a democratic government that employs free enterprise policies with a vibrant civil society and was the 11th largest economy in the world at the end of 2015 (World Bank 2016; Foreign & Commonwealth Office 2017). By contrast, North Korea's communist government oversees a controlled economy and has developed into a totalitarian dictatorship with a cult of personality surrounding the ruling Kim family. South Korea gained global recognition of their commitment to democratic market economy, international trade, and economic progress when it became a member of the Organisation for Economic Co-operation and Development (OECD) in 1996. It was the fifth largest export economy in the world, with its exports valued at $515 billion and a positive trade balance of $177 billion in 2016 (Observatory of Economic Complexity 2018). Technology is one of South Korea's main exports and some of the most popular global brands, such as Samsung, Hyundai, and Kia, are South Korean conglomerates. In recent years, its pop-culture, such as its music, beauty products, films, television shows, and fashion, has gained popularity with the younger generations in other parts of Asia as well as in Western countries. South Korea spent the most on research and development (4.29% of GDP) among OECD member countries in 2014 (OECD 2016) and ranks fifth on the most recent Ease of Doing Business index (The World Bank 2019).

South Korea enjoys a high level of wealth, with GDP per capita (PPP, constant 2011 international $) of approximately $36,000 and an unemployment rate of 3.7% (as of 2017) (The World Bank 2016, 2017).[7] It enjoyed less income inequality (2015 Gini coefficient of 0.295) (OECD 2018c) and

---

[7] Although state-level corruption continues to persist, it is undeniable that South Korea also has healthy political and legal systems. For instance, it successfully removed a corrupt but democratically elected president, Park Geun-Hye, from office through nonviolent legal means in 2017 (Caryl 2017; Choe 2017).

experienced less market income inequality in the late 2000s compared to other OECD countries (OECD 2011a, b). South Korea is also one of the most highly skilled and technologically advanced countries. Overall, it ranked second to Japan in (adult) skills proficiency among OECD member countries in 2012 (OECD 2013). Eighty-seven percent of South Korean adults (aged 25–64) have completed upper secondary education, above the OECD average of 74% (OECD 2018b). Out of the 72 countries and economies that participated in OECD's Programme for International Student Assessment (PISA) test in 2015,[8] South Korean teenagers ranked seventh in mathematics, eleventh in science, and sixth in reading.[9] Moreover, South Korea is one of the most digitally connected countries in the world. As of 2016, its citizens enjoyed the highest average Internet speed in the world,[10] approximately 90% of the population had access to the Internet (Statistica 2017), and there are approximately 121 wireless mobile subscriptions per 100 inhabitants (The World Bank 2016). And, many of its teenagers are comfortable with technology; the 2009 PISA test revealed that South Korean teenagers had the highest digital literacy and scored higher on the test when reading on the computer than reading printed test materials (OECD 2011c).

Arguably, the other Korea could not be more economically and politically different. After the separation, North Korea adopted Marxist-Leninist communism with an ideology that emphasizes national self-reliance (*juche*) and prioritizes the military (*songun*). North Korea historically has had little international trade; it depended on Russia and the Eastern Bloc for trade during the Cold War era and has relied heavily on China since the fall of Soviet Union. Although it enjoyed annual growth rates comparable to those of South Korea in the first two decades after the separation, the North Korean economy has since stagnated, averaging −0.52% between 1990 and 2015 (Trading Economics 2018). North Koreans are among the poorest people in the world, with a GDP per capita of $1800 and an unemployment rate of 25.6% (Central Intelligence Agency 2015). Yet, despite the bleak economic performance measures, North Korea has the fourth largest active military and the largest number of military personnel (including the military reserve force) in the world (International Institute for Strategic Studies 2014).

---

[8] PISA assesses skills and knowledge of 15-year-old students in mathematics, reading, and science around the world every three years.

[9] In comparison, American teens ranked 25th in science, tied for 39th in mathematics (below OECD average), and tied for 23rd in reading in the 2015 PISA test.

[10] Average Internet speed in Korea is 27 Mbps. In comparison, the global average Internet speed is 7 Mbps.

As a socialist state, the North Korean government heavily regulates its citizens. According to the Freedom House (2016), North Korea has neither political nor civil rights. North Korea has a one-party political system and prohibits political activities and expressions that criticize the Korean Workers' Party. The North Korean government threatens dissidents and compels obedience from its citizens by threatening them with detention, torture, forced labor, public executions, and even assassinations. For example, it is believed that Kim Jong Un ordered the public execution of his uncle-in-law, Jang Song-Taek, in 2012, and the assassination of his half-brother, Kim Jong Nam, in 2017, to secure his political power by eliminating political opposition from within the North Korean elite (e.g. Choe 2016; Jager 2017). A regime that relies on fear and threats as a means of commanding loyalty, North Korea has publicly executed over a hundred of its senior military leaders and government officials since 2014 according to a report by South Korea's Institute for National Security Strategy (Theisen 2016; Institute for National Security Strategy 2016). Furthermore, it treats all defectors as enemies of the state and regularly employs the three generations of punishment rule, where surviving families of those who are found guilty of committing a crime and the subsequent two generations of family members must live and die in prison (U.S. Department of State 2017; Wright and Urban 2017). North Korea also places harsh restrictions on freedom of information and movement. The state tightly restricts access to independent and foreign media, and the Korean Central News Agency is the sole source of the information for domestic newspapers, television broadcasters, and radio stations (Reporters Without Borders 2016). Today, the Internet is still only available to North Korean elites, resident foreigners, and tourists (Williams 2016). While the North Korean constitution officially permits the freedom to practice any religion, the state takes a hostile approach toward religions in practice (Kang 2014). In fact, those who practice Christianity risk imprisonment in a labor camp if caught (Bandow 2016).

Moreover, social class strictly determines a person's lifestyle in North Korea. The country maintains a rigidly stratified society with a state-assigned class system (*songbun*), within which political loyalty plays a major role. This system determines where citizens may live; the type of accommodations and occupations they may have; the quality of their education, including whether they receive an education; how much food they are rationed;[11] whether they

---

[11] North Korea has a public food distribution system, where an average North Korean worker receives a daily ration of 700 grams of cereals. The World Food Program views a survival ration to be 600 grams per day per person. During periods of extreme food shortages, North Korea has drastically reduced the ration to its ordinary citizens (to as little as 150 grams per person per day) (Large 2011).

are allowed to travel domestically and internationally; and even whom they may marry. In fact, the government has criminalized all travel without permission and requires citizens to obtain permission to even travel domestically. In addition, citizens are required to travel by public transport within the country (United Nations 2014). This social hierarchy has manifested into a type of feudalism where the rural provinces serve as vassal states to Pyongyang, the capital city that is populated only by those who are loyal to the ruling Kim family. There, elites strive to please the ruler and government policies keep privileges and wealth with the elite within the capital city.

In the 1990s, the dissolution of the Soviet Union and a devastating famine and resulting economic crisis (called the Arduous March) dealt severe blows to the North Korean economy. The failure of the public food distribution system to deliver rations to the populace made the situation worse. In response to the dismal living conditions, the populace turned to black markets (*jang-madang*). Around this time, the state also relaxed the collective farming system and permitted the poor to privately own small plots of arable land and engage in subsistence farming in rural areas. In the early days of the famine, the poor supported one another by forming mutual assistance and bartering networks based on trust and solidarity. Eventually, women began to produce clothes, shoes, and food, and sold their surplus to others. These networks evolved into the black markets that exist today. Witnessing the success of these markets in providing its citizens with what they needed during the crisis, the North Korean government was forced to overlook the existence of black markets once the crisis abated. "Now that the black market has become the new normal," Pearson (2015) wrote, "[the North Korean] government has little choice but to continue its fledgling efforts at economic reforms that reflect market realities on the ground." The rediscovery of the market helped the North Koreans to weather the disaster and to even return to pre-disaster levels of consumption (Lankov 2011). As a direct consequence of the black markets, nonelites were able to improve their lives. Some merchants, whose socioeconomic class historically restricted their access to public education, were able to purchase private education for their children (Lankov 2014). Women's social status also rose as a consequence of their vital role in the black markets (Kwon and Chung 2012).

One of the major contributing factors to the Arduous March in North Korea was the inflexibility and inability of their existing economic system to accommodate the sudden and drastic changes in the food supply. As little as 240,000 to as many as 3.5 million people are estimated to have died from starvation and other hunger-related illnesses (Noland et al. 2001; Schwekendiek and Spoorenberg 2012). Had the North Korean government legally permitted markets at the time, the famine may not (and most likely would not) have been as bad because the markets would have been able to quickly respond to the changing circumstances and priorities in the economy.[12] The fact that the state now overlooks the existence of black markets is an acknowledgment of the market's power to allocate resources effectively even under dire circumstances.

The comparison of the two Koreas illustrates how a society that embraces markets tends to achieve higher standards of living and quality of life than a society that shuns them.[13] At the end of World War II, both Koreas were among the poorest countries in the world. They were identical on almost all margins. Seven decades later, South Korea is a prosperous country with a high quality of life. Through markets, South Koreans are able to have better lives. They have access to more and better resources for physical well-being (such as food, clothing, healthcare, sanitation, education, and so on) and thereby achieve higher levels of social and psychological well-being. In contrast, North Korea is one of the poorest and most oppressed countries in the world. Yet, even in North Korea where market activities are formally outlawed, it was the (black) market and not the state that provided the means for the poor to survive a severe famine and it is the (black) market that still allows North Koreans to improve their lives. Both North and South Koreans benefit from their market activities. That South Koreans have greater access to markets than North Koreans largely explains why South Koreans are better off than North Koreans.

---

[12] Adam Smith ([1776] 1981) expressed his confidence in the market's ability to help societies to weather shortages and famines. In fact, using corn production to illustrate his point, Smith (Ibid.: 526) professed that anyone who studies the European history of scarcities and famines would readily conclude that "a famine has never arisen from any other cause but the violence of government attempting, by improper means, to remedy the inconveniences of a dearth" and that "a dearth never has arisen from any combination among the inland dealers in corn." He believed that only by restraining the market from operating freely can a shortage be turned into a famine. According to Smith (Ibid.: 527),

> The unlimited, unrestrained freedom of the corn trade, as it is the only effectual preventative of the miseries of a famine, so it is the best palliative of the inconveniences of a dearth; for the inconveniences of a real scarcity [from war and other such events] cannot be remedied; they can only be palliated. No trade deserves more the full protection of the law, and no trade requires it so much; because no trade is so much exposed to popular odium.

Studies on famines in modern-day economies appear to support Smith's claim. For instance, Frost (2018) discussed how the root cause of the Great Famine (1959–1961) in China was the suppression of markets (thus disrupting the price mechanism and economic calculation) and how the famine may have been prevented had the government permitted markets to function freely.

[13] The relative difference in access to healthcare, nutrition, and other basic necessities has left a mark on the two Koreas. South Korean men are, on average, 3–8 cm (1.2–3.1 in) taller than their North Korean counterparts (Schwekendiek quoted in Knight 2012). More starkly, in South Korea, the life expectancy is 82.4 years, with an infant mortality rate of 3 deaths per 1000 live births and a maternal mortality rate of 11 per 100,000 live births; by contrast, life expectancy for North Koreans is 70.4 years, with infant mortality rate of 22.9 per 1000 live births and a maternal mortality rate of 82 per 100,000 live births (Central Intelligence Agency 2018).

Markets Are Positively Associated with the Things We Like

It is probably not controversial for us to claim that people want wealth, health, happiness, and social connection. Not exclusively and not always primarily, but wealth, health, happiness, and community are things that most of us like. These goods are obviously linked with one another. Wealth, health, and community can be sources of happiness. Or, conversely, the absence of wealth, health, and community can be sources of distress. Wealth makes it more likely that people will seek preventative and restorative healthcare, as well as recognize and deal with health issues. A general sense of happiness has been known to improve healthcare outcomes. Similarly, successful entrepreneurs often benefit from having a positive outlook (Luthans and Youssef 2004; Trevelyan 2008).

People living in market societies are wealthier, healthier, happier, and better connected than people living in nonmarket societies.[14] The tales of slaves in colonial Bahamas, pre- and post-communist Estonia, and the two Koreas are some of the cases that display how people can improve their lives through markets. Examining economic histories of other countries, such as Hong Kong, Singapore, and China, reveals a similar narrative: the adoption of markets improves peoples' lives. Markets do not prevent, but instead are absolutely compatible with and can contribute to, the successful pursuit of wealth, health, happiness, and community.

Wealthier, Healthier, and Happier

Recall, Adam Smith remarked that "little else" than "peace, easy taxes, and a tolerable administration of justice" is needed to lift a country from the "lowest barbarism" to "the highest degree of opulence" (quoted in Stewart [1795] 1829: 64). This institutional and policy environment leads to the emergence and advancement of a market sphere, or, in other words, an economic sphere where people cooperate with one another in the production and exchange of goods and services.

Markets are sources of wealth because they make the division of labor possible. And, as Smith ([1776] 1981) explained, the division of labor is limited by the size and scope of the market. "When the market is very small," Smith (Ibid.: 31) stated, "no person can have any encouragement to dedicate himself entirely to one employment." It is only when individuals can earn enough

---

[14] Leeson (2010) uses a similar approach as we do to advance a similar claim.

through specialization to support themselves that specialization will occur. It is only when a market is large enough so that an individual can find enough buyers for what they produce can they hope to earn enough through specialization to support themselves.

When labor is divided and workers can, thus, specialize in one or a few tasks, each worker is in a better situation than she otherwise would be. Consequently, society as a whole will be better off than it otherwise would be. The division of labor, Smith (Ibid.: 17–21) explained, leads to more wealth because worker productivity increases under the division of labor. This increase in productivity occurs for three reasons: (1) each worker only performs one or a few tasks and thereby improves her dexterity; (2) everyone tends to loiter between tasks and, so, having one or only a few different tasks reduces wasted time; and (3) having one or a few tasks allows people to find ways to innovate and streamline processes.

Importantly, as Smith noted, the division of labor emerges within a market system because people have a propensity to trade with others. And, with the expansion of markets and so the emergence and extension of the division of labor, there is the potential for increased material progress. "[W]ithout the disposition to truck, barter and exchange," and markets of sufficient size and scope to allow individuals to specialize and trade, Smith (Ibid.: 29) noted, "every man must have procured to himself every necessary and conveniency of life which he wanted."

Another mechanism through which markets can lead to human betterment is by extending the scope for entrepreneurship. As Schumpeter ([1911] 1983, 1950) argued, the entrepreneur is a source of innovation and the driving force of economic development. As such, the entrepreneur is more than just a risk bearer and does more than merely stay alert to unrealized profit opportunities. Instead, the Schumpeterian entrepreneur is an innovator—a creative force who initiates enterprise. Her success is never disconnected from what people desire. She is able to earn profits only by developing new combinations (or reconfiguring existing combinations) of resources and so delivering new and improved goods and services that people actually want. Thus, for Schumpeter ([1911] 1983: 65), economic development is, "defined by the carrying out of new combinations." Development refers to positive changes "in the sphere of industrial and commercial life" and involves,

> (1) The introduction of a new good – that is one with which consumers are not yet familiar – or of a new quality of a good. (2) The introduction of a new method of production, that is one not yet tested by experience in the branch of manufacture concerned, which need by no means be founded upon a discovery scientifically new, and can also exist in a new way of handling a commodity

commercially. (3) The opening of a new market, that is a market into which the particular branch of manufacture of the country in question has not previously entered, whether or not this market has existed before. (4) The conquest of a new source of supply of raw materials or half-manufactured goods, again irrespective of whether this source already exists or whether it has first to be created (Ibid.: 66).

Schumpeter was careful to point out that the "carrying out of new combinations" is not merely putting resources that had previously been idle to use. Instead, Schumpeterian development is "the different employment of the economic system's existing supplies of productive means" (Ibid.: 68). By carrying out new combinations, entrepreneurs set the process of economic development in motion.[15]

Market societies outperform nonmarket societies in numerous indicators of material well-being. For instance, on average, market societies have a GDP per capita of $42,545 (PPP, constant 2011 international $), while nonmarket societies have a GDP per capita of $10,984 (Fig. 4.1). Indeed, the relationship between economic freedom (interpreted here as the degree to which a country formally embraces markets) and income per capita is quite robust (Islam 1996; Hanke and Walters 1997; Leschke 2000). Scholars have also found that the level of economic freedom is positively associated with economic growth (Hanson 2000; Ali and Crain 2001; Carlsson and Lundström 2002; Doucouliagos and Ulubaşoğlu 2006) and that increases in economic freedom contribute to economic growth (Gwartney et al. 1999; Sturm and De Haan 2001). Additionally, it is well established that entrepreneurship is a driver of economic development and that there is additionally a positive relationship between economic freedom and entrepreneurship (Nyström 2008).[16]

Market societies also outperform nonmarket societies on other measures of wealth and well-being (Belasen and Hafer 2012, 2013). Market societies, for instance, have a higher average literacy rate (95.48% of people aged 15 and

---

[15] Schumpeter was not alone in his belief that entrepreneurship is essential for economic progress. For example, Murphy et al. (2006: 12) noted that per capita wealth in the West grew exponentially "[w]ith the advent of entrepreneurship." Nelson and Pack (1999) pointed to entrepreneurship (coupled with a favorable policy environment) as an essential ingredient to the rise of Asian Miracle countries in the late twentieth century. Based on 57 empirical studies on entrepreneurship, Van Praag and Versloot (2007) concluded that entrepreneurs serve an important, but specific, role in the economy by spurring innovation, creating more employment, and generating higher productivity growth relative to their counterparts for the economy. Furthermore, at least some outside the academy also seem to agree that entrepreneurs are important for economic growth. For instance, Sappin (2016) detailed the seven ways in which entrepreneurs drive economic development.

[16] Bjørnskov and Foss (2008) complicate this conclusion and found that some measures of economic freedom are not significantly correlated with entrepreneurship.

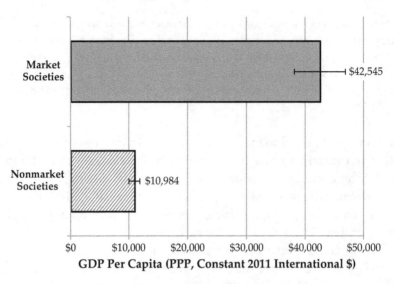

Fig. 4.1 Income per capita is higher in market societies. The error bars represent standard errors. (Data source: *World Bank* Database)

over) than those in nonmarket societies (86.02% of people aged 15 and over) (Fig. 4.2). Children in the market societies also spend more years in school and generally attend better schools. Using the 2012 Index of Economic Freedom (IEF), Roberts and Olson (2013) found that, on average, people in the most economically free countries obtain 15 years of schooling (i.e. some college education, if not a college degree, depending on the country's education system) over their lifetime. On the other hand, people in the least economically free countries only acquire 11 years of schooling (i.e. some high school education) over their lifetime. They also reported that students from more economically free countries tend to score higher than those from less economically free countries on the OECD's Programme for International Student Assessment, a test that evaluates education systems internationally independent of school curriculum. In other words, the quality of the education system is higher in countries with more economic freedom (whose institutions are more supportive of markets) than in countries with less economic freedom. Likewise, Nikolaev's (2014) study involving indicators of OECD's Better Life Index revealed positive correlations between economic freedom and years a country's population spent in formal education, educational attainment (defined as the proportion of a country's population holding at least an upper secondary degree), and student skills (defined as students' reading ability, math skills, and level of science).

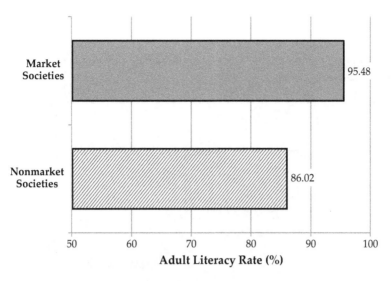

Fig. 4.2 Adult literacy rates are higher in market societies. (Data source: *World Bank Database*)

Overall infrastructure is also better in market societies than in nonmarket societies. Compared to those living in nonmarket societies, more people living in market societies have access to clean drinking water (98.92% vs. 85.03%) (Fig. 4.3). Railway networks are more extensive in market societies than in nonmarket societies (20,030 km vs. 9224 km) (Fig. 4.4). And, more people in market societies are digitally connected than in nonmarket societies (23.78 vs. 5.83 fixed broadband subscriptions per 100 people, and 38.66 vs. 13.31 fixed telephone subscriptions per 100 people) (Fig. 4.5).

Additionally, Roberts and Olson (2013) found a positive correlation between economic freedom and access to better sanitation. They also observed a positive relationship between economic freedom and access to wastewater disposal. While 79.1% of the population had access to wastewater disposal services in countries in the top quartile of 2010 IEF, 59.2% of the population had access to such services in countries in the bottom quartile of IEF. Nikolaev (2014) also observed a positive relationship between economic freedom and the proportion of houses or dwellings with basic facilities for personal hygiene among OECD countries. In addition, more people in market societies reported being satisfied with the quality of their local water (Ibid.).

People in market societies are generally healthier than their counterparts in nonmarket societies. Life expectancy, infant mortality, and maternal mortality are three indicators of health that can provide some insight into a society's ability to offer good healthcare to its citizens; longevity and low infant and

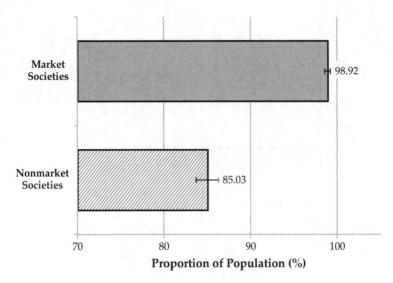

Fig. 4.3 More people in market societies have access to clean drinking water. The error bars represent standard errors. (Data source: *World Bank* Database)

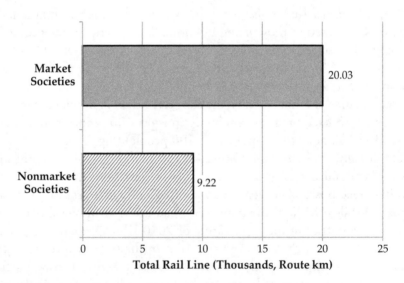

Fig. 4.4 Market societies have more extensive railway networks. (Data source: *World Bank* Database)

maternal mortality rates signal that a society has good healthcare facilities available for various stages of a person's life (Ovaska and Takashima 2006). On average, the life expectancy of those living in market societies was 79.11 years at birth. Compare that to 68.19 years in nonmarket societies (Fig. 4.6). Additionally, on average, 6.63 infants (per 1000 live births) and 22.85 mothers

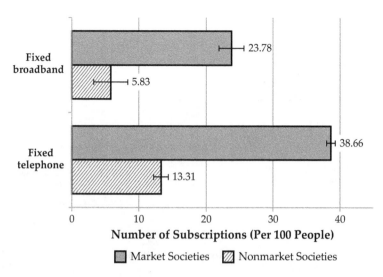

Fig. 4.5 Market societies are better connected digitally. The error bars represent standard errors. (Data source: *World Bank* Database)

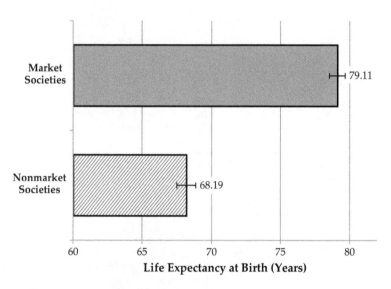

Fig. 4.6 Life expectancy is higher in market societies. The error bars represent standard errors. (Data source: *World Bank* Database)

(per 100,000 live births) die in market societies. By contrast, an average of 31.68 infants (per 1000 live births) and 312.52 mothers (per 100,000 live births) die in nonmarket societies (Figs. 4.7 and 4.8). Also, market societies spend an average of $3239 per person on health expenses annually and nonmarket societies spend an average of $657 per person per year (PPP, constant

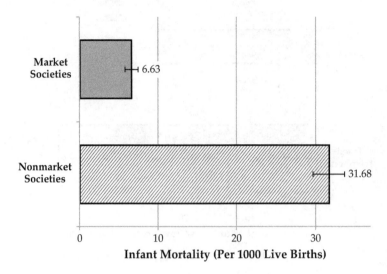

Fig. 4.7 Infant mortality is lower in market societies. The error bars represent standard errors. (Data source: *World Bank* Database)

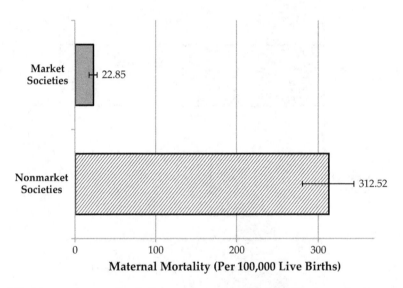

Fig. 4.8 Maternal mortality is lower in market societies. The error bars represent standard errors. (Data source: *World Health Organization* Database)

2011 international $) (Fig. 4.9). Furthermore, those in market societies consume more food per person on a daily basis than those in nonmarket societies (3154 kcal vs. 2706 kcal per capita per day) (Fig. 4.10).

Numerous studies support the conclusion that people in market societies are healthier. Schwekendiek (2009) examined the weight and height differences

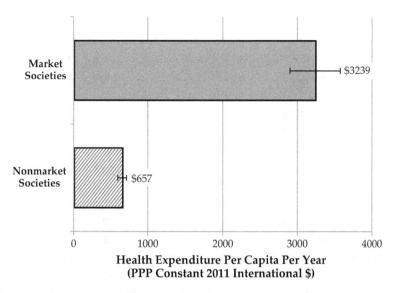

Fig. 4.9 Health expenditure per capita is higher in market societies. The error bars represent standard errors. (Data source: *World Bank* Database)

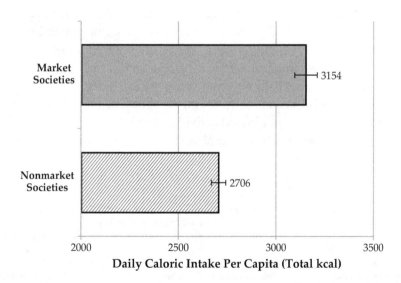

Fig. 4.10 Daily caloric intake per capita is higher in market societies. The error bars represent standard errors. (Data source: *Food and Agriculture Organization* Database)

of North and South Koreans. Using data from 2002, he discovered that pre-school children in North Korea were up to 13 cm shorter (approximately 5.1 in) and up to 7 kg (approximately 15.4 lb) lighter than their South Korean counterparts. North Korean women weighed up to 9 kg (close to 19.8 lb) less than South Korean women. Schwekendiek identified socioeconomic and political factors as the root causes of these discrepancies between North and South Koreans, which manifested into differences in per capita daily caloric intake and, ultimately, differences in height and weight.[17] Given that North and South Koreans were roughly the same height at the time of the separation of the peninsula, it is astonishing to see how large of a divergence occurred for the Korean people from differences in their political and economic systems.[18]

Esposto and Zaleski (1999) and Gwartney and Lawson (2004) reported a positive correlation between economic freedom and life expectancy. Stroup (2007) and Roberts and Olson (2013) found that increases in economic freedom improved life expectancy and lowered infant mortality rates. In fact, Stroup (2007) noticed that increases in economic freedom also corresponded with increases in the proportion of two-year-old children who received adequate vaccinations for diphtheria, pertussis, and tetanus. Naanwaab (2018) showed that an increase in economic freedom decreased maternal mortality. Examining 20 states in India, Razvi and Chakraborty (2016) also corroborated that improvements in economic freedom lowered infant mortality and maternal mortality. There are also a couple of studies that found that people residing in economically free societies may participate in physical activities more. For example, Hall, Humphreys, and Ruseski (2018) noted that people residing in more economically free U.S. states exercised more. Similarly, Ruseski and Maresova (2014) observed that participation in sports and physical activity rose with economic freedom. In addition, they discovered that participation in sports and physical activity appeared to increase with education and income, possibly further explaining why those living in richer market societies are healthier.[19]

---

[17] South Koreans, Schwekendiek (2009) reported, consumed a total of 3040 kcal per capita per day according to FAO 2001–2003 estimates, with daily consumptions of 89 kcal in proteins and 78 kcal in fat, while North Koreans consumed a total of 2160 kcal per capita daily, with daily consumptions of 63 kcal in proteins and 35 kcal in fats.

[18] It is believed that North Koreans were 1.1–1.4 cm (approximately half an inch) taller than South Koreans before the separation of the peninsula (Kimura 1993). If true, then the height and weight differences between the two Koreas would be even more striking. Furthermore, Kimura (1993) and Schwekendiek (2009) were not the only scholars who tied height discrepancies to institutions. For instance, Komlos and Kriwy (2003) discussed how adult East Germans were shorter than West Germans by 1 cm (about 0.4 in); the Berlin Wall physically separated East and West Germanys between 1961 and 1989.

[19] Ljungvall (2013) and Lawson et al. (2016) complicate this relationship. Ljungvall (2013) reported how economic freedom shares a positive (and statistically significant) relationship with the level and changes in average body mass index. Similarly, Lawson et al. (2016) showed that, although life expectancy increased with economic freedom, body mass index, and, thus, obesity increased with economic freedom too. As obesity is linked with numerous health issues, it is a challenge to reconcile their findings with the findings mentioned above.

People who live in market societies are more likely to be happy than people living in nonmarket societies.[20] The proportion of those who are highly satisfied with their lives is, on average, higher in market societies than in nonmarket societies (Fig. 4.11). Furthermore, on average, more people living in market societies believe they are closer to living the best possible life imaginable for themselves than those living in nonmarket societies (Fig. 4.12). There is a happiness gap between market societies and nonmarket societies. Gropper et al. (2011) found a positive relationship between economic freedom and national levels of happiness. Gehring (2013) empirically demonstrated that economic freedom has a positive effect on subjective well-being. Specifically, he argued, developing countries profited the most from economic freedom in terms of subjective well-being.

Additionally, countries that are more tolerant and have a positive attitude toward markets profited the most from economic freedom. Nikolaev (2014) empirically demonstrated that people who live in countries that embrace markets are more likely to find employment, have more job security, live in safe neighborhoods, and are less likely to work long hours. In other words, the drivers of subjective perceptions of well-being appear to improve as the degree of economic freedom increases.

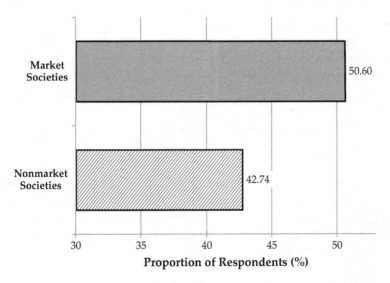

Fig. 4.11 More people in market societies are highly satisfied with life. (Data source: *World Values Survey* Database)

---

[20] Admittedly, the data and literature on happiness and subjective well-being that we cite here are not without issues. See Kahneman and Krueger (2006) for a discussion of the strengths and shortcomings of efforts to measure subjective well-being. See also Badhwar (2014) for a useful neo-Aristotelian account of well-being, where happiness is not reducible to subjective perceptions of well-being but consists in living an objectively worthwhile life.

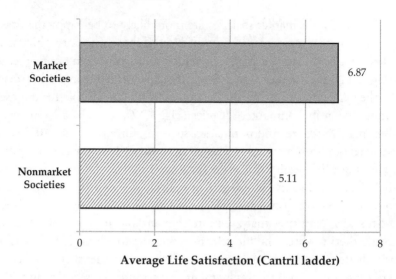

Fig. 4.12 Average life satisfaction is higher in market societies. The error bars represent standard errors. (Data source: *Gallup World Survey* Database published by *World Happiness Report 2017*)

Better Connected

People living in market societies appear to have stronger communities than people living in nonmarket societies. The market, it turns out, is a space that can buttress community. Rather than being a place antithetical to community, markets are social spaces where social bonds can and do develop (Storr 2008; Badhwar 2008).

Arguably, this social potential of markets is well understood. Smith ([1759] 1982: 223–224), for instance, explained that,

> the necessity or conveniency of mutual accommodation [in commercial societies] very frequently produces a friendship not unlike that which takes place among those who are born to live in the same family. Colleagues in office, partners in trade, call one another brothers; and frequently feel towards one another as if they really were so.

Similarly, Hayek (1976: 112) stated that the "interdependence of all men … which tends to make all mankind One World, not only is the effect of the market order but could not have been brought about by any other means." Likewise, Rothbard ([1962] 1993: 85) argued that, it is far more likely that feelings of friendship and communion are the effects of a regime of (contractual) social co-operation rather than the cause … in a world of voluntary social co-operation through mutually beneficial exchanges, where one man's gain is another man's gain, it is obvious that great scope is provided for the development of social sympathy and human friendships.

Seabright (2004) also discussed that under certain institutional arrangements (i.e. within the market) human beings are encouraged to treat strangers as honorary friends.

Our market relationships can develop into meaningful social relationships that can sometimes become deeper than our familial connections. Our market activities also bring us into fellowship with people across the globe and across ethnicities and nationalities that we might not otherwise encounter. The market, thus, makes it possible for diverse individuals to peacefully reconcile their plans and so creates favorable conditions for feelings of friendship.

A variety of social bonds can occur in markets or are strengthened because of markets. For instance,

- Coworkers often develop strong bonds because of their common experiences and circumstances (Zavella 1985; Bridge and Baxter 1992; Argyle and Henderson 1985; Hodson 1997).
- Office romance, that has nothing to do with harassment, is a common phenomenon in the contemporary workplace (Pierce et al. 1996; Williams et al. 1999).
- Principal-client, seller-buyer relationships can develop into deep friendships (Price and Arnould 1999; Butcher et al. 2002; Haytko 2004).
- Master-apprentice and mentor-protégé relationships can sometimes grow into social friendships and even father-son, mother-daughter type relationships (Kram 1983; Gardiner 1998).
- Family businesses can serve the income, fulfillment, and identity needs of family members (Kepner 1991).
- Competitors can even develop relationships with each other (Chamlee-Wright 1997; Ingram and Roberts 2000).
- Shopping and consuming can be social activities that provide an opportunity for friends to deepen their bonds (Feinberg et al. 1989).
- Geographically dispersed communities and friendships are made possible by the communication and transportation services available because of the market (Parks and Floyd 1996).

That these types of relationships are not only possible but are facilitated by the market is all the more important given the growing number of hours that individuals spend both working and shopping outside the home.

Robert Putnam's (2000) *Bowling Alone* is perhaps the most important critique of the social transformation that has accompanied the economic development in the United States in the latter half of the twentieth century. According to Putnam (Ibid.), civic engagement and social capital in the United States are declining.[21] Americans, he wrote, are less active politically, are less likely to join a club, spend less time in church, have fewer friends and acquaintances, and are more isolated from their families than they were in the past. Rather than joining bowling leagues, Putnam argued emblematically, Americans are now even bowling alone.

While acknowledging that workplace and other market-buttressed ties like those mentioned above are possible, Putnam (Ibid.) did not believe that the growth of social bonds formed in markets make up for the loss of community that has occurred because of the growth of markets, the changes in the nature of work, or the technological developments they spawned. Friendships that form around the water-cooler or in the office mailroom, Putnam noted, are in many ways substitutes for friendships that develop elsewhere. "Many people form rewarding friendships at work, feel a sense of community among co-workers, and enjoy norms of mutual help and reciprocity on the job" (Ibid.: 87). But, he insisted, there is "*no evidence whatever* that socializing in the workplace, however common, has actually *increased* over the last several decades" (Ibid.). Putnam (Ibid.) also worried that social connections formed in the workplace "tend to be casual and enjoyable, but not intimate and deeply supportive." Workplace ties, Putnam maintained, are inferior to connections formed in other settings even when they develop beyond merely instrumental relationships. Workplace ties are simply not as important to most Americans as connections to their neighbors and family members.

Admittedly, Putnam's arguments are not without merit. There are, however, several qualifications that should be made. First, the absence of evidence, as the saying goes, is not the evidence of absence. That there is no evidence that workplace connections are increasing as people spend more time at work does not mean that the phenomenon is not occurring. Similarly, that there is no

---

[21] Social capital is a type of capital, much like physical and human capital, that can be used to produce goods and services. It refers to a stock of social relations that are grounded in norms and networks of trust and reciprocity and that facilitate cooperation and collective action between people. Social capital, subsequently, has a direct impact on the economic progress and overall well-being of a country.

evidence that workplace connections are as deep as nonworkplace connections does not mean that these relationships lack meaning. Second, that most Americans are still able to form their most meaningful connections outside the workplace, even as time spent at work is increasing, is evidence of the resilience of nonmarket relationships and is not proof that market ties are inferior substitutes. Third, Putnam himself only attributed 10% of the decline in social connectedness and civic engagement that he observed in the United States to the transformations in the nature of work and the workplace (Ibid.: 283). As he wrote, "neither time pressures nor financial distress nor the movement of women into the paid labor force is *the* primary cause of civic disengagement over the last two decades" (Ibid.: 203). Indeed, Putnam blamed much of the decline in the involvement of Americans in community activities to technological developments, especially television.[22]

Arguably, if it is true that Americans prefer any entertainment and leisure activity to civic engagement and social connection, then this may speak to the undesirability of greater social engagement than what currently exists.[23] If Americans are substituting out of undesirable social connections for more preferable forms of entertainment and leisure, then the loss of community that Putnam identified might actually be for the better. The market also makes it possible for individuals to replace undesirable social connections with preferable forms of sociality. The market and the technological developments that it spurs allow individuals to be more socially selective by making it easier for them to find and communicate with the groups with which they want to be associated. Social networking applications and websites allow individuals to reconnect with old friends with whom they might have lost touch, to deepen their relationships with existing friends, and to form new connections with people, perhaps quite far flung, who share similar attitudes and interests (Rheingold 1993). It is simply not true that these new communities are not "real" communities. Even Putnam acknowledged the potential of social networking sites to promote community (Putnam et al. 2003). As Putnam et al. (Ibid.: 240) stated,

---

[22] According to Putnam (2000: 235–237), changes in the "dependence upon television for entertainment" are closely correlated with the decline in civic engagement because "[t]elevision competes for scarce time … [t]elevision has psychological effects that inhibit social participation … [and s]pecific programmatic content on television undermines civic motivations."

[23] We should note, however, that it is not true that the market or its fruits are standing in the way of community and so making it impossible for Americans to form social bonds or to engage in civic activities. Indeed, the bowling leagues that Putnam celebrates depend on markets for bowling alleys, bowling bowls, bowling shirts, and more.

> [w]ith … [some] qualifications … [these sites can have] elements of community to a surprising degree and … [their] community nature has a great deal of elements that we see in other forms of community: localness, member participation in defining the norms of the group, aims and purposes beyond that of simply being together.

Additionally, blogs and online message boards devoted to particular topics or that express particular perspectives have arguably become a new public sphere, promoting the discussion of topics in a forum where all who have access to the Internet can potentially enter. The communication and transportation services available because of markets (e.g. telephones, email, automobiles, and airplanes) are likewise important tools for building communities and maintaining desirable relationships across sometimes great distances. Relationships that would have had to rely on infrequent contact in the past (i.e. through traditional mail and infrequent visits) now benefit from the possibility of everyday contact.

Rather than hampering the expression of social feelings, markets seem to make it easier for individuals to act on their social feelings and allow for a greater diversity of expression. If we see a decline in community, it is not because markets have made it more difficult for us to build and maintain the communities that we care about. In fact, the reverse is true. We have more tools at our disposal for building and maintaining the relationships that we want to build and maintain. If we see a decline in community, then it is because we are now in a better position to work at building the communities that we want to develop and to opt out of the kinds of community connections that we find undesirable (Florida 2002: 269).

The growth of markets, however, has not led to a decline in community. First, as suggested above, there is evidence to suggest that individuals can form meaningful social bonds in the market place. Second, as Costa and Kahn (2003) contended, Putnam's claims regarding the decline of social capital are somewhat misleading.[24] According to Costa and Kahn, it is not so clear that social capital has declined at all or all that much. "By some measures social capital has declined," they (Ibid.: 26) stated, "and by others it has not." They reported that there are only small declines in the portion of Americans who volunteer or who have organizational memberships (Ibid.: 29). Although there does appear to be a large decline in the time that individuals spend visit-

---

[24] There are numerous studies that also question whether social capital has declined as Putnam described (e.g. Ladd 1996, 1999; Paxton 1999; Rotolo 1999; Clark 2015). See Fischer (2005) for more references to empirical works that oppose Putnam's declining social capital argument.

ing friends and relatives, Americans nonetheless report spending frequent evenings with friends and relatives (Ibid.: 37). Additionally, Costa and Kahn discussed that the movement of women into the workforce explains much of the decline in social capital that we do observe.

Evidence indicates that people living in market societies have more social capital than those living in nonmarket societies.[25] A larger proportion of the population in market societies are active members of organizations and associations compared to nonmarket societies; approximately the same proportion of people in market and nonmarket societies self-report being an active member of a religious organization, but more people in market societies than in nonmarket societies self-report being an active member of a sports or recreational organization (Fig. 4.13).

The Legatum Institute annually releases the Prosperity Index, which investigates prosperity as a combination of wealth and well-being. One of its indicators evaluates social cohesion and engagement, community and family networks, social norms, political participation, and institutional trust. In other words, the index includes an (imperfect, but nonetheless valuable) estimate of the strength of social capital within a society that enables it to

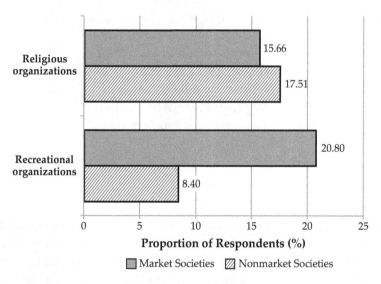

Fig. 4.13 More people in market societies are active members in various organizations. (Data source: *World Values Survey* Database)

---

[25] As we discuss in Chap. 5, evidence from some economic experiments validates this point that subjects from market societies tend to show more trust and other prosocial sentiments than those from nonmarket societies (Henrich et al. 2004; Barr et al. 2009; Ensminger and Cook 2014).

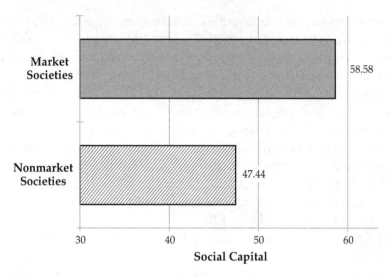

Fig. 4.14 Market societies have stronger social capital. (Data source: Legatum Institute's Prosperity Index)

function effectively. Using data from this index, Fig. 4.14 shows that people living in market societies have significantly stronger social capital (i.e. stronger personal relationships, social network support, and more civic engagement) compared to those living in nonmarket societies.

Concerns about community's decline as a result of the expansion of the market and its accompanying technological innovations appear to be exaggerated. Regarding the possibility that markets can act as a significant barrier to the maintenance and development of social bonds, the evidence suggests that the market is a space that supports community and where social bonds can and do form.

The Things We Want

The evidence presented here cannot definitively offer nor confirm a causal direction between markets and the things that we like. But, it is clear that markets are positively correlated with the things that people want. Evidently, people who reside in market societies—those countries with relatively unhindered markets—are wealthier, healthier, live longer, are better educated, and have access to better sanitation, more infrastructure, and more food. People in market societies are also better connected than individuals in nonmarket societies.

Markets Favor the Poor and They Make the Rich and Powerful Uncomfortable

Markets have an extraordinary ability to enrich the lives of those they touch. People in societies that embrace markets are wealthier, healthier, happier, and better connected.

One set of worries might be that markets only deliver the goods to individuals who are already rich, that the poor suffer in (and because of) markets, and that markets are spaces where the rich get richer and the poor get poorer.[26] Growing economic inequality and social immobility in market societies are offered as proof that markets, left unhindered, will benefit the rich (only) and (mostly) hurt the poor. The reverse, however, appears to be true.

Better to Be Poor in a Market Society

There are numerous accounts of incidences where markets favored the poor and made the rich and powerful uncomfortable. Recall, it was the farmers in rural North Korea who acquired the basic necessities they needed through black markets when the government, which favored the elites, failed them. Some of the disadvantaged in North Korea even accumulated enough wealth to purchase private education and other luxuries historically restricted to the elites in Pyongyang. Most remarkably, black markets were catalysts for social change and raised women's status in the oppressive North Korean society. Similarly, when enslaved Africans in the Bahamas were given access to markets as producers and purchasers and not as possessions, they were able to dramatically improve their standards of living. Remember that some enslaved Africans in the Bahamas were in fact able to earn enough through their market activities that they were able to buy their freedom.

The poor in market societies have vastly superior standards of living than the poor in nonmarket societies.[27] For example, the poorest 10% of the population in market societies earn more than the poorest 10% in nonmarket societies and

---

[26] It is, admittedly, difficult to figure out how to measure poverty and to identify which particular people are poor. For example, Atkinson (1987) specified three issues that arise when measuring and assessing the extent of poverty in a society: where to draw the poverty line; what poverty measure(s) to utilize; and the potential confound between poverty and economic inequality. Certainly, how many people and who are affected will depend on the variable that is chosen and the threshold value that is set.

[27] Still, there is the worry that the poor might be forced to enter into exchanges that they would prefer to avoid because of the power disparities that exist between them and the rich. Munger (2011) pondered a paradox in our moral and ethical understanding of exchange: individual exchanges and their immediate (and potentially and likely unequal) profits that made the involved parties better off were morally good, yet we condemn an aggregated consequence of these exchanges, namely, the unequal distributions of wealth. Munger (Ibid.: 194) rebutted this view, claiming that,

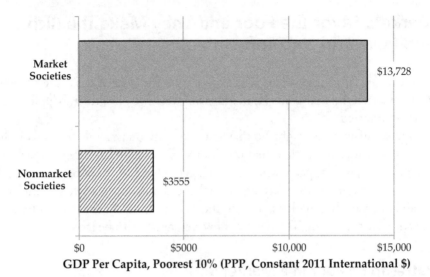

Fig. 4.15 The poorest 10% in market societies earn more than the poorest 10% in nonmarket societies. (Data source: Authors' calculations using data from the *World Bank* Database)

can even earn more than the richest 10% of the population in some nonmarket societies annually (Fig. 4.15). Consider the Netherlands (a market society) and India (a nonmarket society). In 2011, the richest 10% of Indian society earned $13,815 per capita (PPP, constant 2011 international $), but the poorest 10% of Dutch society earned $16,584 per capita. Also think about the poorest 10% in Austria (a market society) who earned $12,891 per capita in 2011. These Austrians earned more than the richest 10% of various nonmarket societies in the same year—Benin ($6282), Chad ($6039), Kyrgyz Republic ($6863), Moldova ($10,239), Niger ($2116), Senegal ($6690), Sierra Leone ($3352), Tanzania ($6581), Togo ($4257), and Zimbabwe ($5635).

While we can never know for sure exactly which of the available opportunities, facilities, and/or benefits each individual can access and take advantage of in their society, we cannot deny that the poor in market societies have access to a much greater array of opportunities, facilities, and benefits (e.g. access to clean water, basic plumbing in homes, and the quality of healthcare and schools) than most people in nonmarket societies.[28]

All objections to the morality and justice of the uses of voluntary market exchange are mistaken, because they are misdirected. Euvoluntary exchanges [i.e. exchanges that are both morally good and truly voluntary] are always justified, and the consequent distributions of wealth are always just. But even exchanges that are not euvoluntary are beneficial, and they benefit most of all the welfare of those who are least well off. Euvoluntary or not, exchange is just, and restrictions on exchange harm the poor and the weak.

[28] OECD's Better Life Index (2018a) and The Economist (2013) reaffirm our point here.

Inequality Might Not Be the Problem That We Think It Is

Thomas Piketty (2014: 8), for instance, feared that absent intervention, capitalist societies could end up in an "endless inegalitarian spiral." Piketty (Ibid.) showed that income and wealth inequality increased, decreased, and then increased again between the late nineteenth century and the first decade of the twenty-first century in both the United States and Europe. But, as Piketty (Ibid.: 324) noted, while the trends were the same for the United States and Europe, wealth and income inequality are generally lower in Europe than they are in the United States, and the dramatic rise of income inequality in the United States over recent years has not occurred in Europe. In 1910, the share of total income earned by the top income decile was just above 45% in Europe and just above 40% in the United States (Ibid.: 323–324). But, by 2010, the share of total income earned by the top income decile was below 30% in Europe and above 45% in the United States. In both regions, the share earned by the top decile dipped considerably in the intervening years (Ibid.). Additionally, in 1910, the share of total wealth controlled by the top wealth decile was around 90% in Europe and around 80% in the United States (Ibid.: 349). By 2010, the share of total wealth controlled by the top wealth decile was above 60% in Europe and about 70% in the United States (Ibid.: 349). However, the share of total wealth controlled by the top wealth decile had been even lower in the United States and Europe in the decades preceding 2010.

Piketty (2015a) admitted that a number of factors can explain these movements in income and wealth inequality and that there are likely forces in both the United States and Europe that push toward equality and away from equality (e.g. families amassing or squandering their fortunes). However, Piketty (Ibid.: 72) attributed the recent explosion of income inequality in the United States to inequalities in labor income that are driven by the supply and demand for skills as well as increases in the returns to higher education.

Additionally, Piketty (Ibid.: 74) identified the size of the gap between the rate of return on capital (r) and the economic growth rate (g) as "one of the important forces that can account for the historical magnitude and variations in wealth inequality." Piketty (Ibid.: 73) acknowledged that the inequality $r > g$ is not by itself a problem; in fact, it is a standard property of most economic models and is likely to be standard feature of most market systems. But, he reasoned, the greater the gap between r and g, the more likely that wealth inequality will be higher and more persistent. Where $r > g$, wealth inequality is likely to be growing. According to Piketty, the gap between r and g at least partially explained why wealth inequality was so extreme around the globe before World War I and partially explains the most recent uptick in wealth inequality.

Piketty (2015b: 4) also asserted that the gap between r and g was artificially low during the periods when wealth inequality was declining (e.g. before the 1980s in the United States) and believed that "several forces might push toward a higher $r–g$ gap (particularly the slowdown of population growth, and rising global competition to attract capital)." Moreover, he argued that income inequality is a particularly worrisome problem when the gap between r and g is large (as might have been the case in the United States in the first decade of the twenty-first century) because in that scenario greater income inequality will lead to greater wealth inequality. Whether wealth inequality will grow or shrink will, thus, depend in part on what happens to r and g; if the gap is widening as Piketty believed, then the inegalitarian spiral he cautions against will occur.

Piketty's analysis and conclusions, however, have been roundly criticized. Mankiw (2015), for instance, clarified that the gap between r and g would have to be substantially large for an unabetted inegalitarian spiral to occur. Besides, he said, three (rather common) forces will limit wealth inequality: (1) the wealthy often have multiple heirs who must share any inherited wealth; (2) the wealthy often consume some of their wealth; and (3) governments tax bequests and capital income. Similarly, Weil (2015) criticized Piketty for focusing almost exclusively on physical capital and for ignoring human capital. According to Weil (Ibid.: 36), there is far less inequality in the distribution of human capital than there is in the distribution of physical capital and "if market wealth is only a part of aggregate wealth, then aggregate wealth is much less unequal than [Piketty] has portrayed it as being." Likewise, McCloskey (2014) chided Piketty for worrying exclusively about relative income and wealth, without any focus on the condition of the poor. "Piketty's vision of a 'Ricardian Apocalypse,' as he calls it," McCloskey (Ibid.: 82) explained,

> leaves room for the rest of us to do very well indeed, most non-apocalyptically, as in fact since 1800 we have. What is worrying Piketty is that the rich might possibly get richer, even though the poor get richer too. His worry, in other words, is purely about difference, about the Gini coefficient, about a vague feeling of envy raised to a theoretical and ethical proposition.[29]

---

[29] McCloskey also pointed out several errors in Piketty's analysis and directly challenged his ethical presuppositions. His analysis, she (2014: 82) claimed,

> is conclusive, so long as the factual assumptions are near-enough true: namely, only rich people have capital; human capital does not exist; the rich reinvest their returns—they never lose it to sloth or someone else's creative destruction; inheritance is the main mechanism, not creativity raising g for the rest of us just when it results in r shared by us all; and we care ethically only about the Gini coefficient, not the condition of the working class.

The central question for us here, however, is not whether or not Piketty's analysis of past inequality is accurate or if his prediction of future inequality is correct, but whether or not his underlying claim that extreme income and wealth inequality is a natural and so inevitable feature of markets is well founded. Even his own analysis did not settle this point because markets exist in a number of the places where he affirmed that extreme income and wealth inequalities do not. If extreme inequalities are in fact natural and inevitable feature of markets as he insisted, then we should expect to see greater inequalities in market societies than in nonmarket societies.

Consider the Gini coefficients of 21 countries from 1980 to 2015. A Gini coefficient is a measure of the income or wealth distribution of a nation's residents; a higher Gini coefficient value denotes a higher degree of inequality. With the exception of the Latin American countries, economic inequality generally appears to have increased during this time. The United Kingdom had a coefficient value of 26.11 in 1961 and 33.99 in 2014. For the United States, the coefficient increased from 38.8 in 1961 to 45.6 in 2014. Likewise, Sweden also experienced increased economic inequality with a coefficient of 22.1 in 1980 and 33 in 2013 (Atkinson et al. 2017). OECD (2015: 15) observed this trend across its member countries:

> In most countries, the gap between rich and poor is at its highest level since 30 years. Today, in OECD countries, the richest 10% of the population earn 9.6 times the income of the poorest 10%. In the 1980s, this ratio stood at 7:1 rising to 8:1 in the 1990s and 9:1 in the 2000s. In several emerging economies, particularly in Latin America, income inequality has narrowed, but income gaps remain generally higher than in OECD countries. During the [Great Recession in the late 2000s], income inequality continued to increase, mainly due to the fall in employment; redistribution through taxes and transfer partly offset inequality. However, at the lower end of the income distribution, real household incomes fell substantially in countries hit hardest by the [Great Recession].

A study by OECD (2015) on inequality discovered that the benefits from economic growth tended to be concentrated amongst the rich and did not reach as much as 40% of the population at the lower end of the income distribution in the recent decades. For example, the average pre-tax income of the richest 1% in the United States rose at the rate of 1% per year between 1970s and the Great Recession in the late 2000s. In comparison, the remaining 99% saw their incomes grow by 0.6% in the same time period. In addition, while the overall real household income increased between 1985 and 2010 in OECD countries, the richest 10% watched their real household incomes rise by more than 50% while the poorest 10% watched their real household incomes rise by about 15% in the same time period (Ibid.: 108).

Growing inequality is not just a problem for the poor; it is potentially a problem for the society writ large. A widening gap between the poor and the rich can harm the overall prosperity of a country. Societies with high levels of economic inequality can hamper talented individuals from impoverished families in their efforts to attain an education and the poor could disproportionately miss more economic opportunities due to inequality. This, in turn, may motivate them to redirect their efforts into undesirable social activities, such as crime, thereby eroding social cohesion. Widening inequality could also generate pressure for the government to implement redistributive policies, which could create subsequent distortions within the economy.

Contrary to popular belief, however, markets do not seem to exaggerate economic inequality. In fact, there are reasons to believe that the levels of economic inequality that today's market societies suffer are not substantially worse than they were in those of countries and empires prior to industrialization. Milanovic et al. (2007) compared income inequality in modern societies to income inequality in those same societies prior to the beginning of the Industrial Revolution and other nonindustrialized societies up to the early twentieth century. They concluded that the underlying distribution of income inequality of developing countries today and that of countries in pre-industrial times are comparable; "both the dispersion and the mean of inequality statistics across countries, at pre-industrial times and today, are similar" (Ibid.: 268).[30] Or, in other words, the economic inequality we observe today may have pre-dated the Industrial Revolution. Furthermore, that market societies suffer from less inequality than nonmarket societies echoes Adam Smith's ([1776] 1981: 24) observations of eighteenth-century Europe; "it may be true, perhaps, that the accommodation of an European prince does not always so much exceed that of an industrious and frugal peasant, as the accommodation of the latter exceeds that of many an African king, the absolute master of the lives and liberties of ten thousand naked savages."

On average, the Gini coefficient of market societies was 31.08 while that of nonmarket societies was 38.62 in 2011 (Fig. 4.16). Again, a higher Gini coefficient value denotes a higher degree of inequality.

---

[30] Economic inequality in the United Kingdom, for which information on income distribution from as far back as the Middle Ages is available, also shows an overall decline in economic inequality as the country modernized (Roser and Ortiz-Ospina 2017).

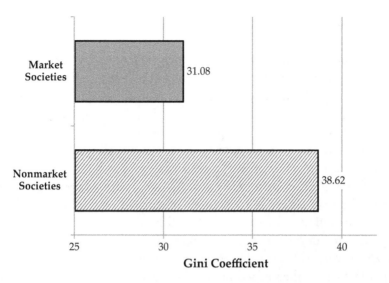

Fig. 4.16 Market societies have less economic inequality. (Data source: *World Bank* Database)

Multiple studies also suggest that markets do not exacerbate economic inequality. That said, the literature on economic freedom and inequality is somewhat ambiguous. Carter (2007) asserted that inequality is a nonlinear function of economic freedom, where the relationship is negative at low levels of economic freedom and where the relationship is positive at high levels of economic freedom. Scully (2002) discussed how economic freedom and inequality have a complicated relationship, detailing how economic freedom exerts a negative and direct effect on economic inequality but a positive (indirect) effect on inequality through growth. Empirical analyses by Clark and Lawson (2008) and Apergis and Cooray (2017) revealed a negative relationship between economic freedom and inequality. Results from several other studies examined the relationship between state-level economic freedom and inequality in the United States and found that they shared a negative relationship (e.g. Ashby and Sobel 2008; Apergis et al. 2014; Bennett and Vedder 2013; Webster 2013; Wiseman 2017).[31]

---

[31] Several studies complicate these results. Bergh and Nilsson (2010) empirically showed that a positive relationship between country-level economic freedom and inequality exists, as did Bennett (2016) for the relationship between state-level economic freedom and inequality in the United States. However, Sturm and De Haan (2015) found no effect of economic freedom on inequality. Bennett and Nikolaev (2017) attributed the inconsistent and ambiguous results in this literature to the use of different econometric models and measures of inequality.

Market Societies Are Mobile Societies

Social mobility refers to the extent to which individuals or groups can move within or between social strata in a society and reflects equality of opportunities across groups. Whether a society is more or less socially mobile depends on the strength of economic classes across generations. Specifically, an individual's level of income, educational achievement, and occupation will be strongly tied to those of her parents in relatively immobile societies. Low mobility in a society is a concern, as (1) such a society is unlikely to utilize its labor and physical force optimally and (2) inequality of opportunities may diminish the motivation and efforts of its citizens at the lower end of the income distribution, which ultimately affects the overall productivity, efficiency, and growth potential of an economy (OECD 2010).

In *The Wealth of Nations*, Smith pointed to what appeared to be a higher turnover rate within the socioeconomic elite class in more commercial societies. Smith ([1776] 1981: 421–422) remarked that,

> very old families, such as have possessed some considerable estate from father to son for many successive generations, are very rare in commercial countries. In countries which have little commerce, on the contrary, … they are very common. … In countries where a rich man can spend his revenue in no other way than by maintaining so many people as it can maintain, he is not apt to run out, and his benevolence it seems is seldom so violent as to attempt to maintain more than he can afford. But where he can spend the greatest revenue upon his own person, he frequently has no bounds to his expence, because he frequently has no bounds to his vanity, or to his affection for his own person. In commercial countries, therefore, riches, … very seldom remain long in the same family.

Corak (2013) calculated intergenerational mobility by approximating the relationship between the earnings of men and those of their fathers. The father-son earnings elasticity estimates the extent to which men's earnings are impacted by their fathers' earnings. A highly elastic value indicates a strong relationship between men and their fathers' earnings, thereby implying low mobility within the country. A low elasticity value, on the other hand, denotes high mobility. In both the United States and United Kingdom, social mobility is low with respective values of 0.47 and 0.5; about half of the advantages from the fathers' earnings are enjoyed by their sons. These elasticities imply that it would take an average of six generations for a family's economic advantage to disappear in the United States and United Kingdom. On the other hand, most of Scandinavian countries (Denmark, Norway, and Finland) and Canada have high mobility measures (with values of 0.15, 0.17, 0.18, and

0.19, respectively), with less than 20% of the fathers' income advantages being passed onto their sons. We could interpret Corak's (2013) estimates to mean that Americans and Brits tend to inherit their socioeconomic statuses from their fathers while Scandinavians and Canadians tend to obtain them largely through their own efforts.[32]

Despite the large variation in father-son earnings elasticity among market societies, market societies collectively outperform nonmarket societies in terms of social mobility. On average, about 33% of fathers' income advantages are passed onto their sons in market societies while over half of fathers' income advantages are passed onto their sons in nonmarket societies (Fig. 4.17).

Additionally, the majority of today's affluent class in the United States seems to be *nouveau riche*. U.S. Trust (2016) is an annually conducted comprehensive study that looks at the attitudes, behaviors, goals, and needs of high-net- and ultra-high-net-worth adults in the United States. According to their study, only one in ten of these adults is wealthy through an inheritance. Nearly three quarters of the survey respondents grew up in a middle class or poorer family, with approximately one in five adults in the study having grown up poor. The

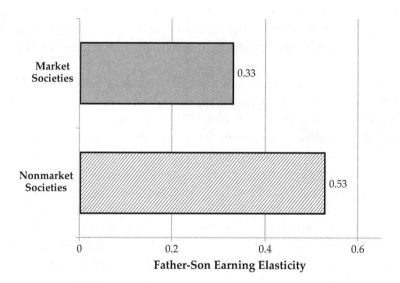

Fig. 4.17 Market societies have more social mobility. (Data source: Corak 2013)

---

[32] This statement should not be read as meaning no American or British man has ever worked for his socioeconomic status or that no Scandinavian or Canadian man has ever inherited his socioeconomic status. There are, of course, "self-made" American and British innovators and there are Scandinavian and Canadian heirs. We merely intend to illustrate what the different values of father-son earnings elasticities mean with this statement.

Millennial generation (18–35 years old) in the study was most likely to have grown up in wealthy families than older generations, but 55% of the Millennial respondents still grew up in the middle class or lower. Over half of the respondents (52%) reported amassing their wealth through earned income and a third of the respondents through investments. Most of the business owners founded their own companies (77%) and only 3% inherited or were transferred ownership of their businesses.

While everyday discourse treats millionaires as a stable class of individuals, both U.S. Trust (2016) and other studies suggest that the millionaire status (defined as tax returns with adjusted gross incomes of $1 million and higher) can be ephemeral. There is a high turnover rate in the millionaire status, which is confirmed by the substantial fluctuations in the number of millionaire tax returns year to year (Hodge 2012, 2014). In fact, the number of millionaires doubled from 2001 to 2007 (193,229 millionaires in 2001 and 392,220 millionaires in 2007), but this number dwindled by about a quarter by 2011 (299,269 millionaires in 2011) (Hodge 2014). Many individuals temporarily gain millionaire status due to a one-time event (such as a sale of a business or stocks). In fact, a study by the Williams Group wealth consultancy suggests that 70% of rich families lose their wealth by the second generation and 90% by the third generation (Taylor 2015). The rich, simply, cannot be confident that they will be able to maintain their wealth in market societies.

A similar story emerges in the top tier of firms based in the United States; even highly successful companies have difficulty maintaining their status in the market. The *Fortune 500* (Fortune 2017), first published in 1955, is an annually published list that ranks the 500 of the largest companies in the United States by total revenue within a fiscal year. While some companies remain on the list year after year, new companies appear and others disappear each year. For example, United States Rubber Company (also known as Uniroyal), a manufacturer of tires and other rubber-related products, ranked 32nd in the Fortune 500 list in 1955 and dropped from the top 500 in 1986 when it underwent a leveraged buyout and was later broken up and sold. Amstar Corporation, a manufacturer and distributor of nutritive sweeteners, ranked 96th in 1955 and dropped from the list when Atlas Copco Group acquired it in 1995. (Atlas Copco Group, a Swedish group, announced in January 2017 its plans to split into two corporations.) Amazon, an American Internet-based retailer, was established in 1994 and was ranked 18th on the Fortune 500 list in 2016 with a revenue of approximately $136 billion. Paypal Holdings Inc., a company founded in 1998 that offers an online payment system as an alternative to checks and cash, made its debut on the Fortune 500 at rank 307 in 2016 with total revenue of $9.25 billion. Others dropped from the list all together and then reemerged years later.

Stangler and Arbesman (2012) observed that the average number of companies that turnover on the Fortune 500 list has increased since the 1980s. For example, it took approximately 25 years for half of the initial cohort of 500 companies from 1955 to fall off the list and only took about 12 years for half the firms to fall off the list from the cohort of firms from 1995. While some of the turnover is certainly due to changes in productivity and innovations,[33] it largely "reflects a kaleidoscopic process of sectoral change and greater efficiencies at the level of individual firms, as well as some less sanguine economic developments" (Ibid.: 2).[34] In fact, only 12% of the top 500 firms in 1955 remained on the list in 2016 (Perry 2016). Or, in other words, nearly nine out of ten Fortune 500 companies in 1955 have merged or are no longer on the list today. Fligstein (1990: 335) reconstructed the decennial turnover of the top 100 American companies over a 60-year period and found that, on average, 21.5 companies leave the list every decade (and thus an average of 21.5 new ones enter the list). Of course, these turnover rates can be misleading, since they do not take mergers, acquisitions, and the like into account. Regardless, this serves to convey how firms (and individuals for that matter) cannot remain at complete ease regarding their financial status in market societies.

Due to issues of data availability, it is perhaps unsurprising that the empirical literature on social mobility and economic freedom is rather sparse. However, available evidence is suggestive of a positive relationship between economic freedom and social mobility. For instance, using a pool of 20 countries, Yaish and Andersen (2012) analyzed the occupational status of survey respondents and their fathers across 20 countries and found that cross-country variation in the respondents and their fathers' correlated positively with GDP per capita. Since, as we saw earlier, market societies tend to be the more affluent societies, we may (cautiously) extrapolate that market societies tend to be more socially mobile.[35]

---

[33] Companies such as Paypal Holdings Inc., Amazon, and Apple Inc. could not have existed in 1955 prior to the invention of the Internet in 1983 and the technological improvements to the computer.

[34] By less sanguine economic developments, they mean changes in antitrust policies and deregulations of certain industries that lead to a high volume of hostile takeovers, divestitures, and leveraged buyouts in the late 1990s.

[35] Goldthorpe and Erikson (1992: 388) challenged the view of systematic differences in social mobility across countries and maintained that cross-country variation in social mobility largely reflects "effects specific to particular societies at particular times."

As Milton and Rose Friedman (1980: 148–149) argued,

> so long as [economic] freedom is maintained, it prevents those positions of
> privilege from becoming institutionalized. Freedom means diversity, but also
> mobility. It preserves the opportunity for today's disadvantaged to become
> tomorrow's privileged and, in the process, enables almost everyone, from top to
> bottom, to enjoy a fuller and richer life.

Current relative social immobility often arises from nonmarket barriers to
social mobility not from the existence of markets. For example, minimum
wage laws and other labor market regulations raise the costs of hiring and fir-
ing employees, thereby making it more difficult for new workers (and members of lower socioeconomic classes) to find employment (e.g. Lazear 1990;
Heckman and Pagés-Serra 2000; Botero et al. 2004; Neumark and Wascher
2004). Stringent business regulations make it difficult for people to start businesses (e.g. Klapper et al. 2006; Van Stel et al. 2007; The World Bank 2019).
In short, markets do not prevent social mobility; rather, nonmarket factors are
more likely to stand in the way of social mobility.

Why Markets Favor the Poor

The reason that markets are more likely to improve the lives of the poor than
to harm them, to reduce inequality rather than exacerbate it, and to increase
rather than dampen social mobility is because markets are a competitive space
where individuals succeed by serving and supporting rather than suppress-
ing others.

Hayek (1937, 1945, 2002) accurately argued that the more competitive the
market the more likely it is that entrepreneurs will discover and deliver what
consumers desire. This is because the only way to succeed in a competitive
market is to do a better job than your competitors at satisfying consumer
demands. In a less competitive market, those pressures to discover and deliver
what people truly want are dampened. As Hayek (2002: 13) explained,
"[w]hich goods are scarce, however, or which things are goods, or how scarce
or valuable they are is precisely one of the conditions that competition should
discover: in each case it is the preliminary outcomes of the market process that
inform individuals where it is worthwhile to search." The market communi-
cates this information to its participants through the price system; it relays
"what kinds of goods and services are demanded, and how urgently" (Ibid.).
By doing so, it allocates resources to people who value them the most within

an economy and encourages them to specialize according to their talents, skills, and abilities. Market competition thus triggers a continuous process, which constantly updates participants with newly discovered information, and ultimately generates wealth for them.

Of course, market competition cannot guarantee that everyone's needs will be met. Market competition has the capacity to "frustrat[e] certain intentions and disappoin[t] certain expectations" (Ibid.: 10). It "does not in general ensure that what most people regard as more important ends are always satisfied before less important ones" and cannot ensure that certain (worthy) individuals will benefit—and certain other (unworthy) individuals will be harmed—from the competitive process (Ibid.: 14). When disappointments do occur in markets, however, alert entrepreneurs will recognize and seize these opportunities. "It is an outcome of the market mechanism," Hayek (Ibid.: 18) explained, "that someone is induced to fill the gap that arises when someone else does not fulfill the expectations on the basis of which a third party has made plans." Competition is, therefore, indispensable if countries are going to develop (Ibid.). Arguably, markets are even more important in less developed countries where a far greater number of unexplored possibilities exists than in highly developed countries. In less developed countries, competition will not only expose the productive extent of their labor and physical forces, but also encourage both innovation and imitation, and provide more opportunities to improve the lives of the poor.

Competition ensures that only those who serve others can maintain and accumulate wealth. Stated another way, the more competitive the market, the more becoming and staying wealthy depends on discovering what consumers (including poor consumers) want. The more competitive the market, the more that those who sub-optimally utilize acquired knowledge, lack entrepreneurial spirit, and/or actively prevent others from expressing this spirit will be penalized with losses and ultimately lose their wealth. Markets, thus, offer *less* protection of the rich's wealth than nonmarket contexts and disproportionately help individuals and countries that are poor.

Additionally, competition will also drive down prices and ensure that competition intensifies over time. At the same prices, cars, televisions, and computers in the United States today are safer, larger, and more powerful than they have ever been. We carry devices that possess the same, if not superior, processing and computational power as the first supercomputer from the 1960s in our pockets in the form of smartphones at a far cheaper price. Over time this means that the poor will be able to afford the "luxuries" that were once enjoyed exclusively by the rich.

Material Improvement Has Moral Implications

People can improve their lives through markets. Moreover, it is not only rich people but poor people as well who can improve their lives by engaging in market activity. Critically, that people's lives are improved through markets has moral implications.[36] That markets make us wealthier, healthier, happier, and better connected means that we (1) are able to avoid many difficult moral dilemmas, (2) are better positioned to actually improve the lives of others (through our market and nonmarket activities), and (3) are more willing to focus on the well-being of others.

Arguably the richer we are, the less likely we are to be confronted with real-world trolley problems. Trolley problems are a class of thought experiments in moral philosophy that describe difficult moral situations where hard moral choices have to be made. The general form of the problem, first articulated by Philippa Foot (1967), asks us to imagine a runaway tram that will hit and kill five people working the track if it is not switched from its present course. The driver cannot stop the tram, but he can switch the tram to another track where only one person is working. The choice the driver confronts concerns what, if anything, he is morally required to do in this situation. Is he morally obligated to intervene to save the five lives that are already in peril by sentencing the one worker who is not currently in any danger to death? Does his obligation change if either the single worker or the five workers were negligent in some way and so not entirely innocent? Does his obligation to act change if, rather than being the driver of the tram, he is a bystander who nonetheless can switch the tram tracks by say pulling a nearby lever? These questions force the answerers to clarify and confront the limits and implications of their moral positions.

The original trolley problem has been compared to other similar morally fraught situations. Foot, for instance, likened the position of the trolley driver to the position of a judge facing a riotous mob that can either knowingly convict an innocent man or allow the mob to harm and kill many innocent people. Judith Thomson (1976) presented another parallel. Suppose, she (Ibid.: 206) began, that a skilled transplant surgeon can save the lives of five of his patients who have a rare blood-type if he harvests the organs from a

---

[36] Cowen (2018) offered a moral argument for economic growth that is consistent with our own here: wealthier societies are happier, live longer, are more autonomous, and live more fulfilling (or fun, as he wrote) lives. However, Cowen was primarily concerned with how "[w]e have strayed from the ideals of a society based on prosperity and the rights and liberties of the individual, and [that] we do not know how to return to those ideals" (Ibid.: 15). Proposing pluralism as a core moral intuition, he sought to reconcile the seeming inconsistency between the "messiness" of a pluralistic moral core and the rigid ideals of prosperity and liberty (Ibid.: 17).

healthy but unwilling person (necessarily killing him) who happens to also have the same blood-type. Is the surgeon, Thomson then asked, permitted to kill the healthy person to save the five unhealthy people? Like the trolley problem, the judge facing the mob and the transplant doctor are in situations where our moral intuitions seem to be in conflict, that is, our obligation not to harm innocent others versus our obligation to help those who we can help. Arguably, being rich allows us to buy ourselves out of some of these moral dilemmas. Being wealthy allows us to avoid many of the trolley problems that we might otherwise confront. The richer the country, for instance, the more likely the tram will be frequently inspected, be better maintained, and have more advanced and even redundant braking systems, the more likely there will be warning systems to alert the workers that the tram is heading toward them, the less likely the tram driver will be confronted with such a horrible choice (i.e. to allow five people to die or to kill one person).[37]

There are a number of moral dilemmas that the poor confront that the rich simply escape. The rich can adequately care for their families without engaging in theft; the poor might not be able to do so. The rich can help a stranger in need without it hurting their families in any significant way; the poor might not have that option. The rich tend to have the flexibility and means to take time off from work (or leave work early) to go to a doctor's appointment or to visit extended family for major holidays; the poor likely need to forgo a substantial portion of their pay to enjoy the same "luxuries." The rich never need confront the decision of whether to care for themselves or their families (at least materially); many of the poor confront this or similar problems every day. Confronting a trolley problem places us in a kind of moral hell that we would prefer to avoid rather than pass through, even if our moral philosophy offers us a clear answer.[38] Arguably, the rich are less likely to spend time in that particular kind of moral hell.[39]

Peter Singer ([1979] 2011) formulated a trolley-like problem where the costs associated with helping others are so low that our obligation to help others becomes more pronounced. Imagine, Singer (Ibid.: 199) wrote, that on his way to give a lecture he sees a small child who has fallen into a shallow pond

---

[37] All the parties are also more likely to be insured in wealthy societies which mitigate some of the tragedy that would result from any loss of life.

[38] Rennix and Robinson (2017) called the trolley problem thought experiment a horror show that we are forced into.

[39] Russell (2014), similarly, spoke to the role of "good institutions" in allowing us to escape social dilemmas. As Russell (Ibid.: 268) wrote, "without [good institutions], the everyday challenges of feeding, clothing, and sheltering ourselves become daily dilemmas. With them, we have better things to do with our time than coping with dilemmas—and a lot less to regret." By good institutions, Russell had in mind private property and the rule of law, the institutions that undergird market societies.

and is danger of drowning. Imagine also that no one else is around. In that scenario, Singer contended, it is clear that he has an obligation to wade into the pond to save the child, even if doing so will mean that his shoes are ruined, and he has to postpone or cancel his lecture. The costs of canceling the lecture and losing the shoes are insignificant compared to the avoidable death of a child. According to Singer (Ibid.), "a plausible principle that would support the judgment that I ought to pull the child out is this: if it is in our power to prevent something very bad happening, without thereby sacrificing anything of comparable moral significance, we ought to do it. This principle seems uncontroversial." This principle, Singer (Ibid.) claimed, should be acceptable to consequentialists (for obvious reasons) and nonconsequentialists (because there is only an obligation to prevent bad outcomes when "nothing comparably significant is at stake").

Singer (Ibid.: 200) argued that this situation (i.e. preventing the death of a child at the price of a pair of shoes and a missed lecture) is akin to the situation that those of us in wealthy societies are in. Extreme poverty is an obvious and preventable bad. The affluent can prevent this bad in some circumstances, "without sacrificing anything of comparable moral significance" and so ought to do what they can "to prevent some extreme poverty" (Ibid.). There are, however, several objections to Singer's formulation, some of which he successfully anticipated.[40] Importantly, Singer overlooked the potential of markets to eliminate extreme poverty among the one billion who still suffer from it, as it did the billions more who were saved from extreme poverty by markets. Indeed, Singer assumed that charity is the only way or the most effective way for the rich to help the poor and that money spent on luxury goods are purely hedonistic with no socially beneficial outcomes. As McCloskey (2016: 6–7) highlighted, however, "[s]ince 1800 the ability of humans to feed and clothe and educate themselves, even as the number of humans increased by an astonishing factor of seven, has risen, per human, by an even more astonishing factor of ten." As markets developed and, importantly, because markets expanded, the number of human beings living in poverty (measured as a percentage of the world's population, and in total numbers) has declined. The market has done more to alleviate extreme poverty than any other (economic or political) system.

A key caveat that Singer recognized, however, is that the size of the sacrifice required of each individual diminishes the more individuals who can help others in need join in the effort to help. According to Singer (Ibid.: 215),

---

[40] See, for instance, Schmidtz (2000) and Schaler (2009).

This surprising outcome – that if everyone with abundance were to contribute to the effort to reduce extreme poverty and all that goes with it, the amount each of us would need to give would be quite modest – shows that the argument [that the relatively rich should help the relatively poor] … is demanding only because so few of those with the ability to help the poor are doing anything significant to help them. … If few are helping, those few have to cut very deep before they get to the point at which giving more would involve sacrificing something of comparable moral significance to the life saved by their gift. If we all, or even most of us, gave according to the much more modest scale I have suggested, none of us would have to give up much.

Singer believed that the obligation to help those in extreme poverty only requires large sacrifices when there is a free rider problem. If everyone who could help could be convinced or coerced into helping, then each of us would have to do very little to satisfy our obligation to help. It seems plausible that the more of us there are who are trying to save the drowning child, the less likely that any of our shoes will be destroyed as a result.

Relatedly, the richer we are, the more that we can sacrifice, and the more people in extreme poverty that we can help (through our charitable giving). Of course, Singer would suggest that this heightens our obligation to help. But, we cannot be morally indifferent to the increased potential to help others that accompanies prosperity.

Not only do markets make it so that we are better positioned to actually improve the lives of others (through our market and nonmarket activities), they make us more willing to focus on the well-being of others. At their core, successful market transactions require our recognizing how our actions or possessions can improve the lives of others. Recall, Smith ([1776] 1981: 27) explained that in proposing a trade, "[w]e address ourselves, not to [our potential trading partner's] humanity but to their self-love, and never talk to them of our own necessities but of their advantages." If we are to succeed, then, we must know how our potential trading partners perceive of their interests.

Two additional observations by Adam Smith are helpful here. Smith ([1759] 1982: 136) observed that a person who suffered from "the most frivolous disaster" would suffer "more real disturbance" than if that person were to learn that a hundred million people he was not otherwise connected to had been "suddenly swallowed up by an earthquake." He (Ibid.: 219) also observed that everyone feels their own pleasures and pains "more sensibly than those of other people" and that, after themselves, they direct their moral attention to their family, then friends, then colleagues, then neighbors, and then fellow citizens.[41]

---

[41] See Nieli (1986: 620). See also Forman-Barzilai (2005) for a criticism of Smith's account.

We are naturally inclined to be concerned with our own ease before we concern ourselves with the suffering of others. Critically, more people in market societies than in nonmarket societies more readily achieve this ease. People in market societies, because they are wealthier, healthier, happier, and better connected, are more likely to be shielded from or insured against "frivolous disasters," and are more likely to have larger and more cosmopolitan spheres of intimacy. Commerce, for instance, connects the cotton farmer in North America with the factory worker in Asia, and those connections might very well be stronger than their connections to their fellow citizens in some other parts of their respective countries.[42]

Is a More Direct Response to the Charge That Markets Are Corrupting Possible?

In *A Theory of Justice*, John Rawls (1971) articulated a conception of justice that could act as a standard against which we might assess the justness of the basic institutional arrangements of a society. To achieve this status, Rawls suggested, the principles of justice must be ones that free and equal individuals would assent to if they were deciding on those principles in a deliberative process that was fair (i.e. they were deciding on the principles behind a veil of ignorance that prevented them from assessing how they might benefit from a particular scheme). According to Rawls (Ibid.: 302), free and equal individuals deciding on the rules of justice in a deliberative process that was fair would choose the following two principles of justice:

First Principle: Each person is to have an equal right to the most extensive total system of equal basic liberties compatible with a similar system of liberty for all.

Second Principle: Social and economic inequalities are to be arranged so that they are both: (a) to the greatest benefit of the least advantaged, consistent with the just savings principle, and (b) attached to offices and positions open to all under conditions of fair equality of opportunity.

---

[42] According to Hayek (1976: 113),

[t]he benefits from knowledge which others possess, including all the advances of science, reach us through channels provided and directed by the market mechanism. Even the degree to which we participate in the aesthetic or moral strivings of men in other parts of the world we owe to the economic nexus.

Rawls further clarified that the first principle (which he described as the greatest equal liberty principle) is lexically prior to the second principle (the first part of which he referred to as the difference principle). By this, he meant that the only justifiable restrictions on liberty are those that strengthen the overall system of liberty and are agreed to by everyone who is affected (Ibid.: 302). The difference principle comes into play as a criterion for comparing the justness of available systems only when those systems that do not satisfy the greatest equal liberty principle have been dismissed as unjust. Additionally, Rawls clarified that he was not talking about the least advantaged individual in any society but a representative member of the least advantaged socioeconomic grouping (Ibid.: 44). He tended to think of this group as the lowest income class or the poorest laborers in a society (Ibid.: 98; see also, Rawls 2001: 139; and Schmidtz 2006: 189). Rawls insisted that the second principle must be prior to any other criteria that we might use to assess the desirability of a set of economic institutions like efficiency or total income. Stated another way, if the rules governing how we bake the pie are to be viewed as just, then (1) every baker must be voluntarily baking the pie and (2) the pie that results must be the pie that offers the most sustenance to the least advantaged even if (a) we used more resources than we might have used to bake the pie and (b) the pie that we baked is not the largest pie that we might have produced, if we were not at all concerned with how much the least advantaged received.[43]

Rawls was, thus, primarily concerned with (1) maximizing the freedoms of all and (2) maximizing the prospects of the least advantaged social group, and he believed that any economic arrangement should be judged by how well it achieved both goals.[44] If the least advantaged will tend to do better in System A than they will tend to do in System B, assuming that both Systems A and B equally ensure that everyone is treated as a free moral person, then System A is to be viewed as *more just* than System B. Rawls acknowledged that justice alone does not settle the question of which economic system we should adopt. And, others have criticized various aspects of Rawls' conception of justice as fairness and its appropriateness for judging the morality of different economic systems (Harsanyi 1975; Schaefer 1979; Sen 1980, 1990; Matsuda 1986). "But," as David Schmidtz (2006: 196) concluded, "at the end of the day, isn't there something fundamentally right (even beautiful) in [Rawls'] grand vision?" A strong case can be made that we should want to live in the society that is the most just on Rawlsian terms.

---

[43] The just savings principle also insists that we must be concerned with future generations.

[44] Rawls also had a concern with equal opportunity (at least regarding our access to positions of power); see the second part of the second principle. This can arguably be recast as a concern about crony capitalism and privileges.

The relevant question for us, then, would be: Is the market system the most just economic system on Rawlsian terms? Is it the economic system that best satisfies the second principle while respecting the first principle? Initially, Rawls argued that justice as fairness does not imply a prior commitment to capitalism or socialism or any of the socioeconomic systems in between. But, ultimately, the question is an empirical one (Ibid.: 193). For his part, Rawls seemed to have believed that a welfare state (i.e. a competitive market paired with a government that provided public goods and engaged in some redistribution) was more likely to satisfy justice as fairness than say a pure market system.[45]

Arguably, the market system is the most just economic system.[46] Markets are arenas where individuals can improve their lives. People residing in market societies are wealthier, healthier, happier, and better connected than people residing in nonmarket societies. Moreover, these advantages do not just accrue to the richest people in these societies. The poor in market societies are better off than the poor in nonmarket societies. Additionally, market societies are more egalitarian and allow for more social mobility than nonmarket societies.[47]

Pointing out that we have good reasons to believe that the market system is the most just economic system available to us—that market societies maximize the freedom and prospects of all people within them including the poorest—is an important response to the most damning critique of markets on moral grounds. By itself, however, it is not an adequate response. Recall that markets, according to this critique, change us for the worse by rewarding our

---

[45] Alternatively, Tomasi (2012) proposed market democracy as the set of social and economic institutions that are most likely to satisfy a Rawlsian style conception of justice as fairness. Stated another way, he argued that market democracy is a system that will both ensure basic liberties and most benefit the least advantaged. "Market democracy," Tomasi (Ibid.: 267) explained,

> takes a fundamentally deliberative approach to the questions of political life. Rather than seeing society as something private, market democracy sees society as an essentially public thing: political and economic structures must be justifiable to the citizens who are to live within them, whatever their social class. … This democratic outlook leads market democracy to affirm a thick conception of economic liberty, with such liberties scoring fully on par with the other basic liberal rights and freedoms.

Similarly, Shapiro (1995) argued that Rawlsian liberals should adopt free market capitalism.

[46] Rawls (2001: 135) contrasted the property-owning democracy that he championed with a capitalist welfare state and a laissez-faire economic system. It is possible, however, that Rawls viewed Western constitutional democracies as coming closest to satisfying justice as fairness (see Rawls 1985; Schmidtz 2006: 195). If so, then we are not disagreeing with him in any fundamental sense. These countries tend to be market societies. Admittedly, this leaves open the question of which kind of market system (e.g. one with a larger welfare state vs. one with a smaller welfare state) comes closest to satisfying justice as fairness.

[47] Alternatively stated, there tend to be more equal shares in market societies than in nonmarket societies and so market societies appear to do a better job of satisfying the difference principle.

worst traits and so, as markets expand, market vices come to replace moral virtues. Markets are a kind of monster that turns market participants into monsters. Engaging in market activity places us in moral jeopardy where we risk losing our souls. As we have noted, however, most moral defenses of markets fail to challenge and some actually endorse the view that markets corrupt our morals. According to these defenses, markets transform *private vice into public virtue*, channel immoral behavior in socially beneficial directions, and generate good results for society like wealth despite (and maybe because of) the bad traits of individuals like greed. If the concern is that market activity leads to moral decline, then a moral defense of markets that stresses its reliance on vice or that speaks to its ability to accommodate and channel vice in socially beneficial directions is not likely to be satisfactory.

Arguably, that people can improve their lives through markets and that this potential for material betterment is not exclusive to the rich is a more direct response to the concern that markets are corrupting. Stressing the moral implications of this potential for material betterment in markets is an additional step toward an adequate response to those who are concerned with how markets transform us. As we argued, the better off we are the more likely we are to avoid difficult moral dilemmas, the more likely our own market and nonmarket activities can and will improve the lives of others, and the more willing we are to concern ourselves with the well-being of others.

In the next chapter, we offer an even more direct response to the concern that markets corrupt our morals than we advance here. We argue that markets are moral spaces that depend on virtue. Additionally, in. Chap. 6, we argue that markets are spaces where moral improvement occurs. We become wealthier, healthier, happier, and better connected as a result of our interactions in the market. We also become better people the greater our exposure to markets.

Bibliography

Ali, A., and W.M. Crain. 2001. Institutional Distortions, Economics Freedom, and Growth. *Cato Journal* 21 (3): 415–426.

Apergis, N., and A. Cooray. 2017. Economic Freedom and Income Inequality: Evidence from a Panel of Global Economies—A Linear and a Non-Linear Long-Run Analysis. *The Manchester School* 85 (1): 88–105.

Apergis, N., O. Dincer, and J.E. Payne. 2014. Economic Freedom and Income Inequality Revisited: Evidence from a Panel Error Correction Model. *Contemporary Economic Policy* 32 (1): 67–75.

Argyle, M., and M. Henderson. 1985. *The Anatomy of Relationships: And the Rules and Skills Needed to Manage Them Successfully*. London: Penguin.

Ashby, N.J., and R.S. Sobel. 2008. Income Inequality and Economic Freedom in the US States. *Public Choice* 134 (3–4): 329–346.

Atkinson, Anthony Barnes. 1987. On the Measurement of Poverty. *Econometrica* 55 (4): 749–764.

Atkinson, A.B., J. Hasell, S. Morelli, and M. Roser. 2017. *The Chartbook of Economic Inequality*. https://www.chartbookofeconomicinequality.com

Badhwar, N.K. 2008. Friendship and Commercial Societies. *Politics, Philosophy & Economics* 7 (3): 301–326.

———. 2014. *Well-Being: Happiness in a Worthwhile Life*. Oxford: Oxford University Press.

Bahama Gazette, 29 November 1799.

Bandow, D. 2016. North Korea's War on Christianity: The Globe's Number One Religious Persecutor. *Forbes*, October 31. https://www.forbes.com/sites/dougbandow/2016/10/31/north-koreas-war-on-christianity-the-globes-number-one-religious-persecutor/

Barr, A., J. Ensminger, and J.C. Johnson. 2009. Social Networks and Trust in Cross-Cultural Economic Experiments. In *Whom Can We Trust?: How Groups, Networks, and Institutions Make Trust Possible*, ed. K. Cook, M. Levi, and R. Hardin, 65–90. New York: Russell Sage Foundation.

Belasen, A.R., and R.W. Hafer. 2012. Well-Being and Economic Freedom: Evidence from the States. *Intelligence* 40 (3): 306–316.

———. 2013. Do Changes in Economic Freedom Affect Well-Being? *Journal of Regional Analysis & Policy* 43 (1): 56–64.

Bennett, D.L. 2016. Subnational Economic Freedom and Performance in the United States and Canada. *Cato Journal* 36: 165–186.

Bennett, D.L., and B. Nikolaev. 2017. On the Ambiguous Economic Freedom–Inequality Relationship. *Empirical Economics* 53 (2): 717–754.

Bennett, D.L., and R.K. Vedder. 2013. A Dynamic Analysis of Economic Freedom and Income Inequality in the 50 U.S. States: Empirical Evidence of a Parabolic Relationship. *Journal of Regional Analysis & Policy* 43 (1): 42–55.

Bergh, A., and T. Nilsson. 2010. Do Liberalization and Globalization Increase Income Inequality? *European Journal of Political Economy* 26 (4): 488–505.

Bjørnskov, C., and N.J. Foss. 2008. Economic Freedom and Entrepreneurial Activity: Some Cross-Country Evidence. *Public Choice* 134 (3–4): 307–328.

Botero, J.C., S. Djankov, R. La Porta, F. Lopez-de-Silanes, and A. Shleifer. 2004. The Regulation of Labor. *The Quarterly Journal of Economics* 119 (4): 1339–1382.

Bridge, K., and L.A. Baxter. 1992. Blended Relationships: Friends as Work Associates. *Western Journal of Communication* 56 (3): 200–225.

Butcher, K., B. Sparks, and F. O'Callaghan. 2002. On the Nature of Customer-Employee Relationships. *Marketing Intelligence & Planning* 20 (5): 297–306.

Carlsson, F., and S. Lundström. 2002. Economic Freedom and Growth: Decomposing the Effects. *Public Choice* 112 (3–4): 335–344.

Carter, J.R. 2007. An Empirical Note on Economic Freedom and Income Inequality. *Public Choice* 130 (1–2): 163–177.

Caryl, C. 2017. South Korea Shows the World How Democracy Is Done. *The Washington Post*, March 10. https://www.washingtonpost.com/news/democracy-post/wp/2017/03/10/south-korea-shows-the-world-how-democracy-is-done/?utm_term=.66c9c74330ae

Central Intelligence Agency. 2015. The World Factbook 2015. https://www.cia.gov/library/publications/download/download-2015/index.html

———. 2018. The World Factbook 2018. https://www.cia.gov/library/publications/the-world-factbook/index.html

Chamlee-Wright, E. 1997. *The Cultural Foundations of Economic Development: Urban Female Entrepreneurship in Ghana*. London/New York: Routledge.

Choe, S. 2016. In Hail of Bullets and Fire, North Korea Killed Official Who Wanted Reform. *The New York Times*, March 12. https://www.nytimes.com/2016/03/13/world/asia/north-korea-executions-jang-song-thaek.html

Choe, S.-H. 2017. South Korea Removes President Park Geun-hye. *The New York Times*, March 9. https://www.nytimes.com/2017/03/09/world/asia/park-geun-hye-impeached-south-korea.html

Chong, Z. 2018. Apple Supplier Guilty of Unsafe Work Conditions, Report Finds. *CNet*, January 18. https://www.cnet.com/news/china-labor-watch-finds-harsh-work-conditions-at-apple-supplier/

Clark, A.K. 2015. Rethinking the Decline in Social Capital. *American Politics Research* 43 (4): 569–601.

Clark, J.R., and R.A. Lawson. 2008. The Impact of Economic Growth, Tax Policy and Economic Freedom on Income Inequality. *The Journal of Private Enterprise* 24 (1): 23–31.

Corak, M. 2013. Inequality from Generation to Generation: The United States in Comparison. In *The Economics of Inequality, Poverty, and Discrimination in the 21st Century*, ed. R. Rycroft. Santa Barbara: ABC-CLIO, LLC.

Costa, D.L., and M.E. Kahn. 2003. Understanding the American Decline in Social Capital, 1952–1998. *Kyklos* 56: 17–46.

Cowen, T. 2018. *Stubborn Attachments: A Vision for a Society of Free, Prosperous, and Responsible Individuals*. San Francisco: Stripe Press.

Craton, M., and G. Saunders. 1992. *Islanders in the Stream: A History of the Bahamian People: Volume One: From Aboriginal Times to the End of Slavery*. Athens: University of Georgia Press.

Doucouliagos, C., and M.A. Ulubaşoğlu. 2006. Economic Freedom and Economic Growth: Does Specification Make a Difference? *European Journal of Political Economy* 22 (1): 60–81.

Ehrenkranz, M. 2018. Tesla Whistleblowers Say Carmaker Failed to Report Serious Injuries at Its Factory. *Gizmodo*, April 16. https://gizmodo.com/tesla-whistleblowers-say-electric-carmaker-failed-to-re-1825292358

Eltis, D. 2017. A Brief Overview of the Trans-Atlantic Slave Trade. *Voyages: The Trans-Atlantic Slave Trade Database*. http://www.slavevoyages.org/assessment/essay. Accessed 5 July.

Ensminger, J., and K. Cook. 2014. Prosociality in Rural America: Evidence from Dictator, Ultimatum, Public Goods, and Trust Games. In *Experimenting with Social Norms: Fairness and Punishment in Cross-Cultural Perspective*, ed. J. Ensminger and J. Henrich, 445–465. New York: The Russell Sage Foundation.

Goldthorpe, J.H., and R. Erikson. 1992. *The Constant Flux: A Study of Social Mobility in Industrial Societies*. Oxford: Oxford University Press.

Esposto, A.G., and P.A. Zaleski. 1999. Economic Freedom and the Quality of Life: An Empirical Analysis. *Constitutional Political Economy* 10 (2): 185–197.

Feinberg, R.A., B. Sheffler, J. Meoli, and A. Rummel. 1989. There's Something Social Happening at the Mall. *Journal of Business and Psychology* 4 (1): 49–63.

Fischer, C.S. 2005. Bowling Alone: What's the Score? *Social Networks* 27 (2): 155–167.

Fligstein, N. 1990. *The Transformation of Corporate Control*. Cambridge: Harvard University Press.

Florida, R. 2002. The Economic Geography of Talent. *Annals of the Association of American Geographers* 92 (4): 743–755.

Food and Agricultural Organization of the United Nations. *Statistics*. http://www.fao.org/statistics/en/. Accessed 15 Mar 2016.

Foot, P. 1967. The Problem of Abortion and the Doctrine of the Double Effect. *Oxford Review* (5): 5–15.

Foreign & Commonwealth Office. 2017. Guidance: Overseas Business Risk—South Korea. *Foreign & Commonwealth Office*, June 5. https://www.gov.uk/government/publications/overseas-business-risk-south-korea/overseas-business-risk-south-korea

Forman-Barzilai, F. 2005. Sympathy in Space(s): Adam Smith on Proximity. *Political Theory* 33 (2): 189–217.

Fortune. 2017. Fortune 500 List. http://fortune.com/fortune500/list/

Freedom House. 2016. *Freedom in the World 2016: The Annual Survey of Political Rights and Civil Liberties*. Maryland: Rowman & Littlefield.

Friedman, M., and R.D. Friedman. 1980. *Free to Choose: A Personal Statement*. San Diego: Harcourt.

Frost, A. 2018. The Disciplinary Role of Market Prices: A Hayekian Critique of Maoist China. In *Exploring the Political Economy and Social Philosophy of F. A. Hayek*, ed. P.J. Boettke, J.S. Lemke, and V.H. Storr, 13–33. New York: Rowman & Littlefield International.

Gardiner, C. 1998. Mentoring: Towards a Professional Friendship. *Mentoring & Tutoring: Partnership in Learning* 6 (1–2): 77–84.

Gehring, K. 2013. Who Benefits from Economic Freedom? Unraveling the Effect of Economic Freedom on Subjective Well-Being. *World Development* 50: 74–90.

Greenhouse, S. 1997. Nike Shoe Plant in Vietnam Is Called Unsafe for Workers. *New York Times*, November 8. https://www.nytimes.com/1997/11/08/business/nike-shoe-plant-in-vietnam-is-called-unsafe-for-workers.html

Gropper, D.M., R.A. Lawson, and J.T. Thorne Jr. 2011. Economic Freedom and Happiness. *Cato Journal* 31: 237–256.

Gwartney, J.D., and R. Lawson. 2004. *Economic Freedom of the World: 2004 Annual Report*. Vancouver: Fraser Institute. https://www.fraserinstitute.org/research/economic-freedom-of-the-world-2004-annual-report

Gwartney, J.D., R. Lawson, and R.G. Holcombe. 1999. Economic Freedom and the Environment for Economic Growth. *Journal of Institutional and Theoretical Economics* 155 (4): 643–663.

Hall, J.C., B.R. Humphreys, and J.E. Ruseski. 2018. Economic Freedom and Exercise: Evidence from State Outcomes. *Southern Economic Journal* 84 (4): 1050–1066.

Handler, J.S. 2009. The Middle Passage and the Material Culture of Captive Africans. *Slavery & Abolition* 30 (1): 1–26.

Hanke, S.H., and S.J.K. Walters. 1997. Economic Freedom, Prosperity, and Equality: A Survey. *Cato Journal* 17 (2): 117–146.

Hanson, J.R. 2000. Prosperity and Economic Freedom: A Virtuous Cycle. *The Independent Review* 4 (4): 525–531.

Harsanyi, J.C. 1975. Can the Maximin Principle Serve as a Basis for Morality? A Critique of John Rawls's Theory. *The American Political Science Review* 69 (2): 594–606.

Hayek, F.A. 1937. Economics and Knowledge. *Economica* 4 (13): 33–54.

———. 1945. The Use of Knowledge in Society. *American Economic Review* 35 (4): 519–530.

———. 1976. *Law, Legislation and Liberty, Vol. 2: The Mirage of Social Justice*. Chicago: University of Chicago Press.

———. 2002. Competition as a Discovery Procedure. *The Quarterly Journal of Austrian Economics* 5 (3): 9–23.

Haytko, D.L. 2004. Firm-to-Firm and Interpersonal Relationships: Perspectives from Advertising Agency Account Managers. *Journal of Academy of Marketing Science* 32: 312–328.

Heckman, J., and C. Pagés-Serra. 2000. The Cost of Job Security Regulation: Evidence from Latin American Labor Markets. *Economia* 1 (1): 109–154.

Helliwell, J., R. Layard, and J. Sachs. 2017. *World Happiness Report 2017*. New York: Sustainable Development Solutions Network.

Henrich, J., R. Boyd, S. Bowles, C. Camerer, E. Fehr, and H. Gintis. 2004. *Foundations of Human Sociality: Economics Experiments and Ethnographic Evidence from Fifteen Small Scale Societies*. Oxford: Oxford University Press.

Hodge, S. 2012. Raising Revenue: The Least Worst Options. *Tax Foundation*, December 5. https://taxfoundation.org/raising-revenue-least-worst-options/

———. 2014. The Number of Millionaire Tax Returns Fluctuates Every Year. *Tax Foundation*, January 8. https://taxfoundation.org/number-millionaire-tax-returns-fluctuates-every-year/

Hodson, R. 1997. Group Relations at Work: Solidarity, Conflict, and Relations with Management. *Work and Occupations* 24: 426–452.

Inglehart, R., C. Haerpfer, A. Moreno, C. Welzel, K. Kizilova, J. Diez-Medrano, M. Lagos, P. Norris, E. Ponarin, and B. Puranen, et al., eds. 2014. *World Values*

Survey: Round Six—Country-Pooled Datafile Version. Madrid: JD Systems. www. worldvaluessurvey.org/WVSDocumentationWV6.jsp

Ingram, P., and P.W. Roberts. 2000. Friendships Among Competitors in the Sydney Hotel Industry. *American Journal of Sociology* 106 (2): 387–423.

Institute for National Security Strategy. 2016. Kim Jung Eung jipkwon 5nyon silchong baekso 김정은 집권 5년 失政 백서 [Kim Jung Eun's 5 Year in Power]. Seoul: Institute for National Security Strategy. http://www.inss.re.kr/inss/attach/getFile.do?fileId=7401

Islam, S. 1996. Economic Freedom, Per Capita Income and Economic Growth. *Applied Economic Letters* 3 (9): 595–597.

Jager, S.M. 2017. What Trump Needs to Know About North Korea's History. *Politico*, August 9. https://www.politico.com/magazine/story/2017/08/09/donald-trump-north-korea-history-215473

Johnson, H. 1991. Friendly Societies in the Bahamas 1834–1910. *Slavery & Abolition* 12 (3): 183–199.

———. 1996. *The Bahamas: From Slavery to Servitude 1783–1933.* Florida: University Press of Florida.

Kahneman, D., and A.B. Krueger. 2006. Developments in the Measurement of Subjective Well-Being and Poverty: An Economic Perspective. *Journal of Economic Perspectives* 20 (1): 3–24.

Kang, J.-M. 2014. Ask a North Korean: Is Religion Allowed? *The Guardian*, July 2. https://www.theguardian.com/world/2014/jul/02/north-korea-is-religion-allowed

Kepner, C.G. 1991. An Experiment in the Relationship of Types of Written Feedback to the Development of Second-Language Writing Skills. *The Modern Language Journal* 75 (3): 305–313.

Kimura, M. 1993. Standards of Living in Colonial Korea: Did the Masses Become Worse Off or Better Off Under Japanese Rule? *The Journal of Economic History* 53 (3): 629–652.

Klapper, L., L. Laeven, and R. Rajan. 2006. Entry Regulation as a Barrier to Entrepreneurship. *Journal of Financial Economics* 82 (3): 591–629.

Knight, R. 2012. Are North Koreans Really Three Inches Shorter than South Koreans? *BBC News*, April 23. https://www.bbc.com/news/magazine-17774210

Komlos, J., and P. Kriwy. 2003. The Biological Standard of Living in the Two Germanies. *German Economic Review* 4 (4): 459–473.

Kram, K.E. 1983. Phases of the Mentor Relationship. *Academy of Management Journal* 26 (4): 608–625.

Kwon, H., and B.H. Chung. 2012. *North Korea: Beyond Charismatic Politics.* Maryland: Rowman & Littlefield.

Ladd, E.C. 1996. The Data Just Don't Show Erosion of America's Social Capital. *The Public Perspective* 7 (4): 5–22.

———. 1999. Peer Relationships and Social Competence During Early and Middle Childhood. *Annual Review of Psychology* 50: 333–359.

Lankov, A. 2011. NK Is No Stalinist Country. *The Korea Times*, October 9. https://www.koreatimes.co.kr/www/news/nation/2011/10/304_96327.html

———. 2014. North Korean Crackdown on Private Education Overlooks the Real Issue. *Radio Free Asia*, February 12. http://www.rfa.org/english/commentaries/lankov-02122014111559.html

Large, T. 2011. Special Report: Crisis Grips North Korean Rice Bowl. *Reuters*, October 7. http://www.reuters.com/article/us-korea-north-food-idUSTRE7956DU20111007

Lawson, R.A., R.H. Murphy, and C.R. Williamson. 2016. The Relationship Between Income, Economic Freedom, and BMI. *Public Health* 134: 18–25.

Lazear, E.P. 1990. Job Security Provisions and Employment. *The Quarterly Journal of Economics* 105 (3): 699–726.

Leeson, P.T. 2010. Two Cheers for Capitalism. *Society* 47 (3): 227–233.

Legatum Institute. 2010. *The 2011 Legatum Prosperity Index: An Inquiry into Global Wealth and Wellbeing*. London: Legatum Institute.

Leschke, M. 2000. Constitutional Choice and Prosperity: A Factor Analysis. *Constitutional Political Economy* 11 (3): 265–279.

Ljungvall, Å. 2013. *The Freer the Fatter? A Panel Study of the Relationship Between Body-Mass Index and Economic Freedom*. Unpublished Paper, Lund University.

Luthans, F., and C.M. Youssef. 2004. Human, Social, and Now Positive Psychological Capital Management: Investing in People for Competitive Advantage. *Organizational Dynamics* 33 (2): 143–160.

Mankiw, G.N. 2015. Yes, $r > g$. So What? *American Economic Review* 105 (5): 43–47.

Matsuda, M.J. 1986. Liberal Jurisprudence and Abstracted Visions of Human Nature: A Feminist Critique of Rawls' Theory of Justice. *New Mexico Law Review* 16: 613–630.

McCloskey, D.N. 2014. Measured, Unmeasured, Mismeasured, and Unjustified Pessimism: A Review Essay of Thomas Piketty's *Capital in the Twenty-First Century*. *Erasmus Journal for Philosophy and Economics* 7 (2): 73–115.

———. 2016. *Bourgeois Equality: How Ideas, Not Capital or Institutions, Enriched the World*. Chicago: University of Chicago Press.

Milanovic, B., P.H. Lindert, and J.G. Williamson. 2007. *Measuring Ancient Inequality*. World Bank Policy Research Working Paper, No. 4412.

Munger, M.C. 2011. Euvoluntary or Not, Exchange Is Just. *Social Philosophy and Policy* 28 (2): 192–211.

Murphy, P.J., J. Liao, and H.P. Welsch. 2006. A Conceptual History of Entrepreneurial Thought. *Journal of Management History* 12 (1): 12–35.

Naanwaab, C. 2018. Does Economic Freedom Promote Human Development? New Evidence from a Cross-National Study. *The Journal of Developing Areas* 52 (3): 183–198.

Nelson, R.R., and H. Pack. 1999. The Asian Miracle and Modern Growth Theory. *The Economic Journal* 109 (457): 416–436.

Neumark, D., and W. Wascher. 2004. Minimum Wages, Labor Market Institutions, and Youth Employment: A Cross-National Analysis. *ILR Review* 57 (2): 223–248.

Nieli, R. 1986. Spheres of Intimacy and the Adam Smith Problem. *Journal of the History of Ideas* 47 (4): 611–624.

Nikolaev, B. 2014. Economic Freedom and Quality of Life: Evidence from the OECD's Your Better Life Index. *Journal of Private Enterprise* 29 (3): 61–96.

Noland, M., S. Robinson, and T. Wang. 2001. Famine in North Korea: Causes and Cures. *Economic Development and Cultural Change* 49 (4): 741–767.

Nyström, K. 2008. The Institutions of Economic Freedom and Entrepreneurship: Evidence from Panel Data. *Public Choice* 136 (3–4): 269–282.

Observatory of Economic Complexity. 2018. South Korea. https://atlas.media.mit.edu/en/profile/country/kor/

Organisation for Economic Co-operation and Development. 2010. A Family Affair: Intergenerational Social Mobility across OECD Countries. In *Economic Policy Reforms: Going for Growth.* Paris: OECD Publishing.

———. 2011a. *Divided We Stand: Why Inequality Keeps Rising.* Paris: OECD Publishing. https://www.oecd.org/els/soc/49499779.pdf

———. 2011b. *Growing Income Inequality in OECD Countries: What Drives It and How Can Policy Tackle It.* Paris: OECD Publishing. http://www.oecd.org/social/soc/47723414.pdf

———. 2011c. *PISA 2009 Results: Students on Line: Digital Technologies and Performance.* Vol. VI. Paris: OECD Publishing. https://doi.org/10.1787/9789264112995-en.

———. 2013. *Skilled for Life? Key Findings from the Survey of Adult Skills.* Paris: OECD Publishing. https://www.oecd.org/skills/piaac/SkillsOutlook_2013_ebook.pdf

———. 2015. *In It Together: Why Less Inequality Benefits All.* Paris: OECD Publishing.

———. 2016. *Research and Development Statistics (RDS) Database.* https://www.oecd.org/sti/rds. Accessed 15 Mar 2016.

———. 2018a. *OECD Better Life Index.* Paris: OECD Publishing. http://www.oecd-betterlifeindex.org

———. 2018b. Korea. In *OECD Better Life Index.* Paris: OECD Publishing. http://www.oecdbetterlifeindex.org/countries/korea/

———. 2018c. *OECD Income Distribution Database: Gini, Poverty, Income, Methods and Concepts.* Paris: OECD Publishing. http://www.oecd.org/els/soc/IDD-ToR-Until2011.pdf

Ovaska, T., and R. Takashima. 2006. Economic Policy and the Level of Self-Perceived Well-Being: An International Comparison. *The Journal of Socio-Economics* 35 (2): 308–325.

Parks, M.R., and K. Floyd. 1996. Making Friends in Cyberspace. *Journal of Computer-Mediated Communication* 1 (4). https://doi.org/10.1111/j.1083-6101.1996.tb00176.x.

Paxton, P. 1999. Is Social Capital Declining in the United States? A Multiple Indicator Assessment. *American Journal of Sociology* 105 (1): 88–127.

Pearson, J. 2015. North Korea's Black Market Becoming the New Normal. *Reuters,* October 28. http://www.reuters.com/article/us-northkorea-change-insight-idUSKCN0SN00320151029

Perry, M.J. 2016. Fortune 500 Firms 1955 v. 2016: Only 12% Remain, Thanks to the Creative Destruction that Fuels Economic Prosperity. *American Enterprise Institute*, December 13. http://www.aei.org/publication/fortune-500-firms-1955-v-2016-only-12-remain-thanks-to-the-creative-destruction-that-fuels-economic-prosperity/

Pierce, C.A., D. Byrne, and H. Aguinis. 1996. Attraction in Organizations: A Model of Workplace Romance. *Journal of Organizational Behavior* 17 (1): 5–32.

Piketty, T. 2014. *Capital in the Twenty-First Century*. Trans. A. Goldhammer. Cambridge: Harvard University Press.

———. 2015a. Putting Distribution Back at the Center of Economics: Reflections on *Capital in the Twenty-First Century. Journal of Economic Perspectives* 29 (1): 67–88.

———. 2015b. About *Capital in the Twenty-First Century. American Economic Review: Papers & Proceedings* 105 (5): 1–6.

Price, L.L., and E.J. Arnould. 1999. Commercial Friendships: Service Provider-Client Relationships in Context. *Journal of Marketing* 63 (4): 38–56.

Putnam, R.D. 2000. *Bowling Alone: The Collapse and Revival of American Community*. New York/Philadelphia: Simon and Schuster.

Putnam, R.D., L.M. Feldstein, and D. Cohen. 2003. *Better Together: Restoring the American Community*. New York: Simon and Schuster.

Raun, T.U. [1987] 2002. *Estonia and the Estonians*. Stanford: Hoover Institution Press, Stanford University.

Rawls, J. 1985. Justice as Fairness: Political Not Metaphysical. *Philosophy & Public Affairs* 14 (3): 223–251.

———. 2001. *Justice as Fairness: A Restatement*. Cambridge: Harvard University Press.

———. [1971] 2009. *A Theory of Justice*. Cambridge: Harvard University Press.

Razvi, S., and D. Chakraborty. 2016. Does Economic Freedom Influence Major Health Indicators in India? Cross-State Panel Estimation Results. *Journal of Development Policy and Practice* 1 (2): 203–221.

Rennix, B., and N.J. Robinson. 2017. The Trolley Problem Will Tell You Nothing Useful about Morality. *Current Affairs*, November 3. https://www.currentaffairs.org/2017/11/the-trolley-problem-will-tell-you-nothing-useful-about-morality

Reporters Without Borders. North Korea. *Reporters Without Borders*. https://rsf.org/en/north-korea. Accessed 15 Mar 2016.

Rheingold, H. 1993. *The Virtual Community: Homesteading on the Electronic Frontier*. New York: Basic Books.

Roberts, J.M., and R. Olson. 2013. *How Economic Freedom Promotes Better Health Care, Education, and Environmental Quality*. Washington, DC: The Heritage Foundation.

Roser, M., and E. Ortiz-Ospina. 2017. Global Extreme Poverty. *Our World in Data*, March 27. https://ourworldindata.org/extreme-poverty

Rothbard, M.N. [1962] 1993. *Man, Economy, and State*. Auburn: Ludwig von Mises Institute.

Rotolo, T. 1999. Trends in Voluntary Association Participation. *Nonprofit and Voluntary Sector Quarterly* 28 (2): 199–212.

Royal Gazette, 4 September 1804.

Ruckinski, T. 2018. Toys 'R' Us Plans to Close All U.S. Stores; 33,000 Jobs at Risk: Source. *Reuters*, March 14. https://www.reuters.com/article/us-toys-r-us-bankruptcy/toys-r-us-plans-to-close-all-u-s-stores-33000-jobs-at-risk-source-idUSKCN1GQ36S

Ruseski, J.E., and K. Maresova. 2014. Economic Freedom, Sport Policy, and Individual Participation in Physical Activity: An International Comparison. *Contemporary Economic Policy* 32 (1): 42–55.

Russell, D.C. 2014. What Virtue Ethics Can Learn from Utilitarianism. In *The Cambridge Companion to Utilitarianism*, ed. B. Eggleston and D.E. Miller, 258–279. Cambridge: Cambridge University Press.

Sappin, E. 2016. 7 Ways Entrepreneurs Drive Economic Development. *Entrepreneur*, October 20. https://www.entrepreneur.com/article/283616

Satz, D. 2010. *Why Some Things Should Not Be for Sale: The Moral Limits of Markets*. Oxford: Oxford University Press.

Schaefer, D.L. 1979. *Justice or Tyranny?: A Critique of John Rawls's a Theory of Justice*. New York: Kennikat Press.

Schaler, J.A., ed. 2009. *Peter Singer Under Fire: The Moral Iconoclast Faces His Critics*. Chicago: Open Court Publishing.

Schmidtz, D. 2000. Islands in a Sea of Obligation: Limits of the Duty to Rescue. *Law and Philosophy* 19 (6): 683–705.

———. 2006. *The Elements of Justice*. Cambridge: Cambridge University Press.

Schumpeter, J.A. 1950. The March into Socialism. *American Economic Review* 40 (2): 446–456.

———. [1911] 1983. *The Theory of Economic Development: An Inquiry into Profits, Capital, Credit, Interest, and the Business Cycle*. New Brunswick: Transaction Publishers.

Schwekendiek, D. 2009. Height and Weight Differences Between North and South Korea. *Journal of Biological Sciences* 41 (1): 51–55.

Schwekendiek, D., and T. Spoorenberg. 2012. Demographic Changes in North Korea: 1993–2008. *Population and Development Review* 38 (1): 133–158.

Scully, G.W. 2002. Economic Freedom, Government Policy and the Trade-Off Between Equity and Economic Growth. *Public Choice* 113 (1–2): 77–96.

Seabright, P. 2004. *Continuous Preferences Can Cause Discontinuous Choices: An Application to the Impact of Incentives on Altruism*. CEPR Discussion Paper, No. 4322.

Sen, A. 1980. Plural Utility. *Proceedings of the Aristotelian Society* 81: 193–215.

———. 1990. Justice: Means Versus Freedoms. *Philosophy & Public Affairs* 19 (2): 111–121.

Shapiro, D. 1995. Why Rawlsian Liberals Should Support Free Market Capitalism. *Journal of Political Philosophy* 3 (1): 58–85.

Singer, P. [1979] 2011. *Practical Ethics*. Cambridge: Cambridge University Press.

Smith, A. [1776] 1981. *An Inquiry into the Nature and Causes of the Wealth of Nations*. Indianapolis: Liberty Fund.

———. [1759] 1982. *The Theory of Moral Sentiments*. Indianapolis: Liberty Fund.

———. [1763] 1982. *Lectures in Jurisprudence*. Indianapolis: Liberty Fund.

Smith, D.J. 2001. *Cultural Autonomy in Estonia. A Relevant Paradigm for the Post-Soviet Era?* One Europe or Several? Working Papers, No. 19, One-Europe Programme.

Stangler, D., and S. Arbesman. 2012. *What Does Fortune 500 Turnover Mean?* Kansas City: Ewing Marion Kauffman Foundation.

Statistica. 2017. *Internet Usage in South Korea—Statistics & Facts*. Hamburg: Statistics.

Stewart, D. [1795] 1829. *The Works of Dugald Stewart. Vol. 7. Account of the Life and Writings of Adam Smith*. Cambridge: Hilliard and Brown.

Storr, V.H. 2004. *Enterprising Slaves & Master Pirates: Understanding Economic Life in the Bahamas*. New York: Peter Lang Publishing.

———. 2008. The Market as a Social Space: On the Meaningful Extraeconomic Conversations that Can Occur in Markets. *The Review of Austrian Economics* 21 (2–3): 135–150.

Stroup, M.D. 2007. Economic Freedom, Democracy, and the Quality of Life. *World Development* 35 (1): 52–66.

Sturm, J.-E., and J. De Haan. 2001. How Robust Is the Relationship Between Economic Freedom and Economic Growth? *Applied Economics* 33 (7): 839–844.

———. 2015. Income Inequality, Capitalism, and Ethno-Linguistic Fractionalization. *American Economic Review* 105 (5): 593–597.

Taagepera, R. 1993. *Estonia: Return to Independence*. Boulder: Westview Press.

Taylor, C. 2015. 70% of Rich Families Lose Their Wealth by the Second Generation. *Reuters*, June 17.

The Economist. 2013. The Examined Life. *The Economist*, May 28. https://www.economist.com/graphic-detail/2013/05/28/the-examined-life

The International Institute for Strategic Studies. 2014. *The Military Balance*. London/New York: Routledge.

The World Bank. 2016. *World Bank Open Data*. https://data.worldbank.org/. Accessed 15 Mar 2016.

———. 2017. *World Development Indicators, GDP Ranking*. Accessed 15 Mar 2017. https://datacatalog.worldbank.org/dataset/gdp-ranking

———. 2019. *Doing Business 2019: Training for Reform*. Washington, DC: The World Bank.

Theisen, W. 2016. Report: North Korea Dictator Kim Jong Unresponsible for 340 Executions While in Power. *Jurist*. https://www.jurist.org/news/2016/12/kim-jong-un-story/

Thiagarajan, K. 2017. The Lives of the Salt Harvesters of Thoothukudi in a Warming World. *The Wire*, August 22. https://thewire.in/environment/salt-pans-thoothukudi-dehydration-groundwater-climate-change

Thomson, J.J. 1976. Killing, Letting Die, and the Trolley Problem. *The Monist* 59 (2): 204–217.

Tomasi, J. 2012. *Free Market Fairness*. Princeton: Princeton University Press.

Trading Economics. 2018. North Korea GDP Annual Growth Rate. https://tradingeconomics.com/north-korea/gdp-annual-growth-rate

Trevelyan, Rose. 2008. Optimism, Overconfidence and Entrepreneurial Activity. *Management Decision* 46 (7): 986–1001.

U.S. *Department of State.* 2017. Prisons in North Korea. https://www.state.gov/documents/organization/273891.pdf

U.S. *Trust.* 2016. 2016 US Trust Insights on Wealth and Worth Survey. http://doingmorethatmatters.com/wp-content/uploads/2016/09/US_Trust-Wealth-and-Worth-Study-2016.pdf

United Nations. *UNData.* http://data.un.org/. Accessed 15 Mar 2017.

United Nations, General Assembly. 2014. *Report of the Commission of Inquiry on Human Rights in the Democratic People's Republic of Korea*, A/HRC/25/63, February 7. Available from https://www.ohchr.org/en/hrbodies/hrc/coidprk/pages/reportofthecommissionofinquirydprk.aspx

Van Praag, C. Mirjam, and P.H. Versloot. 2007. What Is the Value of Entrepreneurship? A Review of Recent Research. *Small Business Economics* 29 (4): 351–382.

Van Stel, A., D.J. Storey, and A.R. Thurik. 2007. The Effect of Business Regulations on Nascent and Young Business Entrepreneurship. *Small Business Economics* 28 (2–3): 171–186.

Webster, A.L. 2013. The Relationship Between Economic Freedom and Income Equality in the United States. *The International Business & Economics Research Journal (Online)* 12 (5): 469–479.

Weil, D.N. 2015. Capital and Wealth in the Twenty-First Century. *American Economic Review* 105 (5): 34–37.

Wilkie, L.A., and P. Farnsworth. 2005. *Sampling Many Pots: An Archaeology of Memory and Tradition at a Bahamian Plantation.* Gainesville: University Press of Florida.

Williams, M. 2016. How the Internet Works in North Korea. *Slate*, November 28. http://www.slate.com/articles/technology/future_tense/2016/11/how_the_internet_works_in_north_korea.html

Williams, C.L., P.A. Giuffre, and K. Dellinger. 1999. Sexuality in the Workplace: Organizational Control, Sexual Harassment and the Pursuit of Pleasure. *Annual Review of Sociology* 25: 73–93.

Wiseman, T. 2017. Economic Freedom and Growth in U.S. State-Level Market Incomes at the Top and Bottom. *Contemporary Economic Policy* 35 (1): 93–112.

World Health Organization. *Global Health Observatory (GHO) Data.* https://www.who.int/gho/database/en/. Accessed 15 Mar 2016.

Wright, M., and D. Urban. 2017. Brutal and Inhumane Laws North Koreans Are Forced to Live Under. *The Telegraph*, September 19. https://www.telegraph.co.uk/news/2017/09/19/brutal-inhumane-laws-north-koreans-forced-live/

Yaish, M., and R. Andersen. 2012. Social Mobility in 20 Modern Societies: The Role of Economic and Political Context. *Social Science Research* 41 (3): 527–538.

Zavella, P. 1985. 'Abnormal Intimacy': The Varying Work Networks of Chicana Cannery Workers. *Feminist Studies* 11 (3): 541–557.

5

Markets Are Moral Spaces

So many of the successful market participants that we encounter in our literary fiction and our news media are entirely motivated by gain and are often calculating and corrupt. Consider, for instance, Antonio and Shylock, the main protagonist and antagonist in Shakespeare's *The Merchant of Venice*. Antonio is a wealthy Venetian merchant. One of his closest friends, Bassanio, is a young nobleman who has squandered his wealth and is deeply in debt (to Antonio and others) but wants to borrow even more money in order to court a wealthy heiress. Unfortunately, Antonio is unable to provide the funds because his money is tied up in investments. "Thou know'st that all my fortunes are at sea. / Neither have I money nor commodity / To raise a present sum," (I.i. 179–181) Antonio reminds Bassanio, but agrees to secure a loan, if Bassanio can find a lender.

Bassanio approaches Shylock, a Jewish moneylender, to borrow the 3000 ducats that he needs,[1] promising to pay it back in three months and naming Antonio as the guarantor. Shylock, however, has a grudge against Antonio because Antonio is a Christian who has railed against Shylock in the marketplace for usury, calling Shylock a "misbeliever, cut-throat dog" (I.iii. 109) and spitting on him. Antonio is also a competitor who brings down the interest rates that Shylock and others can charge by lending money without charging interest. Ultimately, it is actually Shylock's antagonism toward Antonio and not

---

This chapter borrows from Storr (2009), Langrill and Storr (2012), and Choi and Storr (2017).

---

[1] A ducat contains 3.5 grams of gold and would have been worth about $161 in December 2010. As such, 3000 ducats would approximately be worth over $480, 000 today.

© The Author(s) 2019
V. H. Storr, G. S. Choi, *Do Markets Corrupt Our Morals?*,
https://doi.org/10.1007/978-3-030-18416-2_5

the possibility of earning a profit or repairing their relationship that pushes Shylock into making the deal. Rather than charging interest, Shylock tricks Antonio into agreeing to a harsh penalty if he should default.

> Go with me to a notary, seal me there
> Your single bond; and, in a merry sport,
> If you repay me not on such a day,
> In such a place, such sum or sums as are
> Express'd in the condition, let the forfeit
> Be nominated for an equal pound
> Of your fair flesh, to be cut off and taken
> In what part of your body pleaseth me (I.iii. 142–149).

Although Shylock claims that he wants the provision added as a joke ("a merry sport"), in accepting it, Antonio is (likely) agreeing to forfeit his life should he forfeit on the loan. Although Bassanio cautions against making the deal, Antonio is confident that he will avoid that risk because of the returns that he expects from his investments.

But, a ship rich with Antonio's cargo is wrecked at sea and Antonio is unable to repay the debt. Shylock is almost giddy that he will be able to extract his pound of flesh from Antonio. Explaining what use he will make of Antonio's flesh, Shylock exclaims,

> To bait fish withal: if it will feed nothing else,
> it will feed my revenge. He hath disgraced me, and
> hindered me half a million; laughed at my losses,
> mocked at my gains, scorned my nation, thwarted my
> bargains, cooled my friends, heated mine
> enemies; and what's his reason? I am a Jew.
>
> … If a Jew wrong a Christian,
> what is his humility? Revenge. If a Christian
> wrong a Jew, what should his sufferance be by
> Christian example? Why, revenge. The villany you
> teach me, I will execute, and it shall go hard but I
>   will better the instruction (III.i. 49–61).

Antonio has repeatedly wronged Shylock and, in taking his pound of flesh, Shylock will get his revenge. Shylock intends to insist that Antonio pay his bond. And, refuses to listen to the entreaties by Antonio or others. Shylock, in fact, refuses offers that would pay him twice and three times the original loan amount.

In a twist of fate, however, Shylock is frustrated in his attempt to get "justice" from Antonio, who he has taken to court. The judge agrees that Shylock is entitled to his pound of flesh but offers a warning.

> This bond doth give thee here no jot of blood;
> The words expressly are 'a pound of flesh:'
> Take then thy bond, take thou thy pound of flesh;
> But, in the cutting it, if thou dost shed
> One drop of Christian blood, thy lands and goods
> Are, by the laws of Venice, confiscate
> Unto the state of Venice (IV.i. 297–303).

Obviously, there was no way for Shylock to extract the pound of flesh without shedding any of Antonio's blood. Recognizing that he has been tricked, Shylock attempts to accept the offer of three times the principal that he had previously rejected. But, he is rebuffed;

> The Jew shall have all justice; soft! no haste:
> He shall have nothing but the penalty.
> …
> Therefore prepare thee to cut off the flesh.
> Shed thou no blood, nor cut thou less nor more
> But just a pound of flesh: if thou cut'st more
> Or less than a just pound, be it but so much
> As makes it light or heavy in the substance,
> Or the division of the twentieth part
> Of one poor scruple, nay, if the scale do turn
> But in the estimation of a hair,
> Thou diest and all thy goods are confiscate (IV.i. 313–324).

Defeated, Shylock attempts to leave the courtroom but is stopped by the judge;

> Tarry, Jew:
> The law hath yet another hold on you.
> It is enacted in the laws of Venice,
> If it be proved against an alien
> That by direct or indirect attempts
> He seek the life of any citizen,
> The party 'gainst the which he doth contrive
> Shall seize one half his goods; the other half
> Comes to the privy coffer of the state;
> And the offender's life lies in the mercy
> Of the duke only, 'gainst all other voice.

In which predicament, I say, thou stand'st;
For it appears, by manifest proceeding,
That indirectly and directly too
Thou hast contrived against the very life
Of the defendant; and thou hast incurr'd
The danger formerly by me rehearsed.
Down therefore and beg mercy of the duke (IV.i. 338–355).

In an act of "mercy," however, the Duke decides to pardon Shylock's life, but states that he intends to confiscate all of Shylock's wealth, with half going to Antonio and half going to the state as the law demands. Shylock, however, protests that without his money, his life was not worth pardoning; "You take my house when you do take the prop / That doth sustain my house; you take my life / When you do take the means whereby I live" (IV.i. 367–369). Antonio, in a further act of "mercy," agrees to let Shylock keep the half of the money that is owed to him so long as Shylock converts to Christianity and agrees to deed his wealth to his daughter who had eloped with a Christian. Shylock agrees.

The portrayals of merchants and commerce in the Shakespeare's *Merchant of Venice* are problematic.[2] The business people in the *Merchant of Venice* are greedy characters. Shylock will accept nothing less than his pound of flesh. The business people in the *Merchant of Venice* seem to view trade as a zero-sum game, as a contest between hostile others where animosities are played out. Shylock knows that Antonio is in a precarious financial position and enters the arrangement hoping that Antonio will forfeit, hoping to eventually ruin him. "If I can catch him once upon the hip," Shylock says, "I will feed fat the ancient grudge I bear him" (I.iii. 38–39).[3] When Antonio does eventually forfeit,

---

[2] Shakespeare's account of Shylock, for instance, is obviously full of negative ethnic stereotypes. Shakespeare offensively depicted Shylock as the greedy Jew who values his wealth more than his own daughter. Shylock is despised and insulted by his Christian enemies, who repeatedly refer to him as "a kind of devil" (II.ii. 23), "the very devil" (II.ii. 26–27), "the devil ... in the likeness of a Jew" (III.i. 19–20), a "cruel devil" (IV.i. 224), a "damn'd, in execrable dog" (IV.i. 130), and an "inhuman wretch" (IV.i. 4). Throughout the play, Shylock is rarely referred to by name; he is simply the Jew. As literary critic Harold Bloom (1998) wrote, "[o]ne would have to be blind, deaf, and dumb not to recognise that Shakespeare's grand, equivocal comedy *The Merchant of Venice* is nevertheless a profoundly anti-Semitic work." The extent of the anti-Semitism in this play is perhaps best described by the fact that Nazi Germany popularly used *The Merchant of Venice* as propaganda (Gross 1993).

Shakespeare's anti-Semitism was nothing unique in his time. Moneylending was one of the few occupations available to Jews in the European Middle Ages and onward, as Christians were forbidden from practicing usury (Ferguson 2008). Jews were also excluded from other fields of work. Christian kings, for instance, banned Jews from owning farm land. And craft guilds tended to refuse to admit Jews as artisans (Gross 1975).

[3] In many ways, the play is a cautionary tale. "This play helps us understand," Page et al. (2017: 39) wrote, "the ramifications of making business decisions based on self-interest, passion, jealousy, revenge, and greed, and how assessments of risk and return can become distorted." A key question is whether or not this kind of distorted decision-making is typical. It is perhaps telling that a 2016 YouGov poll found that

Shylock stubbornly insists on the most extreme option for satisfying the debt. In fact, Shylock rebuffs an offer to pay him *three* times the principal and demands his pound of flesh. The business people in the *Merchant of Venice* are also imprudent. Already in a risky financial situation, Antonio essentially takes on considerable debt, offering his life as collateral. The business people in the *Merchant of Venice* also seem to worship money. When Shylock's daughter elopes with some of his money, Shylock's lament is, "My daughter! O my ducats! O my daughter!," suggesting that the loss of money is on par with the loss of his child (II.viii. 15).[4] And, when Shylock thinks that his wealth will be confiscated, he argues that "You take my life / When you do take the means whereby I live" (IV.i. 368–369).

Beyond Antonio's rampant anti-Semitism, it is also clear in Shakespeare's account that Antonio views Shylock as a means and not an end. In agreeing to the bond with Shylock, Antonio rejects the possibility that trade can or ought to be an exchange between friends. Antonio urges Shylock to forget about the possibility of friendship between them:

> If thou wilt lend this money, lend it not
> As to thy friends, for when did friendship take
> A breed for barren metal of his friend?
> But lend it rather to thine enemy,
> Who, if he break, thou mayst with better face
> Exact the penalty (I.iii. 130–135).

Antonio lends to his friends without interest, in part, because he views lending with advantage and perhaps all profit-making as taking advantage of the borrower's needy condition. For his part, Shylock agrees that there are limits to the social potential of commerce.

> I will buy with you, sell with you, talk with you,
> walk with you, and so following, but I will not eat
> with you, drink with you, nor pray with you (I.iii. 32–34).

The Merchant of Venice was the fifth most popular Shakespeare play (Dahlgreen 2016). That the *Merchant of Venice* has remained popular for centuries and that the play continues to resonate with audiences and readers may indicate that the play captures something that people believe is true about market activity.

[4] Freedman (2009: 181) explained that,

> [Shylock's] worship of money is the natural result of his social stigmatization. Shylock is far from unfeeling. The moral revealed to Portia's suitor—'all that glitters is not gold'—does not elude him. However, as he clings to money in order to define his sense of self, mercenary damage usurps emotional loss: 'my ducats, my daughter', he wails, more concerned that Jessica has disappeared with his riches than that she has disappeared. Shylock's usury is idolatrous because he can't distinguish money-lending (the sign of his identity) from everything he holds dear (his true identity). He worships his profession with the devotion due to his God and the emotion due to his daughter.

Markets, here, are about taking advantage of others. According to Shylock, any and everything is acceptable in the market, so long as you do not steal from your trading partners; "thrift is blessing, if men steal it not" (I.iii. 88). Markets are not about friendship. Friends give to one another, they do not trade with one another. If friendship is about mutuality, markets are only about gain.

The business people in Anglophone African and Caribbean novels are, similarly, compromised figures. Recall, the central characters in Ngugi's *Devil on the Cross* who we discussed in Chap. 2. Ghanaian author Ayi Kwei Armah ([1968] 1988) tells a similar tale in his novel *The Beautyful Ones Are Not Yet Born*, albeit with a more hopeful ending. This is the story of a man who tries to resist the insidious system of bribes and corruption that exists in his country, only to face ridicule from his compatriots and the disappointed looks of his family members. Set in post-independence Ghana, where the "national game" of theft and bribery is so common "that the point of holding out against it escapes the unsettled mind," Armah's (Ibid.: 109) novel is not only an extraordinary exegesis of the deleterious effects of corruption, but it demonstrates vividly how difficult it is to overcome the cultural and institutional pressures that exist in that system. The government officials accept bribes and the business people offer and pay them. Indeed, to his compatriots, he is either a fool or a coward for taking "refuge in honesty" (Ibid.: 51). Even his wife ridicules him, likening him to the confused chichidodo bird, who "hates excrement with all its soul. But the chichidodo only feeds on maggots, and you know the maggots grow best inside the lavatory" (Ibid.: 45). He wants to eat but does not like how and where the food grows. After all, in Armah's description, in Ghana "everybody prospers from the job he does" (Ibid.: 32); and "the foolish ones are those who cannot live life the way it is lived by all around them, those who will stand by the flowing river and disapprove of the current. There is no other way, and the refusal to take the leap will help absolutely no one at any time" (Ibid.: 108).

Several Anglo-Caribbean cultural texts, similarly, link successful entrepreneurship to theft, corruption, and shady dealings. In Lamming's (1970) *In the Castle of My Skin*, the local businessman is named Mr. Slime. Antiguan novelist Jamaica Kincaid's (1988) *A Small Place* also recounts how commonplace it is for the successful entrepreneurs in Antigua to rely on political connections and corruption. She described how even the wives, girlfriends, and associates of politicians are able to become successful entrepreneurs because they benefit from government contracts and are granted exclusive distribution rights over certain imports.

Similarly, the entertainment industry in the United States tends to present markets and market participants in a negative light. Theberge (1981) reported that the U.S. television industry depicts most business characters as criminals, con artists, or clowns. Similarly, in *Watching America*, Lichter et al. (1991) studied 30 years of television programs and found that the antagonists were twice as likely to be businessmen than any other occupation. Examining the portrayal of business and nonbusiness characters (such as their background character traits and plot functions) in 620 episodes of prime-time fictional television series, Lichter et al. (1997) found that a majority of business characters appearing in U.S. television shows were portrayed negatively whereas over two-thirds of nonbusiness characters were positively portrayed. Moreover, they observed that business characters were more likely to engage in both mildly negative behavior (like foolishness) and genuine wrong-doing (like murder and other violent crimes).[5] While the wealthy were portrayed more negatively than those in lower levels of economic status, Lichter et al. (Ibid.) also noticed that the aversion to business was more pronounced than the aversion to wealth. As they (Ibid.: 79) concluded, "the milieu of business itself is treated as one of greed and corruption." Using textual analysis of 281 plot summaries, Hartman (2006) found that depictions of salespeople and selling behavior in movies between 1993 and 2005 tended to be negative. Similarly, Williams (2004: 61) as well as Boyle and Magor (2008: 126) revealed that the popular comedies and dramas on television often portrayed entrepreneurs as unscrupulous.[6] As Lavoie and Chamlee-Wright (2000: 84) summarized, "the messages conveyed by popular culture do not on the whole support the legitimacy of business, rather the majority of such messages perpetuate negative stereotypical images of the businessperson, and indict market activity as inherently base and sinister." The business people we see on television and in the movies tend to have questionable morals.

There is a sense in which the prevalence of these negative views of markets and successful market participants merely reflects popular sentiment regarding markets and market dealings. There is the possibility, however, that these portrayals are coloring the way that viewers see markets. Regardless, there is reason to believe that the dominant portrayals of markets and market dealings are misleading. For instance, an individual's income and socioeconomic status (occupation and education) are negatively correlated with their involvement in criminal activity, except for self-reported drug use (e.g. Ellis et al. 2009: 32–37).

---

[5] For instance, in recent years, think of the unsavory behavior of various characters in *The Social Network*, *The Wolf of Wall Street*, and *Iron Man* in their pursuit of (greater) wealth. Similarly, the protagonist of *The Greatest Showman*, P.T. Barnum, could be viewed as a variant of Adam Smith's ([1759] 1982) story of the poor man's son.

[6] Boyle and Kelly (2012) argued that the representations of business people have changed with the advent of reality television shows that feature businesses and business people.

Market participants are not the villains that the culture industry pretends. Instead, as Paul Zak (2008: xvii) wrote, "most economic exchange, whether with strangers or known individuals, relies on character values such as honesty, trust, reliability, and fairness."

In reality, markets are moral spaces. They are not exploitive and destructive spaces that breed vice and antisocial sentiments, attitudes, and behavior. In Chap. 4, we argued that people can improve their lives through markets and pointed to the moral implications of the market's ability to facilitate material betterment. In this chapter, we argue that market participants tend to be virtuous, exhibiting the virtue of prudence but other virtues as well. We also argue that markets actually depend on the virtuousness of market participants and could not function well if market participants tended to be immoral.

Yes, Prudence Is a Virtue

Prudence is the use of practical wisdom to guide and govern one's actions. Prudence is distinct from book knowledge and is akin to common sense. It refers to practical knowledge, good judgment, know-how, and acumen. It is the virtue associated with reasoning, planning, deliberating, calculating, analyzing, and thinking creatively; it is "the practical wisdom that keeps ... us from injuring or impoverishing ... others and ourselves" (McCloskey 2003: 259). The prudent person is cold not hot, calculating not impulsive, risk averse not careless, thrifty not prodigal, frugal not wasteful, judicious not rash. The prudent person uses reason and research as they recognize opportunities to improve their situations and as they formulate and follow plans of action in order to achieve their goals. The prudent person is rational.

Prudence is a virtue.[7] Plato ([350 BC] 1997: 1679) defined prudence as "the ability which by itself is productive of human happiness; the knowledge of what is good and bad; the knowledge that produces happiness; the disposition by which we judge what is to be done and what is not to be done." Similarly, Aquinas (ST I-II, q. 61, a. 3.) asserted that "any virtue which causes good in reason's consideration is called prudence." Morality is a "habit of choice," Aquinas (ST I-II, q. 58, a. 1.) stated, "a habit of making us choose well." In order for a choice to be morally good, Aquinas (Ibid.) explained,

---

[7] Aristotle (NE VI.12) distinguished between the prudence as a virtue (*phronesis*) which is a virtue of practical reason and mere prudence or cleverness (*deinotes*). Market participants clearly rely on *deinotes*. Admittedly, it is more controversial to claim that markets rely on and reward *phronesis*. See Yuengert (2012) for a helpful discussion of how an Aristotelian conception of practical wisdom compares with the ways that economics tend to account for prudence.

two things are required. First, one must intend a suitable end, and this comes about through moral virtue, which inclines the appetitive power to a good in accord with reason, that is, to a suitable end. Second, one needs to deal rightly with those things that are for the sake of the end, and this can only come about through reason rightly deliberating, judging, and commanding, which is the function of prudence and the virtues allied with prudence.

In other words, a righteous choice requires a moral purpose and a rational plan of action. In order to determine the "right" purpose and an appropriate plan of action, a person must be prudent.

In many respects, prudence is the most important virtue.[8] It is the virtue that enables us to achieve our goals. A soldier may be heroically courageous. If she is reckless and lacks prudence, however, she is unlikely to successfully defend her nation. An adolescent who seeks adventures may be spirited and ambitious. If he is imprudent, he will not be able to assess the potential dangers that confront him. Justice without prudence can become vengeful. Love without prudence can become oppressive. Selflessness without prudence can become self-destructive. Even if a person possessed all other virtues, "an imprudent person … is a menace to his friends and family, and to his fuller self" (McCloskey 2003: 552). Moral behavior cannot exist without prudence. It is the necessary virtue.

Adam Smith expressed the value of prudence as a virtue.[9] "The care of the health, of the fortune, of the rank and reputation of the individual, the objects upon which his comfort and happiness in this life are supposed principally to depend," as Smith ([1759] 1982: 213) explained, "is considered as the proper business of that virtue which is commonly called Prudence." Prudence secures the material conveniences and resources we require for a good life and helps us to form meaningful connections with our peers within our community in ways that give purpose and add satisfaction to our lives. According to Smith (Ibid.: 189), prudence is composed of two qualities;

first of all, superior reasoning and understanding, by which we are capable of discerning the remote consequences of all our actions and of foreseeing the advantage or detriment which is likely to result from them: and secondly, self-command, by which we are enabled to abstain from present pleasure or to endure present pain, in order to obtain a greater pleasure or to avoid a greater pain in some future time.

---

[8] See Nelson (1992) for an argument in favor of ascribing a central role to prudence in our virtue ethics. See also Russell (2009) for his discussion of *phronesis*.

[9] See Sen (1986), Griswold (1999), Hanley (2009), and Viganò (2017a, b) for a discussion of Smith's treatment of prudence.

Consequently, we need prudence in order to maintain our current states and to save ourselves from anguish. As Smith (Ibid: 213) described,

> Security, therefore, is the first and the principal object of prudence. It is averse to expose our health, our fortune, our rank, or reputation, to any sort of hazard. It is rather cautious than enterprising, and more anxious to preserve the advantages which we already possess, than forward to prompt us to the acquisition of still greater advantages. The methods of improving our fortune, which it principally recommends to us, are those which expose to no loss or hazard; real knowledge and skill in our trade or profession, assiduity and industry in the exercise of it, frugality, and even some degree of parsimony, in all our expences.

Since people have an innate desire to earn the "respect of our equals, our credit and rank in the society we live in," which in turn depends on the "advantages of external fortune" and on "our character and conduct," prudence facilitates our endeavor to behave in ways that makes us truly worthy of the respect we receive (Ibid.: 212–213).

Prudence provides foresight and astuteness in preserving and increasing our material wealth; in fact, *The Wealth of Nations* (Smith [1776] 1981) is an extensive exploration of how prudence can materially improve the lives of individuals and societies. There, he explained how people leverage their comparative advantages and specialize in certain activities in their quest to acquire individual prosperity, and explored how their interactions through a system of mutual interdependence unintentionally promote general societal welfare.

Prudence supports and enhances the other virtues, and it leads people to want to be virtuous. As Smith ([1759] 1982: 216) wrote,

> We talk of the prudence of the great general, of the great statesman, of the great legislator. Prudence is, in all these cases, combined with many greater and more splendid virtues, with valour, with extensive and strong benevolence, with a sacred regard to the rules of justice, and all these supported by a proper degree of self-command. This superior prudence, when carried to the highest degree of perfection, necessarily supposes the art, the talent, and the habit or disposition of acting with most perfect propriety in every possible circumstance and situation. It necessarily supposes the utmost perfection of all the intellectual and of all the moral virtues. It is the best head joined to the best heart. It is the most perfect wisdom combined with the most perfect virtue.

According to Smith (Ibid.: 214), the prudent person "hates the thought of being guilty of any petulance or rudeness" and is "an exact observer of decency, and respects with an almost religious scrupulosity, all the established decorums and ceremonials of society."[10] In her business dealings, she is more likely to rely on her talents and training to succeed than on her connections.[11] Additionally, Smith (Ibid.: 215) wrote,

> He is not a bustler in business where he has no concern; is not a meddler in other people's affairs; is not a professed counselor or adviser, who obtrudes his advice where nobody is asking it. He confines himself, as much as his duty will permit, to his own affairs, and has no taste for that foolish importance which many people wish to derive from appearing to have some influence in the management of those of other people.

Smith ([1759] 1982: 213–216) argued that the prudent person is genuine, simple, modest, guileless, honest, frugal, industrious, far-sighted, dutiful, and averse to conflicts. Smith's image of a prudent person is someone who is admirable and reserved, keeps to himself, has impeccable manners, and never oversteps his boundaries with his peers.

Markets depend on prudence.[12] Moreover, prudence flourishes in the marketplace. Prudent entrepreneurs, for instance, will notice and exploit opportunities to earn a profit by buying a good at a lower price and selling that good at a higher price. That the same good is selling at different prices is an error in need of correction; the price discrepancy means that some producer is selling her wares for too low a price and some consumer is buying the goods he wants at too high a price. Prudent entrepreneurs will be alert to the existence of these errors and will exploit these arbitrage opportunities because of their desire for profits. Prudent entrepreneurs will engage in market research, will formulate and modify their business plans on the basis of sound market data, will search for ways to reduce costs, will invest in research and development, and will reinvest their profits in their enterprises in order to improve their businesses' long-term profitability. Prudent entrepreneurs are mindful of market trends and developments but are not tempted by market fads. On the

---

[10] On the other hand, Smith ([1759] 1982: 216) explained, "When combined with other vices, however, [imprudence] aggravates in the highest degree the infamy and disgrace which would otherwise attend them." "As prudence combined with other virtues, constitutes the noblest; so imprudence combined with other vices, constitutes the vilest of all characters" (Ibid.: 217).

[11] Smith ([1759] 1982: 213) described that "[f]or reputation in his profession he is naturally disposed to rely a good deal upon the solidity of his knowledge and abilities; and he does not always think of cultivating the favour of those little clubs and cabals."

[12] Note that the argument here is not that people in market societies are more reliant on prudence (defined as *deinotes* or *phronesis*) than people in nonmarket societies. Instead, the argument here is simply that prudence is not incompatible with, and in fact is critical to, life in market societies.

other hand, imprudent entrepreneurs will ignore market signals and continue to waste resources in an enterprise that is not profitable. Imprudent entrepreneurs may misinterpret (or, worse, completely ignore) market cues about the relative desirability of their products and risk the livelihoods on which they and their families depend.

Prudence serves as a guiding force in a market setting.[13] Naughton (2017), for instance, argued that practical wisdom is the essential virtue for the successful business leader. Additionally, Oliven and Rietz (2004) concluded that rational traders were the source of market efficiency in competitive markets.[14] Market efficiency, they discovered, relies on market-marking traders (i.e. traders who determine the market price by posting the best bid or ask) who were more rational, less prone to biases, and less likely to make mistakes than average traders. Similarly, Callon and Muniesa (2005) concluded that real markets depend on the existence of calculating agents with calculative capacities who can and do calculate the values and efficiency of tradable goods. And, of course, Mises ([1920] 1935), Hayek (1942), and others have pointed out the critical role that rational economic calculation, that is, the ability to determine the profitability of projects, plays in the market process.

Again, prudence is that virtue that encourages an entrepreneur to spot an opportunity to buy low and sell high, pushes the producer to economize on costs, motivates the inventor to dream up new projects and processes, and prevents the consumer from spending all of his earnings on an impulse. Without prudence, market participants are unlikely to be successful. And, without prudent market participants, markets are unlikely to work well.

Happily, a successful commercial life, because it depends on prudence and because prudence is a virtue, can be a virtuous life. It is also possible to be a market participant and exhibit virtues beyond prudence.

---

[13] Arguably, even those studies that downplay the role of rationality in bringing about market efficiency do so by assuming and enforcing at least a "basic" level of rationality. Becker (1962: 8), for instance, argued that "households may be irrational and yet markets quite rational." Deploying a market experiment where human participants were replaced by zero-intelligence programs subject to a budget constraint, Gode and Sunder (1993) similarly found that markets can function well even when the individual participants are not rational. Stated another way, zero-intelligence traders submitting random bids and offers in a double auction would converge toward the predicted prices and quantities. Markets, it seems, might survive and even achieve allocative efficiency without prudent market participants. But it is important to note that Gode and Sunder imposed a budget constraint (i.e. buyers could not spend more than their budgets and sellers could not accept offers below their costs). As such, these traders could not be completely imprudent. Additionally, while markets can survive imprudent market participants, it is unlikely that imprudent market participants could survive (let alone thrive) in the market. Moreover, while we might achieve allocative efficiency with only minimally prudent market participants, we suspect that the market is unlikely to achieve dynamic efficiency or even productive efficiency if all of the market participants were completely imprudent.

[14] See also Forsythe et al. (1992) and Forsythe et al. (1999).

And, the Bourgeoisie Are Virtuous

In *The Bourgeois Virtues: Ethics for an Age of Commerce* (2006), *Bourgeois Dignity: Why Economics Can't Explain the Modern World* (2010), and *Bourgeois Equality: How Ideas, Not Capital or Institutions, Enriched the World* (2016), Deidre McCloskey chronicled, analyzed, and defended the material and moral benefits of the market system. The Industrial Revolution and the period of income growth that followed, McCloskey noted, elevated both our material wealth and the human spirit. This phenomenal growth in real incomes achieved unprecedented improvements in the quality of life for almost everyone on our planet. Today, for instance, people in market societies no longer experience the economic deprivation, social cleavages, and political inequalities that were commonplace a few hundred years ago. She also argued that markets not only enriched the world materially but also enriched us morally. "The more common claim is that virtues support the market. Yes, I agree," said McCloskey (2006: 4). But, she (Ibid.) added, "the market supports the virtues" and "[c]apitalism … nourishes lives of virtue in the non-self-interested sense, too." "[F]attening up the people, or providing them with inexpensive silk stockings," McCloskey (Ibid.: 23) asserted, "is not the only virtue of our bourgeois life. The triple revolutions of the past two centuries in politics, population, and prosperity are connected. They have had a cause and a consequence … in ethically *better* people. … Capitalism has not corrupted our souls. It has improved them." Not only is it possible to live a virtuous life in market societies, but markets also depend on virtues and actually shape us into better people.

McCloskey argued that the Great Enrichment, the phenomenal and unprecedented economic growth of the past two centuries, was not due to an economic or material factor. Take, for instance, the factors commonly looked at by economic historians. Foreign trade, literacy, coal, steam, property rights, and population growth all did play a role in explaining the trajectory of the Great Enrichment since the eighteenth and nineteenth centuries in northwestern Europe. But, she explained, they could not fully explain the dramatic rise in real incomes. Foreign trade, aside from having been around throughout history, was too small at the time to explain the income growth. Changes in literacy rates as well as the use of coal and steam were responses to changes in demand and, therefore, could not be causes. Property rights and other such institutions existed long before the Industrial Revolution and, in fact, existed in China before Europe. Population growth also occurred in other places and at earlier times. Most critically, other parts of the world were as rich as and even more scientifically sophisticated than Europe prior to the eighteenth century. As such, wealth and scientific advancement cannot be major sources of industrialization. Indeed, capital accumulation was commonplace around the world and too routine to explain the modern world.

Instead, McCloskey argued, a revolution in the rhetoric surrounding commerce and the bourgeoisie caused the Industrial Revolution. The material progress the world has experienced over the last 200 years was caused by a change in the way market life was conceived of and talked about—a transition away from considering commerce as a disrespectable activity to considering it as a legitimate and even moral activity. A change in the "habits of the lip" caused a great shift that gave birth to industrialization (McCloskey 2010: 7). Specifically, McCloskey (Ibid.: 25) argued,

> the historically unique economic growth on the order of a factor of ten or sixteen or higher, and its political and spiritual correlates, depended on ideas more than on economics. The idea of a dignified and free bourgeoisie led to the ideas of the steam engine and mass marketing and democracy.

A rhetorical change, McCloskey explained, changed the world.[15] As she (Ibid.: 7) wrote,

> three centuries ago in places like Holland and England the talk and thought about the middle class began to alter. Ordinary conversations about innovation and markets became more approving. … In northwestern Europe around 1700 the general opinion shifted in favor of the bourgeoisie, and especially in favor of its marketing and innovating. … People stopped sneering at market innovativeness and other bourgeois virtues exercised far from the traditional places of honor in the Basilica of St. Peter or the Palace of Versailles or the gory ground of the First Battle of Breitenfeld.

All of a sudden, or so it seemed, it became dignified to be a merchant. And, this dignity accorded to the bourgeoisie spurred innovation and dramatic economic growth.

For much of history, both sociopolitical elites and the poor sneered at merchants and condemned commerce and the market. It was not unusual for the typical bourgeois to be depicted as a Godless, corrupt individual "to whom going to Hell is equivalent to not making money" (Carlyle [1843] 2014: 361). Market

---

[15] As Martin and Storr (2012: 787–788) wrote, "contrary to much of the literature on the relationship between discourse and social change which tends to focus on discourse as an artifact rather than a driver of change, we argue … that a change in talk not only tends to accompany but often precedes dramatic social transformation."

activity was believed to be morally suspect and certainly was not believed to be admirable. But, a series of happy accidents in the form of the Renaissance, revolts, and revolutions brought about the Bourgeois Revaluation. This was an era which McCloskey identified by a change in rhetoric induced by liberal ideas, "an attitude toward life and society based on tolerance and coexistence, on respect for the rich history and unique experiences of different cultures, and on a firm defense of liberty" (Llosa 2008: 68). This Revaluation in the eighteenth century in northwestern Europe shifted societal perspectives from damning to admiring the bourgeoisie and their activities. The bourgeoisie were, thus, empowered with a new sense of respect for their activities and innovations, which brought about the "gigantic material enrichment of the modern world," and, in turn, permitted "lives of greater spiritual and intellectual scope for the poorest among us" (McCloskey 2010: 86).

McCloskey argued that giving the bourgeoisie liberty (by not overtaxing and overregulating them) and dignity (by honoring their activities) were both necessary conditions for the modern world. But, while both were necessary, the dignity was something entirely new at the time. Admittedly difficult to disentangle, liberty concerns the laws that constrain a merchant's activities while dignity concerns the opinions about merchants held by other members of the society. "Without the liberty to innovate, no amount of new social prestige for the previously scorned bourgeoisie would have done the trick" (Ibid.: 395). The economic transformation that occurred over the last two centuries would not have happened, even if merchants obtained noble and aristocratic statuses in the eighteenth century, had merchants lacked the ability to profit from their business endeavors. At the time, for instance, France required its merchants to apply for permission to open factories and essentially did not give entrepreneurs complete liberty to innovate as occurred in Britain and Holland. This (albeit partial) constraint on innovation meant that France was slower to enjoy the level of material development that Britain and Holland were enjoying during that period. However, "[w]ithout the new dignity for merchants and inventors," McCloskey (Ibid.: 396) explained, "no amount of liberty to innovate would have broken the old cake [of custom], either." Merchants would have been less motivated to engage in the process of innovation if they continued to be treated with disrespect and viewed as dishonorable by other members of society.

The Great Enrichment required granting the bourgeoisie liberty and dignity. As McCloskey argued, however, it is not just that a bourgeois life came to be viewed as dignified. She was not celebrating the widespread adoption of a false consciousness among ordinary people about the nature of life in a commercial society. Instead, she argued, a bourgeois life deserves to be viewed as an ethical life.

McCloskey (2006) explained that capitalism requires and nurtures a virtuous life. As McCloskey (Ibid.: 28–29) elaborated,

> The richer, more urban, more bourgeois people, one person averaged with another, … have larger, not smaller, spiritual lives than their impoverished ancestors of the pastoral. They have more, not fewer, real friends than their great-great-great-great grandparents in "closed-corporate" villages. They have broader, not narrower, choices of identity than the one imposed on them by the country, custom, language, and religion of their birth. They have deeper, not shallower, contacts with the transcendent of art or science or God, and sometimes even of nature, than the superstitious peasants and haunted hunter-gatherers from whom we all descend. They are better humans – because they in their billions have acquired the scope to become so and because market societies encourage art and science and religion to flourish and because anyway a life in careers and deal making and companies and marketplaces is not the worst life for a full human being.

On net, McCloskey claimed, markets not only make us materially better off, they also make us morally better off.

A virtue is "a habit of the heart, stable disposition, a settled state of character, a durable, educated characteristic of someone to exercise her will to be good" (Ibid.: 64). McCloskey argued that successful markets depend on seven virtues: the four classical virtues—courage, justice, temperance, and, of course, prudence—and the three Christian virtues—hope, faith, and love. Collectively, she (Ibid.: 508) referred to these virtues as the bourgeois virtues, "the seven virtues exercised in a commercial society. They are not hypothetical. For centuries … in a widening array of places … we have practiced them. … It is the way we live now, mainly, at work, on our good days, and the way we should, Mondays through Fridays." Obviously, bourgeois virtues are quite distinct from the martial virtues. But, these are the virtues that are given life in market societies.

Prudence as "good judgment" or "practical wisdom" is, as we already discussed, the dominant bourgeois virtue. Again, prudence is that virtue that encourages the entrepreneur to spot an opportunity to buy low and sell high, that pushes the producer to economize on costs, and that drives the inventor to dream up new projects and processes that she expects to be profitable. Admittedly, prudence alone and unbalanced by any other virtues is not sufficient to guarantee that an individual will behave morally. A prudent social entrepreneur, for instance, may discover and pursue efficient strategies for serving others. A prudent thief, similarly, may adopt strategies that allow her to escape detection. If prudence alone governed the behavior of individuals in a marketplace, distrust, fraud, defection, cheap talk, and other such undesirable activities might be prevalent, just as market critics feared. Happily, other virtues balance prudence in bourgeois life.

McCloskey identified love as a key motivating factor in market activity in explaining how market life is good for everyone. One of the common charges against markets is that they undermine social relationships and social solidarity (e.g. Putnam 2000). From a narrowly economic viewpoint, love is meaningless and only economically disadvantages those that feel it. For McCloskey, however, love drives much of what occurs in markets. It is what inspires the entrepreneur to attempt to acquire a fortune and the worker to show up to work every day to support their families and so that their children's futures could be secure. According to McCloskey (2006: 56–57), "[o]ver half of consumer purchases at point of sale are on behalf of children and husbands and mothers and friends. Love runs consumption."

Love also extends to disinterested solidarity with others. For example, McCloskey (2006) suggested that foreign trade expansion would not have occurred in seventeenth century Europe without love. Love encouraged people to stop being calculating, to extend their trust beyond in-group members (defined by blood relation and religion), and to engage in commercial speech (i.e. to exchange market information and to reveal and discover reputations). In doing so, merchants learned to treat strangers as honorary friends and to develop, maintain, and deepen market relationships. McCloskey strongly believed that the market system permitted us to gain stronger social ties in the market compared to the past or to any other economic system. As she (Ibid.: 138) wrote,

> it's not the case that market capitalism requires or generates loveless people. More like the contrary. Markets and even the much-maligned corporations encourage friendships wider and deeper than the atomism of a full-blown socialist regime or the claustrophobic, murderous atmosphere of a 'traditional' village. Modern capitalist life is love-saturated. Olden life was not loving; communitarian life was not; and actually existing socialist life decidedly was not.

Recall, as we argued in Chap. 4, people in market societies tend to be better connected than people in nonmarket societies. The market does not undermine but instead supports social relationships. Moreover, as Solomon (1992: 104) discussed, we socialize with our colleagues and are delighted to see our colleagues despite the dullness and stress of the work. Indeed, as Storr (2008) argued, the market is a social space where meaningful social bonds can and do develop.

There are other bourgeois virtues that guide market participants and govern market interactions. Faith is a backward-looking virtue that requires a person to adhere to her commitments and duties in the face of temptations and to believe that things will ultimately work out. Faith is what drives investors to continue to support a proven company going through a difficult period and encourages an inventor to continue to pursue a project despite obstacles. Not only can friendships be forged in contractual situations where loyalties coexist with explicit rewards, faith can also strengthen the social bonds between market associates. For example, bonds between market relations who are also friends do not disintegrate at the first sign of financial or other difficulties. Hope, unlike faith, is a forward-looking virtue. Hope is what drives investors to support an unproven venture and what encourages inventors to attempt something they have never attempted before. It is clear that if markets are to thrive, they require actors who have both faith and hope. Of course, unbalanced by prudence, faith and hope are recipes for (financial) ruin. Aided by prudence, however, faith and hope are essential virtues in the marketplace.

Succeeding in markets also requires courage. Entrepreneurs need courage if they are to create and/or discover and exploit profit opportunities in a world where knowledge is necessarily dispersed, and the future is unknown and unknowable. Entrepreneurs, to be successful, must have courage in order to deal with the multiperiod, multicommodity market process where not only ignorance but also uncertainty is endemic. It is needed when negotiating a difficult deal and when borrowing a large sum of money to support a risky venture or when introducing an innovative product. If everyone were paralyzed by the ignorance and uncertainty that characterizes the real world, then social and economic progress would not occur. As Israel Kirzner (1999: 12) agreed, "[e]ntrepreneurial alertness, in this essentially uncertain, open-ended, multi-period world must unavoidably express itself in the qualities of boldness, self-confidence, creativity and innovative ability."[16] Acting entrepreneurially in an uncertain world requires courage.

---

[16] Similarly, Joseph Schumpeter explained that the successful entrepreneur is likely to be intuitive and a leader. According to Schumpeter ([1911] 1983: 85),

> Carrying out a new plan and acting according to a customary one are things as different as making a road and walking along it. ... [I]n economic life action must be taken without working out all the details of what is to be done. Here the success of everything depends upon intuition, the capacity of seeing things in a way which afterwards proves to be true, even though it cannot be established at the moment, and of grasping the essential fact, discarding the unessential, even though one can give no account of the principles by which this is done.

Success also depends on the entrepreneur leading "the means of production into new channels" (Ibid.: 89). "Economic leadership," Schumpeter (Ibid.: 88) explained, "must hence be distinguished from 'invention.' As long as they are not carried into practice, inventions are economically irrelevant."

Temperance is the management of self and a balance of passions, whereas justice is the management of society and a balance of citizens (McCloskey 2006: 286). If markets are to flourish, market actors need to control their own passions and respect and enforce the rules; both internal and external constraints matter.

McCloskey argued that this *system of virtues* is in operation in market societies. In order to function properly, markets need virtues in addition to prudence and people who act consistently with these moral principles. This is not to deny that there are bourgeois vices. Of course, vice exists and is almost always present in almost all people at almost all times in market societies.[17] However, a system of virtues guides the interactions between people in the market.[18] When working in conjunction with one another, the bourgeois virtues can and do characterize life in market society. Ultimately, the people who populate the marketplace are also the people who populate our societies. If the market participants were truly unfettered by a system of virtues, it would be hard to imagine that their nonmarket lives could be moral. If we truly believe that virtuous people inhabit our society, we must believe that the virtuous people also inhabit our markets as well. The market, then, should be conceived of as a moral space that depends on virtue and where people *are* virtuous.

In Addition to the Seven Virtues

In addition to exhibiting the seven bourgeois virtues, people in market societies will tend to be more altruistic, are less likely to be materialistic and corrupt, and are more likely to be cosmopolitan as well as trusting and trustworthy.

---

[17] Additionally, the bourgeois virtues are not always balanced in all people at all times in commercial society. For instance, greed is a vice that develops when prudence alone is not checked by or balanced with other virtues. Selfish individuals may succeed on some margins in the market, but will suffer from missed profit opportunities and lead unfulfilling lives. An interesting example of missed profit opportunities is discussed by Ingram and Roberts (2000) who showed that hotel managers could incur losses by not being friends with their competitors. Love alone could lead to the vice of lust, but alloyed with prudence evokes trust and reciprocity. Hope unrestrained by other virtues transforms a principled business person into a common street thug. A man with courage, without restraint of other virtues, is too easily swayed by pride, envy, and greed. Justice, alone, can morph into anger but produces the bourgeois virtue of honesty when combined with faith and courage.

[18] Again, we are not claiming here that undesirable behavior and vices never occur in a market setting. There are countless instances where promises of higher quality goods and services are unfulfilled and where cheating and fraud happen. But, it is important to remember that the market, just like the community, is a space where people interact with one another (Storr 2008). As such, as spaces of social interactions, people can and do behave and treat each other poorly in both the market and the community; morally corrupt behavior and principles are not uniquely linked to the market.

More Altruistic

Among the high- and ultra-high-net-worth adults in the United States, civic duty and a responsibility to help others were among the highly valued traits encouraged within their families when growing up (U.S. Trust 2016). According to a survey of high- and ultra-high-net-worth Americans by U.S. Trust (Ibid.: 37),

> finding solutions to tough problems in the world, giving back to others less financially fortunate, fueling growth in the economy – making a positive impact – is a core value among wealthy individuals and families. They look for opportunities to make a meaningful difference and do so with intent in all areas of their lives – at home, work and in the community.

The wealthy, U.S. Trust (Ibid.) reported, feel they can make the greatest contribution through giving financially to nonprofit organizations (74%), followed by volunteering (61%), and serving on a board or committee of a nonprofit organization (47%). They care about a variety of social and environmental issues; the issues that matter most to the wealthy include environmental protection and sustainability, healthcare quality and access, access to education, children and youth development, elder care, protection and well-being, social mobility and advancement, and empowerment of women. Additionally, 58% of the respondents agree that social and environmental impact of the companies in which they invest is important for their investment decisions and would rather invest in companies that have a positive social impact.[19]

Indeed, some of the wealthiest members of market societies in recent history have also been philanthropists. For instance, Andrew Carnegie, a business magnate and one of the richest men of all time, devoted his retirement to philanthropy (Davidson 2015). In "The Gospel of Wealth," Carnegie ([1889] 2006) discussed the moral responsibility of philanthropy of the rich and proposed that the thoughtful and prudent use of surplus wealth by the rich could alleviate wealth inequality. He concentrated his philanthropic efforts on education and world peace, and ultimately gave away $350 million—almost 90% of his fortune—during his lifetime (Usbourne 2015). Inspired by Carnegie, John D. Rockefeller donated more than $530 million

---

[19] Interestingly, the U.S. Trust (2016) study proposed that the wealthy might also be a mechanism through which our culture could be preserved because the wealthy view fine art as a profitable investment strategy. Twenty-two percent of the respondents collect fine art, over half of whom believe that fine art is an asset that will maintain (if not increase) its value over time.

(in 1937 U.S. dollars) to various philanthropic causes during his lifetime (The New York Times 1937). Similarly, under the direction of Bill and Melinda Gates and Warren Buffet, the Bill and Melinda Gates Foundation works to improve healthcare and reduce extreme poverty around the world and to expand educational opportunities in the United States (Bill and Melinda Gates Foundation 2018). As of 2017, the foundation had disbursed a total of $45.5 billion in grant payments since its inception (Ibid.). With the birth of their daughter in 2015, Mark Zuckerberg and his wife, Priscilla Chan, pledged to donate 99% of their wealth over their lifetimes (a lifetime donation worth over $44 billion in 2015) through the Chan Zuckerberg Initiative (Usbourne 2015). George Soros, likewise, has donated the majority of his wealth to his charity, Open Society Foundations (Higgins 2017). Chow Yun-Fat, a renowned Hong Kong actor who shared 24th place in Forbes' list of highest paid actors in the world with Russell Crow in 2015 and who is reportedly worth $715 million, vowed to donate his entire fortune to charity after his death (*Al Jazeera* 2018; The Straits Times 2018).

Additionally, the success of today's corporations depends in part on whether or not they adopt business practices and initiatives that are socially responsible. For instance, Starbucks takes a comprehensive approach to ethical sourcing with their Coffee and Farmer Equity (C.A.F.E.) Practices standard, and Toms Shoes engages in charity work where the company donates a pair of shoes to children for each pair sold. Many companies also offer their employees incentives to donate and volunteer. Double the Donation, a firm that consults with nonprofits and companies regarding matching gift programs, reported that 65% of the Fortune 500 companies match employee donations (Scott 2015).

Consumers are also often willing to pay a premium to deal with businesses that they believe to be ethical and refuse to return to establishments that have violated certain moral principles. When issues do occur, firms do their best to make amends. For example, IHOP's president, Darren Rebelez, publicly apologized after an incident in one of their restaurants in Maine, stating that IHOP and its franchises have "zero tolerance for actions that are or allude to discrimination of any type" (Rebelez quoted in Bates 2018). Starbucks closed 8000 stores for racial bias training after an incident in Philadelphia (Abrams 2018). Dairy Queen ended its franchise agreement with a store in Illinois after its owner hurled racial slurs at one of his customers (Abderholden 2017). Likewise, the National Basketball Association banned former Clippers owner, Donald Sterling, for life after he was recorded making racially charged remarks (Boren 2014). Multiple companies stopped advertising on Laura Ingraham's news show after she mocked a school-shooting survivor on Twitter

(Shugerman 2018). And, ABC canceled Roseanne Barr's widely successful show hours after her tweets suggested racial bias (Koblin 2018). Successful businesses not only show they have genuine ethical and social concerns, they also stand by their ethical and social views. Indeed, some companies use commercial advertisement as platforms to convey to their customers their stances on certain social issues, including racial injustice (e.g. Nike's advertisement with Colin Kaepernick) and toxic masculinity and female empowerment (e.g. Proctor & Gamble's Gillette advertisement).[20]

People in market societies are also more charitable than people in nonmarket societies. Using data gathered by Gallup on whether or not subjects volunteered, donated money, or helped a stranger in the past month, the World Giving Index by the Charities Aid Foundation (CAF) ranks 139 countries on the basis of their generosity. Although nonmarket societies like Myanmar, Indonesia, and Kenya are among the most charitable, the majority of the most generous countries in the world are market societies (Table 5.1). While six of the top ten most charitable countries are market societies, all ten countries in the bottom ten are nonmarket societies. Moreover, citizens of market societies donate more often than citizens of nonmarket societies (Fig. 5.1). According to a CAF survey (CAF 2016), on average, almost half of the respondents in market societies self-reported making a donation in the past month, while close to a quarter of the respondents in nonmarket societies self-reported doing so.[21] Furthermore, people in market societies seem to donate more than people in nonmarket societies (Table 5.2). While we cannot extrapolate so heavily from a sample of 23 countries, it hints at a possible relationship between (the size of) charitable giving and market societies.

Combined, these results suggest that there are more altruistic people in market societies than in nonmarket societies and that people in market societies are more altruistic than people in nonmarket societies.

---

[20] The Nike advertisement with Colin Kaepernick and Proctor & Gamble's Gillette advertisement were not without controversy (e.g. Abad-Santos 2018; Hsu 2019; Murphy 2019; Scott 2018; Tiffany 2019; Wang and Siegel 2018). We should clarify that we do not mention these advertisements here to add to the debates and conversations fueled by the advertisements. Instead, we mention these advertisements here to merely communicate that companies do sometimes publicly take stances on social issues, occasionally with some risk.

[21] Interestingly, CAF 2017 World Giving Index also reveals that citizens of market and nonmarket societies help strangers at roughly the same frequency; on average, 51.2% of the respondents in market societies self-reported having helped a stranger in the past month while 49% of the respondents in nonmarket societies self-reported doing so. In short, people in market and nonmarket societies apparently help strangers equally, but people in market societies appear to donate more money and more frequently than people in nonmarket societies. One possible reason for this phenomenon is that those living in market societies have more disposable income than those in nonmarket societies and can afford to donate more.

Table 5.1 Top 10 and bottom 10 countries on the 2017 World Giving Index

Ranking	Country	Market society?
1	Myanmar	No
2	Indonesia	No
3	Kenya	No
4	New Zealand	Yes
5	United States	Yes
6	Australia	Yes
7	Canada	Yes
8	Ireland	Yes
9	United Arab Emirates	No
10	The Netherlands	Yes
Ranking	Country	Market society?
130	Mauritania	No
131	Latvia	No
132	Serbia	No
133	Madagascar	No
134	Cambodia	No
135	Georgia	No
136	Morocco	No
137	Lithuania	No
138	China	No
139	Yemen	No

(Data Source: CAF World Giving Index 2017)

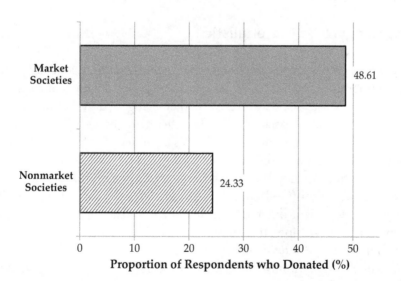

Fig. 5.1 More people in market societies donate to charity. (Data Source: CAF World Giving Index 2017)

Table 5.2 Charitable giving by individuals in 2016

Market society?	Country	Charitable giving by individuals (% of GDP)
Yes	United States	1.44
Yes	New Zealand	0.79
Yes	Canada	0.77
Yes	United Kingdom	0.54
Yes	South Korea	0.5
Yes	Singapore	0.39
No	India	0.37
No	Russia	0.34
No	Italy	0.3
Yes	The Netherlands	0.3
Yes	Australia	0.23
Yes	Ireland	0.22
Yes	Germany	0.17
Yes	Sweden	0.16
Yes	Austria	0.14
Yes	Finland	0.13
Yes	Japan	0.12
Yes	Norway	0.11
Yes	Switzerland	0.09
No	Spain	0.05
No	Czech Republic	0.04
No	China	0.03
No	Mexico	0.03

(Data Source: CAF 2016)

Less Likely to Be Materialistic

People in market societies are less likely to view being rich and successful as being important (Fig. 5.2). On average, 12.11% and 29.45% of the respondents from market societies expressed that being rich and successful were important to them, respectively. On the other hand, on average, 27.29% and 67.91% of those from nonmarket societies expressed that being rich and successful was important to them, respectively.

Neither affluence nor Westernness seems to explain cross-country differences in materialism (Güliz and Belk 1996). Attitudes towards competition, however, may explain differences in materialism. The more someone favors (economic) competition, the more they may be concerned with (material) gain. But, people who reside in nonmarket societies are just as likely to regard (economic) competition to be beneficial to society as people living in market societies (Fig. 5.3). Roughly the same proportion of people regard competition to be beneficial in both market and nonmarket societies. In fact, slightly more people in nonmarket societies (52.35%) hold this opinion than people in market societies (49.42%). However, people in nonmarket societies are

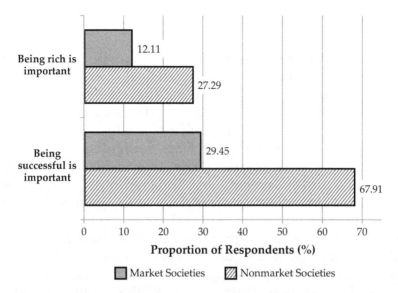

Fig. 5.2 Less people in market societies are materialistic. (Data source: *World Values Survey* database)

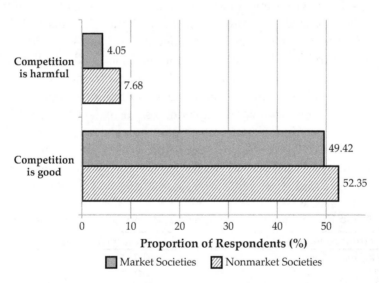

Fig. 5.3 Less people in market societies have a critical view of competition. (Data source: *World Values Survey* database)

almost twice as likely to view competition as harmful to society: 7.68% of the respondents from nonmarket societies expressed that competition is harmful, and 4.05% of the respondents from market societies expressed so.

The evidence (weakly) suggests that people in market societies are less likely to be materialistic than people in nonmarket societies (see Teague et al. 2018).

Less Likely to Be Corrupt

There is also less public corruption in market societies. The Corruption Perception Index (CPI) annually rates 183 countries "according to [the] perceived levels of public-sector corruption" and "draws on different assessments and business opinion surveys" (Transparency International 2011: 3). The index includes topics such as "bribery of public officials, kickbacks in public procurement, embezzlement of public funds, and questions that probe the strength and effectiveness of public-sector anti-corruption efforts" (Ibid.). Each country is rated on a scale of 0 (highly corrupt) to 10 (very clean). All of the top ten least corrupt countries are market societies, and all of the ten most corrupt countries are nonmarket societies (Table 5.3).

Indeed, market societies suffer from less corruption than nonmarket societies (Fig. 5.4). Multiple studies found a negative relationship between economic freedom and corruption (e.g. Chafuen and Guzmàn 2000; Paldam 2002; Graeff and Mehlkop 2003; Shen and Williamson 2005; Carden and Verdon 2010). Shen and Williamson (2005: 340) found that "a very open economy – free of government restrictions [i.e. economically free countries] – is generally associated with lower levels of corruption." Similarly, Goel and Nelson's (2005) analysis revealed that economic freedom was more effective than political freedom in curbing corruption. Graeff and Mehlkop (2003) observed differing patterns of influence of economic freedom on corruption between countries of different income strata, but found that markets consistently improve corruption across all countries. "If market forces are used to allocate capital instead of political or governmental considerations," they (Ibid.: 611) stated, "corruption decreases. This result is valid both for rich and for poor countries." While careful to mention that corruption is pervasive across both developed and developing countries, Shleifer and Vishny (1993: 611)

Table 5.3 Top 10 and bottom 10 countries on 2011 Corruption Perceptions Index

Most corrupt countries		Least corrupt countries	
North Korea	1	New Zealand	9.5
Somalia	1	Denmark	9.4
Afghanistan	1.5	Finland	9.4
Myanmar	1.5	Sweden	9.3
Sudan	1.6	Singapore	9.2
Turkmenistan	1.6	Norway	9
Uzbekistan	1.6	Netherlands	8.9
Haiti	1.8	Australia	8.8
Iraq	1.8	Switzerland	8.8
Venezuela	1.9	Canada	8.7

(Data source: *Transparency International*'s 2011 Corruption Perception Index)

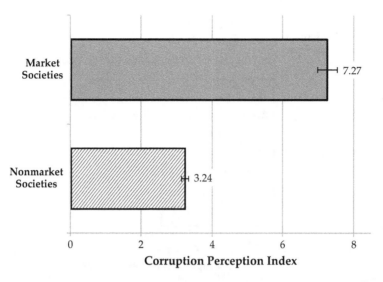

Fig. 5.4 Market societies are less corrupt. The error bars represent standard errors. (Data source: *Transparency International's* 2011 Corruption Perception Index)

wrote how "corruption is bad for development" and frequently used nonmarket societies in Africa, Asia, and Eastern Europe as illustrations.

A possible explanation for why corruption is more pervasive in nonmarket societies could be how the public views briberies and similar activities in these countries. More specifically, it could be the case that government officials in market societies are just as inclined to accept bribes as those in nonmarket societies, but that residents in market societies are more likely to be morally against providing bribes than residents in nonmarket societies. Figure 5.5 provides weak, but suggestive, evidence.[22]

Compared to market societies, more than twice the number of people in nonmarket societies than in market societies expressed that avoiding paying the fare on public transport (6.69% vs. 3.15%) and cheating on taxes (5.71% vs. 2.35%) can be justified. Stealing property and accepting bribes in the course of one's duties are also more accepted by those in nonmarket societies (2.45% and 2.93%) than by those in market societies (1.68% and 1.4%).

Market societies are less corrupt than nonmarket societies. Moreover, people in market societies are less likely to be corrupt and are less likely to be accepting of corruption than people in nonmarket societies.

---

[22] We want to note that, fortunately, the majority of the residents in both market and nonmarket societies view avoiding fares on public transport, stealing, cheating on taxes, and bribery as unjustifiable actions.

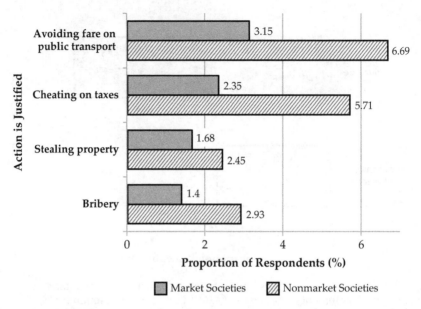

Fig. 5.5 Less people in market societies think unethical actions are justifiable. (Data source: *World Values Survey* database)

More Likely to Be Cosmopolitan

People in market societies are also more likely to be tolerant of differences than people in nonmarket societies. Gary Becker, in *The Economics of Discrimination* ([1957] 1971), explained why there tends to be less discrimination in market settings over time.[23] The existence of employers with a taste for discrimination will mean that members of a racially oppressed group will tend to have lower wages on average than their counterparts from nonoppressed groups. So, for instance, in the United States of the 1950s, the existence of white employers with a disinclination to hire blacks resulted in the wages paid to black workers being lower than the wages paid to whites. In a market system, racist employers likely have to pay a premium to indulge their prejudices against blacks and employers who do not have a taste for discrimination have an incentive to hire the lower paid black workers. Because markets

---

[23] See Arrow (1972) for a modification and extension of Becker's model. See also Marshall (1974) for a survey of the literature on the economics of racial discrimination and a critique of Becker's model of discrimination. Ikeda (2018) offered a useful extension to Becker's model noting that markets not only mean that individuals pay a price for discrimination, but also empowers entrepreneurs to discover past errors that they and others have made, including errors in assessing the productivity of different racial groups.

force market participants to pay for their taste for discrimination, over time, market forces will tend to close the wage gap between blacks and whites as racist employers who refuse to hire blacks are undercut by nonracist employers who do hire blacks. Becker's model of racial discrimination in a market setting relies on self-interest to counter immoral practices.[24]

While Becker focused his efforts in analyzing racial discrimination in a market setting, his framework can be equally applicable to various types of discrimination. The same market mechanisms can, over time, minimize discrimination based on sex, ethnicity, sexual orientation, and other characteristics. They could also curb positive discrimination like nepotism. It remains an open question whether or not Becker's observation of the market's power to suppress repugnant conduct over time through competition also means that the market can lead to genuine changes in people's attitudes, preferences, and behavior for the better.

People who live in markets societies, however, are significantly less likely to be prejudiced than those who live in nonmarket societies (Fig. 5.6). One of the survey questions in the World Values Survey (WVS) asked respondents about who they would not like to have as neighbors. On average, significantly less people in market societies than nonmarket societies mentioned that they would not want as neighbors: people of different races (12.33% vs. 20.69%), homosexuals (32.41% vs. 55.71%), people of different religions (11.35% vs. 22.18%), cohabitating unmarried couples (14.84% vs. 30.46%), and people who spoke a different language (12.24% vs. 17.63%).[25] People in market societies appear to be more accepting of people of diverse backgrounds and characteristics than people in nonmarket societies. Interestingly, while Berggren and Nilsson (2013) did not find a relationship between economic freedom and tolerance toward people of different races, they found a positive relationship between economic freedom and tolerance toward homosexuals.

---

[24] Despite his clear predications about the connection between discrimination and wages, Becker's (1957) model remained empirically untested for decades (to the best of our knowledge). Charles and Guryan (2008) speculated that Arrow (1972) may have contributed to this occurrence. Arrow (Ibid.: 192) criticized that Becker's model of discrimination "predicts the absence of the phenomenon it was designed to explain" because it states that prejudiced employers would ultimately be driven out of the market for sacrificing profits in exchange for indulging their prejudiced preferences. Charles and Guryan (2007, 2008) do attempt to empirically examine Becker's model. Charles and Guryan (2007) demonstrated that racial discrimination and its resultant wage gap could survive perfect competition scenarios; in other words, even if the market drove out racist employers, the prejudiced tastes and the resultant wage gap can persist so long as racist employers can transfer their tastes into their new market role as employees. Charles and Guryan (2008), however, tested and confirmed Becker's key predictions about the relationship between prejudice and wages.

[25] While statistically no different, on average, less people in market societies also mentioned that they would not want to have foreign workers as neighbors (20.26%) than those in nonmarket societies (24.55%).

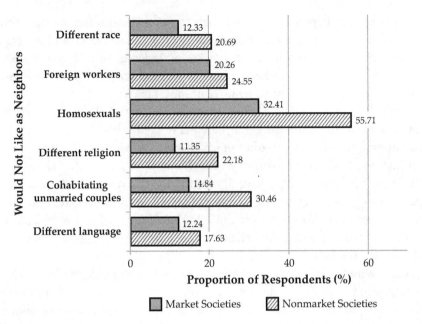

Fig. 5.6 Market societies are less prejudiced. (Data source: *World Values Survey* database)

Women in market societies voluntarily participate in the labor market more, face less discrimination, and enjoy more freedom than their counterparts in nonmarket societies. Fike (2018), for instance, found that women in economically free countries are nearly twice as likely to (voluntarily) participate in the labor market, three times less likely to have vulnerable occupations, and three times more likely to have a bank account. Also, the share of women in a country who earned wages is more than three time higher in countries with high levels of economic freedom than in countries with low levels of economic freedom. Studies by Neumayer and De Soysa (2007, 2011) and Stroup (2008, 2011) have pointed to how economic freedom and openness to trade have improved gender equality. Most notably, Neumayer and De Soysa (2011) observed that increased trade openness has improved women's social rights, such as their right to initiate a divorce, the right to an education, freedom from forced sterilization, and freedom from female genital mutilation without consent.

People in market societies are also more likely to hold profemale views than people in nonmarket societies (Fig. 5.7). As demonstrated in Fig. 5.7, people who live in market societies are more likely to disagree that a university education is more important for boys than girls. Less people from market

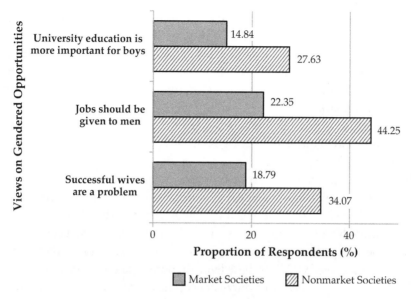

Fig. 5.7 More people in market societies hold pro-female oriented views. (Data source: *World Values Survey* database)

societies agreed that a university education is more important for boys compared to those from nonmarket societies (14.84% and 27.63%). Similarly, approximately a fifth of the respondents from market societies agreed that a man should have more rights to a job than a woman when jobs are scarce (22.35%), and less than a fifth agreed that it is problematic if a woman earned more income than her husband (18.79%). On the other hand, more than 40% of the respondents from nonmarket societies agreed men should have more rights over jobs than women (44.25%), and over a third agreed that successful wives are problematic (34.07%).[26]

In addition, women residing in market societies tend to have rights to travel domestically and internationally and tend to have equal legal rights to inheritance and parental rights (i.e. legal guardianship of a child during a marriage and custodial rights over a child after divorce as a woman). Human Freedom Index (HFI) is a numerical snapshot of the state of human freedom

---

[26] This is interestingly contrasted by views on the importance of equal gender rights for a democracy. Seventy-three percent of the respondents from market societies and 72.8% of those from nonmarket societies agreed that women having equal rights as men is an essential characteristic of a democracy (see Appendix for the definition of the variable and how we calculated our statistics). While equal gender political rights are just as important for those living in nonmarket societies as it is for those living in market societies, it appears as if people living in nonmarket societies do not believe women deserve the same access to economic opportunities, nor economic success, as men.

within a country and measures personal, economic, and civil freedom (Vásquez and Porcnik 2015). For instance, according to 2011 HFI (Ibid.: 62), the market society of Sweden scored the maximum score of 10 in Personal Freedom Index categories pertaining to women,[27] implying that Swedish women have equal rights to inheritance and parental rights, and can freely travel. Women in many nonmarket societies have unfavorable rights to inheritance and parental rights, as well as merely moderate mobility rights. Also, same-sex relationships have complete legal rights in Sweden. Again, this is not the case in many nonmarket societies.

Importantly, children and women appear to have more security in market societies. Corporal punishment of children and domestic violence against women are less likely to be accepted in market societies (Fig. 5.8). On average, 8.8% of those living in nonmarket societies find the act of parents beating children to be acceptable, while only 4.74% of those living in market societies do. And, on average, 3.93% of those living in nonmarket societies find domestic violence to be acceptable, while only 1.9% of those living in market societies do.

Furthermore, individuals residing in market societies are more likely to be open toward religious, sexual, and cultural differences. In fact, respondents from market societies are more likely to be accepting of homosexuality (Fig. 5.9).

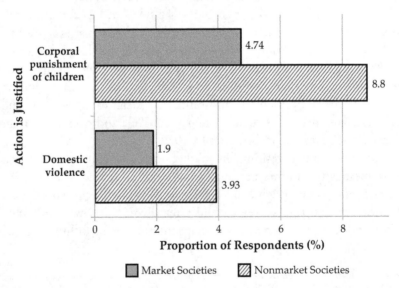

Fig. 5.8 Less people in market societies are accepting of violence. (Data source: *World Values Survey* database)

---

[27] More specifically, Sweden scored the maximum score in Personal Freedom Index categories of Women's Security and Safety—Equal Inheritance Rights, Women's Freedom of Movement, and Women's Parental Rights.

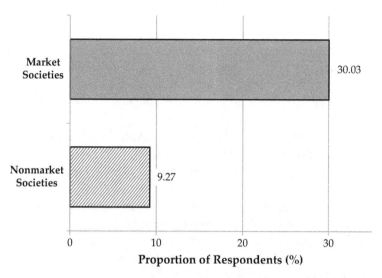

Fig. 5.9 More people in market societies are accepting of homosexuality. (Data source: *World Values Survey* database)

People living in market societies are less likely to be prejudiced and more likely to be tolerant of differences than people living in nonmarket societies.

More Trusting

The relationship between trust and economic development is well established. Trust has been shown to be a key ingredient of almost all social interactions including our interactions in the market (Misztal 1996). While proper contracting and the enforcement of contracts may seem to be alternatives to relying on the parties to a contract acting trustworthily, writing contracts that provide adequate protection when parties are likely to be dishonest is very costly. As John Mueller (1999: 23) pointed out, "it is impossible, or nearly so, to create a perfect written contract … in its day to day dealings, business requires, and inspires, integrity, honesty, trustworthiness, and reliability in order to achieve its vaunted efficiency and growth." Ensuring that there is little or no room for the parties to a contract to engage in bad faith without facing some penalty requires that one meticulously works through the details of those contracts. Additionally, contracting parties in a low-trust environment must frequently rely on an outside enforcer who, in a low-trust environment, is also unlikely to be trusted by contractors. As Fukuyama (1995: 26) similarly argued,

> while contract and self-interest are important sources of association, the most effec-
> tive organizations are based on communities of shared ethical values. These com-
> munities do not require extensive contract and legal regulation of their relations
> because prior moral consensus gives members of the group a basis for mutual trust.

Any community where there are high levels of trust, thus, has an advantage in coordinating activity because it is cheaper to coordinate activities in these communities. "By contrast," Fukuyama (Ibid.: 27–28) continued,

> people who do not trust one another will end up cooperating only under a sys-
> tem of formal rules and regulations, which have to be negotiated, agreed to, liti-
> gated, and enforced, sometimes by coercive means.... Widespread distrust in a
> society, in other words, imposes a kind of tax on all forms of economic activity,
> a tax that high-trust societies do not have to pay.

Trust and honesty lower the cost of market transactions. Dishonesty, if rampant, might sharply curtail the capacity of markets to promote social cooperation.

Trust, then, is now widely accepted as being essential to the development of a successful market economy, and it has been demonstrated that economic per-formance is positively related to social capital in the form of norms of civic cooperation and interpersonal trust (e.g. Banfield 1958; Putnam 1993; Fukuyama 1995; Knack and Keefer 1997; La Porta et al. 1997; Zak and Knack 2001; Friedman and McNeill 2013). Arrow (1972: 357), for instance, asserted, "it can be plausibly argued that much of the economic backwardness in the world can be explained by the lack of mutual confidence." Similarly, Knack and Keefer (1997) found that trust and civic norms exhibit strong relationships to economic growth. Additionally, Zak and Knack (2001) demonstrated that three factors impact levels of investment and economic growth through trust. More homogenous societies and societies with more egalitarian distributions of income exhibit more trust, which thereby improves economic performance, while discrimination based on race, religion, or country of origin reduces trust and thereby worsens economic performance. Consequently, "trust is higher in 'fair' societies" and developing countries could suffer from a low-trust poverty trap (Ibid.: 296). La Porta et al. (1997) showed that trust correlates with better government performance, greater participation in civic and professional societ-ies, and GDP growth across countries. According to Guiso et al. (2009), trade volume between two European countries increases with greater trust shared by the citizens of both countries. Furthermore, high-trust societies are also associ-ated with large-scaled, flexible business organizations (Fukuyama 1995), efficient judicial systems (Berggren and Jordahl 2006), high-quality government bureaucracies (Putnam 1993), less government intervention (Aghion et al. 2010), less corruption and better financial markets (La Porta et al. 1997; Guiso et al. 2004), less crime (Wilson 1987), and better health (Putnam 2000).

Furthermore, recent studies have shown that there is, indeed, a causal effect of trust on economic growth (e.g. Tabellini 2008; Algan and Cahuc 2010) and that citizens of high-trust societies tend to be more cooperative (e.g. Herrmann et al. 2008; Johnson and Mislin 2011). Many other studies revealed that social norms like generalized trust can play a powerful role in constraining the interactions of group members (e.g. Conlin et al. 2003; Shang and Croson 2006; Bicchieri and Xiao 2009), increasing overall cooperation (e.g. Andreoni 1995; Fehr and Gächter 1999; Fischbacher et al. 2001; Henrich et al. 2001; Fehr and Fischbacher 2004a, b; Bicchieri 2006) and solving coordination problems (e.g. Mehta et al. 1994; Sugden 1995; Krupka and Weber 2009). In markets, as Boettke (2007: 85) explained, people "put trust in strangers and bring them into the extended order of division of labour from which we benefit. Trust and friendship are both the foundation of the market economy and the by-product of the expansion of the market economy." On the other hand, as Akerlof (1970) showed, markets would not survive if rampant dishonesty undermines the mechanisms for overcoming adverse selection.

People in market societies display more trust in others than those of nonmarket societies (Figs. 5.10 and 5.11). While everyone appears to equally trust those at a short social distance (i.e. trust in family and neighbors) in both market and nonmarket societies, trust appears to deteriorate as social distance increases and appears to deteriorate quicker in nonmarket societies. Compared to those living in nonmarket societies, on average, more people in market societies express that they at least somewhat trust their known associates (including friends and colleagues), those they meet for the first time and strangers. Stated alternatively, people around the world seem to have equally strong core networks, but those living in market societies seem to have stronger periphery networks.

Several experimental studies have also suggested a positive link between an individual's exposure to markets and their performance in laboratory experiments that explain trust. Market integration can explain a large portion of prosocial behavior variation across societies; subjects from a community with greater market integration display higher levels of prosocial behavior in standard experimental games (Henrich et al. 2004, 2005; Tracer 2004). Exposure to markets, found Ensminger (2004), was a reliable predictor of offer size within ultimatum and dictator games. Not only is trust positively associated with labor participation (Tu and Bulte 2010), but chief executives and senior managers of businesses also show substantially more trust and trustworthiness than undergraduate students in the standard trust game (Fehr and List 2004).

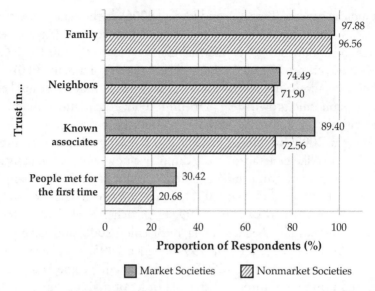

Fig. 5.10 Market societies have stronger interpersonal trust. (Data source: *World Values Survey* database)

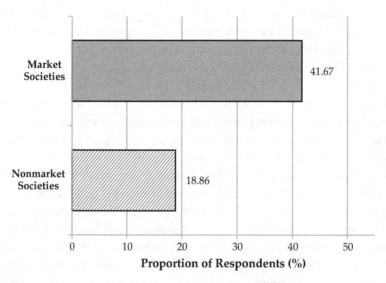

Fig. 5.11 More people living in market societies trust strangers. (Data source: *World Values Survey* database)

According to Al-Ubaydli et al. (2013), encouraging subjects to think about markets can boost trust in a laboratory experiment. Furthermore, a person's particular experience in a market can influence their fairness views (Herz and Taubinsky 2017). Again, the evidence suggests that people in market societies are more trusting than people in nonmarket societies.

It Is Possible for Market Participants to Be Moral

Market activity has almost always been viewed as morally questionable. Market exchanges, it is widely believed, can actually taint the goods and services being traded within them. Similarly, it is widely believed that engaging in market transactions can morally taint market participants. Markets, goes this view, promote materialism, reward selfishness, and encourage greed.

That markets are morally problematic is certainly the view of many market critics. Recall that concerns about usury and calls by Aquinas and others for a just price spoke to this belief that the only way that people can gain through trade is to engage in fraud or to take advantage of others' needy conditions. Indeed, Aquinas (ST II-II, q. 77, a. 4.) explicitly condemned arbitrage. Marx, likewise, worried that markets were inherently alienating and exploitative. Marx ([1821] 1994: 49) asserted that, the greater the scope of market exchange relations "the more *egoistic* and asocial man becomes." More recent critiques have echoed these concerns. Remember, Sandel (2012: 7), for instance, worried about the expansion of the market and its values into "spheres of life where they don't belong." Sandel (Ibid.) concluded that "economists often assume that markets are inert, that they do not affect the goods they exchange. But this is untrue. Markets leave their mark. Sometimes, market values crowd out nonmarket values worth caring about."

Not only do market critics highlight the morally problematic aspects of markets, market apologists have also suggested that markets are opposed to or undermine virtues. Recall that Mandeville ([1714, 1732] 1988) in the *Fable of the Bees* argued that human desires led to private vices like greed but that the market transformed these private vices into public benefits. Moreover, Mandeville suggested through his poem that the public benefits we get from thriving markets actually depend on these private vices. Similarly, Smith ([1776] 1981: 782) worried that as the division of labor expanded in commercial society that the typical worker,

> generally becomes as stupid and ignorant as it is possible for a human creature to become.... The uniformity of his stationary life naturally corrupts the courage of his mind. ... His dexterity at his own particular trade seems, in this manner, to be acquired at the expense of his intellectual, social, and martial virtues.

For Smith, markets are the reason that countries are wealthy and are also potentially corrupting.

Our markets and societies would look vastly different had the moral concerns about the market been true. The evidence suggests that markets and morality are not inconsistent. In fact, markets function better when populated with virtuous people. If markets are to flourish, actors need to control their own passions as well as respect the rules. Markets cannot thrive if entrepreneurs are comfortable with circumventing the rules of the game or are principally engaged in political entrepreneurship (i.e. rent seeking) rather than commercial entrepreneurship (i.e. profit seeking). Markets, thus, require temperance—the management of self, and a balance of our hot and cold passions—and justice—the management of society and a balance between citizens. Temperance encourages people to tame their desires and impulses, and, by extension, to act toward others cordially and respectfully. Justice motivates individuals to abide by laws, respect the market process, and not attempt to subvert it with political processes; it refers to "insist[ing] on private property honestly acquired… [I]t is also the justice to pay willingly for good work, to honor labor, to break down privilege, to value people for what they can do rather than for who they are, to view success without envy" (McCloskey 2006: 508). Justice, said Suri Ratnapala (2003), equips us with a sense of duty and holds us accountable for our actions toward others. "The rules of justice," he elaborated (Ibid.: 220), "are the coordinating principles of social life without which the social structure collapses; they are determined by the nature of the spontaneous order of society." As Ratnapala (Ibid.: 230) concluded, "just conduct is a necessary condition for commerce." Market participants must be virtuous (which includes justice, beneficence, and temperance) if they are to succeed (in the long term) and, so, the necessary tension between morality and markets simply does not exist (Ibid.: 230).

We should clarify that we are not suggesting here that moral people are both necessary and sufficient for markets to thrive. There are, of course, individuals we might describe as being virtuous or moral who exhibit a different set of virtues (e.g. priestly virtues) who we do not suggest must exist in thriving markets. Rather, our claim is that individuals with a certain set of virtues (what McCloskey called the "bourgeois virtues") are necessary though not sufficient for markets to thrive.

McCloskey proposed that markets actually create and cultivate the morality that it needs to function. While the market depends on virtues to function optimally, "our ethics depend on our business. Commerce is a teacher of ethics" (McCloskey 1998: 310). In the next chapter, we argue that market interactions have the ability to make us more virtuous and describe the mechanisms through which commerce teaches us virtues.

Bibliography

Abad-Santos, A. 2018. Why the Social Media Boycott Over Colin Kaepernick Is a Win for Nike. *Vox*, September 6. https://www.vox.com/2018/9/4/17818148/nike-boycott-kaepernick

Abderholden, F.S. 2017. Dairy Queen Ending Franchise Agreement with Zion Store After Racial Slur Incident. *Chicago Tribune*, January 7. http://www.chicagotribune.com/suburbs/lake-county-news-sun/news/ct-lns-dairy-queen-racial-slurs-zion-st-0107-20170106-story.html

Abrams, R. 2018. Starbucks to Close 8,000 U.S. Stores for Racial-Bias Training After Arrests. *The New York Times*, April 17. https://www.nytimes.com/2018/04/17/business/starbucks-arrests-racial-bias.html

Aghion, P., Y. Algan, P. Cahuc, and A. Schleifer. 2010. Regulation and Distrust. *The Quarterly Journal of Economics* 125 (3): 1015–1049.

Akerlof, G.A. 1970. The Market for 'Lemons': Quality Uncertainty and the Market Mechanism. *The Quarterly Journal of Economics* 84 (3): 488–500.

Al Jazeera. 2018. Hong Kong Actor Chow Yun-fat Vows to Donate His Entire Fortune. December 24. https://www.aljazeera.com/news/2018/12/hong-kong-actor-chow-yun-fat-vows-donate-entire-fortune-181224142911854.html

Algan, Y., and P. Cahuc. 2010. Inherited Trust and Growth. *American Economic Review* 100 (5): 2060–2092.

Al-Ubaydli, O., D. Houser, J. Nye, M.P. Paganelli, S.X. Pan, and F. Krueger. 2013. The Causal Effect of Market Priming on Trust: An Experimental Investigation Using Randomized Control. *PLoS One* 8 (3): e55968.

Andreoni, J. 1995. Cooperation in Public-Goods Experiments: Kindness or Confusion? *American Economic Review* 85 (4): 891–904.

Aquinas, T. [1485] 1918. *Summa Theologica*. Translated by the English Dominican Province. London: Burns, Oates & Washbourne.

Aristotle. [340 BC] 1984, 2013. *Nicomachean Ethics*. Translated by Robert Bartlett and Susan Collins. Chicago and London: University of Chicago Press.

Armah, A.K. [1968] 1988. *The Beautyful Ones Are Not Yet Born*. Johannesburg: Heinemann.

Arrow, K.J. 1972. Gifts and Exchanges. *Philosophy & Public Affairs* 1 (4): 343–362.

Banfield, E. 1958. *The Moral Basis of a Backward Society*. New York: Free Press.

Bates, J. 2018. IHOP Apologizes for Waitress Who Asked Group of Black Teens to Pay Upfront. *ABC News*, March 18. https://abcnews.go.com/US/ihop-apologizes-waitress-asked-group-black-teens-pay/story?id=53739093

Becker, G.S. 1962. Irrational Behavior and Economic Theory. *Journal of Political Economy* 70 (1): 1–13.

———. [1957] 1971. *The Economics of Discrimination: An Economic View of Racial Discrimination*. Chicago and London: University of Chicago Press.

Berggren, N., and H. Jordahl. 2006. Free to Trust: Economics Freedom and Social Capital. *Kyklos* 59 (2): 141–169.

Berggren, N., and T. Nilsson. 2013. Does Economic Freedom Foster Tolerance? *Kyklos* 66 (2): 177–207.

Bicchieri, C. 2006. *The Grammar of Society: The Nature and Dynamics of Social Norms*. Cambridge: Cambridge University Press.

Bicchieri, C., and E. Xiao. 2009. Do the Right Thing: But Only If Others Do So. *Journal of Behavioral Decision Making* 22 (2): 191–208.

Bill & Melinda Gates Foundation. 2018. Foundation Fact Sheet. https://www.gates-foundation.org/Who-We-Are/General-Information/Foundation-Factsheet

Boettke, P.J. 2007. Deirdre McCloskey's the *Bourgeois Virtues: Ethics for an Age of Commerce*. *Economic Affairs* 27 (1): 83–85.

Boren, C. 2014. Clippers Owner Donald Sterling Banned for Life from NBA. *The Washington Post*, April 29. https://www.washingtonpost.com/news/early-lead/wp/2014/04/29/clippers-owner-donald-sterling-banned-for-life-from-nba/?utm_term=.9d139a71c246

Boyle, R., and L.W. Kelly. 2012. *The Television Entrepreneurs: Social Change and Public Understanding of Business*. London/New York: Routledge.

Boyle, R., and M. Magor. 2008. A Nation of Entrepreneurs? Television, Social Change and the Rise of the Entrepreneur. *International Journal of Media & Cultural Politics* 4 (2): 125–144.

Bloom, H. 1998. *Shakespeare: The Invention of the Human*. New York: The Berkley Publishing Group.

Callon, M., and F. Muniesa. 2005. Peripheral Vision: Economic Markets as Calculative Collective Devices. *Organization Studies* 26 (8): 1229–1250.

Carden, A., and L. Verdon. 2010. When Is Corruption a Substitute for Economic Freedom? *The Law and Development Review* 3 (1): 40–63.

Carlyle, T. [1843] 2014. In *The Selected Works of Thomas Carlyle*, ed. F.R. Ludovico. Bibliotheca Cakravarti Foundation.

Carnegie, A. [1889] 2006. In *The "Gospel of Wealth" Essays and Other Writings*, ed. D. Nasaw. New York: Penguin.

Chafuen, A., and E. Guzmàn. 2000. Economic Freedom and Corruption. In *2000 Index of Economic Freedom*, ed. G. O'Driscoll, K. Holmes, and M. Kirkpatrick, 51–63. Washington, DC: The Heritage Foundation.

Charities Aid Foundation. 2016. CAF World Giving Index: A Global View of Giving Trends. https://www.cafonline.org/about-us/publications/2016-publications/caf-world-giving-index-2016

Charity Aid Foundation. 2017. CAF World Giving Index 2017: A Global View of Giving Trends. https://www.cafonline.org/docs/default-source/about-us-publications/cafworldgivingindex2017_2167a_web_210917.pdf?sfvrsn=ed1dac40_10

Charles, K.K., and J. Guryan. 2007. Prejudice and The Economics of Discrimination. *NBER Working Paper*, no. 13661.

———. 2008. Prejudice and Wages: An Empirical Assessment of Becker's *The Economics of Discrimination*. *Journal of Political Economy* 116 (5): 773–809.

Choi, S.G., and V.H. Storr. 2017. Markets as Moral Training Grounds. In *Annual Proceedings of the Wealth and Well-Being of Nations Volume IX*, ed. W. Palmer. Wisconsin: Beloit College Press.

Conlin, M., M. Lynn, and T. O'Donoghue. 2003. The Norm of Restaurant Tipping. *Journal of Economic Behavior & Organization* 52 (3): 297–321.

Dahlgreen, W. 2016. Shakespeare 400 Years on: Every Play Ranked by Popularity. *YouGov*, April 22. https://yougov.co.uk/topics/lifestyle/articles-reports/2016/04/22/shakespeare-400

Davidson, J. 2015. The 10 Richest People of All Time. *Money*, July 30. http://money.com/money/3977798/the-10-richest-people-of-all-time-2/

Ellis, L., K.M. Beaver, and J. Wright. 2009. *Handbook of Crime Correlates*. Amsterdam: Academic Press.

Ensminger, J. 2004. Market Integration and Fairness: Evidence from Ultimatum Dictator, and Public Good Experiments in East Africa. In *Foundations of Human Sociality: Economic Experiments and Ethnographic Evidence from Fifteen Small-Scale Societies*, ed. J. Henrich, R. Boyd, S. Bowles, C. Camerer, E. Fehr, and H. Gintis, 356–382. Oxford: Oxford University Press.

Fehr, E., and J.A. List. 2004. The Hidden Costs and Returns of Incentives—Trust and Trustworthiness Among CEOs. *Journal of the European Economic Association* 2 (5): 743–771.

Fehr, E., and U. Fischbacher. 2004a. Social Norms and Human Cooperation. *Trends in Cognitive Sciences* 8 (4): 185–190.

———. 2004b. Third-party Punishment and Social Norms. *Evolution and Human Behavior* 25 (2): 63–87.

Fehr, E., and S. Gächter. 1999. Collective Action as a Social Exchange. *Journal of Economic Behavior & Organization* 39 (4): 341–369.

Ferguson, N. 2008. The Money-lender's Plight. *National Post*, December 10. https://www.pressreader.com/canada/national-post-latest-edition/20081210/281908769002240

Fike, R. 2018. *Impact of Economic Freedom and Women's Well-Being*. Vancouver: Fraser Institute.

Fischbacher, U., S. Gächter, and E. Fehr. 2001. Are People Conditionally Cooperative? Evidence from a Public Goods Experiment. *Economics Letters* 71 (3): 397–404.

Forsythe, R., F.D. Nelson, G.R. Neumann, and J. Wright. 1992. Anatomy of an Experimental Political Stock Market. *American Economic Review* 82: 1142–1161.

Forsythe, R., T.A. Rietz, and T.W. Ross. 1999. Wishes, Expectations and Actions: A Survey on Price Formation in Election Stock Markets. *Journal of Economic Behavior & Organization* 39 (1): 83–110.

Freedman, L. 2009. The Narrative of Consumption: Greed and Literature. In *Greed*, ed. A. Brassey and S. Barber, 170–187. London: Palgrave Macmillan.

Friedman, D., and D. McNeill. 2013. *Morals and Markets: The Dangerous Balance*. New York: Springer.

Fukuyama, F. 1995. *Trust: The Social Virtues and the Creation of Prosperity*. New York: Free Press Paperbacks.

Gode, D.K., and S. Sunder. 1993. Allocative Efficiency of Markets with Zero-Intelligence Traders: Market as a Partial Substitute for Individual Rationality. *Journal of Political Economy* 101 (1): 119–137.

Goel, R.K., and M.A. Nelson. 2005. Economic Freedom Versus Political Freedom: Cross-Country Influences on Corruption. *Australian Economic Papers* 44 (2): 121–133.

Graeff, P., and G. Mehlkop. 2003. The Impact of Economic Freedom on Corruption: Different Patterns for Rich and Poor Countries. *European Journal of Political Economy* 19 (3): 605–620.

Griswold, C.L., Jr. 1999. *Adam Smith and the Virtues of Enlightenment*. Cambridge: Cambridge University Press.

Gross, N. 1975. *Economic History of the Jews*. New York: Schocken Books.

Gross, J. 1993. THEATER; Shylock and Nazi Propaganda. *The New York Times*, April 4. https://www.nytimes.com/1993/04/04/theater/theater-shylock-and-nazi-propaganda.html

Guiso, L., P. Sapienza, and L. Zingales. 2004. The Role of Social Capital in Financial Development. *American Economic Review* 94 (3): 526–556.

———. 2009. Cultural Biases in Economic Exchange? *The Quarterly Journal of Economics* 124 (3): 1095–1131.

Güliz, G., and R.W. Belk. 1996. Cross-cultural Differences in Materialism. *Journal of Economic Psychology* 17 (1): 55–77.

Hanley, R.P. 2009. *Adam Smith and the Character of Virtue*. Cambridge: Cambridge University Press.

Hartman, K.B. 2006. Television and Movie Representations of Salespeople: Beyond Willy Loman. *The Journal of Personal Selling & Sales Management* 26 (3): 283–292.

Hayek, F.A. 1942. Scientism and the Study of Society. Part I. *Economica* 9 (35): 267–291.

Henrich, J., R. Boyd, S. Bowles, C. Camerer, E. Fehr, H. Gintis, and R. McElreath. 2001. In Search of Homo Economicus: Behavioral Experiments in 15 Small-Scale Societies. *American Economic Review* 91 (2): 73–78.

Henrich, J., R. Boyd, S. Bowles, C. Camerer, E. Fehr, and H. Gintis. 2004. *Foundations of Human Sociality: Economics Experiments and Ethnographic Evidence from Fifteen Small Scale Societies*. Oxford: Oxford University Press.

Henrich, J., R. Boyd, S. Bowles, C. Camerer, E. Fehr, H. Gintis, R. McElreath, M. Alvard, A. Barr, J. Ensminger, N.S. Henrich, K. Hill, F. Gil-White, M. Gurven, F.W. Marlowe, J.Q. Patton, and D. Tracer. 2005. 'Economic Man' in Cross-cultural Perspective: Behavior Experiments in 15 Small Scale Societies. *Behavioral and Brain Sciences* 25 (6): 795–855.

Herrmann, B., C. Thöni, and S. Gächter. 2008. Antisocial Punishment Across Societies. *Science* 319 (5868): 1362–1367.

Herz, H., and D. Taubinsky. 2017. What Makes a Price Fair? An Experimental Study of Transaction Experience and Endogenous Fairness Views. *Journal of the European Economic Association* 16 (2): 316–352.

Higgins, T. 2017. George Soros Just Gave Almost 80 Percent of His Wealth to His Charity. *CNBC*, October 17. https://www.cnbc.com/2017/10/17/philanthropist-george-soros-donates-most-of-his-net-worth-to-charity.html

Hsu, T. 2019. Gillette Ad With a #MeToo Edge Attracts Support and Outrage. *The New York Times*, January 15. https://www.nytimes.com/2019/01/15/business/gillette-ad-men.html

Ikeda, S. 2018. The Nature and Limits of Gary Becker's Theory of Racial Discrimination. *The Review of Austrian Economics* 31 (4): 403–417.

Inglehart, R., C. Haerpfer, A. Moreno, C. Welzel, K. Kizilova, J. Diez-Medrano, M. Lagos, P. Norris, E. Ponarin, B. Puranen, et al., eds. 2014. *World Values Survey: Round Six-Country-Pooled Datafile Version*. Madrid: JD Systems. www.worldvaluessurvey.org/WVSDocumentationWV6.jsp.

Ingram, P., and P.W. Roberts. 2000. Friendships Among Competitors in the Sydney Hotel Industry. *American Journal of Sociology* 106 (2): 387–423.

Johnson, N.D., and A.A. Mislin. 2011. Trust Games: A Meta-analysis. *Journal of Economic Psychology* 32: 865–889.

Kincaid, J. 1988. *A Small Place*. New York: Farrar Straus and Giroux.

Kirzner, I.M. 1999. Creativity and/or Alertness: A Reconsideration of the Schumpeterian Entrepreneur. *The Review of Austrian Economics* 11 (1–2): 5–17.

Knack, S., and P. Keefer. 1997. Does Social Capital Have an Economic Payoff? A Cross-Country Investigation. *The Quarterly Journal of Economics* 112 (4): 1251–1288.

Koblin, J. 2018. After Racist Tweet, Roseanne Barr's Show Is Canceled by ABC. *New York Times*, May 29. https://www.nytimes.com/2018/05/29/business/media/roseanne-barr-offensive-tweets.html

Krupka, E., and R.A. Weber. 2009. The Focusing and Informational Effects of Norms on Pro-social Behavior. *Journal of Economic Psychology* 30 (3): 307–320.

La Porta, R., F. Lopez-de-Silanes, A. Shleifer, and R.W. Vishny. 1997. Trust in Large Organizations. *American Economic Review* 87 (2): 333–338.

Lamming, G. 1970. *In the Castle of My Skin*. Ann Arbor: University of Michigan Press.

Langrill, R., and V.H. Storr. 2012. The Moral Meaning of Markets. *Journal of Markets and Morality* 15 (2): 347–362.

Lavoie, D., and E. Chamlee-Wright. 2000. *Culture and Enterprise: The Development, Representation and Morality of Business*. London/New York: Routledge.

Lichter, S.F., L.S. Lichter, and S. Rothman. 1991. *Watching America*. Upper Saddle River: Prentice Hall.

Lichter, S.F., L.S. Lichter, and A. Amundson. 1997. Does Hollywood Hate Business or Money? *Journal of Communication* 47 (1): 68–84.

Llosa, M.V. 2008. *The War of the End of the World*. London: Macmillan.

Mandeville, B. [1714, 1732] 1988. *The Fable of the Bees or Private Vices, Publick Benefits*. With Commentary by F.B. Kaye. Indianapolis: Liberty Fund.

Marshall, R. 1974. The Economics of Racial Discrimination: A Survey. *Journal of Economic Literature* 12 (3): 849–871.

Martin, N., and V.H. Storr. 2012. Talk Changes Things: The Implications of McCloskey's *Bourgeois Dignity* for Historical Inquiry. *The Journal of Socio-Economics* 41 (6): 787–791.

Marx, K. [1821] 1994. *Karl Marx: Selected Writings*, ed. L.H. Simon. Indianapolis: Hackett Publishing.

McCloskey, D.N. 1998. Bourgeois Virtues and the History of P and S. *The Journal of Economic History* 58 (2): 297–317.

———. 2003. Why Economists Should Not Be Ashamed of Being the Philosophers of Prudence. *Eastern Economic Journal* 28: 551–556.

———. 2006. *The Bourgeois Virtues: Ethics for an Age of Commerce*. Chicago: University of Chicago Press.

———. 2010. *Bourgeois Dignity: Why Economics Can't Explain the Modern World*. Chicago: University of Chicago Press.

———. 2016. *Bourgeois Equality: How Ideas, Not Capital or Institutions, Enriched the World*. Chicago: University of Chicago Press.

Mehta, J., C. Starmer, and R. Sugden. 1994. The Nature of Salience: An Experimental Investigation of Pure Coordination Games. *American Economic Review* 84 (3): 658–673.

Mises, L. [1920] 1935. Economic Calculation in the Socialist Commonwealth. In *Collectivist Economic Planning: Critical Studies on the Possibilities of Socialism by N.G. Pierson, Ludwig von Mises, Gerog Halm, and Enrico Barone*, ed. F.A. Hayek, 87–130. London: Routledge & Kegan Paul Ltd.

Misztal, B. 1996. *Trust in Modern Societies: The Search for the Bases of Social Order*. Cambridge: Polity Press.

Mueller, J. 1999. *Capitalism, Democracy, and Ralph's Pretty Good Grocer*. Princeton: Princeton University Press.

Murphy, N. 2019. Gillette Advert Against 'Toxic Masculinity' Faces Backlash for 'Attacking Men'. *The Mirror*, January 15. https://www.mirror.co.uk/news/us-news/gillette-advert-metoo-faces-backlash-13858189

Naughton, M. 2017. Practical Wisdom as the Sine Qua Non Virtue for the Business Leader. In *Handbook of Virtue Ethics in Business and Management*, ed. A.J.G. Sison, G.R. Beabout, and I. Ferrero. Amsterdam: Springer Netherlands.

Nelson, D.M. 1992. *The Priority of Prudence: Virtue and Natural Law in Thomas Aquinas and the Implications for Modern Ethics*. University Park: Pennsylvania State University Press.

Neumayer, E., and I. De Soysa. 2007. Globalisation, Women's Economic Rights and Forced Labour. *The World Economy* 30 (10): 1510–1535.

———. 2011. Globalization and the Empowerment of Women: An Analysis of Spatial Dependence Via Trade and Foreign Direct Investment. *The World Development* 39 (7): 1065–1075.

Oliven, K., and T.A. Rietz. 2004. Suckers Are Born but Markets Are Made: Individual Rationality, Arbitrage, and Market Efficiency on an Electronic Futures Market. *Management Science* 50 (3): 336–351.

Page, R.A., S.K. Andoh, and R.A. Smith. 2017. Classical Literature Gives Life to Business Paradox and Systems Integration. *Administrative Issues Journal* 7 (2): 23–46.

Paldam, M. 2002. The Cross-country Pattern of Corruption: Economics, Culture and the Seesaw Dynamics. *European Journal of Political Economy* 18 (2): 215–240.

Plato. [350 BC] 1997. *Plato: Complete Works*. Translated by J.M. Cooper and D. S. Hutchinson, ed. Indianapolis: Hackett Publishing.

Putnam, R.D. 1993. *Making Democracy Work: Civic Traditions in Modern Italy*. Princeton: Princeton University Press.

———. 2000. *Bowling Alone: The Collapse and Revival of American Community*. New York/Philadelphia: Simon and Schuster.

Ratnapala, S. 2003. Moral Capital and Commercial Society. *The Independent Review* 8 (2): 213–233.

Russell, D.C. 2009. *Practical Intelligence and the Virtues*. Oxford: Oxford University Press.

Sandel, M.J. 2012. *What Money Can't Buy: The Moral Limits of Markets*. London: Macmillan.

Schumpeter, J.A. [1911] 1983. *The Theory of Economic Development: An Inquiry into Profits, Capital, Credit, Interest, and the Business Cycle*. New Brunswick: Transaction Publishers.

Scott, R. 2015. Which Companies Match Gifts Most? *Forbes*, May 21. https://www.forbes.com/sites/causeintegration/2015/05/21/which-companies-match-gifts-most/

Scott, E. 2018. The Most Powerful Brand in Sports Follows the Most Powerful Man in the World into the Anthem Protest Debate. *The Washington Post*, September 4. https://www.washingtonpost.com/politics/2018/09/04/most-powerful-brand-sports-follows-most-powerful-man-world-into-anthem-protest-debate/?utm_term=.f3a808578a22

Sen, A. 1986. Adam Smith's Prudence. In *Theory and Reality in Development*, ed. S. Lall and F. Stewart, 28–37. London: Palgrave Macmillan.

Shakespeare, W. [1564–1616] 1994. *The Merchant of Venice*. London: Pearson Longman.

Shang, J., and R. Croson. 2006. The Impact of Social Comparisons on Nonprofit Fund Raising. In *Experiments Investigating Fundraising and Charitable Contributors*, ed. R.M. Isaac and D.D. David, 143–156. Bingley: Emerald Group Publishing Limited.

Shen, C., and J.B. Williamson. 2005. Corruption, Democracy, Economic Freedom, and State Strength: A Cross-national Analysis. *International Journal of Comparative Sociology* 46 (4): 327–345.

Shleifer, A., and R.W. Vishny. 1993. Corruption. *The Quarterly Journal of Economics* 108 (3): 599–617.

Shugerman, E. 2018. David Hogg, Laura Ingraham Advertisers Dropped. *Independent*, March 30. https://www.independent.co.uk/news/world/americas/david-hogg-laura-ingraham-advertisers-drop-fox-news-show-hulu-tripadvisor-nestle-expedia-a8282101.html

Smith, A. [1776] 1981. *An Inquiry into the Nature and Causes of the Wealth of Nations*. Indianapolis: Liberty Fund.

———. [1759] 1982. *The Theory of Moral Sentiments*. Indianapolis: Liberty Fund.

Solomon, R.C. 1992. *Ethics and Excellence: Cooperation and Integrity in Business*. Oxford: Oxford University Press.

Storr, V.H. 2008. The Market as a Social Space: On the Meaningful Extraeconomic Conversations That Can Occur in Markets. *The Review of Austrian Economics* 2 (2–3): 135–150.

———. 2009. Why the Market? Markets as Social and Moral Spaces. *Journal of Markets and Morality* 12 (2): 277–296.

Stroup, M.D. 2008. Separating the Influence of Capitalism and Democracy on Women's Well-being. *Journal of Economic Behavior & Organization* 67 (3–4): 560–572.

———. 2011. Does Economic Freedom Promote Women's Well-being? In *Economic Freedom of the World: 2011 Annual Report*, ed. J.D. Gwartney, R. Lawson, and J.C. Hall. Vancouver: Fraser Institute.

Sugden, R. 1995. A Theory of Focal Points. *The Economic Journal* 105 (430): 533–550.

Tabellini, G. 2008. Institutions and Culture. *Journal of the European Economic Association* 6 (2–3): 255–294.

Teague, M., R. Fike, and V.H. Storr. 2018. *Markets, Money and Materialism*. Working Paper.

The New York Times. 1937. Rockefeller Gifts Total $540,853,632. *The New York Times*, May 24. http://movies2.nytimes.com/books/98/05/17/specials/rocke-feller-gifts.html

The Straits Times. 2018. Chow Yun Fat Vows to Donate Fortune After He Dies. *The Strait Times*, December 24. https://www.straitstimes.com/lifestyle/entertainment/chow-yun-fat-vows-to-donate-fortune-after-he-dies

Theberge, L.J., ed. 1981. *Crooks, Conmen and Clowns: Businessmen on T.V. Entertainment*. Washington, DC: The Media Institute.

Tiffany, K. 2019. Why Gillette's Toxic Masculinity Ad Is Annoying Both Sexists and Feminists. *Vox*, January 15. https://www.vox.com/the-goods/2019/1/15/18184072/gillette-toxic-masculinity-ad-super-bowl-feminism

Tracer, D.P. 2004. Market Integration, Reciprocity, and Fairness in Rural Papua New Guinea: Results from a Two-Village Ultimatum Game Experiment. In *Foundations of Human Sociality: Economic Experiments and Ethnographic Evidence from Fifteen Small-Scale Societies*, ed. J. Henrich, R. Boyd, S. Bowles, C. Camerer, E. Fehr, and H. Gintis, 232–259. Oxford: Oxford University Press.

Transparency International. 2011. *Corruption Perceptions Index 2011*. Berlin: Transparency International. https://www.corruptionwatch.org.za/wp-content/uploads/migrated/Corruption-perecptions-index-2011-report_0.pdf.

Tu, Q., and E. Bulte. 2010. Trust, Market Participation and Economics Outcomes: Evidence from Rural China. *World Development* 38 (8): 1179–1190.

U.S. Trust. 2016. 2016 US Trust Insights on Wealth and Worth Survey: Key Findings. http://doingmorethatmatters.com/wp-content/uploads/2016/09/US_Trust-Wealth-and-Worth-Study-2016.pdf

Usbourne, S. 2015. The world's Most Generous Billionaires: Mark Zuckerberg Isn't the Only One to Give Away a Large Chunk of His Fortune. *Independent*, December 2. https://www.independent.co.uk/news/business/analysis-and-features/the-worlds-most-generous-billionaires-mark-zuckerberg-isnt-the-only-one-to-give-away-a-large-chunk-a6758066.html

Vásquez, I., and T. Porcnik. 2015. *The Human Freedom Index: A Global Measurement of Personal, Civil, and Economic Freedom*. Vancouver: Fraser Institute.

Viganò, E. 2017a. Adam Smith's Theory of Prudence Updated with Neuroscientific and Behavioral Evidence. *Neuroethics* 10 (2): 215–233.

———. 2017b. Not Just an Inferior Virtue, nor Self-Interest: Adam Smith on Prudence. *Journal of Scottish Philosophy* 15 (1): 125–143.

Wang, A.B., and R. Siegel. 2018. Trump: Nike 'Getting Absolutely Killed' with Boycotts Over Colin Kaepernick's 'Just Do It' Campaign. *The Washington Post*, September 5. https://www.washingtonpost.com/business/2018/09/04/people-are-destroying-their-nike-gear-protest-colin-kaepernicks-just-do-it-campaign/?utm_term=.535518198759

Williams, J. 2004. *Entertaining the Nation: A Social History of British Television*. Stroud: Sutton Publishing.

Wilson, J.W. 1987. *The Truly Disadvantaged: The Inner City, the Underclass, and Public Policy*. Chicago: University of Chicago Press.

Yuengert, A. 2012. *Approximating Prudence: Aristotelian Practical Wisdom and Economic Models of Choice*. London: Palgrave Macmillan.

Zak, P. 2008. *Moral Markets: The Critical Role of Values in the Economy*. Princeton: Princeton University Press.

Zak, P., and S. Knack. 2001. Trust and Growth. *The Economic Journal* 111 (470): 295–321.

6

Markets Are Moral Training Grounds

The Aesopica is a collection of fables and proverbs that are credited to Aesop, a Greek slave and storyteller who was born in Thrace in the seventh century BC. Often, these fables contain an ethical lesson. The *Aesop Fable* "The Farmer and his Sons" (Perry 42), for instance, tells the story of the owner of a farm who had three sons. Before his death, he called his sons together and said to them, "My children, there is a treasure buried in one of my vineyards." After the farmer's death, rather than selling the farm, "his sons took plows and mattocks and dug up the entire farm." Although they did not find any treasure, their efforts did improve the farm; "the vineyard paid them back with a greatly increased harvest." By tricking his sons, the farmer taught them an important lesson about the value of hard work. To be sure, the sons were originally motivated by greed. But they ended up learning that the market rewards industry.

If the story of "The Farmer and His Sons" is a story about the virtue of industry, "The Woman and Her Two Daughters" (Perry 94) is a story about prudence. A mother married one of her daughters to a gardener and the other to a potter. The daughter married to the gardener asked her mother to pray for rain so that her husband's crops would flourish. The daughter married to the potter asked her mother to pray for sunshine so that her husband's pots would dry quickly. The mother realized that she would not be able to pray for either daughter given their competing interests. Success, this fable teaches, is only possible if you are not working at cross-purposes.

Several of the other fables offer cautionary tales about the perils of vice. "The Man, the Pig and the Miracle" (Perry 5) as well as "The Sick Man and His Wife" (Perry 34), for instance, warn that people will sometimes be dishonest to further their interests. Additionally, "The Two Frogs at the Well"

© The Author(s) 2019
V. H. Storr, G. S. Choi, *Do Markets Corrupt Our Morals?*,
https://doi.org/10.1007/978-3-030-18416-2_6

(Perry 43) and "The Weasel and the File" (Perry 59) warn against imprudence. Likewise, "The Sparrow and the Myrtle Berries" (Perry 86) speaks about the dangers of greed. The sparrow stays in a berry tree gorging himself on sweet berries and is killed by a bird catcher. The fables of "The Goatherd and the Wild Goats" (Perry 6) and "The Widow and Her Hen" (Perry 58) offer similar warnings. The goatherder let his own goats go hungry and die while trying to capture wild goats to enlarge his flock. The widow overfed her hen hoping that it would lay more eggs, but the hen grew so fat that it stopped laying eggs.

These fables capture some of the lessons that people undoubtedly learn during their market interactions. It is easy to see how the lessons transmitted through these fables would benefit their readers as they engaged in market activity. It is also easy to imagine that Aesop learned some of these lessons in the agora. Some of these lessons are explicitly about the advantages of being virtuous or the disadvantages of engaging in vice in market settings. Because we can learn from our experiences in markets, those experiences have the potential to change us.

A key question, then, is what lessons about virtues and vice are we likely to learn in the market? If our market activities can and do change us, are they likely to make us more moral or more immoral than we would otherwise be? These questions are particularly important since, if markets are indeed morally corrupting, then they might very well contain the seeds to their own destruction. It is possible, for instance, that markets benefit from and even require the existence of virtuous people (as we argued in Chap. 5), and that markets still transform formerly virtuous people into atomistic individuals concerned with only their narrow self-interest. It is possible that the virtues that markets rely on must be imported from outside of markets and that markets also undermine the growth of these virtues. It is possible that markets are compatible with morality, and that they still encourage us to be immoral.

Markets, we argue, are moral training grounds. Rather than corrupting us, markets make us better people. Recall, the idea that the market improves conduct is called the *doux commerce thesis*. Smith ([1776] 1981), for example, raised the possibility that the market teaches individuals to act honorably. "Of all the nations in Europe," Smith (Ibid.: 538) observed, "the Dutch, the most commercial, are the most faithful to their word" and "[w]henever commerce is introduced into any country, probity and punctuality always accompany it." Montesquieu ([1748] 1989), similarly, explained that the market gentles relations between trading partners. "Commerce," Montesquieu (Ibid.: 338) explained, "cures destructive prejudices, and it is an almost general rule that everywhere there are gentle mores, there is commerce and that everywhere there is commerce, there are gentle mores." Hirschman (1992: 109) echoed this sentiment and argued that commerce is a "powerful moralizing agent which brings many nonmaterial improvements to society even though a bit of hypocrisy may have to be accepted into the bargain." The market, according to Hirschman, (mostly) improves us. Samuel Ricard, quoted by Hirschman (2013: 217–218), likewise explained how commerce has an ability to make individuals unpretentious and humble. As Ricard explained,

> Through commerce, man learns to deliberate, to be honest, to acquire manners, to be prudent and reserved in both talk and action. Sensing the necessity to be wise and honest in order to succeed, he flees vice, or at least his demeanor exhibits decency and seriousness so as not to arouse any adverse judgment on the part of present and future acquaintances.

The market is a moral teacher.

In this chapter, we argue that market interactions have the ability to make us more virtuous through at least two mechanisms. First, every market transaction serves as an opportunity to learn about our trading partners and to discover those market participants who have the moral qualities that we admire. Second, markets allow us to reward market participants with the ethical qualities we appreciate and to punish those who behave immorally. Consequently, the market can train individuals to become more virtuous, at least in the long run.

The Relevance and Irrelevance of Schumpeter's Warning

Schumpeter ([1942] 2010: 72) stressed that the market system is an evolutionary system. As such, change is endemic in the market. The primary sources of market changes, he explained, are the introduction of new products and production methods, the continual turnover of market participants, and frequent changes in the social and natural environments in which markets exist. Schumpeter has described this process of constant transformation as *Creative Destruction*. As Schumpeter (Ibid.: 73) wrote,

> [this] process of industrial mutation … incessantly revolutionizes the economic structure from within, incessantly destroying the old one, incessantly creating a new one. This process of Creative Destruction is the essential fact about capitalism. It is what capitalism consists in and what every capitalist concern has got to live in.

The market system is an economic system where new things and new ways of doing things are constantly being introduced and where older things and older ways of doing things are constantly becoming obsolete. The progress and prosperity that we observe in market societies is the result of this process of Creative Destruction.

In addition to destroying old products and practices, and replacing them with new and better products and practices, Schumpeter warned that the "perennial gale of Creative Destruction" can also destroy the social, institutional, and moral foundations on which the whole process depends or at least once depended. According to Schumpeter, as the market system develops, the entrepreneurial function and so the entrepreneur become increasingly obsolete. In a world of constant innovation, innovation itself becomes routine (Ibid.: 117). While in the early days of the market system the entrepreneur had to be bold and courageous and willing to go against the grain, "it is much easier now than it has been in the past to do things that lie outside familiar routine" (Ibid.). The boldness and courage that once propelled the entrepreneur is now less important. The maverick inventor who was essential in an earlier period has been replaced by a team of research and development specialists. "Since capitalist enterprise, by its very achievements, tends to automatize progress," Schumpeter (Ibid.: 119) stated, "we conclude that it tends to make itself superfluous—to break to pieces under the pressure of its own success."[1]

By making the social function of the entrepreneur superfluous, the prestige of the entrepreneur is also impaired in a market society. By making the entrepreneur obsolete and diminishing the prestige of the bourgeoisie, support for private property and free contracting declines. Recall, McCloskey (2010) argued that it was only when the bourgeoisie (i.e. the capitalist, the merchant, the inventor, the skilled artisan, etc.) was given liberty and dignity that the rapid economic development associated with markets in the last few centuries occurred. According to Schumpeter, however, the market undermines the dignity and then the liberty of the bourgeoisie. In so doing, the market undermines the very factors that it needs to succeed.

---

[1] Cowen (2017) appeared to support Schumpeter's prediction that the vibrant entrepreneurial spirit which was so important to the (early) economic success of commercial societies like the United States would eventually dampen in these societies. Complacency, Cowen (Ibid.: 1) explained, has "sapped us of the pioneer spirit that made America the world's most productive and innovative economy." "Americans," (Ibid.) he continued,

> are in fact working much harder than before to postpone change, or to avoid it altogether, and that is true whether we're talking about corporate competition, changing residences or jobs, or building things. In an age when it is easier than ever before to dig in [i.e. to desire more success or be ambitious], the psychological resistance to change has become progressively stronger.

The spread of market societies did not only erode support for the institutions that undergird the market system and taint the social prestige of the entrepreneurs who drive the market system. Schumpeter believed that the advancement of market societies also caused outright hostility toward the market system. There are two reasons why he believed that this occurred. First, Schumpeter argued, the market system is unable to cultivate the kind of emotional attachment that other social orders are able to cultivate. There are very few odes to capitalism, very few novels where the capitalist is the hero, very few protests to defend capitalism. Advocating for markets is not a popular policy stance. Second, while the market system weakened and replaced illegitimate authority in the first instance, it eventually weakens all authority. Indeed, its growth meant an end to the feudal system and mercantilism. It was only a matter of time, Schumpeter wrote, before the market system turned that force onto itself. The market system,

> creates a critical frame of mind which, after having destroyed the moral authority of so many other institutions, in the end turns against its own; the bourgeois finds to his amazement that the rationalist attitude does not stop at the credentials of kings and popes but goes on to attack private property and the whole scheme of bourgeois values. (Ibid.: 128)

Schumpeter predicted that, as soon as the moral authority of the market system and the institutions that undergird it were destroyed, the market system would become like an undefended fortress that is rich in booty. "Defenseless fortresses," Schumpeter ([1942] 2010: 128) maintained, "invite aggression especially if there is rich booty in them. Aggressors will work themselves up into a state of rationalizing hostility—aggressors always do. No doubt it is possible, for a time, to buy them off. But this last resource fails as soon as they discover that they can have all." In other words, there is very little hostility toward the market system when the bourgeoisie have a strong social position. But, the hostility toward the market system is extreme when the bourgeoisie have a weak social position. Once market actors lose their moral status, the market system would then lose its moral authority, become hated, and become vulnerable.

Schumpeter added that the market system also destroys the family, one of the institutions that might mitigate this self-destructive drive of the market. "To men and women in modern capitalist societies," Schumpeter (Ibid.: 140) wrote, "family life and parenthood mean less than they meant before and hence are less powerful molders of behavior." Furthermore, echoing an observation made by Smith, Schumpeter claimed that market society offers tempting alternatives to familial life. Recall, Smith ([1759] 1982: 223) reasoned that a social transformation accompanies the transition from a pastoral to a commercial society. According to Smith, family is especially important in a pastoral society, since survival in these societies can often depend on your membership in a kinship group. However, it is possible to survive and even thrive without familial connections in a commercial society. In fact, Smith predicted that it is possible for two relatives to meet in the market and not even be aware of their family connections. Schumpeter's point, however, was slightly different from Smith's. Schumpeter insisted that the market is destroying something that it needs by undermining the family, not destroying something that is simply a vestige of earlier times. "As soon as [family concerns] fade out from the moral vision of the businessman," Schumpeter (Ibid.: 143) gravely stated, "we have a different kind of *homo oeconomicus* before us who cares for different things and acts in different ways." The entrepreneur who is unconcerned about his family is, just simply, a different kind of creature: an entrepreneur unattached to family has a shorter-term time horizon than one who has a family; and an entrepreneur with a short-term time horizon because she is unattached to a family has no reason to guard the market system against attacks.

Additionally, Schumpeter argued that the market's ability to defend itself against its critics is complicated by the fact that the strongest arguments in favor of the market system are always those that emphasize how markets outperform other economic systems on relevant margins in the long run. Also, the persuasiveness of any existing or hypothetical defense of the market system is limited because the case for markets must always point to how markets benefit most people without being able to offer guarantees to every person (or even any particular person).[2] "Any pro-capitalist argument," noted Schumpeter (Ibid.: 130),

> must rest on long-run considerations. In the short run, it is profits and inefficiencies that dominate the picture. In order to accept his lot, the leveler or the chartist of old would have had to comfort himself with hopes for his great-grandchildren. In order to identify himself with the capitalist system, the unemployed of today would have completely to forget his personal fate and the politician of today his personal ambition.

In Schumpeter's view, markets are always failing, at least in the short term, to deliver the (material, social, and moral) goods to someone, especially the poorest. Unfortunately for the standing of markets, only the relatively wealthy

---

[2] Arguments in favor of basic income guarantees are often motivated by this concern. For example, Munger (2015: 504) wrote that "[a]ll too often the 'other side'—my side—loses this debate [on basic income guarantees] because we say that doing *nothing* is better than having a welfare state. Then we get told we must hate the poor." See also Zwolinski (2011, 2015).

can really afford to focus on the long term. Moreover, because the market system is unable to inspire the emotional attachment that other social systems are able to produce, market participants tend to blame, not defend, the market system whenever they suffer even the slightest injuries. And, because of the competitive nature of the market, market participants are especially worried about being caught on the destruction side of the perennial gale of creative destruction.

There is also a tendency, Schumpeter lamented, for people living in market societies to take the benefits of markets for granted. As we discussed in Chaps. 4 and 5, there are very real material, social, and moral benefits associated with market societies. People living in market societies are generally wealthier, healthier, happier, and better connected than people living in nonmarket societies. Market societies also outperform nonmarket societies on measures of morality. Unfortunately, it is common, Schumpeter suggested, for market participants to assume that these benefits are inevitable and that they will continue even if the market system ceases to exist. "Secular improvement that is taken for granted and coupled with individual insecurity that is acutely resented," Schumpeter (Ibid.: 130) wrote, "is of course the best recipe for breeding social unrest."[3]

Instead, argued Schumpeter, the market system depends on the very extra-market factors that it destroys. It not only contains the seeds to its own destruction, it is the author of its own demise;

> the same economic process that undermines the position of the bourgeoisie by decreasing the importance of the functions of entrepreneurs and capitalists, by breaking up protective strata and institutions, by creating an atmosphere of hostility, also decomposes the motor forces of capitalism from within. Nothing else shows so well that the capitalist order not only rests on props made of extra-capitalist material but also derives its energy from extra-capitalist patterns of behavior which at the same time it is bound to destroy. … there is inherent in the capitalist system *a tendency toward self-destruction* (Ibid.: 144).

The market system, in Schumpeter's view, eventually destroys the very things that it needs to survive.

There are, of course, reasons to be suspicious of Schumpeter's predictions. After all, many of his predictions have not come to pass, although it appears

---

[3] However, this is not enough to explain the active hostility toward the market system. The active hostility toward the market system also requires a group of people "whose interest it is to work up and organize resentment, to nurse it, to voice it and to lead it" (Schumpeter [1942] 2010: 130).

that his prediction of a growing hostility toward markets among the least well-off has transpired.[4] But, as we have demonstrated, people in market societies—including the poorest in market societies—are wealthier, healthier, happier, better connected, and more moral than those in nonmarket societies. Additionally, some of these societies have been market societies for decades (and even centuries) and the market systems in these societies have yet to destroy their very foundations.

Schumpeter, however, raised an important concern: it is possible that markets contain the seeds to their own destruction. It is possible that the market both relies on certain virtues (as we argued earlier) and that it erodes the very virtues on which it depends.

The relevant question, then, is what moral lessons do markets teach us? Or, asked another way, can and do markets transform us? And, if they do change us, do markets make us morally better or do they corrupt our morals?

Markets Do Change Us

The most worrisome critique of markets on moral grounds is that markets can corrupt our morals. On that view, we enter markets as virtuous creatures but emerge from them as immoral monsters; we enter markets honest and become dishonest as we navigate through them; we enter markets connected to one another but grow detached as we engage in market activity. There is, on that view, a worrisome moral risk associated with engaging in market activity. This concern can certainly be found in the writings of Aquinas, Rousseau, Marx, and many of the modern critics of markets. Ironically, as we have also explained, many of the moral defenses of markets have dismissed or endorsed— rather than challenged—the notion that markets are linked with immorality. Instead, they have stressed that the market transforms private vice into public virtue and have advanced that the greed that drives market activity is the source of all the wealth generated by the market. Writers like Adam Smith, for instance, pointed to the potential of markets to not only benefit from our moral shortcomings but to also cause our moral decline.[5]

---

[4] According to Pew Research Center (2011), more Americans have a positive reaction (50%) to the term "capitalism," than a negative reaction (40%). But, while only 28% of the richest Americans (defined as those with a family income more than $75,000) have a negative reaction to the term "capitalism," 47% of the poorest Americans (defined as those with a family income less than $30,000) have a similar negative reaction. Likewise, while a majority of people in 38 of the 44 countries examined believed that people are "better off in a free market economy," people's economic situation affects their attitude toward market economies (Pew Research Center 2014).

[5] Recall, for Adam Smith ([1759] 1982: 181–183), the poor man's son's self-deceit is the cradle of industry and the division of labor in commercial society, which ultimately leads to moral corruption.

Interestingly, there is not a great deal of discussion about why engaging in markets would (negatively) impact our moral sentiments. More critically, the mechanisms through which markets affect our moral sentiments remain underexplored. At a minimum, in order for market activity to be either morally corrupting or beneficial, our moral makeups cannot be cemented during our childhoods. Moral development or regress in adulthood (when the bulk of people's market interactions occur) must be possible.[6]

Several theorists have tried to explain how moral development or regression occurs in adults. Lawrence Kohlberg (1984), for instance, proposed that moral development continues beyond adolescence and into adulthood. Specifically, he described six stages of moral development:[7]

- Stage 1: Individuals egoistically deem an action as immoral because they were punished for engaging in that action in the past.
- Stage 2: Individuals egoistically deem an action as moral if and only if engaging in it will benefit them (narrowly conceived).
- Stage 3: An action is moral if it conforms to social norms and rules because conforming to social norms is likely to engender social approval.
- Stage 4: An action is moral if it conforms to social norms because of the belief that conforming to social norms and rules is likely to advance the interests of society.
- Stage 5: An action is moral when it truly advances the interests of society whether or not they conform to social norms and rules (though they frequently will).
- Stage 6: An action is moral only if they are consistent with moral rules that are grounded in some universal ethical principles.[8]

Interestingly, in Kohlberg's original studies, he presented his subjects with a market-based moral dilemma. He asked them to evaluate the decision of a desperate husband to steal a lifesaving drug for his wife from a price gouging

---

[6] Alfred Marshall, the economist, agreed that people cannot help but to be altered (even a tiny bit) by their interactions in the marketplace. "[M]an's character has been molded by his every-day work, and the material resources which he thereby procures, more than by any other influence unless it be that of his religious ideals; and the two great forming agencies of the world's history have been the religious and the economic" (Marshall [1890] 1920: 1).

[7] Kohlberg and Ryncarz (1990) added a seventh stage where individuals begin to contemplate questions related to the meaning of life. See also Gilligan (1979, 1982) and Rest et al. (1999) for alternative theories of moral development.

[8] Because Kohlberg and his associates were unable to confirm the existence of Stage 6, it is said that he was forced to revise his six-stage model into a five-stage model (Colby et al. 1983; see also Flanagan and Jackson 1987).

drug developer. The responder whose moral development is at Stage 1 condemns the stealing because theft receives a specific sanction or endorses it because the price gouging druggist has charged too high a price. The responder in Stage 2 endorses or condemns the theft based on a comparison of the joy that the husband will likely gain from saving his wife's life to the pain he will experience by being imprisoned for his crime. The responder in Stage 3 will condemn the theft because the husband is likely to receive disapprobation from breaking the law or will endorse the theft because the husband is likely to receive approval for being a husband who does all he can to save his dying wife. The responder in Stage 4 will condemn the crime simply because it is against the law or endorse it so long as the husband is willing to incur the prescribed punishment. The responder in Stage 5 will condemn the theft because, say, it is a violation of the drug developer's property rights or will endorse the theft because, say, the man's wife has a right to life. The responder in Stage 6 will condemn the theft because, in stealing the drug, the husband elevated his wife's life above others or will endorse the crime because respecting human life is a more fundamental value than protecting private property.

Individuals, Kohlberg explained, use the moral reasoning associated with the stage of moral development they have achieved as a kind of "filter" through which they understand the world and decide on the moral course of action. As such, Kohlberg's theory is not meant to be predictive; people's moral conclusions are not necessarily linked to their stage of moral development. Additionally, Kohlberg did not believe that there was a strict correspondence between people's moral reasoning and their moral behavior. Opposite responses to the same situation could both be considered moral because different moral judges can have different perspectives.[9] The same response to a situation could be considered moral by some and immoral by others. The different moral judgments, Kohlberg proposed, must be considered as equally moral.

Individuals, according to Kohlberg, pass through these stages sequentially during the course of their lives (see Crain 1985: 118–136). The latter stages, he believed, were only possible in teenagers and adults. Kohlberg also argued, however, that moral development was not inevitable. Not everyone passes through the various stages at the same rate. Not everyone reaches the highest

---

[9] Kohlberg (1958: 337) wrote that "[a] Zulu and a Frenchman might do very different things and yet their choices are equally moral in terms of our criteria, criteria of internality, universality, etc. For the sake of labelling we said our criteria were those of form as opposed to those of content." And, Kohlberg and Mayer (1972: 479, italics in original) stated, "What is one person's *integrity* is another person's *stubbornness.*"

stages. In fact, most people never move beyond Stage 4. Also, not everyone uses the moral judgment associated with their highest level of moral development at all times and in all contexts (Colby et al. 1987). Instead, the stage of moral development that a person has achieved speaks to their moral capacity, not to the type of moral judgment they would deploy in any particular situation. Moreover, what resembles moral regression is possible; it is possible to move back to an earlier stage (Kohlberg and Kramer 1969).[10]

In describing the stages of moral development, Kohlberg was more interested in the form of a person's moral development than the content of their moral reasoning. The content of a person's moral judgments (i.e. what that person considers moral) does not depend on a person's stage of moral development but, instead, will depend on their cultural background and their experiences.[11]

Several recent studies have criticized and/or extended Kohlberg's theory of moral development. While Kohlberg believed that the highest stages of moral development would only be achieved by the reflective adult, Gibbs (1979: 94) noted that adolescents can also be reflective. Others have challenged Kohlberg's insistence that the sequence of the stages of moral development was invariant (e.g. Bloom 1977; Buck-Morss 1975; Edwards 1975, 1982; Guidon 1978; Shweder 1982a, b; Simpson 1974; Sullivan 1977; see also Snarey 1985). Additionally, Kreps et al. (1997) argued that real-life moral judgments very rarely involve the kinds of moral dilemmas that Kohlberg focused on.[12] Moreover, Kreps et al. (Ibid.) concluded that people's moral decisions varied

---

[10] Kohlberg (1973a, b) later modified this claim, suggesting instead that the apparent regression pointed to an issue with the definition of the various stages rather than evidence of actual regression in moral development.

[11] Kohlberg et al. (1983) distinguished between two distinct moral types: individuals who make type A, heteronomous, moral judgments and individuals who make type B, autonomous, moral judgments. (Moral type analysis primarily concentrates on the content of moral reasoning.) Those who make type A moral judgments have no clear moral hierarchy; hold an instrumental view of people; perceive moral duty as instrumental or hypothetical; validate their judgments on external bases; display unilateral obedience; can only view the moral dilemma from one point of view; have a rigid view of rules and laws; and do not choose or justify choices in terms of fairness. On the other hand, those who make type B moral judgments have a clear hierarchy of moral values; view people as ends in themselves and hold respect for autonomy and dignity; perceive moral duty as a moral obligation; do not rely on external authority or tradition; believe in cooperation among equals; are capable of understanding the other's perspective; hold a flexible view of rules and laws; and generally choose solutions seen as just or fair (Logan et al. 1990: 75). Logan et al. (Ibid.) found that there were significant and persistent differences across cultures in the proportion of their populations that belonged to the two different moral types. They also found that as people moved to higher stages of moral development, they tended to move from heteronomous to autonomous moral types.

[12] For example, most of our market decisions are not choices between engaging in theft and allowing our spouses to die.

depending on the kinds of dilemmas they face, their involvement in the dilemma, and the context in which they are making the moral determination.

Likewise, Gilligan (1979, 1982) claimed that Kohlberg's theory did an inadequate job of explaining women's moral development. In fact, Gilligan accused Kohlberg of misunderstanding women's moral development. The fact that women perform as well as (and even outperform) men when studying moral development along Kohlbergian lines does not weaken this complaint. In addition to highlighting the gender bias inherent in Kohlberg's theory, others have found that there is also a cultural bias in his theory.[13] Additionally, Henry (2001) highlighted and criticized the structural-functionalist roots of Kohlberg's theory, and challenged its widespread use in educational practice.

These issues aside, these studies collectively indicate that Kohlberg usefully raised the possibility that moral development can continue beyond adolescence. His theory of moral development not only speaks to the various channels through which moral development occurs but also speaks to the different kinds of moral judgments that people engage in. Additionally, Kohlberg and the critical literature he inspired address the importance of people's experiences in shaping both the extent of people's moral development and the content of their moral judgments. The more complex the environment that people experience, the more diverse the others that people encounter, the more advanced their moral development will tend to be.

Engaging in market activity, then, is likely to affect our moral judgments in predictable ways to the extent that (1) certain actions are consistently punished and other actions are consistently rewarded within markets, and (2) certain types of behavior consistently receive disapproval and certain other types of behavior consistently win approval in markets. Moreover, market activity is likely to impact our moral development to the extent that it shelters or exposes us to situations where we face moral dilemmas and are forced to

---

[13] See, for instance, Bloom (1977). Gibbs et al. (2007) evaluated Kohlberg's cultural claims. Kohlberg (1981), for his part, proposed that individuals in some cultures (e.g. preliterate cultures) could not achieve the highest stages of moral development, and that the modal stages of moral development were likely to differ across cultures. But he did not believe directly in "deriving" a person's stage of moral development based on their culture and believed that his stages of moral development were universal. Snarey (1985) contended that only the first four stages of Kohlberg's theories are universal. According to Edwards (1986: 427), "while the available data cannot positively demonstrate invariant sequence, taken together they strongly suggest that development change is generally gradual and positive throughout the childhood and adolescent years, in a wide variety of cultural groups." And, Snarey (1985: 226) concluded that,

the evidence suggests that Kohlberg's interview [method] is reasonably culture fair when the content is creatively adapted and the subject is interviewed in his or her native language. The invariant sequence proposition was also found to be well-supported, because stage skipping and stage regressions were rare and always below the level that could be attributed to measurement error.

make moral choices, and to the extent that it increases or limits our contact with others who have different moral intuitions and reasonings.

To say that markets are morally corrupting, then, is to say that engaging in market activity distorts our moral judgments or impedes our moral development. When critics of the morality of markets assert that engaging in markets is morally corrupting, they are implying that markets tend to reward vice and punish virtue, that immoral actors tend to win approbation and moral actors tend to suffer disapprobation, and that immoral attitudes tend to be cultivated within markets. These critics are also implying that markets limit the opportunities for market participants to make and reflect on their moral choices.

Markets, as we argue below, teach the opposite lessons.[14] In fact, markets reward good behavior and good actors gain social approval. Similarly, markets punish bad behavior and bad actors suffer social disapproval. Additionally, markets constantly place participants in situations where they have to exercise their moral judgments.

An Experiment that Explores the Moral Teachings of Markets

In order to explore how markets might act as moral training grounds, we conducted an economic experiment in the laboratory that investigated whether or not markets allowed individuals to learn about whom to trust and to reward or punish others based on their trustworthiness.

Specifically, we assigned our subjects experimental aliases, by which they were recognizable by other subjects throughout the experiment, and then utilized a two-stage experimental design. In the first stage of the experiment, our subjects were placed in a market setting where several features of real-world markets were retained. Essentially, this market allowed our subjects, as buyers or sellers, to freely, repeatedly, and simultaneously send and receive offers to purchase or sell an experimental good to anyone in the opposite market role.[15] This feature of our market was critical; by allowing the subjects

---

[14] Storr (2018) elaborated that our exposure to markets is likely to positively impact our morality. Our morality, he explained, is a product of our experiences and the people we know. Markets consistently place us in circumstances where we can benefit by serving others and come in contact with an expanding range of diverse others. As such, our moral sentiments are improved for the better in the market. Also, in Chap. 4, we argued that people in market societies are more likely to avoid trolley problems than people in nonmarket societies. This does not mean that they can avoid moral choices, just that the moral dilemmas that they encounter are not likely to be as dire as those in nonmarket societies.

[15] Other popularly used markets in experimental economics (e.g. double auctions) do not give the subjects such degree of freedom to choose with whom to trade. Also, we were able to eliminate any possibility of collusion by forcing our subjects to negotiate with those in the opposite market role.

to freely choose with whom to negotiate, we also gave the subjects the complete freedom to choose whom to avoid trading with in the future. Whenever a subject received an offer, she had the option to accept, reject, ignore, or send a counteroffer. As clarification, an offer constituted a proposed trading price in our experiment.

Once an offer was accepted, the subject who sent the accepted offer had the option to follow through on the trade or to cheat on their trading partner by refusing to pay or to deliver the good. If she decided to execute the trade, the experimental good and the experimental cash (i.e. agreed trading price) were exchanged with her trading partner. In this case, the seller earned the difference between the agreed trading price and her costs while the buyer earned the difference between her endowed budget and the agreed trading price, plus the value of the good. On the other hand, if the subject who sent the offer decided to abandon the trade (i.e. to defect and so default on her agreement), she kept both the good and the cash while his trading partner earned nothing for that particular trade.[16] Our subjects had the opportunity to interact and negotiate with one another as buyers and sellers in this experimental market for ten separate trading rounds.

It is important to note that the payoffs in this experimental market were designed not only to ensure that cheating was profitable but also to heighten the sense of betrayal that subjects would feel when their trading partner cheated them, thereby making dealing with a cheater costly. As such, it should be harder to develop positive relationships characterized by trust and reciprocity in our trading game than in actual markets.

In the second stage of the experiment, our subjects were placed in a trust game. The trust game, as originally developed by Berg et al. (1995), traditionally involves two subjects—a trustor and a trustee—who make decisions sequentially and who are both endowed with ten tokens at the beginning of the game. First, the trustor decides how to split her endowment with the trustee; she could send as little as zero tokens and as much as all ten tokens. The trustor's transfer is often denoted as x. Whatever amount she decides to send, it is tripled before the trustee receives her transfer ($3x$). Finally, the trustee decides how to split this tripled amount and sends a portion (or none or all) of the tripled amount back to the trustor; the trustee's transfer is often denoted as y. The trust game ends with the trustee's decision. At the end of the

---

[16] In this case, the round payment depended on the market role of the subject who sent the offer. If he was a seller, he earned the agreed trading price plus the cost while the buyer earned zero for that particular trade. If he was a buyer, he earned his budget plus the good (valued at E$10) while the seller earned zero for that particular trade.

trust game, the trustor earns a payment equivalent to her leftover endowment plus the amount sent by the trustee (calculated as $10 - x + y$). In turn, the trustee earns a payment equivalent to her entire endowment of 10 tokens plus the portion of the trustor's tripled amount she kept for herself (calculated as $10 + 3x - y$). In our experiment, every buyer played a trust game with every seller. Since subjects were identifiable by their experimental aliases throughout the entire experiment, the subjects knew with whom they were playing trust games at all times.

The trustor's transfer is popularly interpreted as measuring trust; she is trusting, or willing to bet, that the other person will reciprocate her decision, which is risky as it was made at a cost to herself. The trustee's transfer is popularly interpreted as measuring trustworthiness; she reciprocates the trust shown to her with a decision that is also costly to her.[17]

There are at least two mechanisms through which markets might promote trust in this experiment. First, our experimental market might give subjects an opportunity to learn about specific others. Subjects can specifically learn whether or not someone is a fair dealer and a promise keeper. Stated another way, our market gives subjects an opportunity to reveal themselves to be trustworthy or not. This knowledge about the nature of particular trading partners might impact future interactions with them both inside and outside the market. Second, our market might give subjects an opportunity to learn about others in general.[18] As our subjects have more positive experiences in our market, the more likely they are to develop positive relationships with specific others in our market setting, the more likely they are to trust and to reciprocate to others. In other words, successful dealings in our market might condition subjects to the possibility of mutually beneficial exchanges and, so, promote the development of prosocial attitudes.

Given this setup, it was possible for our subjects to have formed a total of four types of relationships with one another after the first stage of our experiment. A buyer and a seller were regarded as sharing a *positive (trading) relationship* if the proportion of successful (i.e. executed) trades between them exceeds half of their total number of trades. Conversely, a buyer and a seller were regarded as sharing a *negative (trading) relationship* if the proportion of successful trades between them is less than half of the total. If the proportion

---

[17] In experimental economics, trustworthiness is popularly viewed to be essentially the same as reciprocity (e.g. Croson and Buchan 1999; Fehr and Gächter 2000b; Ostrom and Walker 2003). Although some have challenged this view (e.g. Kramer 1999; Dufwenberg and Gneezy 2000; Cox 2004), we will follow the popular view and interchangeably use trustworthiness and reciprocity.

[18] See, for instance, Fehr and Gächter (2000a, b, 2002).

of successful trades between a buyer and seller was exactly half of their total number of trades, these relationships were labeled as *ambiguous (trading) relationships*. Since ambiguous relationships could be perceived as either positive or negative relationships, we deemed it more appropriate to separate them from positive and negative relationships for our analysis. Finally, a buyer and a seller were described as *strangers* if they never successfully negotiated a trade in our experimental market over the ten trading rounds.

Our results demonstrate that market interactions promote the emergence of interpersonal trust and that the observed heterogeneity in trust is directly correlated with the perceived quality of a subject's particular market interactions. Our key finding is that individuals exhibited higher levels of trust and trustworthiness in the trust game to those with whom they shared positive relationships compared to those with whom they shared negative relationships. These results are summarized and interpreted below.

Result 1 *Trustors sent larger transfers to trustees with whom they developed positive relationships in the experimental market than to those with whom they developed negative relationships.*

As Fig. 6.1 shows, trustors sent significantly larger transfers to those with whom they developed positive relationships (5.3 tokens) than to those with

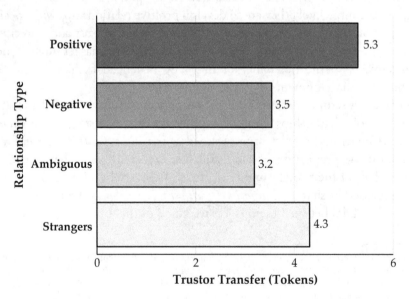

Fig. 6.1 Trustor behavior by relationship type. The maximum trustor transfer is 10 tokens

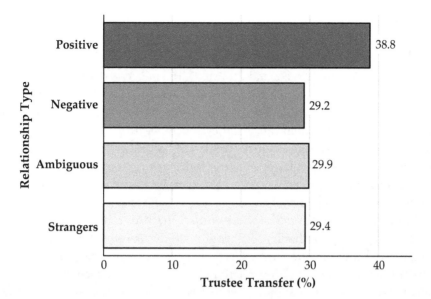

Fig. 6.2 Trustee behavior by relationship type. Trustee transfer is calculated as trustee's token transfer divided by the respective trustor's tripled token transfer (i.e. $\frac{y}{3x} * 100$)

whom they developed negative relationships (3.5 tokens). In fact, trustors transfer roughly 50% (1.8 tokens) more to those with whom they developed positive relationships than to those with whom they share negative relationships. Trustors transferred less tokens to those with whom they shared negative relationships (3.5 tokens) than to strangers (4.3 tokens). This suggests that while trustors were certainly rewarding good (i.e. trustworthy) behavior, they may have also been punishing bad (i.e. untrustworthy) behavior.

Result 2 *Trustees sent larger transfers to trustors with whom they developed positive relationships in the experimental market than to those with whom they developed negative relationships.*

As Fig. 6.2 shows, trustees reciprocated with significantly larger transfers to those with whom they developed positive relationships (38.8%) than to those with whom they developed negative relationships (29.2%).[19] Trustees transfer

---

[19] Following convention in the trust game literature, we converted the trustee's transfer from tokens to percentage of the respective trustor's tripled transfer (i.e. $\frac{y}{3x} * 100$).

roughly 33% (9.6 percentage points) more to those with whom they developed positive relationships than to those with whom they developed negative relationships. Trustees treated strangers and those with whom they share negative relationships equally (29.4% and 29.2%).[20] This suggests that trustees treated those with whom they developed positive relationships better than how they treated others. Additionally, this result is not consistent with subjects punishing individuals with whom they had developed negative relationships (as they are treating them the same as they treat strangers). In short, trustees appeared to have rewarded market friends but not to have punished market enemies.[21]

Arguably, our experiment suggests that it is possible for individuals to develop positive relationships characterized by trust and trustworthiness within a market setting and for those positive market-originated relationships to carry over into nonmarket settings. Recall, our subjects both trusted and reciprocated more in the trust games when paired with other subjects with whom they developed positive relationships in the experimental market. In our market setting, our subjects learned who could be trusted. They, then, rewarded or punished others in the trust game based on their revealed trustworthiness in the market setting.

Our experimental environment also suggests that not all markets are equal in their ability to facilitate the development of trust and trustworthiness. For instance, in another experiment, we eliminated the option to cheat once the offers were accepted in the experimental market while retaining all other aspects of the experiment we described above (Choi and Storr 2018). Specifically, in this new experimental market, buyers and sellers were able to freely, repeatedly, and simultaneously send and receive offers from one another. But once an offer was accepted, the good and experimental cash was immediately exchanged between the involved seller and buyer; the seller earned the difference between the agreed trading price and his cost and the buyer earned the difference between his budget endowment and the agreed trading price, plus the good. Because we removed the ability to cheat, the subjects could only form positive relationships or remain strangers in this new experimental market.

---

[20] See Appendix for statistical tests comparing trustor and trustee transfer sizes across relationship types.

[21] There are, however, limits to how much we can make of these results, especially with regards to strangers. We define two market participants as strangers if they never successfully negotiated a trade during the ten rounds of our experimental market. This definition prevents us from distinguishing between "true" strangers (those market participants who never sent offers to each other) and "unfortunate" strangers (where at least one of the participants sent an offer that was never accepted). As such, we cannot exclude the possibility that subjects can learn about each other by their negotiation behavior even if at the end of the day they never successfully transact.

We found that our subjects treated strangers and those others with whom they developed positive relationships equally in this new experimental market.[22] In other words, a culture where everyone treated others more or less equally and indiscriminately emerged in this new experimental market while a culture where people discriminated between the trustworthy and untrustworthy emerged in the original experimental market. This indicates that individuals can learn something about the trustworthiness of others through market interactions, but only if they have distinct opportunities to learn about each other. While allowing the opportunity to renege on an existing agreement could be viewed as being a pessimistic feature of our experiment, it nonetheless gave our subjects an opportunity to observe and learn about their trading partners.[23]

As we discussed in Chap. 2, some scholars have expressed the view that markets, on net, corrupt social bonds and erode the community. This experiment challenges this view; it suggests that an erosion of community should only occur if markets are, on net, peopled with dishonest traders who cheat others more often than not. In that sort of environment, most of people's market experiences would be trades where at least one party did not live up to their commitments. Happily, as we discussed in Chap. 5, most market societies are not peopled with more dishonest than honest traders. Moreover, these results give us cause to hope that honest traders can discover honest partners even in markets where interacting with a dishonest person is more likely than interacting with an honest person.

We designed our experimental market to specifically allow for the development of interpersonal relationships characterized by trust and reciprocity as

---

[22] In the treatment with the new experimental market, the trustors transferred an average of 4.96 tokens to those trustees with whom they developed positive relationships and transferred an average of 4.38 tokens to strangers. The trustees transferred an average of 34.3% back to those trustors with whom they developed positive relationships and transferred an average of 32.5% to strangers. Both trustor and trustee transfers to positive relationships and strangers were statistically identical in this new experimental market. See Choi and Storr (2018) for more details.

[23] According to Zak (2008: xvii), "the very freedom to exchange in markets celebrates individual dignity and choice but also allows for transgressions." As he (Ibid.) detailed,

Reliance on these values [such as honesty, trust, reliability, and fairness] … arise in the normal course of human interactions, without overt enforcement – lawyers, judges, or the police are present in a paucity of economic transactions. Indeed, we show that legal regulation may perversely lead to an increase in immoral behaviors by crowding out our innate sense of fair play.

To be sure, Zak was not endorsing the absence of legal enforcement; "cheating does occur," he (2008: xvii) continued, "and the institutional rules of exchange and their enforcement are a critical reinforcement of [moral] values." Our experiment suggests that the possibility of cheating makes learning about the trustworthiness of trading partners possible.

well as to allow for the myopia and ability to cheat that we sometimes observe in real-world markets. Subjects had no ability to communicate with one another except through their offers and counter offers. And, they knew nothing about the other subjects in the experimental market (e.g. their legal names, sex, religious affiliations, etc.) except for an experimental identity that made them recognizable to other subjects throughout the experiment. Subjects did, however, have the ability to directly experience and learn about each other's trustworthiness. That our subjects were able to learn about others, rewarded others for their trustworthiness, and developed positive relationships in our experimental context hints at the potential for people in real-world markets to discover whom to trust, to reward trustworthiness, and to develop market friendships.

Why Do Markets Tend to Make Us Better People?

The way in which the market operates encourages virtuous behavior and ensures that unethical behavior is held in check in at least two ways. First, every market transaction represents an opportunity to discover market participants who have the moral qualities that we admire; markets have mechanisms for revealing and sharing information about the moral character of market actors. Second, markets have mechanisms for rewarding and punishing market actors depending on their moral characters. In particular, markets allow us to reward market participants with the ethical qualities we appreciate and to punish those who behave viciously. As Langrill and Storr (2012: 357) stated, "markets increase the benefit of being virtuous and lower the costs of doing so. As we would expect, there is more virtue than there otherwise would be." Markets not only help us to achieve an efficient allocation of goods and services, they also help us maintain and can even enhance our morality.

Markets Are Spaces Where We Discover Whether the People with Whom We Are Interacting Are Good or Bad People

The market is comprised of individuals who have limited and imperfect knowledge and who do not and cannot know what will happen in the future. "[T]he future," as Lachmann (1976: 55) reminded us, "is to all of us unknowable." Nonetheless, we must make plans since many of our goals cannot be accomplished in a single period.[24] And, we must often coordinate our actions with others if our plans are to be successful. Because we are radically ignorant, however, many of the plans that we make will only partially succeed or will fail outright. The success or failure of our plans acts as a feedback mechanism; plans that fail get scrapped, plans that only partially succeed get revised, and even plans that are successful but not yet fully realized get modified as circumstances change. As Kirzner (1973: 10) taught us, "[t]he market process ... is set in motion by the results of the initial market-ignorance of the participants. The process itself consists of the systematic plan changes generated by the flow of market information released by market participation – that is, by the testing of plans in the market." The market process is, at root, an *adjustment process*.

The market process is also a *competitive process*. "[C]ompetition," Kirzner (Ibid.: 13) argued, "is inseparable from the market process itself." The market participants, who are systematically adjusting their plans so that they can coordinate their activities with others, are simultaneously competing with one another. Buyers are vying with each other for resources. Similarly, sellers are vying with each other for customers. As Kirzner (Ibid.: 11–12) stated,

> each market participant, in laying his buying or selling plans, must pay careful heed not only to the prospective decisions of those to whom he hopes to sell or from whom he hopes to buy, but – as an implication of the latter – also to the prospective decisions of others whose decisions to sell or to buy may compete with his own.

It is this rivalry that explains why sellers are constantly attempting to offer more attractive opportunities to their customers and why resources tend to flow to their most highly valued use.

The market can also be described as an *entrepreneurial process*. "[E]ntrepreneurship," as Kirzner (Ibid.: 17) wrote, "is inherent in the competitive process." The entrepreneur performs at least two key functions in the market: she is a coordinating force and promotes innovation.[25] The entrepreneur brings about coordination in the market by being alert to profit opportunities and by taking actions to exploit them through arbitrage—that is, by buying a given good (or its constituent elements) at a lower price than it is

---

[24] Lachmann wrote quite extensively about the centrality of the plan. See, for instance, his book titled *The Legacy of Max Weber* (1971). See, also, Lachmann ([1940] 1977: 68–69).

[25] We often use the shorthand of talking about the entrepreneur as if he was a person with some prescribed role in the market. But, as Kirzner (1973: 15) often reminded us, entrepreneurship is in fact an element in every action.

expected to go for in the market. In this way, entrepreneurs bridge the gap (of knowledge) between the owners of resources and the consumers. However, arbitrage here should not be thought of as just mere arbitrage. As Holcombe (2003: 18) explained, entrepreneurship "is more than just being alert to price discrepancies in the market. It is spotting alternative methods of production, and spotting ways in which output characteristics can be altered to better satisfy the demands of purchasers." Innovation—the creation of new products, production processes, and distribution methods in an attempt to exploit perceived profit opportunities—is also a part of entrepreneurship. The entrepreneurial promoter is necessarily an innovator.

The market process, then, is ultimately a *discovery process*. As Kirzner (1979: 150) described, "we now see [the market] process much more deeply as a process whereby the general tendency for continued spontaneous discovery of available information is powerfully nudged into its most effective and expeditious channels."[26] Discovery is quite different than deliberate search. In a "deliberate act of learning," (1) we recognize that there is something that we do not yet know, (2) we know where, how, and at what cost we can gain the desired knowledge, and (3) we believe that the benefit of knowing is greater than the cost of finding out (Kirzner 1992: 46). In contrast, discovery involves genuine surprise. It does not begin with an awareness of one's ignorance and does not end with the "possession of the sought-after knowledge" (Ibid.). Instead, "the kind of discovery steps we have described as making up the market process … are characterized precisely by the surprise involved by the discovery, and by the corresponding earlier unawareness of the nature of one's ignorance" (Ibid.).[27] The market process, as Kirzner (1979: 151) explicated, is "a systematic but wholly unplanned process of un-deliberate discovery … [which] disseminates knowledge whose very existence has not been known to its spontaneous learners."[28]

Arguably, markets are spaces where we not only discover profit opportunities but also where we discover whether or not the people with whom we are interacting are good or bad people. Recall, every market transaction is an opportunity for opportunism.[29] In a market transaction, the buyer typically

---

[26] Note that adjustments of the sort discussed earlier are possible because the market is ultimately a discovery process.

[27] See Klein (1999) for an interesting discussion of Kirznerian discovery.

[28] Lavoie (1986) argued persuasively that much of the knowledge that is discovered and transmitted through the market is inarticulate knowledge. This is knowledge that we possess but cannot describe in any concrete and detailed way, such as the kind that most of us have regarding how to ride a bike or throw a curve ball in baseball.

[29] Rose (2018) has reasoned that culture is what stops any opportunism that cannot be constrained by rules. Our argument is that not only do markets have mechanisms for constraining opportunism but also that a culture that resists opportunism can emerge in markets.

agrees to pay some specific amount by a specific date for a specific good or service. Often the seller has to deliver the good or perform the service before being paid. As such, the buyer could accept the good or service and still refuse to pay the agreed upon sum and/or refuse to pay by the agreed upon date. Similarly, in a market transaction, the seller typically agrees to deliver some specific good or service of at least some specified quality on or before a specific date. Often the buyer has to pay for the good or service before it has been delivered or performed and before the buyer can be certain of the quality of the good or service. As such, the seller could accept payment and still refuse to deliver the good or service all together or refuse to deliver a good or service of the expected quality by the agreed upon date.

Obviously, as we noted in Chap. 5, markets could not function if opportunism occurred as frequently as it might occur (Akerlof 1970). In a market rife with opportunism, buyers would refrain from buying and sellers would refrain from selling, without robust guarantees. Of course, these guarantees would quickly become cost-prohibitive if they had to underlie every transaction.[30]

The folk theorem is often invoked in the economics literature to explain why we do not see unchecked opportunism in markets. For instance, consider the classic prisoner's dilemma. Imagine two members of a criminal gang who have been arrested. Their imprisoners suspect they have committed a major crime but only have enough evidence to convict them on a lesser charge; they need a confession in order to convince a jury of their involvement and culpability in this major crime. If both prisoners stay silent, they will likely only be convicted of the lesser crime and each will only serve a short sentence in prison. Suppose, however, the imprisoner offers both of them a deal: betray the other prisoner by offering evidence against him and obtain immunity, so long as the other prisoner remains loyal. If, by chance, both prisoners betray each other, they will each receive a sentence even longer than what they would have received had they both refused to betray their comrade. If both prisoners assume that this will be the only time that they will be in this situation with one another, the rational move in this situation for both prisoners would be to betray their fellow prisoner. But the folk theorem implies that neither prisoner will betray their comrade if this situation is likely to be repeated, since

---

[30] Leeson (2007) described how it was possible to trade peacefully with even bandits. In the absence of governments, it is cheaper for some economic agents to violently steal what they desire from weaker economic agents due to their sheer superior strength (such as was the case in pre-colonial west central Africa). In response, agents employed two mechanisms: (1) they used credit to alter the cost-benefit structures of bandits to encourage them to trade, not plunder; and (2) they demanded risk premiums from traveling traders to minimize their risk of transacting with them. But, note that the "market" that Leeson described here is not a thriving market.

they both know that should they betray their comrade that they will likely be betrayed the next time that they are in the same situation. Because of a possibility that market interactions will be repeated, buyers and sellers know that they risk future gains by engaging in opportunism. Even if they believe they are truly unlikely to meet their current trading partner in the future, market participants know that it is possible if not likely that others will find out about their opportunism.

Still, while unchecked opportunism is unlikely in markets, opportunism is still possible and could still be a potentially profitable action. Consequently, a person can still learn something about the trustworthiness of a trading partner by observing whether or not that partner engages in fraud or theft. Recall, the subjects in our experiment did not differentiate between trading partners with whom they shared positive relationships and strangers in the trust game when we did not allow them to cheat one another in the experimental market (Choi and Storr 2018).

As the choice to engage in opportunism is a deliberate decision, the honest or opportunistic trading partner reveals some information about the type of person that they are with every exchange. Thus, in a hostile market environment where deceitful behavior is rampant, a virtuous individual will receive poignant attention. Conversely, in a well-functioning market, the unethical individual will be noticed. The conclusion of each market interaction, whether it is ultimately successful or unsuccessful, will reveal to individuals whom to trust and/or whom to avoid.

Of course, many of the trades that occur in large societies are between strangers and are unlikely to result in repeated interactions. Additionally, some trades (e.g. buying or selling a house) are trades that people engage in only a few times in their lifetime. Markets, however, have evolved systems that communicate reputations of businesses and individual market participants (e.g. brand reputations as well as rating systems such as the ones we see on Amazon, Airbnb, and Uber). These reputation systems allow us to learn about others without having to transact with them. In our roles as consumers as well as sellers, we prefer to deal with trading partners who will not engage in opportunism, all else equal. As consumers, we vet reputations by referring to credible sources and seeking informal reports from close associates before committing to transactions with unknown sellers and firms. As sellers, we check credit ratings and inquire about the reputation of potential trading partners by asking for references. These information-sharing methods raise the stakes for individuals engaging in unethical behavior. When individuals behave improperly in one-on-one market interactions, there are forums where this information can be shared with others.

Business partners inquire about potential partners and offer referrals based on what they have discovered through their market experiences. It would be unrealistic for the unethical businessperson to expect their conduct to never be shared in such a context.[31] After examining a large data set of eBay transactions from 1999, for instance, Resnick and Zeckhauser (2002) concluded that trust between buyers and sellers on eBay, an e-commerce website, emerged as a result of eBay's feedback system. They found that the majority of the transactions were one-time interactions and that sellers with better reputations were more likely to sell their goods.[32] A subsequent field experiment by Resnick et al. (2006) showed that, on average, buyers on eBay demonstrated a higher willingness to purchase from well-established sellers compared to new sellers with little to no reputation. In fact, buyers were 12.5% more likely to purchase from sellers with strong reputations than from new sellers; while buyers bought 56% of the listings posted by new sellers, they bought 63% of the listings posted by sellers with strong reputations. In short, buyers appear to be deliberately seeking out sellers with better reputations when making a purchasing decision, even for one-time purchases. As another example, Jin and Leslie (2003) observed how restaurants endeavored to improve their reputations with patrons once the Los Angeles County government began requiring them to display their hygiene grade cards in 1997. Even in our decisions about where to purchase dinner, reputation—not only in the form of the quality of service and food but also in the form of hygiene—appears to matter to us.

Through e-commerce and e-ratings websites like eBay, Amazon, Airbnb, Uber, Angie's List, Yelp, and others, people can now easily share their experiences and opinions of past and current partners with a large group of individuals. For the ethical, reputation and rating systems help them to stand out from relatively unethical individuals and enterprises. For the unethical, it even further raises the likelihood of their being caught or known for unscrupulous behavior.[33] And, if we mistakenly placed our trust in a swindler or just

---

[31] Recall, according to Smith ([1763] 1982: 538–539),

> A dealer is afraid of losing his character, and is scrupulous in observing every engagement. When a person makes perhaps 20 contracts in a day, he cannot gain so much by endeavouring to impose on his neighbours, as the very appearance of a cheat would make him lose. Where people seldom deal with one another, we find that they are somewhat disposed to cheat, because they can gain more by a smart trick than they can lose by the injury which it does their character.

[32] Interestingly, this higher probability did not translate into a price premium; while sellers with better reputations were more likely to sell their goods compared to others, they did not benefit from a boost in the prices of the goods sold (Resnick and Zeckhauser 2002). This is contradicted by Houser and Wooders (2006), who found that the seller's reputation had a statistically significant effect on the prices of goods sold through eBay.

[33] Gregg and Scott (2006: 95) demonstrated that "recent negative feedback posted in an on-line reputation system is useful in predicting future on-line auction fraud" and that "experienced on-line auction buyers are in a better position to use reputation system data to avoid potentially fraudulent auctions."

simply misread someone, markets have developed instruments such as insurance to reduce the cost of experiencing betrayal. These instruments allow us to take risks while we learn.

It is worth noting that it is probably not enough for unscrupulous market actors to simply pretend to be virtuous. Because individuals prefer to repeat interactions with those who are unlikely to engage in fraud or theft and who are more likely to work toward mutually beneficial outcomes in the long run, game theoretic predictions tell us that unethical business people might be lured by the larger expected profitability associated with being virtuous and will attempt to mimic the behavior of the ethical businessperson. Consequently, the market can incentivize the falsely virtuous to adopt the mannerisms, attitudes, and sentiments of the truly virtuous. While this mimicry may succeed at first, disingenuous individuals are rarely successful at impersonating authentically good people for a long time and do not survive in business. That it is still newsworthy in many market societies when an individual or company engages in and gets away with fraud over a long period of time suggests that it is quite rare. "[P]eople who are genuinely honest, fair, civil, and compassionate are more likely to succeed in business than those who simply fake it" (Mueller 1999: 21). Inauthentic people can sometimes, though rarely, pass for people who are authentically good, but these inauthentically virtuous people do not avoid discovery indefinitely. (Think, for instance, of Bernard Madoff, Robert Allen Stanford, and others who were convicted of running Ponzi schemes over the past few decades.) Although difficult to define precisely, people seem to have an uncanny ability to detect the *authentically virtuous* from the *inauthentically virtuous*. We react to our vague impressions and assessments of others as if by gut instinct and tend to seek out the authentically reliable and virtuous trading partners, particularly in uncertain and risky situations.

Markets Are Conversations About Right and Wrong

A conversation can be thought of as a process, as a dialectic of seeing and saying, as a game involving the to-and-fro play of questions and answers, as bids and asks. As Gadamer (1989: 385) stated, a "conversation is a process of coming to an understanding." Each dialogical participant who enters into a genuine conversation arrives already possessing certain prejudices and opinions as well as a particular knowledge of time and place, but also open to the potential rightness of the other's position and a willingness to listen to the other's views. "It belongs to every genuine conversation," Gadamer (Ibid.) wrote, "that each person opens himself to the other, truly accepts his point of view as valid and transposes himself into the other to such an extent that he understands not the particular individual but what he says." Through a back-and-forth of queries and replies, a "fusion of horizons" comes about.

This process of adjusting and clarifying one's own views and asking for clarification and explanation of the other's views is an indeterministic one.[34] As Gadamer (Ibid.: 383) explained, "[n]o one knows in advance what will 'come out' of a conversation. Understanding or its failure is like an event that happens to us." In a genuine conversation, the dialectic of questionable statements begging for a response and reactions to those statements has "a spirit of its own" and "allows something to 'emerge' which henceforth exists" (Ibid.), but which previously did not exist and could not have been purposely brought into existence. "We say that we 'conduct' a conversation, but the more genuine a conversation is," Gadamer (Ibid.) argued, "the less its conduct lies within the will of either partner … The way one word follows another, with the conversation taking its own twists and reaching its own conclusion, may well be conducted in some way, but the partners conversing are far less the leaders of it than the led."[35]

If we appreciate that the market is an open-ended process out of which a spontaneous order emerges, it makes sense to view the market as a kind of conversation.[36] This analogy is particularly apt because it captures the notion that the market is something that arises out of the interactions of individuals; some trying to understand one another, some talking at cross-purposes, and some unable or unwilling to reach agreement. Moreover, this analogy reminds us that in markets, as in conversations, the details of the resulting order cannot be known by anyone in advance.

Several scholars have profitably employed this analogy of the market as a dialogical process and have described the price mechanism provided by the market as a communications system. Hayek ([1948] 1980: 86–87), for instance, stated that "it is more than a metaphor to describe the price system as … a system of telecommunications." Yeager (1998), similarly, concluded that there are tremendous gains to be had from comparing the market to linguistic processes. "Markets convey information through prices," Yeager (Ibid.: 20) noted,

---

[34] See Gadamer (1989: 375) for a discussion of the indeterminacy of a rightly put question. Notably, this process of mutual adjustment is also very similar to the process of moral development described by Smith in *The Theory of Moral Sentiments* ([1759] 1982).

[35] See Lavoie (1990) for a discussion of hermeneutics and how it may be useful in helping us to understand markets.

[36] Like a conversation, a market can also be described in terms of the play of questions and answers as well as the "fusion of horizons" that can result from open discourse. Note that there is nothing inconsistent about talking about conversations or markets in these two ways—that is, by focusing on the process that leads to order or the nature of the order that results. This analogy captures both critical aspects of the market. It is a process (i.e. play) and an emergent order (i.e. the result of that play).

"in ways that resemble how language conveys information … they play a coordinating role." Markets and language are both spontaneous orders that help us to coordinate our activities with our fellows and to communicate our particular knowledge of time and place. Although linking markets and language can be worthwhile, it quickly becomes clear from Yeager's analysis that language is a closer kin to money than it is to markets. Indeed, the analogy fits more neatly if we link money to language, prices to words, and markets to conversations. As Yeager (Ibid.: 26) maintained, "[s]ome analogies, particularly between money and language, are illuminating." We speak and understand in dollar values and we figuratively and sometimes literally say prices when we make a sale or a purchase. The market is meaningfully thought of as a conversation between consumers and producers.

Horwitz (1995) also pointed out several connections between money and language. Both money and language, he (Ibid.: 164) wrote, "mediate social processes … money is the 'medium of exchange' … while language is the 'medium of experience.'" Both money and language allow us to convey information about our particular circumstances to others (Ibid.: 165). And, both are, in at least one sense, inescapable. "Just as we cannot help but think in terms of the words that language provides us," Horwitz (Ibid.) argued, "we cannot help but act in the market in terms of the money prices of what we want to exchange … Just as a thought that cannot be expressed in words is difficult to communicate in a conversation … so an economic want not expressed in money is difficult to communicate in the market process." It is possible to extend the metaphor even further; "[i]f money is analog to language, then price is analog to word" (Ibid.: 166). Words carry knowledge. We use words to express what we think, what we want, and how we feel. The words spoken by our fellows shape our expectations and guide our activities. Prices likewise convey knowledge. When goods become more scarce prices rise. When goods become less scarce prices fall. "A market price," as Horwitz (Ibid.) wrote, "embodies knowledge made available by exchanges through the medium of money, just as a word is knowledge made available by speaking or writing in a language."

In addition to being conversations about capabilities and desires, conversations about quantities and prices, markets are also conversations about right and wrong. Indeed, markets allow us to tell others that we appreciate them being virtuous or that we disapprove of them being immoral. Markets reward virtuous market participants and punish those who are not virtuous. For this reason, the market is fairly good at inspiring virtuous behavior. Entrepreneurs assess their partners' characters and personalities by observing and judging their negotiating strategies, their communication, their demeanor, and their behavior within and outside the negotiations and other business-related processes. Entrepreneurs, then, adjust their expectations, actions, and decisions to continue (or discontinue) their relationships with particular partners. This cycle of readjustments not only affects the profitability of specific business relationships, but also the opportunities to build new relationships through referrals. How a businessperson conducts herself could determine whether or not she is recommended to others by her trading partner and, thus, could define her future business opportunities.

Consider, for example, Greif's discussion of the Maghribi traders. Greif (1993) documented how a market institution affects individual behavior, business practices, and social structure. Importantly, his study showed that markets work in part because they reward honest traders. The Maghribi traders in pre-modern international trade faced an agency problem. In order to conduct trade internationally in the eleventh century, a merchant had to either travel with his merchandise, or hire agents based overseas to handle his merchandise. It was perhaps efficient for merchants to hire agents to deliver goods to their trading partners abroad, but they also faced the risk of the agents acting opportunistically and embezzling the goods. The Maghribi traders were able to overcome this agency problem by setting up an institution (which Greif called the coalition) that monitored the traders and their agents, regulated their pay, and facilitated information sharing among members. The coalition also exercised multilateral punishment strategies that were costly to embezzling agents. When an agent was suspected of fraud, all business with him was suspended until the coalition came to a verdict regarding his innocence. When an agent was proven to have engaged in fraud, the community of merchants within the coalition "practiced community punishment, and ostracized agents who were considered cheaters until they compensated the injured" (Ibid.: 530). Because the lifetime gains from continuing business with Maghribi merchants far exceeded the gains from a one-time fraud, agents worked toward remaining in good standing with the coalition. By being trustworthy and acting honorably, the member agents benefited from higher wages compared to nonmember agents as well as repeat business within this institution. These traders exemplified how the market, left untethered, can act as a space where people learn to at least mimic virtuous behavior.

In market societies, people's behavior is improved through this process of rewarding one another with future business when there are positive interactions and sanctioning one another when negative business interactions occur. In contexts where it is normal to see our high expectations met, we are sensitive to disappointments and moral transgressions. Again, news of profits and losses hardly makes ripples in the business world, but news (and rumors) of betrayal and fraud disseminate very quickly and widely.[37] Because entrepreneurs within a competitive market process face incentives to distinguish themselves on both price and nonprice margins, even the most prudential individuals will invest in building and maintaining their social networks through good customer service and goodwill.[38]

Beyond rewarding honest and fair business dealing, other virtues are rewarded in the market. Indeed, virtuous behavior can be profitable. Take, for example, courage and hope on which entrepreneurship, the driving force of the market, depends. Without the hope that a better machine can be invented or a new way of doing things can be discovered, entrepreneurship cannot get off the ground. Similarly, entrepreneurs must have the courage to test their new ideas in the marketplace, to persevere in the face of obstacles, and to break out of the status quo. The market rewards these virtues and in so doing encourages them.

In markets, it pays to be virtuous. Surveying the management literature, Mueller (1999) examined some of the attributes the market encourages: fairness, civility, compassion, and "heroism." Because the market became a much larger place in Britain and Germany, "business behavior … became noticeably more honest during the course of the nineteenth century" (Ibid.: 44). Contrary to common belief that successful business people are greedy individuals who lie, cheat, and steal from customers and employees,

> capitalism actually tends, all other things being equal, systematically, though not uniformly, to reward business behavior that is honest, fair, civil, and compassionate, and it inspires a form of risk taking behavior that can often be credibly characterized as heroic. … Under capitalism, as it happens, virtue is considerably more than its own reward. (Ibid.: 5)

---

[37] Corporate, or business, fraud makes headline news. Business people who engage in fraud also face legal sanctions. For instance, Cendant's decade-long accounting fraud was discovered in 1998 (Norris 2000). It was uncovered that Bernard Madoff, once a well-respected investor, operated a US$85 billion Ponzi scheme in 2008 (Aitken 2018). Former CEO of WorldCom, Bernard Ebbers, was convicted of securities fraud, conspiracy, and falsifying reports in 2005 (Ackman 2005). In late 2018, Carlos Ghosn, once celebrated as an automobile industry icon and who served as the CEO and chairman of Renault, Nissan, Mitsubishi Motors, and the Renault-Nissan-Mitsubishi Alliance, was arrested in Japan for allegedly falsifying his financial reports and misusing corporate funds (Ganley 2018; Greenfield 2018).

[38] Maintaining good relationships with customers is one way for a firm to demonstrate its integrity and dependability. Moreover, there are reasons to believe that good customer service can have a considerable effect on revenue. For instance, Chick-fil-A was the politest fast food chain according to QSR Magazine's 2016 report on drive-thrus and made the most revenue of all fast food chains in 2015 (Taylor 2016). "While small pleasantries are easy to dismiss in the multi-billion dollar restaurant business, these little things have played a key role in setting Chick-fil-A apart from the competition" (Ibid.). The literature on customer relationship management further demonstrates how customer relations matter for business performance (e.g. Knox et al. 2002; Buttle 2004).

Moreover, Mueller (Ibid.: 42) pointed out, "cutting a deal with a nice guy will usually generate some pleasure and so one might be quite rationally willing to give in a bit more in a deal with a nice guy than in one with a non-nice guy." Indeed, business partners and consumers alike often pay a premium (and workers are often willing to work at a discount) in order to transact with honest, trustworthy, faithful, and caring (i.e. loving) people.

Markets also punish vice. Recall, Becker ([1957] 1971) outlined how an employer who wishes to discriminate pays a price for his taste in discrimination. An employer who wishes to discriminate faces an increasing cost for his taste as other profit-maximizing, nondiscriminatory employers who opt to hire employees from the group that is being discriminated against are able to recruit qualified employees at lower wages. As such, an employer who wishes to discriminate would earn less profit than an employer who does not wish to discriminate. In order to keep his product competitive, the discriminating employer would then be compelled to hire employees from the group being discriminated against. Over time, through the repetition of this process, markets can dissuade market participants from committing immoral or morally dubious acts. As Friedman ([1962] 2002: 109) argued, "the preserves of discrimination in any society are the areas that are most monopolistic in character, whereas discrimination against groups of particular color or religion is least in those areas where there is the greatest freedom of competition." Similarly, as Steven Landsburg (1997: 185) showed, when there is discrimination within an industry, there is such a huge incentive for hiring a full work force of the discriminated class of workers that, given free entry, there would likely be at least one employer willing to do so.[39]

Through this mechanism of rewards and punishments, the market discourages a racist employee from discriminating against a black employer, a sexist consumer from refusing to purchase a good from a female producer, and a homophobic producer from refusing to sell to homosexual consumers. The business that refuses to hire the most productive workers or serve potential customers who are most willing and able to pay because of race, ethnicity,

---

[39] In his memoir, for instance, Alan Greenspan recounted how his firm benefited by engaging in less gender discrimination than his competitors in the market. "Townsend-Greenspan," he (2007: 74) explained,

> was unusual for an economics firm in that the men worked for the women. … My hiring of women economists was not motivated by women's liberation. It just made great business sense. I valued men and women equally, and found that because other employers did not, good women economists were less expensive than men. Hiring women did two things: it gave Townsend-Greenspan higher-quality work for the same money, and it marginally raised the market value of women.

sexual identity, or sexual orientation will lose out to its competitors. This is, obviously, not to say that we should never expect to observe intolerance in a market setting. It is instead to suggest that indulging in this behavior in a market setting comes at a cost and that the more competitors there are in a market the less likely it is to occur.

This market mechanism can also curb other vices. Vices, no matter what they are, simply cannot flourish in the long run in a market society.

Furthermore, markets have the capacity to make us *authentically virtuous*. People's desire to appeal and gain each other's approval and recognition in society generates a type of contagion effect. Specifically, a man who primarily associates with virtuous people will learn to appreciate and acquire some of their values, even if he himself never becomes perfectly virtuous. As Smith ([1759] 1982: 224) explained,

> The man who associates chiefly with the wise and the virtuous, though he may not himself become either wise or virtuous, cannot help conceiving a certain respect at least for wisdom and virtue; and the man who associates chiefly with the profligate and the dissolute, though he may not himself become profligate and dissolute, must soon lose, at least, all his original abhorrence of profligacy and dissolution of manners. The similarity of family characters, which we so frequently see transmitted through several successive generations, may, perhaps, be partly owing to this disposition, to assimilate ourselves to those whom we are obliged to live and converse a great deal with.

It is likely that a person will acquire the disposition and habits of his virtuous associates. Of course, no human institution, not our churches, governments, schools, or families, can inspire perfectly virtuous agents. However, by rewarding virtue and punishing vice, the market promotes virtue.

Markets Do Teach Us to Be Better People

The market has the potential to change us. If markets reward bad behavior, engaging in market activity will change us for the worse. If they had not started out that way, for instance, the bees in Mandeville's hive would have eventually become immoral given how common and lucrative immorality was in that setting. If markets reward good behavior, however, they have the potential to make people more virtuous than they would otherwise be.

Intriguingly, as we have argued, there is almost a consensus among commentators that markets reward our worst traits. For many, materialism and greed are synonymous with markets. There is disagreement, however, when it comes to assessing whether or not the moral costs that many believe are so clearly associated with market activity outweigh the obvious material benefits of market activity. Some point to the moral corruption that occurs in markets and recommend that market activity be circumscribed. Others point to the potential of markets to harness private vice and transform it into public virtue and so argue against curtailing market activity. Still others worry that the virtues that markets depend on are under threat. Moreover, the threat, they argue, is not an external threat. The market, they claim, needs morals but undermines and erodes them. The market, they fear, contains the seeds to its own destruction.

But the evidence suggests that the consensus is wrong. Markets do not corrupt our morals. Not only are people wealthier, healthier, happier, and better connected in market societies, market activity makes us better people. Markets are spaces where we discover who is virtuous and can expect many of our vices to be revealed. Additionally, markets reward virtue and punish vice. As such, markets are moral training grounds.

In the next chapter, we discuss some of the implications of our argument that market activity is not morally corrupting but leads to moral improvement. Importantly, we are silent on the possibility or problem of noxious markets. You can agree with everything we say about the potential of markets to make us better people and still maintain that markets in certain goods and services are morally problematic. Nothing that we have argued suggests that there should be markets in everything. Our argument does have implications for how we should think about culture. If people in market country A are more moral than people in nonmarket country B, then our arguments suggest that this is likely to have more to do with their economic system than their cultures. The reason that we observe more virtue and less corruption in market societies than in nonmarket societies, as we discussed in Chap. 5, is not because of any cultural advantages that people in market societies happen to enjoy over people in nonmarket societies.[40] Instead, we see more virtue and less corruption in market societies than in nonmarket societies because of the

---

[40] The experience of immigrant entrepreneurs in market societies is also telling in this regard. For instance, Tuttle (2015: 1) implied that "the fiscal contribution of foreign-born households increases the longer these households remain in the [United States]." Given that most of the immigrants to the United States are originally from nonmarket societies, the fact that these immigrants prospered and grew even more prosperous over time would seem to contradict this absolute cultural advantage of market societies argument. Similarly, Powell et al. (2017) argued that the institutional improvement that Israel observed in the 1990s could not have occurred to the same degree without the mass migration to Israel from the former Soviet Union (which increased Israel's population by 20% in the 1990s).

moral advantages associated with markets. Also, if our argument that markets can be a source of moral development is correct, then in addition to the widely recognized economic costs associated with restricting markets, there are potentially moral costs associated with restricting markets. If markets are really spaces where we discover whether the people we are interacting with are good or bad people, then limiting our access to markets or hampering markets might actually limit our ability to discover virtuous others. If markets are really conversations about right and wrong, then moves to truncate that conversation might limit our ability to learn to be virtuous.

Bibliography

Ackman, D. 2005. Bernie Ebbers Guilty. *Forbes*, March 15. https://www.forbes.com/2005/03/15/cx_da_0315ebbersguilty.html

Aitken, R. 2018. After U.S. SEC Shuts Down $85M Ponzi Scheme, Can They Ever Be Eradicated? *Forbes*, May 4. https://www.forbes.com/sites/rogeraitken/2018/05/04/after-u-s-sec-shuts-down-85m-ponzi-scheme-can-they-ever-be-eradicated/

Akerlof, G.A. 1970. The Market for 'Lemons': Quality Uncertainty and the Market Mechanism. *The Quarterly Journal of Economics* 84 (3): 488–500.

Becker, G.S. [1957] 1971. *The Economics of Discrimination: An Economic View of Racial Discrimination*. Chicago/London: University of Chicago Press.

Berg, J., J. Dickhaut, and K. McCabe. 1995. Trust, Reciprocity and Social History. *Games and Economic Behavior* 10 (1): 122–142.

Bloom, A.H. 1977. Two Dimensions of Moral Reasoning: Social Principledness and Social Humanism in Cross-Cultural Perspective. *The Journal of Social Psychology* 101 (1): 29–44.

Buck-Morss, S. 1975. Socioeconomic Bias in Piaget's Theory and its Implications for the Cross-Cultural Controversy. *Human Development* 18 (1–2): 35–49.

Buttle, F. 2004. *Customer Relationship Management: Concepts and Tools*. Oxford: Elsevier Butterworth-Heinemann.

Choi, G.S., and V.H. Storr. 2018. Market Institutions and the Evolution of Culture. *Evolutionary and Institutional Economics Review* 15 (2): 243–265.

Colby, A., L. Kohlberg, J. Gibbs, M. Lieberman, K. Fischer, and H.D. Saltzstein. 1983. A Longitudinal Study of Moral Judgment. *Monographs of the Society for Research in Child Development* 48 (1–2): 1–124.

Colby, A., L. Kohlberg, B. Speicher, D. Candee, A. Hewer, J. Gibbs, and C. Power. 1987. *The Measurement of Moral Judgement: Volume 2, Standard Issue Scoring Manual*. Cambridge: Cambridge University Press.

Cowen, T. 2017. *The Complacent Class: The Self-Defeating Quest for the American Dream*. New York: St. Martin's Press.

Cox, J.C. 2004. How to Identify Trust and Reciprocity. *Games and Economic Behavior* 46 (2): 260–281.

Crain, W.C. 1985. *Theories of Development: Concepts and Applications.* Englewood Cliffs: Prentice-Hall.

Croson, R., and N. Buchan. 1999. Gender and Culture: International Experimental Evidence from Trust Games. *American Economic Review* 89 (2): 386–391.

Dufwenberg, M., and U. Gneezy. 2000. Measuring Beliefs in an Experimental Lost Wallet Game. *Games and Economic Behavior* 30 (2): 163–182.

Edwards, C.P. 1975. Societal Complexity and Moral Development: A Kenyan Study. *Ethos* 3 (4): 505–527.

———. 1982. Moral development in comparative cultural perspective. In *Cultural Perspectives on Child Development*, ed. D. Wagner and H. Stevenson, 248–278. San Francisco: WH Freedman.

———. 1986. Cross-Cultural Research on Kohlberg's Stages: The Basis for Consensus. In *Lawrence Kohlberg: Consensus and Controversy*, ed. S. Modgil and C. Modgil, 419–430. Sussex: Falmer Press Limited.

Fehr, E., and S. Gächter. 1999. Collective Action as a Social Exchange. *Journal of Economic Behavior & Organization* 39 (4): 341–369.

———. 2000a. Cooperation and Punishment in Public Goods Experiments. *American Economic Review* 90 (4): 980–994.

———. 2000b. Fairness and Retaliation: The Economics of Reciprocity. *Journal of Economic Perspectives* 14 (3): 159–181.

———. 2002. Altruistic Punishment in Humans. *Nature* 415 (6868): 137–140.

Flanagan, O., and K. Jackson. 1987. Justice, Care, and Gender: The Kohlberg-Gilligan Debate Revisited. *Ethics* 97 (3): 622–637.

Friedman, M. [1962] 2002. *Capitalism and Freedom: Fortieth Anniversary Edition.* Chicago: University of Chicago Press.

Gadamer, H.G. [1960] 1989. *Truth and Method.* London: Sheed & Ward.

Ganley, E. 2018. Carlos Ghosn: From Auto Industry Icon to Scandal. *The Associated Press*, November 26. http://www.wsfa.com/2018/11/26/nissan-ghosn-auto-industry-icon-scandal/

Gibbs, J.C. 1979. Kohlberg's Moral Stage Theory: A Piagetian Revision. *Human Development* 22: 89–112.

Gibbs, J.C., K.S. Basinger, R.L. Grime, and J.R. Snarey. 2007. Moral Judgment Development Across Cultures: Revisiting Kohlberg's Universality Claims. *Developmental Review* 27 (4): 443–500.

Gilligan, C. 1979. Woman's Place in Man's Life Cycle. *Harvard Educational Review* 49 (4): 431–446.

———. 1982. *In a Different Voice: Psychological Theory and Women's Development.* Cambridge: Harvard University Press.

Greenfield, R. 2018. Dazzled by Ghosn's Star, Investors Ignored Lessons of History. *Bloomberg*, November 23. https://www.bloomberg.com/news/articles/2018-11-23/dazzled-by-ghosn-s-star-investors-ignored-lessons-of-history

Greenspan, A. 2007. *The Age of Turbulence: Adventures in a New World*. New York: Penguin.

Gregg, D.G., and J.E. Scott. 2006. The Role of Reputation Systems in Reducing On-Line Auction Fraud. *International Journal of Electronic Commerce* 10 (3): 95–120.

Greif, A. 1993. Contract Enforceability and Economic Institutions in Early Trade: The Maghribi Traders' Coalition. *American Economic Review* 83 (3): 525–548.

Guidon, A. 1978. Moral Development: A Critique of Kohlberg's Sequence. *University of Ottawa Quarterly* 48 (3): 232–263.

Hayek, F.A. [1948] 1980. *Individualism and Economic Order*. Chicago: University of Chicago Press.

Henry, S.E. 2001. What Happens When We Use Kohlberg? His Troubling Functionalism and the Potential of Pragmatism in Moral Education. *Educational Theory* 51 (3): 259–276.

Hirschman, A.O. 1992. *Rival Views of Market Society and Other Recent Essays*. Cambridge: Harvard University Press.

———. 2013. In *The Essential Hirschman*, ed. J. Adelman. Princeton: Princeton University Press.

Holcombe, R.G. 2003. The Origins of Entrepreneurial Opportunities. *The Review of Austrian Economics* 16 (1): 25–43.

Horwitz, S. 1992. Monetary Exchange as an Extra-Linguistic Social Communication Process. *Review of Social Economy* 50 (2): 193–214. Reprinted in D.L. Prychitko, ed. 1995. *Individuals, Institutions, Interpretations: Hermeneutics Applied to Economics*, 154–175. Aldershot: Avebury Publishing.

Houser, D., and J. Wooders. 2006. Reputation in Auctions: Theory, and Evidence from eBay. *Journal of Economics and Management Strategy* 15 (2): 353–369.

Jin, G.Z., and P. Leslie. 2003. The Effect of Information on Product Quality: Evidence from Restaurant Hygiene Grade Cards. *The Quarterly Journal of Economics* 118 (2): 409–451.

Kirzner, I.M. 1973. *Competition and Entrepreneurship*. Chicago: University of Chicago Press.

———. 1979. *Perception, Opportunity, and Profit: Studies in the Theory of Entrepreneurship*. Chicago: University of Chicago.

———. 1992. *The Meaning of the Market Process: Essays in the Development of Modern Austrian Economics*. London and New York: Routledge.

Klein, P.G. 1999. Entrepreneurship and Corporate Governance. *The Quarterly Journal of Austrian Economics* 2 (2): 19–42.

Knox, S., A. Payne, L. Ryals, S. Maklan, and J. Peppard. 2002. *Customer Relationship Management: Perspectives from the Market Place*. London/New York: Routledge.

Kohlberg, L. 1958. *The Development of Modes of Moral Thinking and Choice in the Years 10 to 16*. PhD dissertation, University of Chicago.

———. 1973a. Continuities in Childhood and Adult Moral Development Revisited. In *Life-Span Developmental Psychology: Personality and Socialization*, ed. P.B. Baltes and K.W. Schaie, 179–204. Orlando: Academic Press.

————. 1973b. Stages and Aging in Moral Development—Some Speculations. *The Gerontologist* 13 (4): 497–502.

————. 1981. *The Philosophy of Moral Development: Moral Stages and the Idea of Justice (Essays on Moral Development, Volume 1)*. San Francisco: Harper & Row.

————. 1984. *The Psychology of Moral Development: The Nature and Validity of Moral Stages (Essays on Moral Development, Volume 2)*. San Francisco: Harper & Row.

Kohlberg, L., and R. Kramer. 1969. Continuities and Discontinuities in Childhood and Adult Moral Development. *Human Development* 12 (2): 93–120.

Kohlberg, L., and R. Mayer. 1972. Development as the Aim of Education. *Harvard Educational Review* 42 (4): 449–496.

Kohlberg, L., and R.A. Ryncarz. 1990. Beyond Justice Reasoning: Moral Development and Consideration of a Seventh Stage. In *Higher Stages of Human Development: Perspectives on Adult Growth*, ed. C.N. Alexander and E.J. Langer, 191–207. Oxford: Oxford University Press.

Kohlberg, L., C. Levine, and A. Hewer. 1983. *Moral Stages: A Current Formulation and a Response to Critics (Contributions to Human Development, Vol. 10)*. Basel: S. Karger.

Kramer, R.M. 1999. Trust and Distrust in Organizations: Emerging Perspectives, Enduring Questions. *Annual Review of Psychology* 50 (1): 569–598.

Krebs, D.L., K. Denton, and G. Wark. 1997. The Forms and Functions of Real-Life Moral Decision-Making. *Journal of Moral Education* 26 (2): 131–145.

Lachmann, L.M. 1971. *The Legacy of Max Weber-Luckmann*. Berkeley: Glendessary Press.

————. 1976. From Mises to Shackle: An Essay on Austrian Economics and the Kaleidic Society. *Journal of Economic Literature* 14: 54–62.

————. [1940] 1977. *Capital, Expectations, and the Market Process: Essays on the Theory of the Market Economy*. Kansas City: Sheed, Andrews and McMeel.

Landsburg, S.E. 1997. *Fair Play*. New York: Free Press.

Langrill, R., and V.H. Storr. 2012. The Moral Meaning of Markets. *Journal of Markets and Morality* 15 (2): 347–362.

Lavoie, D. 1986. Euclideanism Versus Hermeneutics: A Reinterpretation of Misesian Apriorism. In *Subjectivism, Intelligibility and Economic Understanding: Essays in Honor of Ludwig M. Lachmann on His Eightieth Birthday*, ed. I.M.M. Kirzner, 192–210. London: Macmillan.

————. 1990. Understanding Differently: Hermeneutics and the Spontaneous Order of Communicative Processes. *History of Political Economy*, Annual Supplement to Vol. 22: 359–377.

Leeson, P.T. 2007. Better off Stateless: Somalia before and after Government Collapse. *Journal of Comparative Economics* 35 (4): 689–710.

Logan, R., J. Snarey, and D. Schrader. 1990. Autonomous Versus Heteronomous Moral Judgment Types: A Longitudinal Cross-Cultural Study. *Journal of Cross-Cultural Psychology* 21 (1): 71–89.

Marshall, A. [1890] 1920. *Principles of Economics: An Introductory Volume*. London: Palgrave Macmillan.

McCloskey, D.N. 2010. *Bourgeois Dignity: Why Economics Can't Explain the Modern World.* Chicago: University of Chicago Press.

Montesquieu. [1748] 1989. *Montesquieu: The Spirit of the Laws*, editor A.M. Cohler, B.C. Miller and H.S. Stone. Cambridge: Cambridge University Press.

Mueller, J. 1999. *Capitalism, Democracy, and Ralph's Pretty Good Grocer.* Princeton: Princeton University Press.

Munger, M. 2015. One and One-Half Cheers for a Basic-Income Guarantee: We Could Do Worse, and Already Have. *The Independent Review* 19 (4): 503–513.

Norris, F. 2000. Cendant Says Accounting Firm Knew of Fraudulent Practices. *The New York Times*, June 20. https://www.nytimes.com/2000/06/20/business/cendant-says-accounting-firm-knew-of-fraudulent-practices.html

Ostrom, E., and J. Walker, eds. 2003. *Trust and Reciprocity: Interdisciplinary Lessons for Experimental Research.* New York: Russell Sage Foundation.

Perry, B.E., ed. [1952] 2007. *Aesopica: Greek and Latin Texts.* Urbana: University of Illinois Press.

Pew Research Center. 2011. Little Change in Public's Response to 'Capitalism,' 'Socialism': A Political Rhetoric Test. *Pew Research Center*, December 28. http://www.people-press.org/2011/12/28/little-change-in-publics-response-to-capitalism-socialism/?src=prc-number

———. 2014. Emerging and Developing Economies Much More Optimistic than Rich Countries about the Future. *Pew Research Center*, October 9. http://www.pewglobal.org/2014/10/09/emerging-and-developing-economies-much-more-optimistic-than-rich-countries-about-the-future/#free-market-seen-as-best-despite-inequality

Powell, B., J.R. Clark, and A. Nowrasteh. 2017. Does Mass Immigration Destroy Institutions? 1990s Israel as a Natural Experiment. *Journal of Economic Behavior & Organization* 141: 83–95.

Resnick, P., and R. Zeckhauser. 2002. Trust among Strangers in Internet Transactions: Empirical Analysis of eBay's Reputation System. In *The Economics of the Internet and E-Commerce*, ed. M.R. Baye, 127–157. Oxford: Elsevier Science.

Resnick, P., R. Zeckhauser, J. Swanson, and K. Lockwood. 2006. The Value of Reputation on eBay: A Controlled Experiment. *Experimental Economics* 9 (2): 79–101.

Rest, J.R., S.J. Thoma, and M.J. Bebeau. 1999. *Postconventional Moral Thinking: A Neo-Kohlbergian Approach.* London: Psychology Press.

Rose, D.C. 2018. *Why Culture Matters Most.* Oxford: Oxford University Press.

Schumpeter, J.A. [1942] 2010. *Capitalism, Socialism, and Democracy.* London/New York: Routledge.

Shweder, R.A. 1982a. Beyond Self-Constructed Knowledge: The Study of Culture and Morality. *Merrill-Palmer Quarterly* 28 (1): 41–69.

Shweder, R. 1982b. Liberalism as Destiny: Review of Kohlberg (1981). *Contemporary Psychology* 27: 421–424.

Simpson, E.L. 1974. Moral Development Research: A Case Study of Scientific Cultural Bias. *Human Development* 17 (2): 81–106.

Smith, A. [1776] 1981. *An Inquiry into the Nature and Causes of the Wealth of Nations.* Indianapolis: Liberty Fund.

———. [1759] 1982. *The Theory of Moral Sentiments.* Indianapolis: Liberty Fund.

———. [1763] 1982. *Lectures in Jurisprudence.* Indianapolis: Liberty Fund.

Snarey, J.R. 1985. Cross-Cultural Universality of Social-Moral Development. A Critical Review of Kohlbergian Research. *Psychological Bulletin* 97 (2): 202–232.

Storr, V.H. 2018. The Impartial Spectator and the Moral Teachings of the Market. In *The Oxford Handbook of Freedom*, ed. D. Schmidtz and C.E. Pavel, 456–474. Oxford: Oxford University Press.

Sullivan, E.V. 1977. A Study of Kohlberg's Structural Theory of Moral Development: A Critique of Liberal Social Science Ideology. *Human Development* 20 (6): 352–376.

Taylor, K. 2016. Chick-fil-A is Beating Every Competitor by Training Workers to Say 'Please' and 'Thank You'. *Business Insider*, October 3. https://www.businessinsider.com/chick-fil-a-is-the-most-polite-chain-2016-10

Tuttle, J. 2015. *Immigration, Income Tax, and Social Assistance: Examining the Fiscal Contribution of Foreign Born and Native Born Households in the U.S.* George Mason University Institute for Immigration Research.

Yeager, L.B. 1998. Are Markets Like Language? *The Quarterly Journal of Austrian Economics* 1 (3): 15–27.

Zak, P. 2008. *Moral Markets: The Critical Role of Values in the Economy.* Princeton: Princeton University Press.

Zwolinski, M. 2011. Classical Liberalism and the Basic Income. *Basic Income Studies* 6 (2): 1–14.

———. 2015. Property Rights, Coercion and the Welfare State: The Libertarian Case for a Basic Income for All. *The Independent Review* 19 (4): 515–529.

7

What If Markets Are Really Moral?

Many people think of Ebenezer Scrooge from *A Christmas Carol* (Dickens [1843] 2013) as an archetype of a market participant. Scrooge, we learn at the start of Charles Dickens' novel, is a callous and calculating businessman. According to Dickens (Ibid.: 1.7–8),

> he was a tight-fisted hand at the grindstone, Scrooge! a squeezing, wrenching, grasping, scraping, clutching, covetous, old sinner! Hard and sharp as flint, … The cold within him froze his old features, … A frosty rime was on his head, and on his eyebrows, and his wiry chin. He carried his own low temperature always about with him; he iced his office in the dog-days; and didn't thaw it one degree at Christmas. External heat and cold had little influence on Scrooge. No warmth could warm, no wintry weather chill him.

Scrooge is a harsh, solitary, selfish figure who cares more about money than other people. His external appearance and his imperviousness to the elements reflect his internal coldness.

Early in the novel, we find Scrooge in his counting-house, keeping a suspicious eye on his clerk. Just as Smith and Marx would have predicted, Scrooge treats his worker as poorly as possible. He denies his clerk a decent fire, despite the cold weather. And, he only begrudgingly gives his clerk the day off at Christmas. Scrooge also criticizes his nephew's Christmas cheer, as he finds no profit in it. Additionally, Scrooge at the beginning of the novel is uncharitable. He, for instance, rejected the entreaties of the two gentlemen who came to his office to solicit donations for the poor. "It's not my businesses," Scrooge remarks, explaining his indifference to the lot of the poor (Ibid.: 1.65). "It's

© The Author(s) 2019
V. H. Storr, G. S. Choi, *Do Markets Corrupt Our Morals?*,
https://doi.org/10.1007/978-3-030-18416-2_7

enough for a man to understand his own business, and not to interfere with other people's. Mine occupies me constantly" (Ibid.).

During the course of the novel, Scrooge is visited by the ghost of Marley, his former partner, and three additional spirits (the ghosts of Christmas past, present, and future). With the help of the ghosts, Scrooge is reminded that there is a purpose to life beyond earning a profit, that there is genuine suffering and sorrow in his community, and that he will have lived an empty and lonely life if he continues on his current course. The novel ends with a repentant and transformed Scrooge. He raises the salary of his employee, he is generous to the less fortunate, and his coldness melts away. According to Dickens (Ibid.: 5.70), Scrooge "became as good a friend, as good a master, and as good a man as the good old city knew, or any other good old city, town, or borough in the good old world." The greedy character we met at the beginning of the novel becomes his opposite by the end of the novel.

Market participants, however, are simply not Scrooges. In fact, the typical market participant has less in common with the Ebenezer Scrooge that we meet at the beginning of the novel than the Scrooge that emerges at the end of Dickens' *A Christmas Carol*. The central moral criticism of markets (i.e. that markets corrupt our morals) is not correct. If markets are really morally corrupting, then we should expect the social scientific models and concepts which (best) explain how markets function to allow for the likelihood of moral corruption. If markets really do crowd out virtue and corrupt the virtuous, this should be borne out in the evidence. Our theoretical understanding of how markets can and should work, however, points in the opposite direction. Moreover, the evidence suggests that markets are not the *immoralizing* spaces that some have imagined them to be. People who live in market societies tend to be wealthier, healthier, happier, and better connected than people who live in nonmarket societies. Additionally, on average, people who live in market societies exhibit more virtue and less vice than people who live in nonmarket societies.

Markets, in fact, are *moralizing* spaces. As we navigate markets as customers, producers, clients, principals, colleagues, and competitors, we discover who can be trusted and are rewarded for being trustworthy. Our direct interactions with our colleagues, customers, competitors, suppliers, employees, bosses, and others provide first-hand knowledge (sometimes tacit and inarticulate) about their dispositions, personalities, moral priorities, and more. We also have numerous opportunities to observe them interact with others in market settings and to acquire secondhand knowledge that sometimes confirms or opposes our existing impressions of them. This knowledge of what other market actors are like informs our decisions regarding whom to engage and avoid in future market transactions. Since people will want to do business with people who are virtuous, and to avoid dealings with people who are immoral, markets will tend to reward virtuous behavior and punish immoral behavior.

In challenging the view that markets are morally corrupting, we have not only argued that markets are compatible with morality but also that markets support moral improvement. The argument we advance here, however, has nothing to say about the problem of noxious markets or the role of governments and government programs in promoting morality. If markets are *moralizing*, as we suggest, that does have implications for how we should think about culture and how we should think about market interventions. This chapter will discuss some of the implications of our argument that markets can be and tend to be moral.

Nothing to Say About Noxious Markets

Almost nobody believes that everything should be for sale. Some markets—such as markets in healthcare or necessary items after a disaster—strike many as problematic. Some goods and services—such as sex, addictive drugs, human organs, and items made with child labor—strike many as repugnant. Debra Satz (2010) in *Why Some Things Should Not Be for Sale: The Moral Limits of Markets* described these markets as noxious markets. As Satz (Ibid.: 3) explained, "[m]arkets in these goods are seen as fundamentally different from, and elicit very different reactions than, markets in automobiles or soybeans. Such markets … strike many people as noxious, toxic to important human values. These markets evoke widespread discomfort and, in the extreme, revulsion." The discomfort and revulsion that noxious markets elicit, Satz (Ibid.) suggested, might be sufficient reason to regulate or block such markets. She offered a framework through which we can analyze noxious markets and think through the various current controversies about how to respond to them.

Noxious markets, Satz (Ibid.: 93) argued, are markets where the parties to the exchange are not able to interact with each other as equals. "A market exchange based in desperation, humiliation, or begging or whose terms of remediation involve bondage or servitude," Satz (Ibid.) noted, "is not an exchange between equals. … lurking behind many, if not all, noxious markets are problems relating to the *standing* of the parties before, during, and after the process of exchange." She (Ibid.: 94–97) highlighted four characteristics of noxious markets that people find particularly offensive:

(1) harmful outcomes to involved parties or third parties (e.g. a market that leaves a person destitute);
(2) harmful outcomes for the society (e.g. a market whose operation weakens the social structure that allows people to interact as equals);
(3) weak agency, which refers to the feature of markets that relies on the asymmetry in agency of some market participants (due to information asymmetry, imperfect knowledge, or asymmetry in their ability to understand the consequences of a particular trade); and
(4) vulnerability, which refers to how some markets pivot around the vulnerability of one of the parties to the trade (e.g. a market whose participants have very unequal needs for the good being exchanged).

A truly noxious market, Satz explained, would score highly on one or more of these four parameters. A market for votes, for instance, might be viewed as noxious because of the harm some believe it will cause to society. Similarly, the sale of sex might be thought of as noxious because of concerns about the harm to the parties involved in and affected by the exchange. A market for addictive drugs, likewise, might be considered noxious because drug addiction is harmful to the drug addict, because drug addicts are harmful to society, because drug addicts have a diminished capacity to make informed decisions, and because drug addicts might have a heightened vulnerability to all sorts of abuse. Once we as a society have resolved whether or not a particular market is noxious and have also established the source(s) of its noxiousness, we can then tailor a policy that addresses the particular problems with that market.

Jason Brennan and Peter Jaworski (2016) objected to the complaints about market activity of the kind advanced by Satz and others. Their claim is that there is no morally significant difference between selling something and giving it away. Stated another way, Brennan and Jaworski argued that introducing buying and selling can do nothing to transform an item or an activity that is morally unproblematic into something that is morally problematic. According to Brennan and Jaworski (Ibid.: 10),

if you may have, use, possess, and dispose of something (that does not belong to someone else) for free, then—except in special circumstances—it is permissible for you to buy and sell it. Another way of expressing our thesis is that the market does not transform what were permissible acts into impermissible acts. It does not introduce wrongness where there was not any already.

Notice that this is a conditional claim. Brennan and Jaworski did not argue that there should be markets in everything. They would, however, recommend markets in multiple areas where Satz and others would question the existence of markets or at least the existence of unregulated and unrestrained markets. And, Brennan and Jaworski would not bar the buying or selling of anything that it was permissible to exchange for free. Moreover, Brennan and Jaworski argued that when there is a problem with the sale of some good or service, the problem is often not that it was for sale but how it is being sold. Additionally, they acknowledged that markets in some items and activities (because markets will lead to increased production and lower costs over time) could increase the problems associated with these otherwise morally permissible items or activities.

Ironically, Brennan and Jaworski's position is not fundamentally different than Satz's position. Satz (2010: 6) never advocated the complete elimination of markets; "markets make an important contribution to the possibility of [a society of equals], but to do so they need limits, and some goods need to be guaranteed to all." Furthermore, "[m]arkets allow people to accomplish many important social and individual tasks under modern conditions of interdependence and diversity" (Ibid.: 91). As Brennan and Jaworski (2016: 28) acknowledged, their disagreement with Satz was over how and which markets should be limited, not over whether (some) markets should be limited.

Still, we believe, the difference between a gift and an exchange is a morally critical distinction. The radical subjectivism of the kind we embrace demands that we be sensitive to the possibility and appropriateness of actors ascribing different meanings to things that they buy and sell from things that they receive or give away.

That said, we are silent on the possibility or problem of noxious markets. It is possible to agree with everything we argued about the potential of markets to make us better people and still maintain that markets in certain goods and services are morally problematic and should not exist. Nothing that we have argued and none of the evidence that we presented suggest that there should be markets in everything. In fact, none of the market societies that we have discussed allow markets in everything.

Silent on the Importance of Democracy

Societies are complex phenomena. As such, it is impossible to isolate one factor as the key factor in bringing about any particular societal outcome. Although our focus has been on the impact of markets, the economic, social as well as moral development that we catalog might depend on a number of factors beyond markets. Several scholars pointed to democracy as being critical to development. Sen (1999: 15), for instance, claimed that democracy is a universal value. The value of democracy includes its *intrinsic importance* in human life, its *instrumental role* in generating political incentives, and its *constructive function* in the formation of values (and in understanding the force and feasibility of claims of needs, rights, and duties). By its intrinsic importance, Sen was referring to the central role that political participation plays in living a flourishing life. By its instrumental role, Sen was stressing the opportunity that democracy gives citizens to express and pursue their political goals. By its constructive function, Sen meant the potential of the political process to promote the exchange of information and perspectives, and the potential of political participation to cultivate the values of citizenship. Our argument that markets are not morally corrupting in no way challenges the belief that democracy is an important source of economic, social, or moral development.[1]

Interestingly, the research on the (direct) relationship between democracy and economic growth remains inconclusive. According to Doucouliagos and Ulubaşoğlu's (2008), meta-analysis of 483 regression estimates from 84 published studies, 73% of the regressions failed to find a positive and statistically significant relationship between democracy and growth.[2] However, numerous studies demonstrate how democracy has enormous indirect effects on growth. For instance, democracies can fuel economic growth by improving access to education, thus increasing the quantity (though not quality) of education supplied and spurring human capital accumulation (e.g. Helliwell 1994; Baum and Lake 2001, 2003; Stasavage 2005; Dahlum and Knutsen 2017). Democratic leaders who rely on votes for re-election are inclined to adopt

---

[1] We, however, strongly disagree with Bowles and Gintis (1978, [1986] 2012) who argued that democracy and capitalism are inherently incompatible systems. Bowles and Gintis ([1986] 2012: 3) argued that "capitalism and democracy are not complementary systems" and that they are sharply contrasting institutions where,

> the one is characterized by the preeminence of economic privilege based on property rights [i.e. promotes and relies on inequalities], the other insists on the priority of liberty and democratic accountability based on the exercise of personal rights [i.e. promotes and relies on an egalitarian principle].

More recently, Kuttner (2018) also defended this argument. A number of market societies, however, are also democracies. Additionally, though not definitive, our analysis does suggest that being a market society is more critical than being a democracy for economic, social, and moral development (see Appendix).

[2] Doucouliagos and Ulubaşoğlu (2008: 62) specified that, of the 483 regression estimates, "15% of the estimates [were] negative and statistically significant, 21% of the estimates [were] negative and statistically insignificant, 37% of the estimates [were] positive and statistically insignificant, and 27% of the estimates [were] positive and statistically significant."

redistributive policies such as welfare spending, progressive tax policies, and minimum wage laws in response.[3] Other studies specified how democracy may impact economic growth through channels such as political stability (e.g. Alesina and Perotti 1996; Feng 1997; Uddin et al. 2017). Democracies also tend to promote political stability by, among other reasons, reducing the likelihood of social unrest by allowing citizens to express dissatisfaction with the incumbent administration through the electoral process and by facilitating smooth transitions of power from one leader to another (Dahl 1991). While mixed overall, some evidence suggested that democracy correlates negatively with income inequality (e.g. Lindert 1994, 2004; Rodrik 1999; Persson and Tabellini 2003; Reuveny and Li 2003).

The research on the relationships between democracy and trust (e.g. Warren 1999; Newton 2001; Bjørnskov 2007) as well as on the relationship between democracy and tolerance (e.g. Sullivan et al. 1982; Peffley and Rohrschneider 2003; Mann 2004) is also inconclusive. The literature on the relationship between democracy and political corruption is similarly mixed. Some aspects of democracy seem to incentivize corruption. Competition between political parties over votes can motivate some politicians to buy votes. Other aspects of democracy, like the protections for free speech and the free press, can check political corruption (Chowdhury 2004). Sung (2004), for instance, found that government corruption can increase in the early stages of political liberalization, but that democratization eventually decreases corruption. Similarly, Saha and Su (2012) and Saha et al. (2014) found that democracy will tend to increase corruption when economic liberalization is low but will lower corruption when economic liberation is high. On the other hand, Sun and Johnston (2009) compared India and China and concluded that democracy in India had not done a better job of checking corruption than the authoritarian development state in China. Jetter et al. (2015), likewise, found that democracy only reduces corruption in countries where income is above a threshold.

Importantly, our argument that markets can promote moral development implies nothing about the importance of democracy or the relationship between democracy and any particular economic, social, or moral outcome. Accepting our argument implies nothing about the role that democracy plays or does not play in our material, social, and moral development nor does it imply anything about the relative importance of democracy as compared to markets in promoting development.

---

[3] See Acemoglu et al. (2015) for a comprehensive overview of the topic of democracy, income redistribution, and income inequality.

Important Things to Say About the Culture

Several scholars have argued that differences in measures of morality across countries can be explained by differences in culture. For instance, Lawrence Harrison (1992) and Samuel Huntington (1996) believed that culture largely explained why some countries prospered and others did not. They advocated the view that societies must possess the "right" kind of culture in order to experience economic progress; possessing the "wrong" kind of culture dooms a society to economic destitution. The apparent differences in morality between market and nonmarket societies that we highlighted, on Harrison and Huntington's view, would be due to systematic differences across the cultures that exist in these societies.

An implication of the sort of argument for cultural determinism advocated by Harrison and Huntington is that a society will blossom or wither as its culture shifts.[4] Consider, for example, two societies, Society A and Society B, with their own distinctive cultures. Now, assume members of Society B immigrate to Society A. We could imagine how the culture in Society A may shift (for better or worse) as more members of Society B move to Society A. If we further assume that Society A was a market society because it had the "right" culture and Society B a nonmarket society because it had the "wrong" culture, the "right/wrong culture" argument would predict that the culture in Society A will become more development-resistant as people immigrate from Society B. On this view, members of Society B possess values and attitudes that are not conducive toward economic progress and will undermine the existing values and attitudes of those in Society A that are conducive toward economic progress.

In sharp contrast, our argument predicts that markets will incentivize individuals immigrating from Society B to modulate their behaviors, attitudes, and values to "what works" in Society A. Recall from our argument and suggestive experimental evidence in Chap. 6 that the market rewards individuals when they exhibit desirable behaviors, attitudes, and values and punishes them when they exhibit undesirable ones. Stated another way, if Harrison and Huntington are correct, we should observe immigrants to market societies from nonmarket societies exhibiting more or less the same level

---

[4]Lavoie and Chamlee-Wright (2000) and Storr (2013) offered extensive critiques of Harrison's view of culture. Rather than viewing culture as a constraint or causal force, for instance, Storr agreed with Geertz that culture shapes but does not cause economic activity. "As interworked systems of construable signs," Geertz (1973: 14) wrote, "culture is not a power, something to which social events, behaviors, institutions, or processes can be causally attributed; it is a context, something within which they can be intelligibly – that is, thickly – described."

of immoral behavior as their counterparts in their countries of origin. However, if our argument holds, we should observe immigrants to market societies from nonmarket societies exhibiting less immoral behavior than their counterparts in their countries of origin.

Unfortunately, there is scant research that focuses on the intergenerational transmission of values that compares immigrants' current values against those of their counterparts in their countries of origin. But the little evidence that does exist hints that the children and grandchildren of those immigrants to market societies exhibit moral values that deviate from those of their counterparts in their ancestors' countries of origin and that approach those of the natively born in their receiving countries. For instance, while Tabellini (2008) found that generalized trust of third-generation immigrants in the United States positively, but imperfectly, correlated with the generalized trust in their ancestors' countries of origin, he also discovered evidence for some immigrants, in particular those whose ancestors immigrated from nonmarket societies such as Hungary, Portugal, Spain, and Yugoslavia, expressing greater generalized trust than those in their ancestors' countries of origin. Although this improvement in generalized trust was not true for all third-generation immigrants whose ancestors originated from a nonmarket society (such as Greece and Portugal), Tabellini's analysis raises doubts about the arguments advocated by Harrison and Huntington.

Moreover, the literature on immigrant entrepreneurship demonstrates that immigrants (from nondeveloped countries) thrive in developed countries. For instance, numerous studies showed that rates of business ownership are generally higher among foreign-born residents than natively born residents in developed countries such as the United States, United Kingdom, Canada, and Australia (e.g. Borjas 1986; Lofstrom 2002; Clark and Drinkwater 2000, 2010; Schuetze and Antecol 2007; Fairlie et al. 2010). Similarly, Fairlie (2012) and Fairlie and Lofstrom (2014) documented an increasing trend in self-employment rates and new business formation among immigrants, while Hunt (2011, 2015) observed that skilled immigrants are more likely to start firms with more than ten employees than their counterparts who were native-born. More narrowly focused on the high-tech sector, Saxenian (1999, 2002) reported that immigrants founded or ran as much as a quarter of the high-tech firms in Silicon Valley in the 1980s and 1990s. Wadhwa et al. (2007) documented similar trends in other industries in the United States for firms founded between 1995 and 2005.

Other empirical studies suggest how formal institutions such as markets have the ability to exert desirable influence on the behavior of immigrants. For example, Fisman and Miguel (2007) investigated the parking violation behavior of United Nations employees in New York City before and after the city implemented a rule that permitted local parking enforcement authorities to seize diplomatic license plates. Diplomatic immunity exempts diplomats and their families from incurring parking fines, so some members of the diplomatic community exploited this privilege to park conveniently regardless of the local rules. Once the plate confiscation rule came into effect and diplomats became subject to local parking rules, even diplomats from highly corrupt countries began abiding by the local rules. In fact, instances of parking illegally and amassing unpaid parking violations by such diplomats reduced by 98%. Choi and Storr (2018) manipulated one institutional rule to experimentally demonstrate that different market structures can facilitate the formation of distinct cultures defined by different levels of trust and trustworthiness. In that economic experiment, a culture where participants more or less treated one another equally and indiscriminately emerged in the treatment where the market automatically enforced all agreements. A culture where participants rewarded trustworthy and punished untrustworthy trading partners emerged in the treatment where the market permitted participants to defect on agreements. We certainly do not deny that culture shapes human behavior and we agree that whether certain types of institutions "stick" also depends on culture (e.g. Boettke et al. 2008; Choi and Storr 2019). But, if we are correct that markets encourage morality, if members of a (market) society exhibit relatively more moral behavior than those in another (nonmarket) society, this difference is likely to have more to do with their economic systems than their cultures.

To explore whether our argument holds, we conducted some regression-based analysis to determine whether culture, not markets, is the source of differences in morality.[5] We operationalized culture as Huntington (1996) defined civilizations and concentrated on whether being a Western civilization affected some of the measures from Chaps. 4 and 5. In addition to culture, we also included ethnic fractionalization, political rights, and civil liberties, which have been identified as being critical factors in explaining economic, social, and moral development. Our analysis revealed that being a market society is statistically significant in explaining the economic, social, and moral outcomes that we explored more consistently than any other factor. While preliminary and by no means definitive, our regression analysis supports our hypothesis that being a market society is associated with more of things that we care about than culture or any other societal characteristic.

---

[5] See Appendix for additional details on and results from the regression analysis.

Culture is not likely the driving force behind the observed differences in morality that we observe across societies. The reason that we observe more virtue and less corruption in market societies than in nonmarket societies, as we discussed in Chap. 5, is not because of any cultural advantages that people in market societies happen to enjoy over people in nonmarket societies. Instead, it is because of the moral advantages associated with markets.

There Are Potentially Moral Costs to Limiting Markets

People in market societies are wealthier, healthier, happier, and better connected than people in nonmarket societies.[6] Markets are positively correlated with economic growth (e.g. Gwartney et al. 1999; Hanson 2000; Ali and Crain 2001; Sturm and de Haan 2001; Carlsson and Lundström 2002; Doucouliagos and Ulubaşoğlu 2006). Measures of social capital are also higher in market societies than they are in nonmarket societies. Additionally, the benefits of markets do not only accrue to the most advantaged in these societies. Market societies have higher social mobility and lower income inequality than nonmarket societies (e.g. Berggren 1999; Scully 2002). Other studies show that people in market societies have higher levels of subjective well-being (Goldsmith 1997) and quality of life as measured by literacy and life expectancy (Esposto and Zaleski 1999). Limiting access to markets and restricting the range of markets are, thus, likely to be (materially and socially) costly.

If markets are morally corrupting, however, we would be confronted with a horrible moral conundrum. The markets that are making us wealthier, healthier, happier, and better connected would, simultaneously, be making us worse people. We would, in effect, be purchasing material and social benefits at the price of our morality. In this scenario, we might want to consider restricting markets despite the material costs associated with doing so. Luckily, we do not appear to have this problem. Rather than being incompatible with morality, markets are not only consistent with morality but seem to promote morality. People in market societies exhibit the seven bourgeois virtues (i.e. prudence, justice courage, temperance, faith, hope, and love). They also tend to be more altruistic, more cosmopolitan, less materialistic, and less corrupt, as well as more likely to be trusting and trustworthy.

---

[6] There now exists a growing literature on the material and social benefits of markets. Recall, for instance, our discussion in Chap. 4. See also Berggren (2003) for a survey of papers on the benefits of economic freedom.

If our argument that markets can be a source of moral development is correct, there are also potentially moral costs associated with restricting markets. If markets are really spaces where we discover whether the people we are interacting with are good or bad people, limiting our access to markets or hampering markets might actually limit our ability to discover virtuous others. If markets are really conversations about right and wrong, then moves to truncate that conversation might limit our ability to learn to be virtuous.

Bibliography

Acemoglu, D., S. Naidu, P. Restrepo, and J.A. Robinson. 2015. Democracy, Redistribution and Inequality. In *Handbook of Income Distribution: Volume 2*, ed. A.B. Atkinson and F. Bourguignon, 1885–1966. Amsterdam: Elsevier.

Alesina, A., and R. Perotti. 1996. Income Distribution, Political Instability, and Investment. *European Economic Review* 40 (6): 1203–1228.

Ali, A., and W.M. Crain. 2001. Institutional Distortions, Economics Freedom, and Growth. *Cato Journal* 21 (3): 415–426.

Baum, M.A., and D.A. Lake. 2001. The Invisible Hand of Democracy: Political Control and the Provision of Public Services. *Comparative Political Studies* 34 (6): 587–621.

———. 2003. The Political Economy of Growth: Democracy and Human Capital. *American Journal of Political Science* 47 (2): 333–347.

Berggren, N. 1999. Economic Freedom and Equality: Friends or Foes? *Public Choice* 100 (3–4): 203–223.

———. 2003. The Benefits of Economic Freedom: A Survey. *The Independent Review* 8 (2): 193–211.

Bjørnskov, C. 2007. Determinants of Generalized Trust: A Cross-Country Comparison. *Public Choice* 130 (1–2): 1–21.

Boettke, P.J., C.J. Coyne, and P.T. Leeson. 2008. Institutional Stickiness and the New Development Economics. *American Journal of Economics and Sociology* 67 (2): 331–358.

Borjas, G.J. 1986. The Self-Employment Experience of Immigrants. *Journal of Human Resources* 21 (4): 487–506.

Bowles, S., and H. Gintis. 1978. The Invisible Fist: Have Capitalism and Democracy Reached a Parting of the Ways? *American Economic Review* 68 (2): 358–363.

———. [1986] 2012. *Democracy and Capitalism: Property, Community, and the Contradictions of Modern Social Thought*. London/New York: Taylor & Francis.

Brennan, J., and P.M. Jaworski. 2016. *Markets Without Limits: Moral Virtues and Commercial Interests*. London/New York: Routledge.

Carlsson, F., and S. Lundström. 2002. Economic Freedom and Growth: Decomposing the Effects. *Public Choice* 112 (3–4): 335–344.

Choi, G.S., and V.H. Storr. 2018. Market Institutions and the Evolution of Culture. *Evolutionary and Institutional Economics Review* 15 (2): 243–265.

———. 2019. A Culture of Rent Seeking. *Public Choice* 181 (1–2): 101–126.

Chowdhury, S.K. 2004. The Effect of Democracy and Press Freedom on Corruption: An Empirical Test. *Economic Journal* 85: 93–101.

Clark, K., and S. Drinkwater. 2000. Pushed Out or Pulled in? Self-Employment Among Ethnic Minorities in England and Wales. *Labour Economics* 7 (5): 603–628.

———. 2010. Patterns of Ethnic Self-Employment in Time and Space: Evidence from British Census Microdata. *Small Business Economics* 34 (3): 323–338.

Dahl, R.A. 1991. *Democracy and Its Critics*. New Haven: Yale University Press.

Dahlum, S., and C.H. Knutsen. 2017. Do Democracies Provide Better Education? Revisiting the Democracy–Human Capital Link. *World Development* 94: 186–199.

Doucouliagos, C., and M.A. Ulubaşoğlu. 2006. Economic Freedom and Economic Growth: Does Specification Make a Difference? *European Journal of Political Economy* 22 (1): 60–81.

Doucouliagos, H., and M.A. Ulubaşoğlu. 2008. Democracy and Economic Growth: A Meta-Analysis. *American Journal of Political Science* 52 (1): 61–83.

Esposto, A.G., and P.A. Zaleski. 1999. Economic Freedom and the Quality of Life: An Empirical Analysis. *Constitutional Political Economy* 10 (2): 185–197.

Fairlie, R.W. 2012. Immigrant Entrepreneurs and Small Business Owners, and Their Access to Financial Capital. *Small Business Administration Office of Advocacy Report #SBAHQ-10-R-0009*. Washington, D.C.: U.S. Small Business Administration.

Fairlie, R.W., and M. Lofstrom. 2014. Immigration and Entrepreneurship. In *Handbook of the Economics of International Migration*, ed. B.R. Chiswick and P.W. Miller, 877–911. Amsterdam: Elsevier.

Fairlie, R.W., J. Zissimopoulos, and H.A. Krashinsky. 2010. The International Asian Business Success Story? A Comparison of Chinese, Indian and Other Asian Businesses in the United States, Canada and United Kingdom. In *International Differences in Entrepreneurship*, ed. J. Lerner and A. Schoar, 179–208. Chicago: University of Chicago Press and National Bureau of Economic Research.

Feng, L. 1997. Democracy, Political Stability and Economic Growth. *British Journal of Political Science* 27 (3): 391–418.

Fisman, R., and E. Miguel. 2007. Corruption, Norms, and Legal Enforcement: Evidence from Diplomatic Parking Tickets. *Journal of Political Economy* 115 (6): 1020–1048.

Geertz, C. 1973. *Interpretations of Culture*. New York: Basic Books.

Goldsmith, A.A. 1997. Economic Rights and Government in Developing Countries: Cross-National Evidence on Growth and Development. *Studies in Comparative International Development* 32 (2): 29–44.

Gwartney, J.D., R. Lawson, and R.G. Holcombe. 1999. Economic Freedom and the Environment for Economic Growth. *Journal of Institutional and Theoretical Economics* 155 (4): 643–663.

Hanson, J.R. 2000. Prosperity and Economic Freedom: A Virtuous Cycle. *The Independent Review* 4 (4): 525–531.

Harrison, L.E. 1992. *Who Prospers: How Cultural Values Shape Economic and Political Success*. New York: Basic Books.

Helliwell, J.F. 1994. Empirical Linkages Between Democracy and Economic Growth. *British Journal of Political Science* 24 (2): 225–248.

Hunt, J. 2011. Which Immigrants Are Most Innovative and Entrepreneurial? Distinctions by Entry Visa. *Journal of Labor Economics* 29 (3): 417–457.

———. 2015. Are Immigrants the Most Skilled US Computer and Engineering Workers? *Journal of Labor Economics* 33 (S1): S39–S77.

Huntington, S.P. 1996. *The Clash of Civilizations and the Remaking of World Order*. New York: Simon & Schuster.

Jetter, M., A.M. Agudelo, and A. Ramírez Hassan. 2015. The Effect of Democracy on Corruption: Income Is Key. *World Development* 74: 286–304.

Kuttner, R. 2018. *Can Democracy Survive Global Capitalism?* New York: W.W. Norton & Company.

Lavoie, D., and E. Chamlee-Wright. 2000. *Culture and Enterprise: The Development, Representation and Morality of Business*. London/New York: Routledge.

Lindert, P. 1994. The Rise of Social Spending, 1880–1930. *Explorations in Economic History* 31 (1): 1–37.

———. 2004. *Growing Public: Social Spending and Economic Growth since the Eighteenth Century*. Cambridge: Cambridge University Press.

Lofstrom, M. 2002. Labor Market Assimilation and the Self-Employment Decision of Immigrant Entrepreneurs. *Journal of Population Economics* 15 (1): 83–114.

Mann, M. 2004. *The Dark Side of Democracy: Explaining Ethnic Cleansing*. Cambridge: Cambridge University Press.

Newton, K. 2001. Trust, Social Capital, Civil Society, and Democracy. *International Political Science Review* 22 (2): 201–214.

Peffley, M., and R. Rohrschneider. 2003. Democratization and Political Tolerance in Seventeen Countries: A Multi-Level Model of Democratic Learning. *Political Research Quarterly* 56 (3): 243–257.

Persson, T., and G. Tabellini. 2003. *The Economic Effects of Constitutions*. Cambridge: MIT Press.

Reuveny, R., and Q. Li. 2003. Economic Openness, Democracy, and Income Inequality: An Empirical Analysis. *Comparative Political Studies* 36 (5): 575–601.

Rodrik, D. 1999. Democracies Pay Higher Wages. *The Quarterly Journal of Economics* 114 (3): 707–738.

Saha, S., and J.J. Su. 2012. Investigating the Interaction Effect of Democracy and Economic Freedom on Corruption: A Cross-Country Quantile Regression Analysis. *Economic Analysis and Policy* 42 (3): 389–396.

Saha, S., R. Gounder, N. Campbell, and J.J. Su. 2014. Democracy and Corruption: A Complex Relationship. *Crime, Law and Social Change* 61 (3): 287–308.

Satz, D. 2010. *Why Some Things Should Not Be for Sale: The Moral Limits of Markets*. Oxford: Oxford University Press.

Saxenian, A. 1999. *Silicon Valley's New Immigrant Entrepreneurs*. San Francisco: Public Policy Institute of California.

———. 2002. Silicon Valley's New Immigrant High-Growth Entrepreneurs. *Economic Development Quarterly* 16 (1): 20–31.

Schuetze, H.J., and H. Antecol. 2007. Immigration, Entrepreneurship and the Venture Start-Up Process. The Life Cycle of Entrepreneurial Ventures. In *International Handbook Series on Entrepreneurship, Vol. 3: The Life Cycle of Entrepreneurial Ventures*, ed. S. Parker, 107–135. New York: Springer.

Scully, G.W. 2002. Economic Freedom, Government Policy and the Trade-Off Between Equity and Economic Growth. *Public Choice* 113 (1–2): 77–96.

Sen, A. 1999. Democracy as a Universal Value. *Journal of Democracy* 10 (3): 3–17.

Stasavage, D. 2005. Democracy and Education Spending in Africa. *American Journal of Political Science* 49 (2): 343–358.

Storr, V.H. 2013. *Understanding the Culture of Markets*. London/New York: Routledge.

Sturm, J.-E., and J. De Haan. 2001. How Robust Is the Relationship Between Economic Freedom and Economic Growth? *Applied Economics* 33 (7): 839–844.

Sullivan, J.L., J. Pierson, and G.E. Marcus. 1982. *Political Tolerance and American Democracy*. Chicago: University of Chicago Press.

Sun, Y., and M. Johnston. 2009. Does Democracy Check Corruption? Insights from China and India. *Comparative Politics* 42 (1): 1–19.

Sung, H.-E. 2004. Democracy and Political Corruption: A Cross-National Comparison. *Crime, Law & Change* 41: 179–194.

Tabellini, G. 2008. Institutions and Culture. *Journal of the European Economic Association* 6 (2–3): 255–294.

Uddin, M.A., M.H. Ali, and M. Alsur. 2017. Political Stability and Growth: An Application of Dynamic GMM and Quantile Regression. *Economic Modeling* 65: 610–625.

Wadhwa, V., A.L. Saxenian, B.A. Rissing, and G. Gereffi. 2007. America's New Immigrant Entrepreneurs: Part I. *Duke Science, Technology & Innovation Paper* (23).

Warren, M.E., ed. 1999. *Democracy and Trust*. Cambridge: Cambridge University Press.

Appendix: Data, Methodology, and Data Analysis

In our view, the most damning critique of markets on moral grounds is that engaging in market activity places us in a kind of moral jeopardy. Moreover, the central moral criticism of markets (i.e. that markets corrupt our morals) cannot be (entirely) evaluated philosophically. Whether or not markets are morally corrupting must be evaluated using our theoretical understanding of how markets can and should work, and on the basis of evidence regarding how markets do in fact work.

This appendix presents our methodology, the data, and the analysis that we use to assess whether or not markets are morally corrupting. Our empirical strategy deploys a number of comparisons of how market societies and nonmarket societies perform on various measures of morality. If markets are morally corrupting, our claim is that we should observe market societies displaying lower levels of virtue and higher levels of vice compared to nonmarket societies. For any causal relationship between two variables to be true, the two variables in question must necessarily correlate with one another. As an illustration, suppose we believe that good weather causes high harvest yield. This argument implies two things: (1) high harvest yield is caused by good weather and (2) high harvest yield is associated (i.e. correlated) with good weather. Thus, if there were some arguments that merely claimed that good weather and high harvest yield are correlated, and others that claimed good weather causes high harvest yield, then it must be true that all of these arguments share one empirical claim: a correlation between good weather and harvest yield exists. If evidence surfaced that suggested a correlation between

© The Author(s) 2019
V. H. Storr, G. S. Choi, *Do Markets Corrupt Our Morals?*,
https://doi.org/10.1007/978-3-030-18416-2

good weather and harvest yield did not exist, then there would be good reason to suspect that good weather did not cause high harvest yield. This is the empirical approach we take; if the collective empirical evidence suggests that markets are not associated with more vice and less virtue, then there are reasons to doubt whether markets engender more vice and less virtue.

In this appendix, we first describe how we measure morality. Next, we discuss how we classify countries as market and nonmarket societies, followed by the list of market and nonmarket societies. Then we offer definitions of the variables we compared throughout the book, along with how we calculated them for the comparisons. We also present the statistical analysis of each comparison. Finally, we perform some regression analysis. This analysis supports our primary argument that market societies outperform nonmarket societies on many of the margins that we, as a society, care about.

Measuring Morality

A virtue is a disposition to act or feel the right way for the right reasons. Our strategy for measuring morality, however, necessarily relies on assessing the existence of various virtue-like traits, the prevalence of various virtue-like behaviors, and expressions of values and beliefs that are consistent with various virtues. While we would want to assess the reasons why individuals act or feel the way that they do, we do not have direct access to people's motivations.

Of course, being virtuous and behaving virtuously are not disconnected. In fact, there are several key links between them:

(a) genuinely virtuous people (i.e. people who do the right things for the right reasons) are likely to consistently act virtuously and to consistently express values and beliefs that are consistent with various virtues;

(b) people who consistently behave virtuously and consistently express values and beliefs that are consistent with various virtues are likely to develop into virtuous people; and

(c) people can nurture or cultivate virtuous dispositions by consistently behaving virtuously and consistently expressing values and beliefs that are compatible with various virtues.

Arguably, (a) is a less controversial claim than (b) and (c). While certainly controversial, (b) and (c) are clearly plausible. Together, however, they point to the appropriateness of looking to people's actions and expressed attitudes as a way of assessing whether or not they are virtuous. Regardless, looking at behavior and expressions of values is the best we can do empirically.

More limiting, our empirical strategy often relies on quantitative measures of moral outcomes and comparisons of the results of cross-country surveys of morally relevant attitudes. That these measures can really "get at" virtue is (admittedly) unlikely. Moreover, it is possible that the results of any comparisons of this sort are misleading. It is possible, for instance, that seemingly virtuous behavior is increasing as virtue is decreasing; more people could be doing the right thing but less of them could be doing the right thing for the right reasons. Still, as our aim is merely to assess the empirical plausibility of an often-unsupported empirical claim rather than to definitively answer an empirical question, we believe the benefits of the approach we adopt outweigh the limits.

Many of our measures and a number of the studies that we reference rely on the answers to virtue-related questions in the World Values Survey (WVS). WVS explores people's beliefs and values in over a hundred countries by interviewing a representative sample of individuals in each county. According to WVS (2019), "[t]he WVS network has produced over 1,000 publications in 20 languages and secondary users have produced several thousand additional publications." While it is not the only (nor the largest) cross-country compilation of information on beliefs and values, WVS is perhaps the most suitable and convenient dataset for quantitative cross-cultural analysis (Chai et al. 2009). For instance, the Human Relations Area Files (HRAF) offers two datasets that contain ethnographic material covering many aspects of cultural and social life. "However, despite its extremely wide coverage and unique tagging and classification system," Chai et al. (Ibid.: 195) wrote that HRAF,

> is primarily a qualitative resource that would require extensive recoding to be comparable to the WVS. While a number of data sets have been generated from the HRAF ethnographies …, the focus of such work has been on small societies rather than countries and on customs and practices such as child rearing rather than on attitudinal variables like values and beliefs.

Perhaps for this reason, using WVS is a standard approach for a number of quantitative studies on cultural, social, and moral topics.

Classifying Countries as Market and Nonmarket Societies

Our strategy for classifying market and nonmarket societies was chosen because we wanted a basis for sorting countries into their respective categories before looking at how they performed materially and morally. Stated another way, we wanted to know whether a society was a market or nonmarket society before looking at the wealth or virtuousness of its members. In determining whether or not market activity is morally corrupting, it is important to know which countries allow the greatest scope and support for market activities, and which countries do not.

We determine whether a country is a market or nonmarket society based on five indices: Fraser Institute's 2011 Economic Freedom of the World index (EFW), Heritage Foundation and The Wall Street Journal's 2011 Index of Economic Freedom (IEF), World Economic Forum's 2011–2012 Global Competitive Index (GCI), World Bank's Doing Business project's 2011 Distance to Frontier (DTF), and World Justice Project's 2012–2013 Rule of Law index. Empirically speaking, we defined a country as a market society if its scores were in the top two-fifths of the range of possible scores in each of the indices for which a score was available for that particular country. Any country whose scores were not in the top two-fifths of the range of possible scores in each of the indices for which a score was available for that particular country is defined as a nonmarket society. Defined in this manner, we have 40 market societies and 150 nonmarket societies. We use data from 2011 unless otherwise noted; doing so allows us to maximize the available data across different sources.

EFW and IEF, as their names suggest, measure the economic freedom of different societies. EFW rates more than 150 countries and territories based on five general areas of economic freedom: size of government; legal structure and security of property rights; access to sound money; freedom to trade internationally; and regulation of credit, labor, and business (Gwartney et al. 2016). IEF ranks over 170 countries on four main aspects of economic freedom: rule of law, government size, regulatory efficiency, and market openness (Miller et al. 2018). GCI measures the factors, policies, and institutions that determine the economic competitiveness and thus the long-term economic growth and prosperity for over 100 countries (Schwab et al. 2017). DTF measures how well a society is performing on the margins pertaining to regulations for commerce or conducting business (World Bank 2019). Finally, the Rule of Law index evaluates how the general public experiences and understands the rule of law in practical, everyday situations in about 100 countries (World Justice Project 2018). It customarily rates each country on a 0-to-1 scale based on eight primary factors: constraints on government powers, absence of corruption, open government, fundamental rights, order and security, regulatory enforcement, civil justice, and criminal justice. Given that our goal here is to better identify market societies versus nonmarket societies, we reconstructed the Rule of Law index by applying the same original methodology but using only three factors: constraints on government powers, fundamental rights, and regulatory enforcement. To minimize confusion, we refer to this reconstructed index as the Modified Rule of Law index.

As the propositions in Chap. 2 highlight, our main purpose with regard to the data is to illustrate how market societies perform in relation to nonmarket societies on a variety of measures. For example, in Chap. 4 and onward, we seek to answer questions of the following format: are members of market societies, on average, wealthier (or less greedy, less selfish, less materialistic, more trustworthy, more tolerant, or better connected) than those of nonmarket societies? Performing such comparisons requires us to use a binary (i.e. discrete) variable. A continuous variable that measures the degree of market-society-ness is not appropriate for our purposes. Of course, a continuous variable that measures market-society-ness has the potential to provide insight into questions like how a one-unit change in the market-society-ness of a country affects various measures. However, this is not our main objective. Instead, we wish to determine whether or not market and nonmarket societies perform differently on various measures. Of course, none of these comparisons alone can ever unquestionably prove or disprove the claim that markets are morally corrupting. Collectively, however, they might give us reasons to support or suspect the view that markets corrupt our morals.

While it would have been most ideal for all five indices to be available for all countries in our dataset, this is unfortunately not the case. In fact, we have scores for only 54 countries for all five indices. This issue of sample size may have been addressed by using only one index, as opposed to multiple indices, but this strategy would have given one particular index too much sway in labeling a country as a market or nonmarket society. As Table A.1 depicts, a country can be regarded as a market society by one index, but as a nonmarket society by another. Furthermore, although it is possible to criticize one of the indices that we used, we find it reasonable (and, in fact, compelling) to classify a country as a market society if all of the independent indices agree that it is a market society. We should note that there are not really any surprises. Using this approach, countries like the United States, Australia, Canada, many of the countries in Western Europe, and some of the noncommunist countries in Asia are classified as market societies. Emerging economies like India as well as the obviously nonmarket societies like Chad and Iran are characterized as nonmarket societies.

Lastly, we recognize that there may be concerns with our decision to designate those who fall into the top two-fifths of the range of possible scores for all indices to be market societies. It can be argued that the concerns pertaining to our choice in threshold value would apply to any and all choices of cutoffs. Hence, we feel comfortable defining market societies as countries in the top two-fifths of the five indices that measure marketness in which the countries appear.

A number of the studies that we reference use various measures of economic freedom. The higher the level of economic freedom, the more that locale embraces markets. In a society that embraces markets, people voluntarily engage in exchanges coordinated by markets and can enter, exit, and compete in markets without excessive restrictions. To ensure this freedom, it is critical that property rights are enforced to protect citizens and their property from the aggression of others. To ensure this freedom, it is also critical that governments are not so large that they crowd out or overburden private enterprise. As we use two of the more popular measures of economic freedom in deciding how to classify locales, from our perspective, the studies that rely on measures of economic freedom speak to the same phenomenon that we are principally concerned with, namely, the scope and support for market activities in a society.

Market and Nonmarket Societies

The five indices on which we rely use different scales; as such, the threshold value for the top two-fifths differs across indices. EFW scores range from 1 to 10; a country is said to be in the top two-fifths if its raw score is greater than or equal to 6.4. IEF scores countries between 0 and 100, so its threshold score is 60. The GCI scores range from 1 to 7. A country is said to be in the top two-fifths when its raw score is greater than or equal to 4.6. Like IEF, DTF is measured between 0 and 100. Finally, the Rule of Law index is measured on a scale from 0 to 1; thus, the relevant threshold value for the Modified Rule of Law index is 0.6.

In Table A.1, a country (name) is shaded in gray if it is a market society. Cells shaded in gray in the columns for indices indicate that the specific scores are greater than or equal to their appropriate threshold values.

Table A.2 defines the variables we use to empirically demonstrate our main argument throughout Chaps. 4 and 5.

In Table A.3, we report the test statistics and the corresponding p-values for the various pairwise or multiple comparisons performed in Chaps. 4 and 5. For comparisons in which the sample size for both market and nonmarket societies was greater than 30 observations, we performed two-sided t-tests and included the standard errors in the figures. Whenever one of the sample sizes fell below 30 observations, we performed a two-sided Mann-Whitney test.

Tables A.4 and A.5 present statistical results from comparisons between different relationship types in trustor and trustee behaviors for the experiment discussed in Chap. 6. In short, trustor and trustees both sent larger transfers

Table A.1 Market and nonmarket societies with their index scores

Market society?	Country	EFW	IEF	GCI	DTF	Modified Rule of Law
No	Afghanistan				37.53	
No	Albania	7.25	64	4.06	61.86	0.50
No	Algeria	5.2	52.4	3.96	48.8	
No	Angola	5.13	46.2	2.96	37.43	
Yes	Antigua and Barbuda				63.61	
No	Argentina	5.67	51.7	3.99	57.17	0.51
No	Armenia	7.71	69.7	3.89	61.59	
Yes	Australia	7.93	82.5	5.11	81.02	0.85
Yes	Austria	7.57	71.9	5.14	76.43	0.83
No	Azerbaijan	6.19	59.7	4.31	62.59	
No	Bahrain	7.76	77.7	4.54	66.26	
No	Bangladesh	6.41	53	3.73		0.40
No	Barbados	6.82	68.5	4.44		
No	Belarus		47.9		54.07	0.45
Yes	Belgium	7.31	70.2	5.2	72.28	0.76
No	Belize	6.6	63.8	3.52	60.71	
No	Benin	6.05	56	3.78	39.64	
No	Bhutan		57.6		55.83	
No	Bolivia	6.39	50	3.82	50.3	0.41
No	Bosnia and Herzegovina	6.73	57.5	3.84	52.89	0.58
No	Botswana	7.23	68.8	4.05	64.85	0.68
No	Brazil	6.58	56.3	4.32		0.62
Yes	Brunei Darussalam			4.78	60.15	
No	Bulgaria	7.38	64.9	4.16	67.84	0.57
No	Burkina Faso	5.95	60.6	3.25	41.5	0.53
No	Burma		37.8			
No	Burundi	5.3	49.6	2.95	35.04	
No	Cabo Verde	6.54	64.6	3.58	55.82	
No	Cambodia	7	57.9	3.85	50.11	0.37
No	Cameroon	6.33	51.8	3.61	44.36	0.34
Yes	Canada	7.87	80.8	5.33	81.3	0.78
No	Central African Republic	5.32	49.3		24.85	
No	Chad	5.07	45.3	2.87	29.05	
Yes	Chile	7.94	77.4	4.7	69.82	0.71
No	China	6.32	52	4.9		0.38
No	Colombia	6.6	68	4.2	65.63	0.54
No	Comoros		43.8		45.29	
No	Costa Rica	7.61	67.3	4.27	55.87	
No	Cote d'Ivoire	5.86	55.4	3.37	40.69	0.47
No	Croatia	6.91	61.1	4.08	61.82	0.59
No	Cuba		27.7			
No	Cyprus	7.69	73.3	4.36	67.45	
No	Czech Republic	7.23	70.4	4.52	67.85	0.70

(continued)

Table A.1 (continued)

Market society?	Country	EFW	IEF	GCI	DTF	Modified Rule of Law
No	Democratic Republic of Congo	5.43	40.7		33.57	
Yes	Denmark	7.64	78.6	5.4	85.26	0.89
No	Djibouti		54.5		44.06	
Yes	Dominica		63.3		63.56	
No	Dominican Republic	7.19	60	3.73	62.7	0.55
No	Ecuador	5.84	47.1	3.83	56.79	0.48
No	Egypt	6.33	59.1	3.88	57.33	0.48
No	El Salvador	7.15	68.8	3.89	60.57	0.53
No	Equatorial Guinea		47.5		44.94	
No	Eritrea		36.7		31.37	
Yes	Estonia	7.68	75.2	4.62	76.31	0.77
No	Ethiopia	5.21	50.5	3.76	47.95	0.38
Yes	Fiji	7.15	60.4		68.09	
Yes	Finland	7.8	74	5.47	81.31	0.87
Yes	France	7.29	64.6	5.14	70.31	0.78
No	Gabon	5.58	56.7		47.93	
No	Georgia	7.62	70.4	3.95	76.18	0.57
Yes	Germany	7.6	71.8	5.41	79	0.79
No	Ghana	6.77	59.4	3.65	59.81	0.65
No	Greece	6.68	60.3	3.92	59.81	0.63
No	Grenada				59.45	
No	Guatemala	7.33	61.9	4	60.24	0.52
No	Guinea		51.7		38.78	
No	Guinea Bissau	5.74	46.5		33.68	
No	Guyana	6.35	49.4	3.73	57.5	
No	Haiti	6.62	52.1	2.9	43.12	
No	Honduras	7.33	58.6	3.98	57.73	
Yes	Hong Kong	8.91	89.7	5.36	88.52	0.73
No	Hungary	7.36	66.6	4.36	67.13	0.65
Yes	Iceland	6.76	68.2	4.75	81.01	
No	India	6.6	54.6	4.3		0.52
No	Indonesia	6.91	56	4.38		0.57
No	Iran	5.94	42.1	4.26	56.98	0.39
No	Iraq				46.57	
Yes	Ireland	7.75	78.7	4.77	82.02	
Yes	Israel	7.32	68.5	5.07	71.65	
No	Italy	7.18	60.3	4.43	65.76	0.65
No	Jamaica	7.03	65.7	3.76	61.67	0.58
Yes	Japan	7.44	72.8	5.4		0.82
No	Jordan	7.77	68.9	4.19	57.13	0.54
No	Kazakhstan	6.98	62.1	4.18	58.5	0.43
No	Kenya	6.98	57.4	3.82	56.66	0.46
No	Kiribati		44.8		58.44	
No	Kosovo				56.36	
No	Kuwait	7.21	64.9	4.62	59.4	

(continued)

Table A.1   (continued)

Market society?	Country	EFW	IEF	GCI	DTF	Modified Rule of Law
No	Kyrgyz Republic	6.66	61.1	3.45	62.87	0.46
No	Laos		51.3		48.36	
No	Latvia	7.24	65.8	4.24	73.43	
No	Lebanon	7.32	60.1	3.95	61.33	0.53
No	Lesotho	6.26	47.5	3.26	51.47	
No	Liberia		46.5		41.94	0.43
No	Libya		38.6			
No	Lithuania	7.45	71.3	4.41	73.31	
Yes	Luxembourg	7.43	76.2	5.03	65.98	
Yes	Macau		73.1			
No	Macedonia	7.09	66	4.05	65.11	0.57
No	Madagascar	6.24	61.2	3.36	44.73	0.50
No	Malawi	6.37	55.8	3.58	49.2	0.47
No	Malaysia	7.03	66.3	5.08	76.53	0.53
No	Maldives		48.3		63.58	
No	Mali	5.91	56.3	3.39	47.08	
No	Malta	7.65	65.7	4.33		
No	Marshall Islands				57.69	
No	Mauritania	5.64	52.1	3.2	42.78	
No	Mauritius	8	76.2	4.31	74.24	
No	Mexico	6.72	67.8	4.29		0.53
No	Micronesia		50.3		50.17	
No	Moldova	6.72	55.7	3.89	58.62	0.45
No	Mongolia	7.12	59.5	3.86	58.9	0.53
No	Montenegro	7.13	62.5	4.27	61.65	
No	Morocco	6.56	59.6	4.16	59.85	0.51
No	Mozambique	5.82	56.8	3.31	53.04	
No	Namibia	6.39	62.7	4	62.19	
No	Nepal	6.23	50.1	3.47	57.84	0.51
Yes	New Zealand	8.15	82.3	4.93	88.92	0.85
No	Nicaragua	7.37	58.8	3.61	52.7	0.43
No	Niger	6.01	54.3	3.45	37.69	0.44
No	Nigeria	6.39	56.7			
No	North Korea		1			
Yes	Norway	7.5	70.3	5.18	81.85	0.88
Yes	Oman	7.17	69.8	4.64	65.06	
No	Pakistan	6.34	55.1	3.58		0.41
No	Palau				56.7	
No	Panama	7.12	64.9	4.35	65.42	0.53
No	Papua New Guinea	7	52.6		57.1	
No	Paraguay	6.81	62.3	3.53	60.95	
No	Peru	7.59	68.6	4.21	68.43	0.61
No	Philippines	7.35	56.2	4.08	53.96	0.55
No	Poland	7.22	64.1	4.46	64.83	0.75
No	Portugal	7.22	64	4.4	72.51	0.68
No	Puerto Rico			4.58	71.8	

(continued)

Table A.1 (continued)

Market society?	Country	EFW	IEF	GCI	DTF	Modified Rule of Law
Yes	Qatar	7.47	70.5	5.24	64.48	
No	Republic of Congo	4.57	43.6		34.45	
No	Romania	7.33	64.7	4.08	62.55	0.62
No	Russia	6.58	50.5	4.21		0.41
No	Rwanda	7.45	62.7	4.19	59.61	
Yes	Saint Kitts and Nevis				61.22	
Yes	Saint Lucia		70.8	5.17	65.02	
Yes	Saint Vincent and the Grenadines		66.9		63.79	
Yes	Samoa		60.6		67.1	
No	Sao Tome and Principe		49.5		40.53	
Yes	Saudi Arabia	7.09	66.2		68	
No	Senegal	5.99	55.7	3.7	40.81	0.59
No	Serbia	6.73	58	3.88	58.2	0.51
No	Seychelles		51.2		62.3	
No	Sierra Leone	6.28	49.6		41.98	0.51
Yes	Singapore	8.66	87.2	5.63	90.4	0.75
Yes	Slovakia	7.43	69.5		69.78	
No	Slovenia	6.57	64.6	4.3	65.22	0.67
No	Solomon Islands		45.9		59.41	
No	South Africa	6.8	62.7	4.34	67.6	0.60
Yes	South Korea	7.48	69.8	5.02	81.77	0.70
No	Spain	7.4	70.2	4.54	67.89	0.76
No	Sri Lanka	6.65	57.1	4.33	55.88	0.56
No	Suriname	6.51	53.1	3.67	44.34	
No	Swaziland	6.8	59.1	3.3	57.34	
Yes	Sweden	7.5	71.9	5.61	82.39	0.91
Yes	Switzerland	8.23	81.9	5.74	75.31	
No	Syria	6.55	51.3	3.85	50.64	
Yes	Taiwan		70.8	5.26	74.8	
No	Tajikistan	6.45	53.5	3.77	44.18	
No	Tanzania	6.84	57	3.56	53.46	0.50
No	Thailand	6.58	64.7	4.52	72.27	0.57
Yes	The Bahamas	7.4	68		65.4	
No	The Gambia	7.07	57.4	3.85	48.88	
Yes	The Netherlands	7.51	74.7	5.41	73.96	0.84
No	Timor-Leste	6.4	42.8	3.35	42.25	
No	Togo	5.45	49.1		39.32	
No	Tonga		55.8		65.27	
No	Trinidad and Tobago	6.97	66.5	4	62.13	
No	Tunisia	6.58	58.5	4.47	67.32	0.56
No	Turkey	7.07	64.2	4.28	64.81	0.50
No	Turkmenistan		43.6			
No	Uganda	7.14	61.7	3.56	51.33	0.42

(*continued*)

Table A.1 (continued)

Market society?	Country	EFW	IEF	GCI	DTF	Modified Rule of Law
No	Ukraine	6.19	45.8	4	44.09	0.43
No	United Arab Emirates	8.06	67.8	4.89	70.91	0.56
Yes	United Kingdom	7.81	74.5	5.39	84.88	0.79
Yes	United States	7.7	77.8	5.43		0.73
No	Uruguay	7.37	70	4.25	58.15	0.72
No	Uzbekistan		45.8		39.79	0.34
No	Vanuatu		56.7		62.12	
No	Venezuela	3.96	37.6	3.51	37.87	0.35
No	Vietnam	6.26	51.6	4.24	58.93	0.43
No	West Bank and Gaza				49.58	
No	Yemen	6.39	54.2	3.06	56.66	
No	Zambia	7.11	59.7	3.67	57.04	0.44
No	Zimbabwe	4.99	22.1	3.33	41.14	0.30

Data source: Agrast et al. (2012–2013), Gwartney et al. (2011), Miller and Holmes (2011), Schwab et al. (2011), and World Bank (2010)

to those with whom they developed a positive relationship in the experimental market than to those with whom they developed negative relationships.

Kruskal-Wallis tests reveal that trustors and trustees behaved identically toward those with whom they share negative relationships, ambiguous relationships and strangers (trustor transfers: $\chi^2 = 1.08$; $p = 0.583$; trustee transfers: $\chi^2 = 0.157$; $p = 0.925$). This implies that there are no statistically meaningful distinctions between the three relationship types for both trustors and trustees.

Regression Analysis

In this section, we test whether market societies outperform nonmarket societies on a variety of the economic and social measures discussed in Chaps. 4 and 5 using regression analysis. Our main explanatory variable is Market Society, which equals 1 when the country is defined to be a market society according to our methodology and equals 0 when the country is defined to be a nonmarket society. In this analysis, we also included some other variables that scholars have identified as being critical in explaining economic

Table A.2 Variable definitions

Variable name	Definition	Source	Corresponding figure in text
GDP per capita	GDP per capita (PPP, constant 2011 international dollars)	World Bank (2016)	Figure 4.1
Adult literacy rate	Adult literacy rate is measured as the percentage of people within a country aged 15 or over who can read and write	World Bank (2016)	Figure 4.2
Access to improved water source	Access to improved water source is defined as the proportion of a country's population with access to improved (drinking) water source and includes piped water on premise (e.g. piped household water connection located inside a person's house, yard, or land) and other improved drinking water sources (e.g. public taps, protected springs, and rainwater collection)	World Bank (2016)	Figure 4.3
Total rail line	Total rail line (thousands, route km)	World Bank (2016)	Figure 4.4
Fixed broadband	Fixed broadband subscriptions refer to the World Bank's fixed (or wired) broadband subscriptions, which is defined as the total number of active subscriptions to the following broadband technologies with download speeds of 256 kbit/s or greater (per 100 people): DSL, cable modem, fiber-to-the-home, and other fixed technologies (such as broadband over power lines and leased lines)	World Bank (2016)	Figure 4.5
Fixed telephone	Fixed telephone subscriptions refer to the World Bank's fixed (or wired) telephone subscription, which is defined as the active number of analogue fixed telephone lines, voice-over-IP subscriptions, fixed wireless local loop subscriptions, integrated services digital network voice-channel equivalents, and fixed public payphones (per 100 people)	World Bank (2016)	Figure 4.5
Life expectancy at birth	Life expectancy at birth, total (years)	World Bank (2016)	Figure 4.6
Infant mortality	Infant mortality rate (per 1000 live births)	World Bank (2016)	Figure 4.7
Maternal mortality	Maternal mortality ratio (per 100,000 live births)	World Health Organization (2017)	Figure 4.8
Health expenditure per capita per year	Health expenditure per capita per year (PPP, Constant 2011 international dollars)	World Bank (2016)	Figure 4.9
Daily caloric intake per capita	Daily caloric intake per capita (total kcal)	Food and Agriculture Organization (2017)	Figure 4.10

Variable	Description	Source	Figure
High life satisfaction	High life satisfaction refers to the proportion of respondents with high life satisfaction and is calculated as the proportion of respondents who answered with an 8 or above on World Values Survey's life satisfaction question (V23: "All things considered, how satisfied are you with your life as a whole these days? Using this card on which 1 means you are 'completely dissatisfied' and 10 means you are 'completely satisfied' where would you put your satisfaction with your life as a whole?")	World Bank (2016)	Figure 4.11
Average life satisfaction	Life satisfaction, or life evaluation, is calculated using Gallup World Poll's Cantril ladder question ("Please imagine a ladder, with steps numbered from 0 at the bottom to 10 at the top. The top of the ladder represents the best possible life for you and the bottom of the ladder represents the worst possible life for you. On which step of the ladder would you say you personally feel you stand at this time?")	Gallup World Survey (2017)	Figure 4.12
Religious organizations	Religious organizations is calculated as the proportion of respondents who self-reported being active members to a religious organization (V25: "Now I am going to read off a list of voluntary organizations. For each organization, could you tell me whether you are an active member, an inactive member or not a member of that type of organization?: Church or religious organization")	World Values Survey (2014)	Figure 4.13
Recreational organizations	Recreational organizations is calculated as the proportion of respondents who self-reported being active members to a sports or recreational organization (V26: "Now I am going to read off a list of voluntary organizations. For each organization, could you tell me whether you are an active member, an inactive member or not a member of that type of organization?: Sport or recreational organization")	World Values Survey (2014)	Figure 4.13
Social capital	Legatum Institute includes social capital as part of its Legatum Prosperity Index, which evaluates the strength of personal relationships, social network support, social norms, and civic participation in a particular country. Legatum Prosperity Index's social capital score is calculated as weighted sum of various variables' distance-to-frontier values	Legatum Institute (2010)	Figure 4.14

(continued)

Table A.2 (continued)

Variable name	Definition	Source	Corresponding figure in text
GDP per capita, poorest 10%	GDP per capita of the poorest 10% is calculated as the income share held by the poorest 10% in a particular country, multiplied by the total GDP per capita (PPP, constant 2011 international dollars) and divided by the total population. GDP per capita of the richest 10% is calculated as the income share held by the richest 10% in a particular country, multiplied by the total GDP per capita (PPP, constant 2011 international dollars) and divided by the total population Note: While we utilize our estimates of income per capita of the richest and the poorest deciles of society here, our values must be interpreted cautiously. Using World Bank data from 2011, we calculated GDP per capita of the poorest (richest) 10% as the income share held by the poorest (richest) 10% in a particular country, multiplied by the total GDP per capita (PPP, constant 2011 international dollars) and divided by the total population. However, according to the World Bank, income shares were estimated using either consumption or income data (whichever was available for a particular country), some of which only pertained to urban areas. Because of the method used by the World Bank to estimate income shares, some of our values are imprecise However, we believe our predicted income per capita of the poorest and richest deciles are nonetheless indicative of actual income earned by different deciles. In an ideal world where we had both income and consumption data for each country, we suspect that the income shares calculated using both data will approximate one another; if the poor earns 5% of the national income, it is also likely that they consume roughly 5% of the national consumption. Since we merely wish to illustrate—not prove beyond a reasonable doubt—that the poorest in the commercial societies could be (and are) richer than the richest in noncommercial societies, we believe our estimated values are still appropriate for this purpose	Authors' calculations using World Bank (2016)	Figure 4.15

Gini coefficient	The Gini coefficient measures the extent to which the distribution of income (or, in some cases, consumption expenditure) among individuals or households within an economy deviates from a perfectly equal distribution. A Gini coefficient of 0 represents perfect equality, while a coefficient of 100 implies perfect inequality	World Bank (2016)	Figure 4.16
Father-son earning elasticity	Father-son earning elasticity, or also referred to as the intergenerational income mobility, refers to the extent to which income levels are able to change across generations. A value of 1 indicates that there is no generational income elasticity and implies that all poor children would become poor adults and all rich children would become rich adults. A value of 0 indicates that there is complete intergenerational mobility and implies that there is no relationship between family background and the adult income outcomes of children. In other words, a child born into poverty would have exactly the same likelihood of earning a high income in adulthood as a child born into a rich family	Corak (2013)	Figure 4.17
Donations	Donations is calculated as the proportion of respondents who self-reported that they had donated money to a charity in the past month on Gallup's World View World Poll	Charities Aid Foundation (2017)	Figure 5.1
Charitable giving by individuals	Charitable giving by individuals is defined as the amount of money donated to not-for-profit organizations by individuals as a percentage of GDP	Charities Aid Foundation (2017)	Table 5.2
Being rich is important	Being rich is important is calculated as the proportion of respondents who answered "Very much like you" or "Like you" on World Values Survey's Schwartz question about being rich (V71: "Now I will briefly describe some people. Using this card, would you please indicate for each description whether that person is very much like you, like you, somewhat like you, not like you, or not at all like you?: It is important to this person to be rich; to have a lot of money and expensive things")	World Values Survey (2014)	Figure 5.2

(continued)

Table A.2 (continued)

Variable name	Definition	Source	Corresponding figure in text
Being successful is important	Being successful is important is calculated as the proportion of respondents who answered "Very much like you" or "Like you" on World Values Survey's Schwartz question about being successful (V75: "Now I will briefly describe some people. Using this card, would you please indicate for each description whether that person is very much like you, like you, somewhat like you, not like you, or not at all like you?: Being very successful is important to this person; to have people recognize one's achievements")	World Values Survey (2014)	Figure 5.2
Competition is harmful	Competition is harmful is calculated as the proportion of respondents who answered 8 or above on World Values Survey's question about competition (V99: "Now I'd like you to tell me your views on various issues. How would you place your views on this scale? 1 means you agree completely with the statement on the left; 10 means you agree completely with the statement on the right; and if your views fall somewhere in between, you can choose any number in between. 'Competition is good. It stimulates people to work hard and develop new ideas' vs. 'Competition is harmful. It brings out the worst in people'")	World Values Survey (2014)	Figure 5.3
Competition is good	Competition is good is calculated as the proportion of respondents who answered 1, 2, or 3 on the World Values Survey's question about competition (V99: "Now I'd like you to tell me your views on various issues. How would you place your views on this scale? 1 means you agree completely with the statement on the left; 10 means you agree completely with the statement on the right; and if your views fall somewhere in between, you can choose any number in between. 'Competition is good. It stimulates people to work hard and develop new ideas' vs. 'Competition is harmful. It brings out the worst in people'")	World Values Survey (2014)	Figure 5.3

Corruption Perceptions Index	The Corruption Perceptions Index ranks each country according to its perceived level of public-sector corruption. Scores range from 0 (highly corrupt) to 10 (very clean)	Transparency International (2011)	Table 5.3 and Figure 5.4
Avoiding fare on public transport	Avoiding fare on public transport is calculated as the proportion of respondents who answered 8 or above for the World Values Survey question: Avoiding fare on public transport (V199: "Please tell me for each of the following actions whether you think it can always be justified, never be justified, or something in between: Avoiding a fare on public transport")	World Values Survey (2014)	Figure 5.5
Cheating on taxes	Cheating on taxes is calculated as the proportion of respondents who answered 8 or above for the World Values Survey question: Cheating on taxes (V201: "Please tell me for each of the following actions whether you think it can always be justified, never be justified, or something in between: Cheating on taxes if you have a chance")	World Values Survey (2014)	Figure 5.5
Stealing property	Stealing property is calculated as the proportion of respondents who answered 8 or above for the World Values Survey question: Stealing property (V200: "Please tell me for each of the following actions whether you think it can always be justified, never be justified, or something in between: Stealing property")	World Values Survey (2014)	Figure 5.5
Bribery	Bribery is calculated as the proportion of respondents who answered 8 or above for the World Values Survey question: Bribery refers to the justifiability of someone accepting a bribe in the course of their duties (V202: "Please tell me for each of the following actions whether you think it can always be justified, never be justified, or something in between: Someone accepting a bribe in the course of their duties")	World Values Survey (2014)	Figure 5.5
Different race	Different race is calculated as the proportion of respondents who mentioned people of a different race as a group of people who the respondent would not want as neighbors (V37: "On this list are various groups of people. Could you please mention any that you would not like to have as neighbors?: People of a different race")	World Values Survey (2014)	Figure 5.6

(continued)

Table A.2 (continued)

Variable name	Definition	Source	Corresponding figure in text
Foreign workers	Foreign workers is calculated as the proportion of respondents who mentioned foreign workers as a group of people who the respondent would not want as neighbors (V39: "On this list are various groups of people. Could you please mention any that you would not like to have as neighbors?: Immigrants/foreign workers")	World Values Survey (2014)	Figure 5.6
Homosexuals	Homosexuals is calculated as the proportion of respondents who mentioned homosexuals as a group of people who the respondent would not want as neighbors (V40: "On this list are various groups of people. Could you please mention any that you would not like to have as neighbors?: Homosexuals")	World Values Survey (2014)	Figure 5.6
Different religion	Different religion is calculated as the proportion of respondents who mentioned people of a different religion as a group of people who the respondent would not want as neighbors (V41: "On this list are various groups of people. Could you please mention any that you would not like to have as neighbors?: People of a difference religion")	World Values Survey (2014)	Figure 5.6
Cohabitating unmarried couples	Cohabitating unmarried couples is calculated as the proportion of respondents who mentioned cohabitating unmarried couples as a group of people who the respondent would not want as neighbors (V43: "On this list are various groups of people. Could you please mention any that you would not like to have as neighbors?: Unmarried couples living together")	World Values Survey (2014)	Figure 5.6
Different language	Different language is calculated as the proportion of respondents who mentioned people who speak a different language as a group of people who the respondent would not want as neighbors (V44: "On this list are various groups of people. Could you please mention any that you would not like to have as neighbors?: People who speak a different language")	World Values Survey (2014)	Figure 5.6

University education is more important for boys	University education is more important for boys is calculated as the proportion of respondents who agreed, or strongly agreed, with the indicated statement (V52: "For each of the following statements I read out, can you tell me how much you agree or disagree with each. Do you strongly agree, agree, disagree, or strongly disagree?: A university education is more important for a boy than for a girl")	World Values Survey (2014)	Figure 5.7
Jobs should be given to men	Jobs should be given to men is calculated as the proportion of respondents who agreed with the indicated statement (V45: "Do you agree, disagree or neither agree nor disagree with the following statements?: When jobs are scarce, men should have more right to a job than women")	World Values Survey (2014)	Figure 5.7
Successful wives are a problem	Successful wives are a problem is calculated as the proportion of respondents who agreed with the indicated statement (V47: "Do you agree, disagree or neither agree nor disagree with the following statements?: If a woman earns more money than her husband, it's almost certain to cause problems")	World Values Survey (2014)	Figure 5.7
Corporal punishment of children	Corporal punishment of children is calculated as the proportion of respondents who answered 8 or above on the World Values Survey's question on the justifiability of parents beating children (V209: "Please tell me for each of the following actions whether you think it can always be justified, never be justified, or something in between: Parents beating children")	World Values Survey (2014)	Figure 5.8
Domestic violence	Domestic violence is calculated as the proportion of respondents who answered 8 or above on the World Values Survey's question on the justifiability for a man to beat his wife (V208: "Please tell me for each of the following actions whether you think it can always be justified, never be justified, or something in between: For a man to beat his wife")	World Values Survey (2014)	Figure 5.8

(continued)

Table A.2 (continued)

Variable name	Definition	Source	Corresponding figure in text
Accepting of homosexuality	Accepting of homosexuality is calculated as the proportion of respondents who answered 8 or above for World Values Survey's question on homosexuality (V203: "Please tell me for each of the following actions whether you think it can always be justified, never be justified, or something in between: Homosexuality")	World Values Survey (2014)	Figure 5.9
Family	Family is calculated as the proportion of respondents who expressed that they completely or somewhat trust their family (V102: "I'd like to ask you how much you trust people from various groups. Could you tell me for each whether you trust people from this group completely, somewhat, not very much or not at all?: Your family")	World Values Survey (2014)	Figure 5.10
Neighbors	Neighbors is calculated as the proportion of respondents who expressed that they completely or somewhat trust their neighbors (V103: "I'd like to ask you how much you trust people from various groups. Could you tell me for each whether you trust people from this group completely, somewhat, not very much or not at all?: Your neighborhood")	World Values Survey (2014)	Figure 5.10
Known associates	Known associates is calculated as the proportion of respondents who expressed that they completely or somewhat trust their known associates (V104: "I'd like to ask you how much you trust people from various groups. Could you tell me for each whether you trust people from this group completely, somewhat, not very much or not at all?: People you know personally")	World Values Survey (2014)	Figure 5.10
People met for the first time	People met for the first time is calculated as the proportion of respondents who expressed that they completely or somewhat trust the people whom they meet for the first time (V105: "I'd like to ask you how much you trust people from various groups. Could you tell me for each whether you trust people from this group completely, somewhat, not very much or not at all?: People you meet for the first time")	World Values Survey (2014)	Figure 5.10

Generalized trust	Generalized trust is calculated as the proportion of respondents who answered, "Most people can be trusted," on World Values Survey's generalized trust question (V24: "Generally speaking, would you say that most people can be trusted or that you need to be very careful in dealing with people?")	World Values Survey (2014)	Figure 5.11
Equal rights for women as an essential characteristic of a democracy	Equal rights for women as an essential characteristic of a democracy is calculated as proportion of respondents who answered 8 or above on the World Values Survey's question about essential characteristic of democracy: Women have the same rights as men (V139: "Many things are desirable, but not all of them are essential characteristics of democracy. Please tell me for each of the following things how essential you think it is as a characteristic of democracy. Use this scale where 1 means 'not at all an essential characteristic of democracy' and 10 means it definitely is 'an essential characteristic of democracy': Women have the same rights as men")	World Values Survey (2014)	Footnote 26 in Chap. 5

Note: This table offers definitions of variables used throughout Chaps. 4 and 5. See figure numbers offered in the column "Corresponding figure in text" for the corresponding figures in the chapters

Table A.3 Two-sample statistical tests

Corresponding figure in text	Variable name	Test statistic	p-value	N_{Market}	$N_{Nonmarket}$
Figure 4.1	GDP per capita	$t = -7.0776$	$p < 0.000$	39	147
Figure 4.2	Adult literacy rate	$Z = -0.554$	$p = 0.580$	3	45
Figure 4.3	Access to improved water source	$t = -10.204$	$p < 0.000$	33	139
Figure 4.4	Total rail line	$Z = -1.256$	$p = 0.209$	22	60
Figure 4.5	Fixed broadband	$t = -9.072$	$p < 0.000$	38	137
Figure 4.5	Fixed telephone	$t = -10.163$	$p < 0.000$	38	147
Figure 4.6	Life expectancy at birth	$t = -12.353$	$p < 0.000$	37	147
Figure 4.7	Infant mortality	$t = 11.494$	$p < 0.000$	37	147
Figure 4.8	Maternal mortality	$t = 9.003$	$p < 0.000$	34	144
Figure 4.9	Health expenditure per capita per year	$t = -7.552$	$p < 0.000$	34	140
Figure 4.10	Daily caloric intake per capita	$t = -5.942$	$p < 0.000$	38	131
Figure 4.11	High life satisfaction	$Z = -2.031$	$p = 0.042$	14	45
Figure 4.12	Average life satisfaction	$Z = -7.107$	$p < 0.000$	27	117
Figure 4.13	Religious organizations	$Z = -1.087$	$p = 0.277$	14	45
Figure 4.13	Recreational organizations	$Z = -3.973$	$p = 0.0001$	14	45
Figure 4.14	Social capital	$Z = -6.328$	$p < 0.000$	29	118
Figure 4.15	GDP per capita, poorest 10%	$Z = -5.534$	$p < 0.000$	16	57
Figure 4.16	Gini coefficient	$Z = 3.576$	$p < 0.000$	17	56
Figure 4.17	Father-son earning elasticity	$Z = 2.786$	$p = 0.005$	7	15
Figure 5.1	Donations	$Z = -6.418$	$p < 0.000$	28	104
Figure 5.2	Being rich is important	$Z = 3.546$	$p = 0.0004$	14	45
Figure 5.2	Being successful is important	$Z = 3.599$	$p = 0.0003$	14	45
Figure 5.3	Competition is harmful	$Z = 2.797$	$p = 0.005$	14	45
Figure 5.3	Competition is good	$Z = 0.517$	$p = 0.605$	14	45
Figure 5.4	Corruption Perceptions Index	$t = -13.527$	$p < 0.000$	36	142
Figure 5.5	Avoiding fare on public transport	$Z = 2.067$	$p = 0.039$	14	45
Figure 5.5	Cheating on taxes	$Z = 1.199$	$p = 0.230$	11	44
Figure 5.5	Stealing property	$Z = 0.891$	$p = 0.373$	14	45
Figure 5.5	Bribery	$Z = 1.621$	$p = 0.105$	14	45
Figure 5.6	Different race	$Z = 2.144$	$p = 0.032$	14	44
Figure 5.6	Foreign workers	$Z = 0.6$	$p = 0.549$	14	44
Figure 5.6	Homosexuals	$Z = 2.707$	$p = 0.007$	13	43
Figure 5.6	Different religion	$Z = 2.558$	$p = 0.011$	14	43

(continued)

Table A.3 (continued)

Corresponding figure in text	Variable name	Test statistic	p-value	N_{Market}	$N_{Nonmarket}$
Figure 5.6	Cohabitating unmarried couple	$Z = 2.354$	$p = 0.019$	14	43
Figure 5.6	Different language	$Z = 1.702$	$p = 0.089$	14	45
Figure 5.7	University education is more important for boys	$Z = 3.011$	$p = 0.003$	13	45
Figure 5.7	Jobs should be given to men	$Z = 3.261$	$p = 0.001$	14	45
Figure 5.7	Successful wives are a problem	$Z = 3.777$	$p = 0.0002$	14	45
Figure 5.8	Corporal punishment of children	$Z = 1.657$	$p = 0.098$	13	45
Figure 5.8	Domestic violence	$Z = 1.892$	$p = 0.058$	13	44
Figure 5.9	Accepting of homosexuality	$Z = -3.447$	$p = 0.001$	13	42
Figure 5.10	Family	$Z = -0.298$	$p = 0.765$	13	45
Figure 5.10	Neighbors	$Z = -0.028$	$p = 0.978$	13	45
Figure 5.10	Known associates	$Z = -4.652$	$p = 0.000$	13	45
Figure 5.10	People met for the first time	$Z = -2.899$	$p = 0.004$	13	45
Figure 5.11	Generalized trust	$Z = -4.276$	$p = 0.000$	14	45

Note: This table offers the test statistics and p-values of various two-sided statistical tests comparing market and nonmarket societies throughout Chaps. 4 and 5. See figure numbers offered in the column "Corresponding figure in text" for the corresponding figures in the chapters

Table A.4 Statistical tests between different relationship types for trustor behavior

Relationship type	Positive (N = 28)	Negative (N = 68)	Ambiguous (N = 16)	Strangers (N = 36)
Positive (N = 28)		2.361 (0.018)	−2.001 (0.045)	−1.091 (0.275)
Negative (N = 68)			−0.258 (0.796)	0.882 (0.378)
Ambiguous (N = 16)				−0.93 (0.353)
Strangers (N = 36)				

Note: This table presents results from two-sided Mann-Whitney tests comparing two relationship types. For each comparison, the Z-score is reported and the corresponding p-value is reported within parentheses. The table also reports sample sizes for various relationship types (N). The maximum trustor transfer is ten tokens

Table A.5 Statistical tests between different relationship types for trustee behavior

Relationship type	Positive (N = 32)	Negative (N = 67)	Ambiguous (N = 18)	Strangers (N = 31)
Positive (N = 32)		1.97 (0.049)	1.142 (0.254)	1.667 (0.096)
Negative (N = 67)			−0.193 (0.847)	0.298 (0.766)
Ambiguous (N = 18)				−0.383 (0.702)
Strangers (N = 31)				

Note: This table presents results from two-sided Mann-Whitney tests comparing two relationship types. For each comparison, the Z-score is reported and the corresponding p-value is reported within parentheses. The table also reports sample sizes for various relationship types (N). Trustee transfer is calculated as trustee's token transfer divided by the respective trustor's tripled token transfer (i.e. $\frac{y}{3x} * 100$)

Table A.6 Definition of independent variables

Variable name	Definition	Source
Market society	This dummy variable is equal to 1 if a country is a market society and equal to 0 if a country is a nonmarket society	Authors' calculation
Ethnic fractionalization	This is defined as the probability that two randomly selected individuals in a country will be from different ethnic groups. This variable is regarded as a measure of ethnic diversity	Fearon (2003)
Political rights	Freedom House rates the political rights in a particular country by analyzing the electoral process, political pluralism, and participation in a particular country. Scores range from 1 to 7, where 1 represents the most free (in terms of political rights) and 7 represents the least free (in terms of political rights)	*Freedom in the World* index by Freedom House (2012)
Civil liberties	Freedom House rates civil rights in a particular country by analyzing the freedom of expression and beliefs, and associational and organizational rights. Scores range from 1 to 7, where 1 represents the most free (in terms of civil liberties) and 7 represents the least free (in terms of civil liberties)	*Freedom in the World* index by Freedom House (2012)
Western culture	We follow Huntington's (1996) definition of Western civilization, which largely comprises countries in Europe, North America, and Australasia. This dummy variable takes on the value of 1 if a country is identified as being part of the Western civilization by Huntington (1996) and takes on the value of 0 otherwise	Huntington (1996)

Note: This table offers the definitions of various independent variables used in our econometric analysis (Table A.7)

Table A.7 Being a market society is a statistically significant explainer of a larger number of dependent variables

Dep. Variables	Market society	Ethnic frac.	Political rights	Civil liberties	Western culture	Constant	N	R^2	Corresponding figure in text
(4.1) GDP per cap.	23,624.28*** (2706.279)	−10,660.5*** (3328.984)	756.739 (1108.744)	−2149.132 (1434.431)	2685.68 (2781.869)	20,501.43*** (2886.427)	148	0.601	Figure 4.1
(4.2) Access to improved water source	7.432** (3.464)	−22.519*** (4.241)	−1.123 (1.452)	−1.168 (1.915)	−2.495 (3.573)	104.663*** (3.751)	146	0.346	Figure 4.3
(4.3) Fixed broadband	11.9*** (1.676)	−10.337*** (2.132)	−0.487 (0.712)	−1.523 (0.937)	5.166** (1.728)	17.857*** (1.833)	141	0.716	Figure 4.5
(4.4) Fixed telephone	15.447*** (2.976)	−16.186*** (3.594)	−0.895 (1.213)	−1.633 (1.557)	5.945* (3.055)	29.861*** (3.167)	150	0.575	Figure 4.5
(4.5) Life exp. at birth	6.089*** (1.775)	−15.003*** (2.144)	−0.121 (0.723)	−1.267 (0.929)	0.717 (1.822)	80.475*** (1.889)	150	0.510	Figure 4.6
(4.6) Infant mortality	−11.079** (5.226)	42.83*** (6.312)	−1.9 (2.13)	6.109** (2.735)	−1.184 (5.365)	−3.909 (5.563)	150	0.448	Figure 4.7
(4.7) Maternal mortality	−91.207 (86.39)	652.361*** (104.342)	−26.662 (35.211)	76.029* (45.206)	−19.077 (88.687)	−176.983* (91.95)	150	0.343	Figure 4.8
(4.8) Health exp. per cap. per yr.	1874.832*** (220.863)	−902.77*** (272.167)	−32.655 (92.124)	−144.21 (120.502)	868.671*** (227.364)	1688.426*** (237.65)	147	0.706	Figure 4.9
(4.9) Daily caloric intake per cap.	184.163* (96.048)	−450.347*** (119.329)	61.568 (40.688)	−127.871** (52.61)	293.032*** (100.198)	3134.238*** (103.358)	141	0.442	Figure 4.10
(4.10) Avg. life satis.	1.441*** (0.22)	−0.577* (0.292)	−0.11 (0.095)	−0.036 (0.124)	−0.025 (0.235)	5.939*** (0.246)	134	0.489	Figure 4.12
(4.11) Social capital	6.585*** (1.633)	0.828 (2.089)	−0.733 (0.697)	−0.367 (0.922)	3.918** (1.749)	50.747*** (1.786)	135	0.436	Figure 4.14
(5.1) Donations	22.26*** (3.824)	8.191 (4.941)	−2.31 (1.659)	1.91 (2.106)	2.852 (4.015)	21.194*** (4.236)	122	0.367	Figure 5.1
(5.2) Corruption Perception Index	3.066*** (0.285)	−0.68** (0.342)	0.161 (0.117)	−0.539*** (0.148)	0.705** (0.292)	4.862*** (0.304)	149	0.755	Figure 5.4

Standard errors are reported in parentheses
***significant at 1%; **significant at 5%; *significant at 10%

development: ethnic fractionalization,[1] political rights and civil liberties,[2] and Western culture.[3] All of our specifications are estimated using ordinary least squares (OLS). For this analysis, we only conduct analysis on dependent variables for which we have more than 100 observations. We list our explanatory and dependent variables in Table A.6, along with their definitions and their sources. We offer our findings in Table A.7. In short, our econometric analysis reveals that being a market society is statistically significant in explaining dependent variables more frequently than any other explanatory variable. While preliminary and by no means definitive, our results, taken in whole, raise doubts that markets are morally corrupting and, in fact, suggest that markets promote morality.

Bibliography

Agrast, M.D., J.C. Botero, J. Martinez, A. Ponce, and C.S. Pratt. 2012–2013. *The World Justice Project: Rule of Law Index 2012–2013*. Washington, DC: World Justice Project. https://worldjusticeproject.org/sites/default/files/documents/WJP_Index_Report_2012.pdf

Alesina, A., and G. Tabellini. 1989. External Debt, Capital Flight and Political Risk. *Journal of International Economics* 27 (3–4): 199–220.

Chai, S., M. Liu, and M.S. Kim. 2009. Cultural Comparisons of Beliefs and Values: Applying the Grid-Group Approach to the World Values Survey. *Beliefs and Values* 1 (2): 193–208.

Charities Aid Foundation. 2017. *CAF World Giving Index 2017: A Global View of Giving Trends*. https://www.cafonline.org/docs/default-source/about-uspublications/cafworldgivingindex2017_2167a_web_210917.pdf?sfvrsn=ed1dac40_10

Easterly, W., and R. Levine. 1997. Africa's Growth Tragedy: Policies and Ethnic Divisions. *The Quarterly Journal of Economics* 112 (4): 1203–1250.

---

[1] For instance, high levels of ethnic fractionalization within a country could hinder a country's economic progress by fostering political instability and social conflict and by encouraging the selection of poor public policies, among others (e.g. Alesina and Tabellini 1989; Shleifer and Vishny 1993; Easterly and Levine 1997).

[2] Political rights and civil liberties protect citizens from the violation of their freedom by governments, social organizations, and other private individuals and are indicators of the prevalence of the rule of law and, consequently, democracy in a society (e.g. Fabro and Aixalá 2012).

[3] Weber ([1905] 2002, [1905] 2011), for instance, emphasized how a Protestant work ethic led to the emergence of modern capitalism and the accumulation of wealth in the West. See also Harrison (1992) and Huntington (1996).

Fabro, G., and J. Aixalá. 2012. Direct and Indirect Effects of Economic and Political Freedom on Economic Growth. *Journal of Economic Issues* 46 (4): 1059–1080.

Fearon, J.D. 2003. Ethnic and Cultural Diversity by Country. *Journal of Economic Growth* 8 (2): 195–222.

Gwartney, J.D., R. Lawson, and J.C. Hall. 2011. *Economic Freedom of the World: 2011 Annual Report.* Vancouver: Fraser Institute. https://www.fraserinstitute.org/sites/default/files/economic-freedom-of-the-world-2011.pdf

———. 2016. *Economic Freedom of the World: 2016 Annual Report.* Vancouver: Fraser Institute. https://www.fraserinstitute.org/sites/default/files/economic-freedom-of-the-world-2016.pdf

Harrison, L.E. 1992. *Who Prospers: How Cultural Values Shape Economic and Political Success.* New York: Basic Books.

Huntington, S.P. 1996. *The Clash of Civilizations and the Remaking of World Order.* New York: Simon & Schuster.

Inglehart, R., C. Haerpfer, A. Moreno, C. Welzel, K. Kizilova, J. Diez-Medrano, M. Lagos, P. Norris, E. Ponarin, and B. Puranen, et al., eds. 2014. *World Values Survey: Round Six – Country-Pooled Datafile Version.* Madrid: JD Systems. www.worldvaluessurvey.org/WVSDocumentationWV6.jsp.

Miller, T., and K.R. Holmes. 2011. *Highlights of the 2011 Index of Economic Freedom: Promoting Economic Opportunity and Prosperity.* Washington, DC: Heritage Foundation. https://www.heritage.org/index/pdf/2011/index2011_highlights.pdf

Miller, T., A.B. Kim, and J. M. Roberts. 2018. *The 2018 Index of Economic Freedom.* Washington, DC: The Heritage Foundation. https://www.heritage.org/index/pdf/2018/book/index_2018.pdf

Schwab, K., X. Sala-Martin, and R. Greenhill. 2011. *The Global Competitiveness Report 2011–2012.* Geneva: World Economic Forum. http://www3.weforum.org/docs/WEF_GCR_Report_2011-12.pdf

Schwab, K., X. Sala-Martin, and R. Samans. 2017. *The Global Competitiveness Report 2017–2018.* Geneva: World Economic Forum. http://www3.weforum.org/docs/GCR2017-2018/05FullReport/TheGlobalCompetitivenessReport2017%E2%80%932018.pdf

Shleifer, A., and R.W. Vishny. 1993. Corruption. *The Quarterly Journal of Economics* 108 (3): 599–617.

The World Bank. 2010. *Doing Business 2011: Making a Difference for Entrepreneurs.* Washington, DC: The World Bank.

———. *World Bank Open Data.* https://data.worldbank.org/. Accessed 15 Mar 2016.

———. 2019. *Doing Business 2019: Training for Reform.* Washington, DC: The World Bank.

Transparency International. 2011. *Corruption Perceptions Index 2011.* Berlin: Transparency International. https://www.corruptionwatch.org.za/wpcontent/uploads/migrated/Corruption-perecptions-index-2011-report_0.pdf

Weber, M. [1905] 2002. *The Protestant Ethic and the "Spirit" of Capitalism and Other Writings*. Trans. P. Baehr and G. Wells. London: Penguin Books.

———. [1905] 2011. *The Protestant Ethic and the "Spirit" of Capitalism: The Revised 1920 Edition*. Trans. S. Kalberg. Oxford: Oxford University Press.

World Justice Project. 2018. *World Justice Project: Rule of Law Index 2018*. Washington, DC: World Justice Project.

World Values Survey. 2019. *World Values Survey Publications*. http://www.worldvaluessurvey.org/WVSContents.jsp?CMSID=Publications. Accessed 12 Mar 2019.

Index[1]

---

[1] Note: Page numbers followed by 'n' refer to notes.

© The Author(s) 2019
V. H. Storr, G. S. Choi, *Do Markets Corrupt Our Morals?*,
https://doi.org/10.1007/978-3-030-18416-2

CPSIA information can be obtained
at www.ICGtesting.com
Printed in the USA
BVHW040212010721
610969BV00016B/152

9 783030 184155